IT Manager's Handbook,
2nd Edition

About the Authors

Bill Holtsnider is an experienced writer, educator, and software professional with more than 22 years of experience working in the computer industry. His IT expertise includes working in such diverse areas as stock portfolio management, biotechnology, identity management, and software development. He is the author of several books and a wide range of technical and marketing documentation.

Brian D. Jaffe is a seasoned veteran in the IT community, with more than 20 years of professional experience. As an IT professional, he has worked for several Fortune 500 companies including Bristol-Myers Squibb, Time Warner, Philip Morris, and The Interpublic Group of Companies. Currently he is Director of IT Services for Time Warner. His articles have appeared in *Computerworld*, *InfoWorld*, *eWeek*, and *The New York Times*.

IT Manager's Handbook, 2nd Edition

Getting Your New Job Done

Bill Holtsnider

Brian D. Jaffe

AMSTERDAM • BOSTON • HEIDELBERG • LONDON
NEW YORK • OXFORD • PARIS • SAN DIEGO
SAN FRANCISCO • SINGAPORE • SYDNEY • TOKYO

Morgan Kaufmann Publishers is an imprint of Elsevier

Publishing Director	Diane Cerra
Assistant Editor	Asma Stephan
Publishing Services Manager	George Morrison
Project Manager	Brandy Lilly
Text Design	Cate Barr
Composition	Charon Tec (A Macmillan Company)
Technical Illustration	Charon Tec (A Macmillan Company)
Interior printer	Maple-Vail Book Manufacturing Group
Cover printer	Phoenix Color

Morgan Kaufmann Publishers is an imprint of Elsevier.
500 Sansome Street, Suite 400, San Francisco, CA 94111

This book is printed on acid-free paper.

Library of Congress Cataloging-in-Publication Data
Holtsnider, Bill, 1956–
    IT manager's handbook : getting your new job done / Bill Holtsnider, Brian D. Jaffe.
      p. cm.
    Includes bibliographical references and index.
    ISBN-13: 978-0-12-370488-7 (pbk. : alk. paper)
    ISBN-10: 0-12-370488-X (pbk. : alk. paper) 1. Industrial management–Data processing.
2. Management information systems. I. Jaffe, Brian D. II. Title.

    HD30.2.H657 2006
    004.068–dc22

                                  2006011119

ISBN 13: 978-0-12-370488-7
ISBN 10: 0-12-370488-X

For information on all Morgan Kaufmann publications, visit our Web site at www.mkp.com or www.books.elsevier.com

Printed in the United States of America
06 07 08 09 10 5 4 3 2 1

For M & D
—B.H.

For my mother and father
—B.D.J.

Brief Table of Contents

Complete Table of Contents

Chapter Eight

IT Compliance and Controls 201

Part Two: The Technology of Being an IT Manager

Chapter Nine

Chapter Ten

Operations   255

Chapter Fourteen

Software and Operating Systems   383

Chapter Seventeen

Preface

Far and away the best prize that life offers is the chance to work hard at work worth doing.

— THEODORE ROOSEVELT

Many technical professionals are eager to join the ranks of management. But as the saying goes, "Be careful what you wish for." This book introduces you to the many key concepts you will face as a new information technology (IT) manager. It also provides you with suggested methods for dealing with many of the large issues that arise, including specific recommendations for actions as well as places to look for further help.

We have seen a lot of technical professionals — developers, programmers, installers, hardware techs — suddenly thrust into positions of management in their IT departments. Not only were they given no formal training or clear idea of what the position entailed, they were also expected to know a great deal about a lot of different things. As senior IT professionals ourselves, we have seen this situation repeated many times. We set out to write a book that would help new IT managers navigate the choppy seas of management.

This book aims to help you with all those responsibilities that are suddenly thrust upon you, that you suddenly acquire, or that you suddenly realize need to be addressed. We don't spend much time talking about the theory of IT management. We spend most of the book describing what you need to worry about when you need to deal with a particular situation, such as creating a budget or writing an ad for an open position.

We wrote the book for *new* IT managers and *future* IT managers. Much of the material in this book will be familiar to experienced IT managers — those people who have been managing IT departments since the space program in the 1960s. But for many individuals, the late 1990s and early 2000s have brought a radical change in responsibilities with little or no help along with it. This book is written to help you identify, deal with, and (if necessary) look for further help on many of the key issues that are suddenly facing you as a new IT manager.

We also recognize that one of the more difficult career steps in the field of Information Technology is moving up from technician to manager. For those hoping to make this leap, this book can be useful in letting you know what awaits you on the other side. By learning more about an IT manager's job, you will know what skill sets to focus on so that you can demonstrate to your company that you're prepared and ready to be a manager.

What is New and Different in this Edition

Our primary goals in writing a new edition of this successful book were to update its technical information and to add new topics that over the past few years have been added to IT managers' responsibilities.

Some of the new topics addressed, and how they affect IT and IT management, in this book include:

◆ Identity Theft, Security Audits, and Security versus Convenience (Chapter 13, Security)

◆ Changing Jobs, Getting Started and Establishing Yourself at a New Company (Chapter 5, Changing Companies)

◆ Managing Vendors (Chapter 7, Managing Vendors)

◆ Directory Services (Chapter 15, Enterprise Applications)

◆ Data Centers (Chapter 11, Physical Plant)

◆ Outsourcing and Offshore Outsourcing (Chapter 3, Staffing Your IT Team)

◆ Sarbanes-Oxley, HIPAA, and the Patriot Act (Chapter 8, IT Compliance and Controls)

In the first edition, the chapter on security was 15 pages long; this time it's more than double that. Similarly, the chapter on project management is much larger and more comprehensive than it was before. The issues of data center (cooling, electricity, space, etc.) weren't even discussed in the first edition, but gets its due attention this time. In the first book, we didn't even mention "compliance" — for this edition we devote an entire chapter to it.

Information Technology has grown to become a critical, complicated, and integral component of corporate life. Things that were the purview of IT experts back then (e.g., configuring a desktop) are commonplace activities for the consumer. Similarly, certain technologies that were worth mentioning in the first edition (e.g., Token-Ring) are now considered antiquities. This edition also incorporates words that weren't even part of the IT lexicon (e.g., "phishing") when we wrote the first edition.

This new edition reflects all these shifts.

How Technical Is This Book?

This book discusses the basic principles of such "non-technical" issues as managing your IT team, staffing, managing projects, and budgeting. It also discusses the more difficult topics of hardware, software, networks, the Net, and so on. Finally, it covers topics that might be considered somewhat "in between" the technical and non-technical: security, disaster recovery, and enterprise applications. For the technical areas, it's designed to cover the basic concepts, but it's certainly not intended to be a technical reference on any of these topics. This book is for technical professionals, but it isn't crammed with code.

The Structure of This Book

We worked hard to write a book that we, as busy technical professionals, would use ourselves. We have structured the material in easy-to-read, easy-to-grab chunks. We don't have any free time and we assume you don't either. The book is designed to be scanned for critical information; it includes many cross-references and page references, because one topic often leads to another and because readers want to make the jump right away, not after looking in the index. We hope you find the structure and format useful and helpful.

Chapter-by-Chapter Summaries

	Chapter	Summary
	The Business of Being an IT Manager	
1	The Role of an IT Manager	Understand the role of an IT manager, why it's so important, and how integral it is to your company.
2	Managing Your IT Team	While it's tempting to think of hardware and software as your most critical IT resources, it is actually the *people* who run, support, and manage the technologies that are the most critical.
3	Staffing your IT Team	Hiring and all of its aspects is one of the classic managerial responsibilities. This chapter talks about the issues and challenges you'll face and offers some concrete suggestions for solving them.
4	Project Management	As an IT manager you'll go from one project to another; some that are miniscule, and others that seem too big to be measured. Your success at being able to manage projects is a critical factor in being successful at your role.

5	Changing Companies	When you take a job in a new company, all that was familiar to you at your old company is suddenly gone. This chapter offers guidance on starting at a new company, how to establish yourself, and what you should be doing those first few weeks and months.
6	Budgeting	It's likely that the IT department has one of the largest budgets in the company. This chapter helps you get a foundation in managing a budget, spending, etc.
7	Managing Vendors	This chapter offers guidance on how to make the most of your vendor relationships so that it's beneficial to both of you.
8	IT Compliance and Controls	Regulations and legislations are increasingly having a major impact on how IT departments operate. In addition to the compliance issues, this chapter offers information about different methodologies being adopted by various organizations.

The Technology of Being an IT Manager

9	Getting Started with the Technical Environment	The IT infrastructure is your foundation. If you don't have a firm grasp on it to manage it and ensure its stability, everything else you do is at risk of toppling over.
10	Operations	Keeping everything up and running is the number one priority of IT. This chapter offers some insights into managing operations.
11	Physical Plant	Air conditioning, raised floors, electrical circuits, and fire suppression are all areas you may not have expected to be involved with as an IT manager, but they are a critical part of the job.
12	Networking	Systems are great, but it is networks that enable us to access all those resources. From LANs to WANs, and routers to switches, this chapter will help you understand important networking technologies and concepts.
13	Security	Security is a 24/7/365 concern that should be an integral part of every decision you make in IT. You need to understand not just the specific threats (because those will change) but the overall concepts behind building your secure IT world.

14	Software and Operating Systems	What's the point of doing it faster if it's being done incorrectly? Whether it's a PDA, a desktop, or a server, it is the software that distinguishes the winners from the losers.
15	Enterprise Applications	These are the applications that virtually everyone in the company relies on. Some are very visible, such as e-mail; others are virtually transparent to the users, such as directory services.
16	Storage and Backup	As the use of IT continues to increase and becomes a more and more important part of our daily lives, the amount of data we need to manage is growing dramatically. This chapter talks about dealing with data storage and backup.
17	User Support Services	While it is tempting to think of hardware and software as your most critical IT resources, the support that you provide to your end-users can be the most vital service you offer, and the one that is the greatest influence on how the IT department is perceived by the rest of the company.
18	Web Sites	Regardless of what kind of business or organization you're in, you need both a "real-world" and an online presence. Determine what kind of Web strategy you need and how to implement it.
19	User Equipment	The equipment that goes to users usually requires the most management, gets the most turnover, and is often the subject of technology envy (from the largest flat-screen to the coolest handheld).
20	Disaster Recovery	With so many, and so much, depending on IT, your company may not be able to survive much downtime if disaster strikes.

Note on URLs and Web Resources

State-of-the-art information is critical to IT managers and IT professionals of all kinds. Many of the sources for this book are Web sites. And, as any Web user, experienced or new, understands, Web content changes quickly. We have included Web addresses whenever we can, knowing full well that sites change, material gets deleted or added, and pointers that worked when we wrote the book may not necessarily work when you read it. Regardless, we thought it best to give you a reference where we found worthwhile information. You can use that information as a starting point for your search for information.

Acknowledgments

Trying to condense the topic of IT management into one book isn't an easy task. It required a delicate touch to both properly balance technical and non-technical issues as well as to determine which topics to focus on in each area.

A large portion of the ideas presented here represent what we've learned from others. Accordingly, we must give credit to those who taught us (often unknowingly) throughout the course of our careers in corporate IT — colleagues, co-workers, those we have reported to, and those who have reported to us. We are indebted to, and grateful for, these accidental mentors.

For this edition, we would like to thank Jonathan Ganz, Frank Calabrese, Brian McMann, Norma Sutcliffe, and Nick Wilde for reviewing our initial proposal. We would especially like to thank Jonathan Ganz, Karen Godshalk, Karen Hitchcock, James Snyder, and Nick Wilde for reviewing the manuscript and providing such insightful and valuable feedback — the final product is radically improved by your suggestions.

We are also greatly indebted to our editor, Diane Cerra, and to our assistant editor, Asma Stephan. Diane made this new edition possible and Asma made it work. We are very grateful for their tireless enthusiasm and efforts.

And most important, we are tremendously indebted to our family and friends for their support and understanding while this book was being written. It's motivating to know that as the final edits are being made and this period of self-imposed exile ends, they are anxious and eager to forget about those declined invitations, missed dinners, and nonexistent weekends. In particular:

Bill would like to thank his partner, wife, and confidante, Polly, for her caring and unwavering support. Writing may be a solitary activity, but no one does it alone.

Brian would like to thank his girlfriend Jenine for her understanding, patience and support — as this project comes to an end, it's time for the beginning we never had.

First Edition Acknowledgements

It isn't possible to mention each and every person that contributed to developing the book that you now hold in your hand. Still, we have to be sure to thank Bruce Caldwell, *Information Week*; Tom Conarty, Bethlehem Steel Corporation;

Dan Deakin, Zentropy Partners; Rob Hawkins, Hofs-Hut, Inc.; Robert Rubin, Elf Atochem NA Inc.; Matt Tavis, Sapient Corporation; Philip Tolley, Matrix Rehabilitation Inc.; and Janet Wilson, Mutual Insurance Company of Arizona, for helping us fine-tune the initial proposal by adding and eliminating various chapters and sections.

We are especially grateful to Curtis Johnsey, O'Connor Kenny Partners; Brian McMann, Tanning Technology Corp.; Curt Wennekamp, Medshares, Inc.; Mark Jones, Boeing; and Janet Wilson, Mutual Insurance Company of Arizona, for reviewing the manuscript and their invaluable suggestions and comments. They helped us keep the book focused on its goals and made certain that important topics, as well as differing perspectives, weren't overlooked or given short shrift. We would also like to thank our editors, Jennifer Mann, who agreed to publish the book, and Karyn Johnson, who kept us on course throughout the long adventure that writing this book became.

Bill Holtsnider
Denver, CO
bholtsnider@gmail.com

Brian D. Jaffe
New York, NY
brian@red55.com

The Business of Being an IT Manager

PART ONE

The Role of an IT Manager

The buck stops here.

—HARRY TRUMAN

What does an IT Manager actually do? Are you glad you got the job? Or do you eventually want to become one yourself? Before we help you answer those questions, we discuss the definition and the pros and cons of being a manager. Clearly management as a career path is well suited for some people, but not for everyone. Is it right for you?

IT Managers need to wear a lot of hats. Different parts of the organization will have different expectations of this position, and you'll have to address them all. Finance expects you to manage costs; Sales and Marketing will want to see IT help to generate revenue; your staff is looking

CHAPTER ONE

for guidance, career development, and a work-life balance; and the administrative assistant down the hall just wants her printer to stop smudging. In this chapter, we will examine the roles and responsibilities of an IT Manager.

1.1   Just What Does an IT Manager Do?

IT Managers now have many responsibilities (data centers, staff management, telecommunications, servers, workstations, Web sites, user support, regulatory compliance, disaster recovery, etc.) and connect with almost all the departments (Accounting, Marketing, Sales, Distribution, etc.) within a company or organization.

This is both the good and the bad news. At some companies, an IT Manager can have direct influence on the strategic direction of the company, suggesting and helping implement e-commerce initiatives, for example. In other companies, an IT Manager is really a technician, a software developer, or network installer. And to complicate things even further, those definitions change quickly over time. Yesterday's network installer is today's e-commerce consultant.

By the way, at this point, "IT" (Information Technology) and "IS" (Information Systems) have now become synonymous terms. While they are often used interchangeably, "IT" is becoming much more widely used. Some people may use "IS" to refer to activity related to business software applications, but this use has waned considerably.

Why All That Change and Flexibility Is Good

The position of IT Manager can be very challenging. It is extremely varied in scope, allows you to come in contact with a large portion of your company, provides you with opportunities to directly affect the overall direction of your organization, and is excellent professional experience to acquire. In addition, you get to increase your range of experience; you are forced to (and get to) keep up with the latest changes in technology (so your skill set will always be in demand); and your network of contacts gets large.

As important as all that is, there is an added bonus: In recent years, IT has taken on a strategic value in the roles companies play in the new economy. Information Technology is now a critical component of many companies and the U.S. economy: "IT is the fastest growing sector in the economy with a 68% increase in output growth rate expected between 2002 and 2012 (*U.S. Bureau of Labor Statistics*)." Not only is your job interesting and rewarding, it is also very important. Dependence on technology is only growing, and issues like security and compliance are making IT more visible throughout the organization. What more could you ask for?

Why All That Change and Flexibility Is Bad

On the other hand, being an IT Manager is a difficult, often thankless, task. Like many service jobs, if you do it superbly, most people don't notice. In addition, the responsibilities differ radically from company to company. Some companies actually have many IT Managers and several layers of management. At others (and this number is shrinking), an IT Manager is a part-time role someone fills while doing their "real" job.

In addition, the role of an IT Manager can often vary widely within an organization, depending on who is making the decisions at the time. While the techniques might vary, the "Western Region Sales Manager" knows what his or her role is — get more sales as soon as possible — and that isn't going to vary much from company to company. An IT Manager, on the other hand, can mean many things to many people, and the job changes as technology and needs advance and evolve. Addressing all these needs and people can mean that time for "extras" like sleep and meals have to be sacrificed.

As a manager, everyone else's crises become yours. People (your users, your staff, etc.) are demanding quick resolutions to problems, and are looking to you to fix them.

In this book, we will discuss in detail the positive and negative elements of the key components of being an IT Manager. If a process is littered with political landmines ("budgeting," for example), we'll warn you about it; if a process has hidden perks (being an unofficial project manager for a project can put you in contact with many different people at many different layers of the organization), we'll tell you that, too. But before you decide if you should be an *IT* Manager, read the next section to determine if you want to be a *manager* at all.

1.2   Managers in General

Before you decide whether or not you want to become an IT Manager, you should decide whether or not you want to become a manager at all. One method of evaluating a potential career is to read books or take introductory classes about how to do it; sometimes, reading a book about a subject will make you realize you *do not* want to pursue that particular career (see Table 1.1).

Like most topics in this book, we present you with both the positive and the negative aspects of being a manager. We'd like to share our experiences and those of other managers we know; managers with over 100 years of combined experience contributed ideas to the following section.

Of course, the comments in this section are extremely subjective. Both positive and negative comments about such a broad topic ("management") are bound to be generalizations that easily can be counter-argued. So take each comment/idea/suggestion as something to be considered, evaluated, and adapted; perhaps it applies to your experience and perhaps not. But remember, everything here has been written by professionals who have been out in the front lines of the corporate world for a long time.

General Definition of a Manager

Management has been defined as "assembling the resources to achieve a mutually agreed upon objective" (G. Puziak, 2005). Or it can be defined as "getting things done through other people" (AMA President, 1980). A more mundane view is the answers.com definition: "authoritative control over the affairs of others." All three views are commonly held beliefs.

Note the radical difference between the definitions: the first two talk about collaboration ("mutually agreed upon" and "through"); the last one defines management as "control." As always, flexibility is key.

Styles of Management

These definitions reflect the two typical management structures American companies now employ: "Command and Control," or "Collaboration." (These styles have many different names: "Authoritarian" and "Participative," or "Military" and "Worker Responsibility.") Few companies, or individuals, are either purely one type or another, of course, but most are *generally* one kind or another. To succeed as a manager, it's best if you determine which type of management your company uses. And determine which type of manager you want to become. But as always, flexibility is key. While one type of style may work well in one situation, a different situation could call for an entirely different approach.

Command and Control

Based on classic military structure, this style was popular for most of American corporate history. You direct your employees and your boss directs you. In its extreme, this style doesn't allow for disagreement or input from subordinates.

It emphasizes clear commands, and rewards staff that follow these commands virtually without question.

This style has lost popularity. While some environments still operate under this style, many corporations are revisiting their commitment to such a rigid method of management. While execution of tasks under command and control systems is often faster and costs less, it is (among other reasons) also often wrong and ends up costing more to implement in the long term. In addition, employees under this system are often unhappy because they exercise little control in their jobs. It is also hard to know what value is lost in an environment where collaboration and teamwork is absent.

Collaboration

This style of management is more modern. All levels of the corporate ladder are actively involved in the execution of a business. It doesn't mean dock workers make decisions on plant relocations (although auto workers are now much more involved in decisions that affect them than they ever have been). But it does mean that many workers who are affected or who can contribute to decisions are now asked to be involved — regardless of where they stand in the company hierarchy.

The benefits of collaboration are increased personal satisfaction for workers and often better and more cost-effective decisions (because the people affected by those decisions are involved). The negatives are summarized by that old adage "paralysis by analysis." Often, too many people involved in a decision don't make the decision or the process better; oftentimes it bogs it down.

Within the collaboration mode, there are also two extremes: managers who micro-manage — they are involved in every decision, consult as many people as possible on even the smallest of issues — and managers who are so distant they provide no guidance or feedback to their team, and ignore even the most pressing of issues.

What Kind of Manager Will You Be?

It's hard to predict, but study the two types of management styles above. Which kind have you experienced as a staff member? Which kind did you like? What kind of style is common in your company? "Management style shock" is not uncommon; a manager comes from another company and, bringing her management toolbox with her, quickly discovers that her "style" and that of the new company radically conflict. She is used to a collaborative approach and this company has no patience for discussion; her bosses dictate what she should do and they expect her to do the same. Or she starts commanding her staff around and they, used to group meetings to make important decisions, are shocked.

Pros and Cons of Being a Manager: Reasons To Become A Manager, and Reasons Not to Become One

Table 1.1 Pros and cons of being a manager

PRO		CON	
	May have more control over your life. You manage others instead of only managing yourself. Of course, you will also have a manager above you.		May have less control over your life (since the problems of others now become your problems).
	Typically make more money than those in non-management roles. Although this, too, is changing. There are technical tracks in many companies that are almost as lucrative as management. But not every company has this option.		Typically (but not always) a manager has more responsibility than a non-manager. There is more credit if things go right and a bigger price to pay if things go wrong.
	Do work on a larger scale. A simplistic example might be: one non-management worker may generate $1000 a day in revenue for the company, but a manager may manage six such workers, generating $6000 daily for the company.		Management looks and sounds a lot easier than it is. Often, managers are seen attending endless meetings or just having casual conversations all the time — not doing "real work." In fact, they carry a great deal of responsibility and have to routinely make difficult decisions.
	Have greater potential to "make a difference."		There are numerous headaches that come with managing people: meeting your project's budget and schedule projections, dealing with challenging employees, and administrative annoyances ("those 200 new PCs arrived, where do we store them until we're ready to work on them?").

(Cont.)

Table 1.1　Pros and cons of being a manager (continued)

PRO		CON	
	Get the credit for all the good work that your team does on your watch...whether it happened because of you, your staff, or by random chance.		You get the blame for all the bad stuff that happens on your watch...whether it happened because of you, your staff, or by random chance.
	Get the opportunity to develop non-IT skills, working with other departments, vendors, partners, etc.		There are tough decisions to make: budget cuts, employee performance, having to choose between Jenine and Peter for the promotion.
	Have the opportunity to determine strategy and to set direction for both a department and the company as a whole.		
	Acquire the ability to add more value to a department and a company.		
	Have the opportunity to develop, coach, and mentor other people.		

The Hidden Work of Management

One aspect of management is that the work is often less apparent and less tangible than the work being done by subordinates.

Management is Sometimes Hard to See

There are, of course, examples of useless and lazy managers. You may be even a victim of one. But management is not, in and of itself, easy. Nor are all of its components visible. A worker may see a manager go out every day for lunch and think: "That guy just eats out every day on company time and money." But the manager may be having "working lunches" with fellow managers and performing some of the tasks discussed in this book: finding resources, hiring personnel, writing a budget, setting objectives and strategies, fighting with Human Resources (HR) and Finance about planned layoffs, or planning a system overhaul. In that scenario, a hard-working manager and a slouch look exactly the same to an outside observer.

Good and Bad Management Often Look Alike — For a While

In addition, because great — or even good — management is often hard to see, the effects of good management are often clear only in retrospect. Consequently, bad management and good management can often look the same. A manager that has a critical meeting with a subordinate that gets that subordinate back on track looks, to the outside observer, exactly like a manager having an intense conversation with a co-worker about weekend party plans. That worker's new attitude may take weeks, or months, to show itself concretely. A key decision not to pursue opening a new plant overseas happens in meeting rooms far from the general employee population; it may cost hundreds of jobs in the short term, but save thousands in long term. Those results will show up in the financial results years after the decision was made.

Resentment Toward Management

If you become a manager, you can assume there may be some resentment toward you in that role. This resentment could be because others in the department had hoped that they would get the job, or some may think that you're not qualified. There are also challenges when you are promoted and now have to manage a group of people that used to be your peers. There can be a tendency for tension between non-managerial staff and managers: the role of one is to direct, steer, or manage the other. Most of the time, that relationship works well and each person knows his/her own role and understands the other's role to some degree. Occasionally, however, that tension needs time and attention by both sides before it disappears.

The key to dealing with this problem is to communicate. Talk with your staff. Build a relationship with each member of your team. Let each person know you recognize their talents and their contributions.

Babysitting versus Managing

There is a portion of any manager's job that is "just babysitting." People are unpredictable, but you can predict they aren't always going to act in ways that will help you and your department. Sometimes their actions will cause you a great deal of stress; anyone who has faced a wrongful termination suit will attest to the pain of delivering a pink slip. Other times employees will drive you crazy with items so mundane you'll scarcely believe you are talking about the issue; many managers know of the enormous "turf wars" that erupt over inches of desk size, who gets the larger monitor, or who is allowed to go to which train-ing classes. Hence the name "babysitting."

Politics

Unlike non-managerial workers, many managers spend a large amount of time dealing with the political elements of the company. While some people dislike any form of politics at work, many others thrive on it. "Politics at work" can mean anything from jockeying for a larger role in an upcoming project to turf wars about who manages which department.

Some politics is necessary: the network support team needs someone to run it, and either a new person has to be hired (see Chapter 3 on Staffing Your Team, page 43) or a current employee needs to be appointed. Some non-objective considerations will eventually come into play, since humans are involved. Does John in Accounting have the right personality for the job? If Mary is given that promotion, will she eventually merge the department with her old one? If Tom is hired, will he want to bring along his friend Chris that he always seems to have working for him?

1.3 The Strategic Value of the IT Department

IT management has become one of the most critical positions in the new econ-omy. As corporations have embraced the efficiencies and excitement of the new digital economy, IT — and IT professionals — have grown dramatically in value. IT is no longer "just" a department, no longer an isolated island like the

---

The CEO's Role in IT

"First, the CEO must be sure to regard information technology as a strategic resource to help the business get more out of its people. Second, the CEO must learn enough about technology to be able to ask good, hard ques-tions of the CIO and be able to tell whether good answers are coming back. Third, the CEO needs to bring the CIO into management's deliberations and strategizing. It's impossible to align IT strategy with business strategy if the CIO is out of the business loop."

—Bill Gates
Business @ the Speed of Thought, p. 318

MIS departments of old corporations where requests for data would flow in and emerge, weeks or months later, in some kind of long, unreadable report. Many companies now make IT an integral part of their company, of their mission statements, and of their spending. Your role is more critical than ever before.

Applications Development versus Technical Operations

Most IT organizations have two primary functional areas: Development and Operations.

Applications Development

Companies often see the real value of IT as only the applications that serve the company's core business. Applications are what allow one business to become innovative, more efficient, and more productive and set itself apart from its competitors. Careers within applications development include analysts, programmers, database administrators, interface designers, testers, etc.

Many people within IT like working in applications development because it allows them to really learn how the business operates. As a result, it may often provide opportunities for increased involvement with people in other departments outside of IT. However, many programmers find the job is too isolating because their daily interactions may only be with the program logic displayed on their screen and the keyboard. Of course, some programmers welcome the isolation and embrace the opportunity to work in the field.

Technical Operations

The technical support function is the oft-forgotten area of IT. The technical operations organization is responsible for making sure that the computers are up and running and operating as they should. Their jobs go well beyond the computer hardware and often include the network (routers, switches, telecommunication facilities, etc.), database administration, operations, security, backups, operating systems, and so on. The Help Desk may be the most visible portion of the Technical Operations group. Within the industry, this infrastructure side of IT is often referred to as the "plumbing." Like most important and underappreciated jobs, when operations is doing their job well you don't even know they exist.

However, those in operations may find the time demands stressful. Some system maintenance can only be done during weekends and evenings when users won't be affected. Similarly, it will be the operations staff that is roused by a mid-REM-sleep phone call when the system crashes in the middle of the night.

(See Chapter 2, Managing Your IT Team, page 19, for a discussion of methods of preventing burnout.)

IT Department Goals

One of your goals as an involved and caring manager is to make sure that your department's aims are in line with those of your organization. It doesn't matter if you're an IT Manager for a non-profit citizen's group or midlevel manager for General Motors; you need to discover what the organization's goals are and make them your own.

If you work for a corporate organization, your IT goals may be measured in the same terms as the business units that you support — reduce per-unit costs of the division's products and increase the capacity and throughput of the business and manufacturing processes. Your tactics must clearly satisfy these goals. If you work in a non-profit or educational organization, your goals — and the way you are measured — will be different.

Your boss should be clear about communicating those goals to you. But they shouldn't be a secret anyway. If your company makes widgets, make sure the company's strategy includes an appropriate use of IT throughout the company. Is the widgets factory truly automated? Can the Accounting Department's systems talk to the HR systems?

The Value of IT Managers

IT is a brave new world to many of today's corporations. Many executives now know how to use Word, Excel, e-mail, and their handheld Blackberry, but some have little or no understanding of the deeper, more complex issues involved in IT. They imagine IT to be a powerful but complex world where rewards can be magically great and risks are frighteningly terrible. These executives, and their corporations, need professionals to both explain and execute in this new world. This is where you come in.

You can leverage your technical knowledge, experience, and interests with your company's direct profit and loss requirements. *Together*, you and your company can provide a powerful business combination. *Alone*, your individual skills and passions can wither into arcane interests, and your business expertise can build models relevant to an economic world decades in the past.

Will your technical expertise and recommendations occasionally clash with the company's needs and vision? Absolutely.

Will your ideas about technical directions sometimes be in direct opposition to their perceptions of "market forces"? Absolutely.

Will you "win some and lose some"? Absolutely.

The purpose of this book, however, is to help you win — and to help your company win as often as it can be done. We want you, your IT department, *and* your company to work together as successfully as possible.

1.4 Develop an IT Strategy

The cosmic question "Why are we here?" applies to corporate departments as well. It is entirely possible that many, if not all, of your staff don't have the full understanding of how the IT department serves the entire organization. When it comes to their job, they may understand what's critical for today. But, while today is important, it's also vital to know about tomorrow and beyond. If they're looking at the trees, you have to be the one to let them know about the forest. The strategy should include feedback from your employees and should be cleared by your boss, but you should drive its formulation.

Without an IT strategy, you won't be able to align your long-term goals with your short-term responsibilities. You need to have these items decided and written down, so that when your boss tells you to do X, and your employee needs Y, and the other manager down the hall that helped you last week needs Z, you have a clear idea of which task should be addressed in which order.

Some companies have huge IT departments, with layers and layers of managers. Organizations of this size have formal IT strategies and sub-strategies. But many smaller companies don't have formal IT departments with managers, budgets, and expectations. Wherever you are on the size and formal structure spectrum, you should have a strategy. And you should write it down.

Your strategy should include the following:

✦ Who are your team members? And what can they do?

✦ Why/how is technology important to your organization?

✦ What are your assets?

✦ Who are your customers?

✦ What are your customers' needs?

✦ How do you plan to satisfy these needs?

While this all sounds simple, it's definitely not. Your customers may not even know what their IT needs are, for example. However, the very act of getting this all down on one or two sheets of paper can be of great value. For more information on the benefits of documentation, see Chapter 8 on IT Compliance and Controls (page 201).

Determine Who Your Team Members Are

This seems like a simple task — just list the people in your department. In fact, your team members may or may not be all the people on your staff. You may have someone on your staff who has part-time responsibilities to another department. This person is on your team, but you can't count on them 100% of the time.

Or, people from other departments, who aren't on your payroll and report to some other remote branch of the organizational chart, could be very useful to your department. They might call you when they hear about certain problems on the system, for example, or help you when someone in your department is out sick. These people aren't on your payroll, and they aren't in your department, but they are on your team.

In addition to determining who the team members are, find out their skill sets and backgrounds. You may know a team member as a cable installer but he may have rudimentary Java skills that the Applications Development team could use. She may be a sales manager who has some project management experience that could help you with the new phone system rollout.

Determine How Important Technology Is to Your Organization

The technology in use can vary tremendously from organization to organization. In a law firm, technology might be used simply for word processing, or it might be used to accurately track client billings. Additionally, it could be used to scan and archive documents, so that every single piece of paper related to a case is online where it can be indexed, cross-referenced, and immediately retrieved. In a retail organization, technology can be used for all the traditional back office activities (billing, purchasing, etc.) but probably serves its most vital function by helping the store managers to know what products are generating the most sales and profits, and which should be dropped from inventory. The store might also use it for space planning so that the shelves are stocked in a way that maximizes space usage, as well as profitability.

Determine Who Your Customers Are and What Their Needs Are

Whether your customers are other employees, suppliers, consumers, or other businesses, they are the ones you need to serve. Find out who your customers are. Figure out what their needs are. Then spend your time addressing those needs.

Issues to consider include:

+ **Your customers are not necessarily *retail* customers (although they could be).** More likely, your customers are other internal departments in the company and your boss. Different jobs have different customers, and there are departments (like Sales and Marketing) who should spend all day figuring out what their external customers need. IT, on the other hand, commonly serves other departments in the company like Sales, Marketing, Accounting, and Management.

✦ **Figure out what your customers' needs are.** Are they products or services? Data and information? Reduced costs? Improved efficiency or productivity?

✦ **Ask your customers directly about their needs.** Set up meetings with representatives from different departments, ask questions, note the answers, and change the way you're doing business to reflect customer needs and concerns.

Keep Your Department Central to the Company's Operations

Make sure the strategy mentioned in the above section is carefully aligned with the goals of the entire organization. This is critical. If the needs of your immediate boss are out of alignment with what the entire company is doing, you have a serious problem.

Let the rest of the organization know what you're doing in IT. To many of the other department managers, IT may not mean much more than "the people at the Help Desk that can reset passwords." Periodically, have a meeting with the other department heads. Let them know what you're doing in IT, what you've accomplished, and what you plan to do. With a little luck, light bulbs will start going off. They may see uses for the technology that you hadn't thought of. Get some good discussion going and you may learn a way to deliver a lot more value by slightly modifying your plans.

The reality is that in today's corporate world, IT departments are, for the most part, by default in the middle of action. Everyone is becoming aware of the values that computerization can bring to an enterprise. Wineries, toy shops, bookstores, and sandwich places — supposed havens for the non-technical — now have sophisticated computerized inventory systems, customer service mechanisms, online ordering counterparts, and — gasp — even fax machines to take preorders. Information technology is everywhere.

1.5   Additional Resources

Web Sites

✦ itmanagement.earthweb.com (IT management site)

✦ www.amanet.org/index.htm (industry organization for managers)

✦ www.informatics.indiana.edu/news/news.asp?id = 131&careers = true (IT Career Growth News)

✦ www.itaa.org/business/it (IT Industry association)

✦ www.managementhelp.org (library of resources for managers)

Books and Articles

✦ Bossidy, Larry, and Charan, Ram, *Execution: The Discipline of Getting Things Done*, Crown Business, 2002.

✦ Hill, Linda, "Becoming a Manager: How New Managers Master the Challenges of Leadership," *Harvard Business School Press*, 2003.

✦ Levinson, Meredith, "Inside an IT Marketing Campaign," *CIO Magazine*, February 1, 2006, p. 47.

✦ Margulius, David L., "Breaking Away: When IT Puts Business In the Lead," *Infoworld*, December 5, 2005, p. 28.

✦ Neff, Thomas, and Citrin, James, *You're in Charge — Now What?: The 8 Point Plan*, Crown Business, 2005.

✦ Robinson, William, *Your First 90 Days In A New Job (How To Make An Impact)*, Lulu, Inc., 2004.

✦ Stettner, Morey, *Skills for New Manager*, McGraw-Hill, 2000.

✦ Watkins, Michael, "The First 90 Days: Critical Success Strategies for New Leaders at All Levels," *Harvard Business School Press*, 2003.

Managing Your IT Team

In leadership, Peter [Drucker]'s enormous contribution has been his insistence that leaders come in all shapes, sizes, races and genders, and that leadership is not some mysterious blend of charisma and luck. Rather, Peter has argued persuasively that leadership most commonly arises from a commitment to serve others rather than self. . .

—FREDERICK HARMON

CHAPTER TWO

Even with the advanced functionality available in today's hardware and software, it's still the human factor that's the biggest influence on how effectively technology is put to use in your environment. The members of your IT team are the ones who will select, implement, configure, monitor, and manage the technology in your corporation.

The technology products in your environment (generally) behave in a fairly predictable manner, but people often don't. Managing a staff is an art, not a science.

The importance of managing a team can't be understated:

✦ Become a great manager and you've found a career path that will serve you well for the rest of your working life.

✦ Fail to manage well, and you'll be back in the non-managerial ranks soon enough.

✦ Become good at it, and it becomes your most valuable skill, and your staff becomes a critical component of the organization.

✦ Without good staff management skills, you'll see your department's goals and objectives become an uphill battle.

2.1   Keeping Employees Focused

IT Managers must set priorities clearly, explain the company and department mission, and communicate often with their team. Throughout this book, specific techniques are detailed to provide you with methods to accomplish these goals. In this section we will discuss the reasons why these goals must be pursued.

Establish Priorities

One of the most important, but often unnoticed, functions of a manager is to set priorities, such as allocating staffing and funding to various projects. Employees who spend months at a time working on a project often wonder what exactly it is that their manager does. In truth, the manager is doing one of the most important parts of his job by deciding *which* projects get worked on, *when* they need to start and finish, and *what* resources are assigned to them. A manager's real worth is in his ability to set goals and objectives and to set priorities and make decisions to achieve them.

Setting goals and priorities means managing your staff and your team so that their work reflects, as close as possible, your own priorities. A manager's merit is found in his staff's work. Of course, your decisions and priorities may be totally off base. Or they may be 100% on target. But if you fail to manage your staff well, the quality of your priorities will not matter: Your goals and objectives will never be realized anyway.

Communicate with Your Team

First and foremost, communicate your vision for the department to your staff. They should understand both where you want the department to go, and the plans you have for getting there. Both are important. You don't want to be the manager who makes the trains run on time, but doesn't know what to put in the freight cars. Similarly, you don't want to be the manager who goes on about the wonders of train travel but never gets the tracks laid.

The communication of your goals and priorities to your team is vital. The way you communicate with them will vary with a project's scope. A two-year project to implement an Enterprise Resource Planning (ERP) application will require different communication than managing a weekend effort to upgrade the company's database servers.

Here are some guidelines when communicating with your team.

Make Sure the Team Understands the Overall Objective and Goals

Explain it in practical terms; for example, "implementing a new accounts payable system might include eliminating all manual processes, thereby reducing turnaround time to 24 hours, and ensuring that no unauthorized payments are made."

Explain How You Envision Achieving the Goal

You don't have to offer too much detail, especially on a large project, but you should have some thoughts, visions, and ideas you can articulate as a type of road map. "Our first milestone is the end of February; by then we should have a prototype system for the users to look at. By mid-year we should have finalized all the details. We're looking to plan for parallel testing in the 4th quarter, with the final cut-over set for December 31st."

Encourage Questions and Input from Your Staff

There are several reasons why you should do this:

- ✦ Asking for your staff's input (and taking it seriously) will make your team feel like a part of the decision-making process; they will work better and harder on a process they feel a part of and understand.

- ✦ They are a lot closer to the work than you are — they'll be the first to recognize an opportunity, a potential landmine, or a dead end.

- ✦ The group will usually have important insight to share.

If the goal or plan is especially challenging, or perhaps it deviates somewhat from the norm, you'll have to be that much more motivating and excited when you communicate with the team.

Ask questions of the team to ensure that they have an appropriate understanding of the project. For example: How do you think we should start? Where do you see danger zones? What are the key milestones? What kinds of resources do you think we will need?

Listen Carefully

Notice the staff's comments, tone, and body language. Use these as clues to determine if your team is behind you. Make sure everyone feels free to air any doubts or concerns. One technique is to go around the table at the end of each meeting and to ask each member to express any concerns they have, and then address them accordingly. Another is to encourage the staff to send you e-mails or meet with you privately if they feel intimidated by speaking in front of a group.

Meet Regularly

Meeting frequencies might vary depending on the work at hand. Weekly and monthly meetings are common. During critical project times, it isn't uncommon to have daily meetings. You can have too many meetings or too few — it depends on the project. Try to establish a rhythm that people can work with; if you establish a meeting time of every Friday morning, the team will work throughout the week with that in mind.

Meetings don't have to always be project oriented. Regular department meetings, as well as individual meetings, with your direct reports can help foster a culture of open communication and sharing of information.

Project Meetings

Project meetings are a separate type of meeting that have both additional benefits and potential problems. See Chapter 4, Project Management (page 95), for a fuller discussion of project management.

Company Mission

Another method of keeping your employees focused is to clearly outline the company's mission, vision, and values. Defining and articulating these shouldn't be your responsibility as an IT Manager; someone else should do that for you (and the rest of the company). But once your company has agreed upon a mission statement, communicate it with your staff. Make it clear how this mission, and the vision statement that details how you are going to achieve that mission, directly affects the actions of every employee.

Company values are the final means you should use to keep your employees on the right track. If your company hasn't made its values clear, ask your management to do so. Again, defining and communicating values isn't your job; you can participate if a company-wide committee is formed, but you should not have to come up with these on your own. "Company values" are defined by the entire company and can be useful guides in determining employee behavior.

In addition to communicating the company's mission, goals, and values to your team, it's also vital that you share with them *the goals and values of the IT department*, objectives that should reflect both the company's mission and your own goals and values.

2.2 Avoiding Burnout

With IT so critical to today's organizations, the demands on the staff can be enormous. Glassy-eyed programmers, cases of Jolt soda, sleeping bags under desks, and 3 a.m. pizza deliveries have become routine.

IT demands are heavy because:

+ Virtually every aspect of an organization is dependent on IT and its services.

+ The tasks and their solutions are hard, complicated, and intense.

+ In the digital world we now live in, the workplace is often 24/7, and the demands are non-stop. The technology allows people to work 24 hours a day, squeezing in time for sleep only when the body refuses to stay awake.

+ The lure of a complex technical challenge often excites people to work 20 hours a day. (In the early days of developing the Macintosh, Steve Jobs handed out T-shirts that read: "Working 90 hours a week and loving it.")

+ IT staff is needed during working hours to ensure systems are running as they should and responding to problems. However, the staff is also needed during off–hours because that's often the only time that certain work (e.g., maintenance, upgrades, etc.) can be done.

◆ Unlike the days of assembly-line labor, the work of IT isn't measured in products produced per unit of time. So there are no clear external indicators of when the work is "complete." ("The IT job is one where you get an 'F' if you fail but only a 'C' if you succeed — this stuff is supposed to work, right?" Bill Gates, *Business @ the Speed of Thought*, p. 322.)

◆ Highly energized and motivated employees may not even realize the condition they are getting themselves into. While it may be tempting to push your staff, or allow them to push themselves to the limit, it's important to remember that you won't get much work out of them once they've hit that wall.

Be as Clear as Possible About Your Real Priorities

It takes more than just stating that something is a priority for everyone on a team to realize that it is a priority. If coding a specific interface is a critical task for a larger project, you have to say so. But also remember that your actions can dilute your words. If the status of the interface barely gets mentioned during staff meetings, or only one person is assigned to work on it part-time, even though you say it is a priority, you'll be sending mixed signals. You can demonstrate the task's importance by focusing on it during meetings, reallocating additional resources to it, sacrificing lesser priorities for it, and so on.

Make Your Employees Aware of the Dangers of Burnout

Often people most susceptible to burnout are the ones unaware of the problem. They work like dogs for two years and then they crash.

Outline the Prices Employees Can Pay

When making them aware of the problem, outline the cost of burnout:

◆ Deterioration of health

◆ Errors on the job

◆ Relationships with co-workers deteriorate

◆ Problems at home with family and with relationships

◆ Loss of job

The short-term gains for working weekends for two years in a row don't outweigh the long-term losses of any of the above.

Deal with the Situation

As the manager, you need to be more aware of the problem of burnout and take steps to monitor and avoid the situation:

✦ Be very clear about your performance and productivity expectations regarding your employees. Define clear measures and metrics and communicate them clearly and often. Get real commitments from your employees regarding time lines and deliverables. And make sure they feel safe in telling you when your expectations are unrealistic.

✦ Be very conscious of the levels of effort all of your team members are putting out. And don't think in absolute numbers. A 10-hour day may not seem like a big deal to you, but it can be an enormous commitment for a single parent or a person just coming off working three demanding projects.

✦ Spread the effort around. The amount of IT work is endless — as a manager, you have a responsibility to your company and your employees to carefully allocate work across the board. Certainly people have different work outputs, just as they have different working and communication styles. Your job is to consider the team as a whole, each person as an important part of that whole, and get the jobs done within that context.

✦ Make changes in personnel to reflect the needs of the jobs your team must perform. Need more people? Ask for them — and do so with concrete, numerical evidence of why you need them. Is one person on the verge of burning out because the company has overworked her? Shift that person's responsibilities. Is one person over his head in his job? Look for other places within the company that this person can contribute. (Care needs to be taken when doing this, as the employee may not understand.) In general, the IT world isn't for the fainthearted.

✦ Be aware of how much different people can give. Some employees can only deliver 40 hours' worth of work in a week, even if they are at their desk 60 hours. Others can easily double their efforts, for short times, in response to direct requests. Often, running at top speed isn't the fastest way to get there. Be sensitive to what motivates your employees, as well as their needs and limitations. Recognize that people can only be pushed, or even push themselves, so far. Recognize when they can be pushed further, and when you have to insist they take a break. Do this well, and you'll be rewarded with a far more productive and motivated team.

2.3 Employee Training

Training is always an issue for managers. While they know that it's a perk that employees often enjoy and it improves employee's skills, they are also concerned about its cost, the employee being away from his full-time responsibilities, and the fear that the employee will use the newly acquired skill to seek another job elsewhere. On the other hand, a few days or a week at a training class can serve as a respite for a hard-working employee as well as increase his skill set.

However, because learning new skills is such a critical part of working in IT, providing training is an important part of managing an IT staff. There are so many IT classes offered that it wouldn't be difficult to have someone spend more time at training classes than they do at work. As a manager you have to balance a few items when doling out training:

✦ Cost

✦ Need

✦ Employee morale

✦ Scheduling demands

Cost

There are two issues involved with the cost of employee training:

1. The cost of the training itself

2. The cost of having the employee away from her full-time responsibilities

Often, the second issue far outweighs the first. The expenses for an employee to attend a training class vary greatly. Some classes are offered either locally or online, and may only be three hours in length. But many training options include cross-country travel, which requires hotel, rental car, and travel expenses that can inflate the cost of the class by a factor of two or more.

Despite those variances, the real cost issue is often the expense of having an employee away from work for a period of time. Can you spare this individual for an entire week? Sometimes several people are sent to training together. Can you spare all of them? Sometimes contractors can fill in for staff members who are at training, in which case the costs are fairly easily measured. But other times, some of your other employees or people from other departments need to fill in; the "cost" of these solutions, while not always visible, is often much higher than a week in a hotel.

Need

What is the short- and long-term value of this kind of training for an employee? Often the needs are well defined: Joe needs a Windows Administrator class because he will back up Maria while she is on vacation. But other times, the issue gets cloudy: Mark wants to take an advanced Java programming class, but that isn't his exact responsibility right now and it isn't clear that the company is going to be using Java anyway.

"Need" may appear to be the clear deciding factor, but often the value of taking a training class is unclear. If that is the case, you need to use some of the other criteria listed in this section to help you decide whether or not to agree to have an employee take a training class.

Employee Morale

Many employees view training as a reward. It provides them with concrete, resume-enhancing skills, sometimes lets them "get out of the house" by traveling to a warm spot in midwinter, and often allows them to interact with professionals with the same interests and questions.

In addition, sending a staff member to a training course — or even suggesting it for yourself — can be an excellent way to motivate employees. Both you and your employees need to aggressively monitor their skill sets to make sure they are current and useful.

Also be aware that sending one person to training can occasionally cause a second person to feel resentment. One of the challenges any manager faces is how to juggle multiple responsibilities, such as how to manage multiple people. Make sure you spread the "wealth" around so that feelings like these have no basis in fact.

Scheduling Demands

This is probably the most difficult issue to deal with. Many of your own staff will find the issue difficult, rightly recognizing that a week away from the office means a week of catching up when they get back. Who will cover for them? If they are overburdened right now (as many IT people are), how are they ever going to make up for a lost week's worth of work? The answer is pretty simple: Evaluate the short-term costs versus the long-term gains. See the above three items; if the direct costs aren't overwhelming, if the employee (and your department) needs the training, and if their morale will be improved, go for it — and have them go for it.

How Do You Know When Your Employees Need Training?

There are three principal ways to identify when an employee needs training:

1. **They tell you.** IT people are deluged by training class offers and by situations where they are aware of their technical shortcomings in one area or another. Asking the boss for a class or two is a common request. (Asking for a week-long class on a cruise ship in the Bahamas is less common, but not unheard of.) You should consider an employee's request for training as a positive indication that they are interested in learning and doing more for the company. (It could also be an indication that they like being out of the office.) In addition, look at your employee's goals. Are they asking for the training to meet the performance goals you both set together?

2. **Your customers tell you.** The IT department's customers can be a variety of groups: they can certainly be outside customers, but they can also be (sometimes exclusively) internal. In either case, if you solicit feedback from your customers about what their IT needs are, you may hear about specific technical services that your department can't provide without either (1) getting more training for current employees or (2) hiring someone else to do the job.

3. **You find out on your own because you are a proactive manager.** Learn to address training needs before they become problems. If you do this, you'll save yourself tremendous time, money, and effort over the long term. You'll anticipate your department's needs for Java developers and start running the ads months in advance, knowing that particular talent is hard to find. You'll budget for a new Help Desk support rep early in the cycle, before the seasonal sales cycle kicks in and all the calls come in. And you'll send your people for training in Windows network administration, for example, before the project to upgrade starts.

Certification

Most IT Managers don't have the luxury of sending people to training just for the sake of training. As such, few IT departments are willing to sponsor their employees for training that leads to vendor or technology certification. This is simply because managers know that some of the classes in a certification program these days are fillers — they are of little or no use to a specific employee's job responsibilities. Of course, there are exceptions. Some managers may use certification as a way of rewarding highly valued employees, or for those employees whose responsibilities are very specialized. Of course, sending an employee to the requisite classes doesn't guarantee certification; the employee still has to pass the exam. (Note that some companies won't even pay for the exam if the employee doesn't pass.)

The value of certification is discussed in Chapter 3, Staffing Your Team (page 43).

What If the Employee Takes a Training Class, and Then Uses His New-Found Skills to Find Another Job?

Be Honest About This Problem

One effective technique is simply to address the issue with the employee beforehand, while you are still making a decision about whether or not they should go to training. As is often the case in business situations, bringing the topic out in the open can go a long way toward easing everyone's fears. Just discussing the issue doesn't create any legal arrangement, of course, but it should let both sides know where the other stands. As a manager, you should openly express your concern about the possibility of the employee "taking the training and running." You hope the employee will reply that the job is much bigger than one skill set, they like the environment, they would work here for free they like it so much, and so on. But if they don't, if they hedge or are evasive, or blurt out a series of negative statements, you've got a problem that a training class isn't going to solve.

Employee Agreements

Many companies have a policy that says an employee has to sign an agreement to reimburse the cost of training if she resigns within X months of taking a class. Of course, many employers and employees are hesitant about even making such an agreement because it creates somewhat of a non-trusting, non-supportive relationship. Before asking your employees to agree to something like this, make sure you discuss the issue with your HR department — there is probably an existing policy about it.

Because the IT world is so fluid, this situation works the other way, too. Employees can spend months on certification programs for a company and then the company changes direction. For example, one IT Manager had his entire Oracle database certification paid for but the company decided (at the last minute) to stay with Microsoft SQL. He eventually left to go to an Oracle shop.

Non-Technical Training

When you think about IT training, you generally think about technical training. It's important to remember that some of your staff may also benefit from non-technical training as a way of expanding their horizons, such as:

- ✦ Time management (for those who have trouble staying organized)
- ✦ Business writing (for those who have to prepare memos and reports)

- ✦ Presentation skills (for those who have to give presentations to groups)

- ✦ Interpersonal skills (communications, conflict management)

- ✦ Supervisory skills (for those who have a staff to manage)

- ✦ Project management (for those responsible for keeping projects on track)

- ✦ Leadership skills (for those who have to manage others)

Non-technical training can have tremendous value. Employees may not appreciate it as much as technical training, but you will value it. You can tell an employee that you're sending him to a non-technical training because you have plans to move him up in the organization, or you might tell him that his deficiencies in these areas are holding him back.

Your HR department can be the best source for non-technical training information. Training options are now more flexible and more accessible than ever before; in addition to the explosion of night and part-time schools, companies that provide on-site training, online courses, and the myriad of different media-based educational options make getting trained a lot more convenient.

Maximizing the Value of Training

If you send an employee for training, it's because you see the need. It's then up to you as their manager to make sure that they're putting these skills to use. You should review the course curriculum to get a feel for what the employee should be able to do after completing the class. If an employee isn't using the skills learned in a class, it could be because the selection of that particular class was a poor one, or that you haven't challenged them to use their newly acquired skills. There are some ways to test technical skills. See Chapter 3, Staffing Your Team (page 43), for tips on conducting technical interviews.

In addition, consider the following training ideas:

- ✦ Have the employee who went to training give an informal ("brown bag lunch") training session to the rest of the team. You can then see how much the employee learned and give your entire team some of the benefits of the training.

- ✦ Have the employee formally train the employees who didn't attend the training; if the employee goes to the initial training with that goal in mind, it can add value to their experience as well as save the company money.

- ✦ Consider on-site training where the content can be more contextually specific to your organization and your configuration.

2.4 Performance Reviews

Performance reviews are probably the single most important discussions you'll have with members of your staff. Although performance reviews are traditionally a once-a-year event, some companies are now doing them twice a year. Regardless of the frequency, a professionally done review should be done just like you should do your taxes: The end result should be the formalization of 12 months of regular discussion, feedback, analysis, and evaluation. Do the work in small bits all year, and you will be ready when the big moment arrives. Neither you nor the employee should be shocked at what is discussed.

The annual review process gives you a chance to document the employee's accomplishments, dedication, commitment, challenges, and opportunities for improvement. Many companies have evaluation forms that have been developed by the HR department. Other companies have no form and leave it up to each manager, or simply rely on a memo-style format. However, a form generally won't help you since a useful evaluation should really consist of descriptive narratives and discussion, not merely checked boxes.

Performance reviews are often used to resolve two other important company issues: rewarding over-performing employees and addressing under-performing employees. Poorly written evaluations make both of these tasks even more difficult, and the costs of failing at this are high:

1. Mishandled terminations can (and often do, these days) end in lawsuits.

2. Mishandled reviews of good performers often lead to the key employee changing jobs to get what they should've received from you.

Key Areas of Evaluation

Areas that you want to consider when reviewing an employee's performance include:

+ Quality of work
+ Flexibility
+ Creativity in solving problems
+ Communication skills
+ Innovation
+ Going above and beyond the requirements of the job
+ Coordination and collaboration with others (particularly those they don't have direct authority over)

✦ Accountability

✦ Ability to complete assignments in a timely manner

✦ Ability to pick up new skills on their own

✦ Ability to work with and enhance the work of other staff members

✦ Ability to manage short- and long-term projects

Quality of Work

Is this person providing excellent or mediocre work? Not every staff member will give you spectacular performances. On the other hand, not every staff member is compensated spectacularly. But your needs as a manager may be such that this person fulfills certain other critical functions: They may be a team member who keeps others enthusiastic about the project, for example, or set a good example for keeping focused, or have a deep knowledge of company history and provide long-term perspective to decisions.

Flexibility

Most roles have job descriptions, some job descriptions are even written down(!), but almost no job description adequately anticipates the real-world demands of the position. It's important for every employee to understand the real goals of the department and how he can help achieve those goals. Changing market conditions, changing project demands and priorities, and changing technical capacities all require employees to be flexible about their tasks. Has this employee adapted well to the fluid requirements of the job?

Creativity in Solving Problems

Along with flexibility about their job descriptions, good employees are often creative in solving problems. Five new employees started Monday, but only four laptops were delivered; a creative employee might find one in the test lab to tide everyone over. The rush order for two new servers needs a manager's signature, but she called in sick today; a creative employee will find a manager from another department or the manager's boss to get the order started.

Communication Skills

Can this person communicate well? Do they send clear, easy-to-read e-mails or do they send rambling e-mails that take 10 minutes to read and are still difficult to understand? Do they speak well in meetings, do they make personal attacks, or do they say nothing at all? Technical people are often not great communicators because their jobs often don't require tremendous amounts of interaction. But there is a base level of information exchange that every job requires, and a base level of interactive behavior that every organization requires. If a person works in a group, there are certain standards that must be met.

Innovation

Today's technology can be used in many different ways. And when multiple technologies are combined, the possibilities can grow exponentially. Innovation is an attribute for finding new ways of doing things — or doing new things. This could be anything related to simplifying processes, reducing errors, or finding additional uses for existing tools.

Going Above and Beyond Requirements of the Job

Many employees view their work as nothing more than a job, a day's work for a day's pay, and have almost an adversarial stance about doing anything more. Can you fault someone for doing only what they are supposed to do? However, for those who view their work as more of a "career" than a "job" and seek to be promoted and move up, going above and beyond the job requirements is one of the best ways to achieve those goals. This can include helping out co-workers, volunteering to do the more challenging tasks, working on items that no one else seems to want to do, etc.

Coordination and Collaboration with Others (Particularly Those They Don't Have Direct Authority Over)

"Plays well with others" is another way to describe this attribute. It simply means that you work well with others on a team. This could apply to situations where a large team is formed for a particular project, as well as the case of individual contributors that periodically have to interact with others. It also includes gaining the respect of those you work with. To do all this well requires a numbers of skills and traits: interpersonal, influencing, leadership, communication/listening, trust, adaptability, compromise, and relationship building.

Accountability

Managers look for accountability in their employees primarily because it makes the manager's job easier. A manager prefers knowing that when an employee is assigned a task, it will be done, and the manager won't have to do regular checks to ensure that work is progressing. (See the next item on completing assignments on time.) Accountability also means that the employee will recognize what their own responsibilities are, and will not sit around waiting for the manager to tell them what to do. If your staff isn't accountable, you end up as a micro-manager. On the other hand, it's up to the manager to make their employees feel accountable through follow-up, project assignments, stated goals and objectives and a clear statement of the job requirements, as well as the impact to others when things don't go as planned.

Ability to Complete Assignments in a Timely Manner

For most companies today, timely performance is critical. Gone are the days when deadlines were approximations and missing them had few consequences. "Just-in-time" no longer refers to an inventory technique; it now is often used to describe how entire departments and companies act in response to market conditions.

Be clear about your expectations for timely performance and let your staff know you'll be using that as a criterion for evaluation. And let them know that you are being evaluated on that basis as well. Installing the new phone system on Monday instead of the Friday before may be suddenly required, but create an environment where people feel comfortable suggesting coming in on Saturday (or at least discussing if it is necessary).

Ability to Pick Up New Skills on Their Own

The IT world changes so quickly that it's an employee's fundamental responsibility to help herself, her department, and her company stay current. Every department has the programmer still resting on his legacy coding skills; encourage your staff not to become that person. See the "Employee Training" section above for details on the issue of training. Some companies provide tuition reimbursement to earn toward a degree.

Ability to Work With and Enhance the Work of Other Staff Members

You may have a Windows Administrator with superlative technical skills but zero people skills. Let him know that your IT department is a team, not a random collection of individuals, and everyone is expected to interact professionally with each other. Snarling or swearing at anyone else who touches the system isn't acceptable.

Many a manager has had to say "You don't have to like all your fellow IT department members, but you have to treat them with respect." This is a common problem with technical people, and one way of solving the issue is to inform them that their behavior in this area is part of their review.

Ability to Manage Short- and Long-Term Projects

Every employee in IT is given projects, some long and complex, some short and simple. Inform your staff that their ability to handle projects is an element you will be evaluating when it comes to review time. Many employees might not think in project-related terms; they think their task is to get the new laptops installed in the Sales department in the next two weeks (and not see how it relates to the bigger goal of a new sales-force automation system implementation). Of course, that is a project, a set task with a specific goal, resources, and a timeline. For some levels and tasks, as long as they finish the projects on time and under budget, it isn't important for them to think in project management terms. But those who do see the bigger picture and take the long view may have brighter futures.

Specific Evaluation Statements

The words used in performance reviews can have a great deal of impact, or no impact at all. You want to be sure that you are clear, and that each statement has meaning and value to the employee. Avoid ambiguity, and use examples to back-up your assessments. See Table 2.1 for some samples.

Useful Metrics

If the individual being reviewed has a position that is operational in nature, you should include quantitative metrics in the review:

- ✦ Network up-time
- ✦ Systems response time
- ✦ Call resolution/response time
- ✦ Number of incidents/calls addressed per hour/day
- ✦ System reliability

Guidelines for Reviews

Don't forget: both you and the members of your IT staff are salaried professionals. Act as such, and treat them that way. Your respect will be rewarded.

Table 2.1 Sample evaluation comments

Statement Type	Example	Description
Almost useless	"Mark is a fine worker with a good attitude; he works hard and has done a good job for the company."	While it may be true, this statement tells Mark nothing concrete about his past performance and gives him nothing to focus on for the future. Nor is the company served by this kind of statement. How valuable an employee is Mark, and how can it help Mark grow?
Positive	"Martha was exemplary in her efforts to complete her implementation of the new health-care plan project on time. In addition to working over several weekends, she also enlisted the help of two departments to meet the October 1 deadline."	This is a very useful comment for Martha; she knows her efforts were noticed and the company knows they have a committed employee.
Negative	"Mary Jane showed no interest in expanding her professional skill set; she turned down several offers for training classes in new programming languages; and refused to move to a new project that would have required her to learn new procedures."	Mary Jane knows exactly what she did wrong and, if she chooses, how she can change her behavior to act differently in the future.

No Surprises

As mentioned above, preparing for a review is often a year-long process that ends with the written evaluation and the meeting with the employee. As such, a performance review shouldn't contain any surprises for the employee, especially bad surprises. Any negative comments that you include in the review should be items that you've discussed with the employee multiple times in the course of the year.

Be Objective

It's important to remember that a performance review is the company's formal assessment of the employee's performance. Be as objective as possible. Remember reviews of your own performance — often the most contentious items are the subjective ones. With this in mind, your performance review should be full of examples and specifics to back up your assessment. Providing quantifiable accomplishments and measurable goals helps you remain objective.

Also, remember that other people will read this review in the future. Other people in the company, for example, may read this review when thinking about transferring the employee into their department. Or the person may leave and may later reapply at your company. Be sure that your comments accurately reflect the employee's performance.

Carefully Record Details

The more specifics you can provide, the more valuable the review will be for the employee. And the more specifics you can provide now, the more understandable it will be in the future. It's hard to recall the incidents you need when you're looking back on the past 12 months. Review your own status reports for ideas. And, during the year, jot quick notes to yourself on scraps of paper that you toss into the employee's file. While this sounds like a great idea in theory, it's in fact something many good managers do on a regular basis. Details matter, and memories fade. Record them as they happen and both you and the recipient of your work — for this is real work that managers have to do — will be better for it.

When reviewing these notes, take the long view. Try and look over the course of the entire year and remember that you probably wrote those notes when something was going particularly well, or particularly poorly. Perhaps those comments are right on target, or perhaps they represent an emotional high or low.

As you prepare the review, you can also ask the employee for her own list of accomplishments (and areas they think they can improve upon) over the past 12 months. This can help jog your own memory and help you understand what the employee considers her greatest achievement. Additionally, it helps you see what the employee thinks were her most important contributions. Getting her input can help you avoid embarrassment by failing to mention something that was important to her.

Negative Reviews

Performance reviews that are mostly or entirely negative are difficult for both the reviewer and the reviewed.

There are four important points to keep in mind if you are in this situation:

1. Be as specific as possible
2. Negative reviews should not be a surprise to anyone
3. Keep HR informed
4. Be professional

Be Specific

Not only will the session(s) probably be very emotional, but the end result can be more positive when you can be very specific about what happened. This detail includes not only past performance but current events; be clear and detailed in your notes about what conversations took place and what each party said. If the employee failed to meet goals, identify what those goals were, and where the employee came-up short. Stick to the facts and be objective.

It Should Not be a Surprise

Follow the guidelines outlined in this chapter; constantly communicate with your staff and record both accomplishments and failures throughout the year. If you do these things, both you and the employee should be aware of the mismatch between their goals and their performance.

Keep HR Informed

Make sure to keep your HR department informed. If your company doesn't have an HR department, find an appropriate third party to keep informed of (or sit in on) the situation — your own boss is a logical choice. If you keep someone else involved and aware of the situation, you will always have a third party to check back with (if required) later in the process.

Be Professional

Take extra care to make sure that what you write comes off in a highly professional manner. Resist the urge to list failures. Instead, cite circumstances where the employee "fell short of expectations" or "needs development" to identify areas where the employee needs to focus his efforts. In some situations, an employee may not be aware of his own weakness; for example, his contributions and involvement at staff meetings are more like speeches instead of discussions. If this is the case, consider it a coaching opportunity for you and a development area for him.

The task of preparing for and conducting performance reviews really shouldn't be emotional, but in some cases it will be stressful and time-consuming.

Example of When You Might Need to Give a Negative Review

Susie did a mediocre job, but more problematic was the fact that she was very difficult to deal with. As a result, most people avoided working with her. To make matters worse, she was used to getting very positive reviews.

When reviewing someone like this, you might want to ask them what they want out of the job. Do they want to move to the next level (e.g., level 3 to level 4), which would mean a raise along with the promotion? If they answer "yes," then you can proceed to list all the things they need to do in their current position that they aren't doing, and then list the things that they need to do to get to the next level. For example, you could say: "You've completed this first project, which is great, but the second one wasn't completed on time. Why?"

After the explanation is given, then you say that you understand, and in the future, they need to report sooner or more effectively about what is going right or wrong. Then, you can add, for example, after they've completed all these tasks (as in the case of Susie), she would need to mentor someone else and/or be the lead on a project. It may be that both you and she know this isn't likely. If that's the case, and she's unable or unwilling to say that, you have given her the motivation to either step up to the task or (honestly) find other work, because the next review will be explicit about this new task.

Have Employees Review Themselves

Many companies have adopted the formal policy of having employees, in addition to their managers, review themselves. The employee uses the same form as the manager and evaluates her performance over the specified period of time. Naturally, self-reviews (like resumes) can contain some elements of (how shall we put it?) "skill inflation"? Nonetheless, the exercise is a very valuable one for both the employee and the manager. The employee gets a chance to express her concerns and talk about what she thought her strengths and weaknesses were. Identifying the gaps between the manager's assessment and the employee's self-assessment can help in figuring out development opportunities, and identify where problems are.

"360" Reviews

The theory behind "360 degree reviews" is that an employee receives feedback from not only his direct supervisor, but from other individuals as well, which include peers and subordinates (see Table 2.2). A person may work on a project run by another department manager, for example; in that case, the other manager can have direct input into the employee's review. Or an employee may work much more with two staff members and may only occasionally see their direct manager. (Some employees have management in other states or other countries.) In that case, 360 reviews allow the individuals who most directly work with the person to provide input on their performance.

When 360 reviews were a new evaluation technique, many companies tried them; how many are still using them isn't clear. If your company is using them, or thinking of using them, be prepared for more feedback — both good and bad — at review time.

Table 2.2   Pros and cons of "360 reviews"

PRO		CON	
	360 reviews provide opportunities for people traditionally not asked for their opinions to express them; customers, for example, often have to be proactive about providing feedback to suppliers.		They generally involve a *lot* more data. And, the feedback from multiple people may be inconsistent, which makes it difficult to identify pluses and minuses and figure out a development plan.
	The quality of review for some workers improves tremendously because the people best suited to evaluate an individual are now involved in the process.		In addition, people who haven't done performance reviews before are suddenly providing detailed review data; you may or may not want information on Ken's workplace cleanliness, for example.

A newer trend is to use 360 assessments not as formal review components but as feedback mechanisms throughout the year. In other words, you may ask the manager from another department for feedback on your staff member once the project ends, store that feedback away, and use it during the review. Or solicit input from project team members at the end of the project and use that data later. But when review time comes around, you don't need to poll five co-workers of the employee or customers that person has talked to; you already have that data. You do a performance review as you normally would using the data you collected throughout the year.

How to Conduct the Actual Review Discussion

When it's time to meet with the employee to go over the performance review, remember it's a discussion — make this an interactive time, not a linear one. Do not simply read the review to him. In fact, you may want to consider giving the employee time to read the review in advance of your meeting, so that he has time to digest it and can then discuss it intelligently and unemotionally. Remember though, as a manager, to discuss it with conviction. This is your "assessment" of his performance. You should be willing to make changes for two reasons: gross error (e.g., a project was completed on time, when you said it wasn't) or language nuances.

Respect Privacy

If you work in a cube farm, make sure you reserve a conference room or arrange for an off-site meeting. You will both want the comfort of knowing the conversation isn't being overheard, regardless of whether everything is positive.

Tone of the Discussion

You need to be clear in your discussion with the employee. Depending on the employee's performance, your tone may need to include hints of motivation, hard-heartedness, and optimism. At the end of the review, there shouldn't be any doubt in the employee's mind as to what you think of his performance, where he has excelled, where he needs to improve, and steps he needs to take to do so.

In certain cases, you might want to have specific follow-up meetings with an employee at regular intervals after the formal performance reviews. If necessary, you may want to consider additional interim informal reviews at certain, pre-specified times.

2.5   Additional Resources

Web Sites

- ✦ *www.humanresources.about.com/od/360feedback* (360 reviews)
- ✦ *techrepublic.com.com/5138-10878_11-729776.html* (360 review templates)
- ✦ *www.pfdf.org/leaderbooks/drucker/bio.html* (Drucker quote)

Books and Articles

✦ Broadwell, Martin M., and Carol Broadwell Dietrich, "The New Supervisor: How to Thrive in Your First Year as a Manager," *Perseus*, 1998.

✦ Fournies, Ferdinand F., *Why Employees Don't Do What They're Supposed to Do and What to Do about It*, McGraw-Hill, 1999.

✦ Jaffe, Brian D., "Following a Few Simple Rules Can Ease the Pain of Employee Reviews," *InfoWorld*, January 26, 1998.

✦ Lewis, Bob, *Bob Lewis's IS Survival Guide*, Sams, 1999.

✦ Maslach, Christina, and Michael P. Leiter (Contributor), *The Truth about Burnout: How Organizations Cause Personal Stress and What to Do about It,* Jossey-Bass Publishers, 1997.

✦ Potter, Beverly, et al., *Overcoming Job Burnout: How to Renew Enthusiasm for Work,* Ronin Publishing, 1998.

✦ Straub, Joseph T., *The Rookie Manager: A Guide to Surviving Your First Year in Management*, Amacom, 1999.

Staffing Your IT Team

We're all either our greatest advocate or our greatest Achilles' heel.

—JONATHAN WYGANT

Your success and failure as an IT Manager is based almost entirely on the people that work for you. Every time you hire a new employee, you have an opportunity to add value to your team and to adjust the balance of skill sets and personality of the team — and to your company as a whole. Therefore, each hire should have your full attention and not be dismissed as another administrative chore. This chapter discusses the important details associated with the various elements involved in hiring for your team.

Hiring a few years ago was difficult because there weren't enough well-qualified candidates available for the open positions. More recently, hiring has been difficult

CHAPTER THREE

because there are now too many well-qualified candidates. The reasons will change, but the difficulty — and importance — of hiring the right people for the right jobs will never change.

3.1   Why IT Managers Need to Deal with Hiring People

You need to deal with hiring because the people on your staff are the single biggest factor in determining whether or not you're going to be successful or not at your job.

Hiring means dealing with recruiting agencies and your HR department, reviewing résumés, conducting interviews, and negotiating an offer. If you secretly wish that the first candidate you meet is *the one* and you're glad your job isn't in personnel, don't worry: you're not alone. That means you feel the same way as every other IT Manager.

It's precisely this urge to "hire first, ask questions later", however, that can easily lead to a decision that you and your company will come to regret. This chapter details some of the issues to watch out for, the questions to ask (both of yourself and interviewees), as well as other items you should be concerned about when you're considering bringing someone new onto your team.

HR Department's Role

Because recruiting for an IT position usually involves dealing with a lot of technical terms, skills, and résumés with acronyms and buzzwords, many HR departments that normally lead recruiting efforts for all other departments will take a back seat and let you drive when it comes to IT recruiting. But this isn't always the case.

Talk to HR and discuss the following:

+ Is there an approved list of recruiters to use? What is the company's policy on their finder's fees?

+ Can you find and use your own recruiters?

+ Who is responsible for placing ads in newspapers and on Web sites? Who pays for the ads?

+ Will HR perform the initial screening of applicants' résumés?

+ Who evaluates the salary range for this position and what is the evaluation process?

✦ Who should be the internal point of contact for agencies and applicants?

✦ Who does background and reference checks?

✦ What is the time frame for the process?

✦ Who is in charge of the process?

As stated above, many HR departments recognize that IT recruiting is a special skill — and one that they might not be particularly good at. Accordingly, they may ask you to take as large a role as possible. If this is the case in your company (and don't assume it is), HR may only want to get involved at the very beginning and then during the final round of interviews.

How to Get Help with Your Hiring

If you're working for a small company, you'll probably have to assume some HR duties, just like you have to assume some administrative, accounting, or travel duties. But once the company reaches a certain size, it should have someone to help with the hiring duties. They don't have to take care of all of the hiring, but they certainly can help.

In particular, you can get the HR department to help you with the screening and recruiting processes:

✦ Once you have written the description (see the section, Write a Position Description, on page 55), they can post it for you. They can work with you to figure out where the position should be posted — general job-sites, industry specific, etc.

✦ Have them identify someone in their department as a contact point. Let them field the initial calls and e-mails.

✦ Have them weed through the initial responses (which can be in the hundreds, even for specifically worded technical jobs) down to a manageable size. Give them strict guidelines ("The candidate must have 5 years of programming experience and must know at least Perl, C++, and Java.") to use to perform the initial screening. Give them a number: You want to look at 15 résumés max and talk to five candidates max. Let them weed the initial responses down to an acceptable size. If the job requires writing skills, HR can give a writing test or have them ask for writing samples.

✦ If interpersonal skills are important, HR can save you valuable time by eliminating those who simply are poor communicators, don't take pride in their appearance, etc.

✦ Once you have done the interviewing and chosen the candidate you like, hand the ball back to HR. They can call the candidate's references and draw up the offer letter. Finally, you (or HR, whichever you prefer) can make sure there is a place for the candidate when he first arrives, that he has work to do, and also that the associated new-hire materials (like the benefits package, company policies, etc.) are covered.

✦ Your HR representative can also be an effective liaison between you and the candidate when the offer is extended and/or negotiated. They have the experience to know how to handle these situations, how to respond, etc. They will check with you before committing to anything and offer you guidance.

Justifying a Hire

Of course, before you hire someone, you may need to get approvals. Whether it is simply replacing someone who recently left, or adding to staff, you may need to convince others that this hire is necessary. If it's a new position, you'll have to explain why this role is needed and what benefit it will deliver. Sometimes the position description (discussed later in this chapter) has enough information; other times you may need to go into more detail.

Some ideas to consider include:

✦ The department's work load has grown by X percent in the past year, and additional staff is needed to keep up. Sometimes you can justify the workload with metrics like the number of calls to the help desk, number of new projects, the company's growth, etc. Also, what about previous downsizing (the "falling further behind" syndrome)?

✦ The department has brought in new technologies and you need to hire people who are already skilled and experienced in order to use the product effectively.

✦ The company can save time and money if certain processes are automated, but you need staff to implement and support this.

✦ You will be able to respond to our users/customers X percent faster if we expand our staff.

Be as specific as you can with your estimates, but also note that they are only estimates. No one expects you to be able to determine to the dollar or to the hour how much savings or productivity improvement a new hire will generate, so note that these are your best guesses. But use numbers in your request. Numbers represent facts, and presenting facts is better than presenting an opinion — don't just say "it would be good to get another guy." Plus, you don't want to be perceived as an "empire-building" manager who thinks he can increase his own status (or ego) simply by managing a larger staff.

Start with Internal and External Referrals

Looking inside is the best method to start your search for a candidate. Does anyone in your department/company/personal network know of a candidate who matches your criteria? Co-workers, other managers, and internal job-posting boards all can provide valuable names. You should *always* start here.

The quality of people you contact through these referrals is generally higher and the candidates are generally better suited for the position. Most people are conscious of putting their reputation on the line when recommending another person, and will do so only if they have some level of confidence that the person merits the recommendation.

Be sure you don't make any promises, though. Ask everyone if they know of someone, but be careful not to make any assurances up front. The most you should promise is that you'll look at their résumé or that you'll make sure the right person looks at the résumé. Some internal referrals can be radically mismatched ("I thought you said you were looking for a C++ programmer, not a Web development person). Aside from the occasional courtesy interview, you shouldn't waste your time, or theirs, by interviewing candidates who are never going to get the job.

Of course, make sure the candidate is treated with respect. If they're referred to you, and they aren't right for the position, make sure they're contacted with that information. You want to be able to reuse your internal contacts, and leaving their recommendations in limbo is a good way to make sure they don't help you next time.

Internal versus External Hires

An internal hire is when someone from within the company, or perhaps even from within your own department, is selected for an opening. In some cases it might be a promotion, and in other cases it might just be a lateral change. Hiring individuals from within your own department or your own company presents its own challenges. Like many other issues dealt with in this book, there are good and bad reasons for hiring inside (see Table 3.1).

Should You Hire a Full-Time Employee or a Consultant?

The answer, of course, is "it depends." It depends on what your needs are. Both types of employees have their strengths and weaknesses.

Table 3.1 Pros and cons of internal hires

PRO		CON	
	The candidate is known. Her strengths and weaknesses have been seen by other people you work with, so there shouldn't be many surprises.		Hiring an internal person may anger other people you work with. If the person has talent and is a contributor to his group, his boss may be reluctant (or downright furious at the idea) for one of their workers to transfer. For personal reasons, many managers are angrier at a worker transferring to another department or division than they are at a person leaving the company altogether. It doesn't make a lot of sense (a lost worker is a lost worker, and going to another division still might benefit the previous manager in some small ways), but it's a fact. Try to determine what the reaction of the manager of the candidate you are interested in will be before you start talking to people. This can range from a simple and casual request at a meeting you are both attending to a formal, pre-interview notification.
	Many companies aggressively promote the concept of hiring/promoting from within (although some don't), so you can get some kudos from upstairs for adding to the company's "internal hire" list.		People who have worked for the company for a while know "where all the bodies are buried." They arrive with many preconceived ideas — maybe even some about your department. New people to the company generally come with their eyes and ears open, ready to absorb and learn. Some internal people arrive like that, and some arrive with lots of hard-to-shake prejudices.

(Cont.)

Table 3.1   Pros and cons of internal hires (continued)

PRO		CON	
	Other employees will appreciate seeing that there is an opportunity to move up. Too often, staff members leave a company simply because they don't believe they see much opportunity for their own growth.		
	There will be a radically shorter introduction term; the benefits package has already been filled out and the candidate knows how the company works, and can start being productive a lot sooner.		

Full-time employees are individuals who work for your corporation. Some are paid by the hour and some are salaried, but in either case, they are hired by, paid by, and report to someone in an organization. In addition to salaries, full-time employees receive additional benefits that can take the form of health insurance coverage, retirement plans, etc. To your Finance and HR people, these individuals are sometimes referred to as W-2s, because they get a W-2 tax form at the end of the year.

Most full-time employees are hired on an "at will" basis, which means that either the employee or the company can terminate the arrangement at any point, for any non-discriminatory reason. However, this can vary from state to state. Regardless, your Legal and HR departments will probably insist on sufficient reasons and due process, though, if you're the one looking to end someone's employment.

Consultants (frequently referred to as "contractors"), on the other hand, are brought in on a temporary basis by companies. They're generally paid by the hour or day, receive no benefits, and aren't on the company's payroll. They aren't necessarily employees of an organization, and are often responsible for handling not only their own insurance but also their own tax issues. You may find an independent contractor through an agency or consulting firm, or you may find them directly through Web searches or personal referrals. Online job boards are popular methods of finding qualified contractors.

These individuals are often referred to as 1099s, because instead of receiving a W-2 tax form, they get a 1099 tax form (either from your company or their agency).

Which type of employee should you hire? See Table 3.2.

Along those lines, it is important to note that IT is a strenuous world, and that IT projects are often complex, multi-person, multi-year adventures. You'll need to get buy-in from everyone on your team for many of the issues you address; contractors may or may not be there for you in the crunch. See Table 3.3 for the pros and cons to using full-time employees.

Table 3.2 Pros and cons to using consultants

PRO	CON
In general, contractors may have more diverse experience. You can find independent contractors with backgrounds in most, if not all, of the obscure corners of technology. Because they aren't locked to one desk and to one organization, they're free to roam and learn what new projects and new companies can teach them.	**On the other hand, consultants often cost more than full-time employees.** Even counting benefits, etc., that a full-time person is paid, contractors can easily cost you more. This is particularly the case if the contractor is hired through an agency, as the pay rate will include the agency's markup. (Contractors have to pay their own Social Security taxes, among other things, so their rates will generally be higher than a full-time person's wages.)
Because contractors often have such varied expertise, they usually require little or no training to become productive. You can see results from contractors in a relatively short amount of time.	**If you hire a consultant, for budgeting purposes you will need to estimate how long the contract will be.** This is sometimes very hard to do; if you are finishing off a company-wide operating system upgrade, you know (roughly) how many machines are involved, how long it will take to do each one, etc. But if you are helping the Development team implement a new Accounts Receivable system, there are many variables that affect the outcome. That process could take a week or three months and sometimes factors nowhere near your control can influence that figure.

(Cont.)

Table 3.2   Pros and cons to using consultants (continued)

PRO	CON
Consultants don't add to "head count." When companies are trying to save money, it looks poorly if they are adding to staff. Although the actual costs are more expensive, upper management and the Finance department frequently would rather pay a contractor as opposed to increasing the employee head count.	**It is easy (and potentially disastrous) to forget that contractors aren't employees of your company: Their loyalty, in the end, is to themselves.** This isn't to say contractors do a poor job; some do spectacular jobs (while others don't, of course). But they care about getting paid and recording hours; their interest in the long-term growth of your department or your company isn't all that high. If a contractor feels that he may not have much of a future with your company, he may start looking for a more reliable revenue stream, and possibly leave you at his convenience, not yours.
Consultants can usually be dedicated to a particular project, whereas full-time employees have many other responsibilities.	
You can terminate a contractor quickly and easily when you need to. Sometimes this is the most significant benefit of a consultant. This might be because the need for the contractor is for a specific time period, or because you want to be able to end the relationship easily (without interference from HR) if the person doesn't work out as planned. Various states have various laws about what you must do in those situations. While professional courtesy says you should give at least two weeks notice when terminating a full-time person, in general, you can fire a contractor the same day.	

Table 3.3 Pros and cons to using full-time employees

PRO	CON
In general, full-time employees are more committed. They're more loyal to your organization because they have a vested interest in its success, of course. They have a better understanding of the context of the work they're doing; they remember the project when it was done five years ago, and they understand why this particular VP's needs are being given priority.	**Full-timers can sometimes be less deadline driven.** They know there is always tomorrow, and many aren't shy about reminding you. Many full-time employees are dedicated, hard-driving workers, but many are not.
Full-time employees are cheaper — in the short term. When you calculate the cost of a worker, you need to include the benefits the employee receives, the cost of office space, etc. But in the short term, even the total of these costs can be less than a pricey consultant.	**Terminating full-time employees is much more complicated than terminating contractors.** There are many laws surrounding the termination of a full-time employee, and this is one area where you are much better off having your HR department deal with the issue. A more detailed discussion of this issue is presented below.
Sometimes, full-time employees are better suited for the specific task at hand. Sometimes the learning curve for a consultant can be severe, whereas a full-time employee brings critical legacy knowledge about the process that can radically affect the time it takes to complete that process. It may be wiser to get an employee trained about a new technology, than to try to get a contractor fully versed in the organization and process of your company.	

Determine Which Type is Best for Your Job

To best determine whether you should hire a consultant or a full-time employee, think about why you're hiring a new employee. Do you need someone for a few months in an area of technology that you have no expertise in and probably won't need in the future? If so, you should hire a contractor. Do you need someone to fill a gaping hole in your team or replace an employee who is leaving? If so, you should hire a full-time employee.

Financial considerations may also play a role here. Not only does the actual cost enter into it, but, as mentioned before, sometimes an organization doesn't want to "add head count" and would prefer you bring someone in as a consultant instead of as a full-time employee.

Consultant or Employee — You Can't Have It Both Ways

Regardless of whether you decide to hire an independent contractor or a full-time employee, make that determination *before* you open the req. In the past ten years several companies (including one that has its headquarters in Redmond, WA) have tried to have it both ways. That is, even though individuals were brought on as contractors, the employer was essentially treating them as full-time employees. These companies have lost lawsuits as a result of this kind of corporate behavior. As such, the individuals were entitled to those things that true full-time employees enjoy, like participating in stock purchase plans (*http://www.bizjournals.com/seattle/stories/2000/12/11/daily7.html*).

Worker status is a tricky issue with many potential legal ramifications. If you have any concerns about the status of your workers or potential employees, take them up with your HR and Legal departments as soon as possible.

Timing Considerations

The circumstances and requirements of the hire will often help you with this decision; if you're looking to fill an entry-level position, late spring is a good time to get this semester's graduates. And, if your company follows the academic calendar (for example, textbook publishing and school supplies companies), you'll be on a more defined schedule. Summer time (due to vacations) and the holiday period at the end of the year are generally quieter times for staffing. This is because people aren't generally looking to make potentially career/life-altering changes during these times. Similarly, at the end of the year, some companies will defer all hiring until the following year, simply for the benefit of making this year's numbers look better.

"When is the best time to hire?" The correct answer to this question is: "At least one month before you *need* to hire." Hiring people takes time, often more time than you expect, and it's not a decision you should leave until the

Why Do Some Organizations Refuse to Increase Full-Time Head Count?

There are reasons why a company may not want to increase its full-time head count that, strangely enough, have nothing to do with money.

+ **Official Size Limits**. Companies may want to stay a certain size to qualify for specific government contracts. There is a 500-employee limit, for example, to qualify as a small business in the manufacturing industry (*http://www.sba.gov/size/indexguide.html*). Hiring consultants or part-time employees does not affect this limit.

+ **Business Model**. Some companies are little more than middlemen, facilitating the flow of business from one sector to another, from one group of companies to another (eBay is a company like this). Companies like this grow or shrink quickly based on their immediate needs; they want to remain very flexible and not be burdened with a lot of overhead. Not only do they not hire full-time workers, they often lease office space on a very short-term basis.

+ **Impressing Investors**. When times are tough, investors like to see a company reducing costs, and that includes staff reductions. Nonetheless, it is all too common to see individuals laid off as employees, only to be brought back very quickly as consultants.

+ **Nature of the Market They Are In**. One author calls it the "Ben and Jerry's vs. Amazon" model. Does your company operate in a market with lots of well-established competitors (like Ben and Jerry's)? If so, slow, organic growth may be your best method of succeeding. On the other hand, if your company enters a new field (like Amazon was doing when it started), getting as much market share as soon as possible may be the best way to approach things. In that case, adding as many personnel as soon as possible may be required.

last minute. And training people takes time, too. Since you brought them on because they had a specific skill set that you needed, contractors should need less training than full-time employees. (You should think twice about paying for a contractor's training expenses. It happens, but it should be when you've exhausted all other options.)

Regardless of what type of employee you have hired, keep in mind that they will need time to become familiar with the environment, how the organization operates, what their role is, when the next meetings are, etc.

3.2 Write a Position Description

Most likely, you're going to have to prepare some type of Position Description (PD), sometimes called a Job Description (JD). A PD is a relatively detailed description of a specific role.

Your HR department may ask you to write a PD so that it can be posted internally within the company, or it may be used to relay the pertinent details to agencies and recruiters. HR may also use the information in PDs to help prepare an ad for the newspaper or for a job-posting site. HR often insists that every employee have a JD so that every individual's responsibilities, accountabilities, etc., are clearly spelled out. In many organizations, the content of the JD is the basis for determining the grade, title, salary range, bonus eligibility, etc., for a position.

Even if you aren't required by your company's procedures to prepare a JD for the hiring process, it's a good idea to do so. Every member of your staff should have a JD of their own job. This way, there is little doubt as to what their responsibilities are.

A PD can also be used for performance evaluations, salary considerations, and staffing justification. If an employee becomes a problem employee, it's good to have a hard-and-fast description of what their official duties are supposed to be. HR can use this information to help resolve difficult personal situations.

Position Descriptions versus Contracts

Along these lines, it's important to remember that the PD is just that: a description. It is *not* a contract. There are several reasons this distinction is important, but the most important ones are:

- ✦ *Many companies have formal contracts with some of their employees* (particularly at the senior levels), and a PD is not designed for that purpose. Some companies — depending on the company, the industry, and the position — have formal, legal contracts that they require employees to sign upon joining the organization. These contracts are generally strong legal instruments with very specific terms. They aren't good methods for determining what a person *should* do; they are often a list of things a person should *not* do (like using company resources for personal needs, or revealing confidential information). A PD doesn't serve this legal function.

- ✦ Goals, responsibilities, and expectations *are* things that should be listed in a PD. These aren't legally enforceable items, but nonetheless are critical components of the position.

✦ *Things change*. While your staff may or may not appreciate change, it's still incumbent on you as a manager to maintain your flexibility. Your boss will demand a wide variety of things from you, often adding or subtracting duties the same week. You'll need to adapt quickly to those new challenges and be able to turn your staff in the new direction. A PD that details exactly what an IT professional can do severely limits that individual's flexibility and radically constrains the manager and the department. You don't want to be in the position of assigning someone a task and hearing them say "that's not in my job description."

The format of the PD can vary. Your HR department may have a standard format that it likes to use. It's often similar to an outline, and is usually kept to one or two pages.

General Requirements

While PDs vary from company to company, there are many similarities. The following are common elements of a PD (see Figure 3.1):

✦ **Job title**. The title should be descriptive about the job and also be one that an employee will be proud to have on his business card. Something along the lines of "IT Associate II" is of little meaning; "Senior Software Developer" is better. Use industry standard titles and descriptions so that both you and the potential employees can readily do comparisons of qualifications versus salary and benefits.

✦ **Position summary**. A high-level, two- or three-sentence description of what the job entails.

✦ **Scope of responsibility**. This provides more detail about the job. It may cover the number or types of systems, requirements for being on call, budgeting responsibilities, personnel responsibilities (hiring, management, performance reviews, etc.), requirements for doing high-level presentations or low-level documentation, etc. This section usually has the most information about the job and what is expected of the employee.

✦ **Immediate supervisor or manager**. Identify the title of the individual the person will be reporting to. This will help give some perspective to where the position is in relationship to the entire IT organization.

✦ **Number of direct reports**. Indicate the size of the staff that reports to this position. It might even help if you provide some simple description of the staff (operators, programmers, other managers, etc.).

✦ **Minimum versus specific requirements**. For all critical issues, list the minimum requirements (and name them as such) as well as any specific requirements. If you must have a programmer with at least three years of development experience, say so clearly. If you need someone with SAP in the background somewhere, be clear about that.

✦ **Education, training, and certification requirements**. If these are a requirement for the job, specify what they are.

✦ **Experience required**. If formal training isn't required, companies often ask for a minimum number of years of "real-world" similar experience in a given field. Sometimes you may want to identify the type of experience that is required. For example, you may want someone with experience in a similar industry, or with very large organizations.

✦ **Travel**. If there is travel required in the position, it's important that it be identified. Traditionally, it's identified as a percentage of time. It's important to be as honest here as possible. Since most candidates look negatively on travel requirements, you might want to be overly careful and overestimate the amount of travel. You may also want to describe the travel in more detail (local/domestic/international, or short trips of two or three days vs. weeks or months at a time).

✦ **Salary**. If you include a salary in a PD, give a range. If there is a bonus, simply say "bonus eligible."

Sample Position Description

Job title: Senior Java Developer

Position summary: Writes application code for company's commercial Web site

Scope of responsibility: Work with systems analysts, customer service, and marketing teams to develop and maintain code for company's e-commerce Web site. Will be responsible for developing, testing, documenting and maintaining code in an environment consisting of approximately 30 systems with 100 modules, 50 servers, two data centers, and receiving approximately 200,000 hits per day. Employee will participate in a rotating on-call schedule to insure that systems are available and reliable on a 24×7 basis.

Immediate supervisor: Robert Smith, Manager of E-commerce Development

Number of direct reports: None

Travel: 10–15% travel required

Specific requirements: Minimum 3 years Java development, 10+ years development in another language (C, C++, Perl, SQL)

Experience required: Minimum 1 year experience in supporting a high-volume retail e-commerce site.

Salary: $75,000–$95,000

Figure 3.1   Position Description

Advertising Options

First, Post Internally

In some companies, you must post open positions internally first. Find out if your company requires you to do so, or allows you to do so only if you wish. Typically, HR feels that existing employees should have the first shot at any new openings, and it is bad form for employees to find out about an opening through external sources. And, sometimes you may want to let people within your department know a job opening is about to be created, but other times you may not want that information known until the last minute.

Whatever you do, don't try and have it both ways; employees will find out that you are advertising behind their backs and your reputation (deservedly) will suffer.

In short, don't advertise (inside or out) until you're ready for everyone to know about it.

Popular Web Sites

There has been a tremendous shakeout in job sites, and after many sites merged, there are only a few left standing. *Monster.com*, *HotJobs.com*, *Dice.com*, *CareerBuildeer.com*, and your local *CraigsList.org* are the most popular. There are now site aggregators, such as *Indeed.com*, that scour all of these sites and consolidate results from most job sites.

Web Posting Issues to Think About

The good news is that your job will be shown to millions of people; the bad news is that your job will be shown to millions of people. And most jobs in IT can't be filled by millions of people.

Be prepared for a large number of responses. It sounds like a nice problem to have until it happens to you. Online postings routinely generate hundreds of responses in the first few days — even if you have the job sites filter the results.

Networking

Filling a job via networking can be a very rewarding process. You simply start by talking to your professional contacts (peers, subordinates, HR representatives, co-workers from former jobs, sales representatives, contacts you meet at conferences and seminars). You don't have to go into great detail, just briefly mention the type of job you have open, along with a brief description of what you're looking for. But your "network" of contacts extends far beyond the people you currently work with, as well as those you used to work with. A little word of mouth can go a long way.

Professional Contacts

- ✦ The HR department may have recently interviewed someone who was rejected for a position in another department, but perhaps fits your requirements.

- ✦ Members of your, or other, departments may know of people at their former jobs.

- ✦ Your vendor representatives, who are probably already familiar with your environment, may know individuals at their other customer sites who would be a good match.

- ✦ Perhaps someone who was a close second for a previous open position can be called back in for this position.

- ✦ Professional organizations that either you or one of your staff belong to.

- ✦ Local schools and universities.

Personal Contacts

- ✦ People on your staff may have friends and colleagues who they can vouch for and know are looking for jobs. This connection brings a double bonus: What higher compliment is there for you as a manager than for one of your subordinates to recommend a friend to work for you?

- ✦ Your community can provide you with a rich source of potential job leads. Let the word get out to your friends, to fellow community members, to neighbors, and to fellow squash players, that you're looking to hire someone.

- ✦ For all you know, the next person you meet at a Fourth of July barbecue softball game could know the ideal candidate for you.

Social Networks Online

There are "social networking" Web sites such as *LinkedIn.com* and *ZoomInfo.com* that allow you to create and join online networks. Many IT professionals are migrating to that method of making contacts.

Effectiveness of Networking

Does networking work? It sure does. Does it work every time? No. It's a matter of luck and timing, the people you contact, and the way you talk about the job, as well as other factors that you can't always identify. You never know the chain of connections that will lead you to the right contact. In fact, one of the co-authors found a job via someone he went to Sunday school with and hadn't spoken to in over 15 years. One of the nice things about networking is that it can be the cheapest way to find candidates, but it may not be the fastest or most effective. However, you can always use networking in conjunction with other recruiting methods.

Job/Recruiting Fairs

While the value of job fairs is often viewed with less than total admiration, a *Computerworld* survey (*Computerworld*, 1/10/2000, "So, When Do I Start?") found that "10% of all IT workers are hired at recruiting events. That's way behind the leading tool — employee referrals, at 25% — but it is fourth on the list, ahead of search agencies (8%) and paid Internet recruiting services (also 8%)."

The article goes on to note: "People use these fairs." And you should, too, given that information. Will all of your needs be filled at the first event you attend? No. But IT professionals attend these events, and you should do the same. You can spend a lot of money and waste a lot of time just going endlessly to events like these (they seem to be offered almost every week these days), but a targeted effort, with specific presenters and detailed planning, can reap big rewards.

On the plus side of job fairs, it's the best opportunity for seeing the greatest number of candidates in the least amount of time. You can glance at a résumé and chat with a candidate for a few seconds or a few minutes, and determine if this is someone you want to bring into the office for a more traditional interview. Candidates are also looking to meet with as many employers as possible. Candidates' feelings aren't hurt if you move on to someone else after exchanging just a few words.

On the other hand, job fairs aren't generally charming places with a warm ambience. This atmosphere may deter many candidates from attending. And, since a typical lunch hour may not provide enough time for a candidate, most people assume that a significant percentage of job seekers at job fairs are out of work and have been unable to find a position through other means. Lastly, job fairs are usually only held in certain geographies — typically larger metropolitan areas.

The (Limited) Value of Print Advertising

The days of choosing one type of job ad over another are fading; many Sunday papers are joining up with job Web sites. Many newspapers are offering print as well as online listings. Although print ads certainly seem to be a dying breed, they aren't dead yet. Very senior positions still often appear in "display ads" in the business section. Some companies choose to use print ads *in addition* to online ads, and some choose to use print *instead* of online, perhaps as a way of attempting to reach a different demographic. One of the co-authors spotted an ad for a CIO in the classified job section of the *New York Times*. Perhaps since the company was obviously looking for a seasoned executive, they thought that the newspaper might be a more targeted medium (maybe assuming that the type of the candidate they're looking for probably grew up in the days when newspapers were pretty much the only venue for job advertisements).

3.3 Recruiters

Whether you call them "recruiters," "agents," or "headhunters," they are a fact of life in the modern corporate hiring world. Recruiters generally don't have a great reputation. Sometimes that poor reputation is deserved; many other times, however, a recruiter can mean the difference between success and failure of a project that is relying heavily on very specific types of staff. Using a recruiter has both advantages and disadvantages. Weigh them carefully before deciding. The costs for making the wrong choice can be high.

In truth, a recruiter is probably going to use some of the same methods (print, Web, and networking) that are discussed in this chapter, and that you could easily use yourself.

Another factor to consider is that recruiters' roles have shrunk dramatically in direct relation to the rise of job sites. Finding a candidate on *Monster. com* may or may not be the right method for you, but using an old-fashioned recruiter has some positives and negatives, too. Details for each option are discussed below in Table 3.4.

If a headhunter's less-than-stellar reputation is deserved, the way in which they are compensated may be one of the reasons. Agents generally receive between 20 and 30% of the annual starting salary of the person they place. With high commissions, coupled with weeks or months between successfully placing a candidate, a headhunter has high incentives to do his best to succeed at every opportunity.

You should also talk to your HR department. There may be specific policies against using headhunters unless all other avenues have been exhausted. Or, they may have negotiated rates with specific recruiters that you can use. Many companies now have a short list of approved recruiters that every hiring manager within the company *must* use.

Finding the Right Recruiter

Finding good recruiters is more of an art than a science, but probably not terribly different from how you found your accountant. You probably took a

Table 3.4 Pros and cons to using a recruiter

PRO		CON	
	Recruiters take the lion's share of the recruiting burden off of you.		Keep an eye out for recruiters who don't appear to be listening to you and your requirements. If they continually send you candidates and/or résumés that clearly aren't suitable matches, change to another recruiter. This is a very common problem. Recruiters have bodies they want to place (and often take the view that if they throw enough things against the wall, the odds are that eventually something will stick), but that isn't your problem. Demand what you are paying for.
	Your HR department may do nothing more than use one or two of the recruiting media mentioned above. The recruiter, on the other hand, will place the ads and work the phones. In addition, he'll do the initial screening of candidates and résumés. He will make sure that the candidates he sends you are in the right salary and skill range. Recruiters will also meet candidates before sending them to you to be sure that they have the appropriate "presentation" for you. The last four sentences above state what the recruiter "will do." More appropriately, they ought to say "should do." It's the "wills" and "shoulds" that separate good recruiters from bad ones.		Some recruiters try to convince you to ignore your own instincts. If you reject an agent's candidate, the recruiter should ask why, so he can learn what you don't like and increase the odds of sending you people you will like. But if your agent tries to argue with you, or convince you that you should consider someone you didn't like, it's time to move on. There are plenty of fish in this sea.
	In large metropolitan areas where there is a large pool of talent, agents can help you separate the wheat from the chaff. In areas where the pool of talent isn't quite so deep, a recruiter may be able to help you find the shade in a desert.		Some recruiters try to increase the odds of success by overwhelming you with résumés. One of their primary functions (as described above) is to separate the wheat from the chaff; if you aren't saving time using a particular recruiter, switch.

(Cont.)

Table 3.4 Pros and cons to using a recruiter (continued)

PRO	CON
If your marketplace is a difficult one to recruit in, agents can help. For example, many downtown metropolitan areas have an intensely competitive hiring IT environment. Qualified IT professionals know they can easily find a job and are generally very savvy about doing so. Are you prepared to find the right avenues, investigate the common sources for this position, etc., by yourself?	In general, working with agents is a mix of personalities — yours and theirs. And since you're the one paying, you can, and should, choose not to work with those who don't seem to work well with you.
A recruiter has his own network and contacts. In addition to posting the ads on Web sites, an experienced headhunter will know lots of people. He will likely know people who may be interested in changing jobs, but who aren't actively searching the job sites. This network will also help him match up the right personality and attitude with the culture of your organization.	
If the job you're hiring for is a complex one with very specific requirements, a recruiter can take on the burden of finding those candidates.	
If the job you're hiring for is a popular one, that a lot of people will be interested in applying for, a recruiter can help narrow down the field.	

recommendation from a friend or relative the first time you needed an accountant. Later, you may have changed accountants, perhaps based on another recommendation, because you weren't 100% comfortable with the first one. You may have gone through a few options before finding one you're comfortable with. In essence, you networked. Finding a good agent to help you find a job or to help fill an open position is the same process.

You can start by asking people you know which headhunters they've used. Ask who they liked, disliked, and why. Your company's HR department can probably offer you some references of agents they've worked with in the past, as well as those they've had bad experiences with. You can also ask others in your department about agents they've used. If you really don't know where to turn, you can always look in your local newspapers' help-wanted sections and see which agents have ads there. Regardless of how you find them, be sure and check out their references before you start using them.

You want to find agents you like working with. You may prefer agents who are fast paced, or those who are more laid back. Because they often conduct their business over the phone or via e-mail, it is entirely possible that you may never meet some of the agents you work with. As such, you'll have to rely on your instincts to judge them as you work with them and speak to them on the phone. As complicated as the world gets, and as competitive as recruiters are, it's somewhat surprising to know that many agreements with recruiters are done verbally. And, if you don't meet them in person, you won't even have the proverbial "handshake."

You may not even have to find recruiters, since they'll often be looking for you. Headhunters earn their keep by establishing contacts with hiring managers, companies, and candidates. Sooner or later (probably sooner) they'll learn that you're a manager and that you have responsibility for staffing. They may hear this from existing contacts they have (like others at your company), or simple cold calls to your switchboard ("Can you transfer me to the IT Manager?").

Technical Abilities

Many recruiters don't have the technical depth required to adequately help you with your search. Recruiters are no different than the rest of the population in this regard: There are many people who are very ignorant about technical matters, there are those who know enough "to be dangerous," and there are truly knowledgeable people. Your concern should be twofold: how much do they understand and how honest are they about their abilities.

Remember that sometimes you will be trying to fill positions that require skill sets that are still being developed. IT is a constantly changing industry. If you want to hire someone with word-processing skills, those metrics are well defined. But you might be trying to find a .Net programmer or VoIP technician. Those technologies are only a few years old.

This means you will find few recruiters who understand your requirements. What you will be looking for is a recruiter who is honest enough to admit what they don't know and willing enough to listen to you tell them what they need to know.

Things to Keep in Mind

Some important things to remember when dealing with recruiters:

✦ Fees generally run 20 to 30% of the annual salary that is offered and are usually negotiable. Some recruiters may not accept less than 20 or 25%. Agree on the fee up front, and preferably in writing. Include terms about when the fee is paid, and what happens if the employee is fired or quits soon after being hired.

✦ Oftentimes, a recruiter will ask what your company normally pays as a finder's fee. If they do, this is a great time to offer up a lower number. Recruiters know that if you use them once, you may use them again. So they may be willing to give up a few percentage points in exchange for a potentially lucrative relationship.

✦ The headhunters' fees are usually paid after a certain period of time. This is to ensure that the candidate doesn't quit, or isn't discovered to be a disaster, immediately after being hired. Agents often request to collect their fees after 30 days. You can usually push that out to 60 or 90 days. Don't pay the fee early based on the promise that you'll be credited with a refund if the new hire bails out before the agreed-upon period. Before using a headhunter, agree on the payment and guarantee terms, preferably in writing.

Using Multiple Recruiters

It's quite common, and not considered unethical, to give the same assignment to multiple recruiters. As long as you can deal with working with several agents, it will increase your odds of finding exactly the right person. On the off chance that two recruiters send you the same candidate, the professional thing to do is work with the recruiter who sent you the candidate first. (If there are two identical résumés on the fax machine, or in your e-mail in-box, use the time stamp to tell you who sent it first.)

3.4   Selecting Candidates

Reviewing Résumés

Résumés come in all shapes and sizes, and there is no science to reviewing them well. What one manager may consider to be a great résumé, another may dismiss immediately. A résumé that's great for a programmer may not be great for a programmer/analyst.

When candidates write résumés, they may agonize over every word, phrase, and formatting choice. There are volumes on the subject of writing résumés. In this section, though, we are addressing the issue of reading résumés.

Things to look out for when you read a résumé include:

◆ **Be on the lookout for spelling and grammar errors**. Most people spend an enormous amount of time getting their résumé just right (and having others review it), so any mistakes should have been filtered out. If it contains a typo, it could mean the candidate isn't focused on detail (or has poor writing skills). Factor this in if your position requires these abilities.

◆ **Take note of the overall appearance**. Does it seem well formatted, or thrown together haphazardly? This could be a reflection of the fact that the candidate thinks that things like appearance are superficial.

◆ **Look at the job history**. Is the candidate a job hopper? Are there gaps that you want to ask about? In IT, while many managers will reject a job hopper, they may also be concerned about those who have been in a job for an extended period of time. They may fear that a candidate with 15 years at his current job only has one view of the world, and may have difficulty adapting to the new job environment.

◆ **Does the level of detail in the résumé match what you're looking for?** For example, if the résumé highlights that the candidate upgraded the operating system on a server, it may indicate he's coming from a very small environment compared to yours; you may have so many servers that an OS upgrade is such a common practice that the task is barely mentioned among technicians, much less seen as a résumé-worthy accomplishment.

◆ **Does the résumé have a laundry list of technologies?** For example, does it list every model of every brand of workstation and server they ever worked with (e.g., IBM PC, XT, AT, Compaq Proliant 5000, 5000R, 5500, 5500R, 6000, 6500, 7000R) along with every version of every software package (e.g., Windows 3.1, 3.11, 95, 98, ME, NT 3.51, 4.0, 2000, XP, 2003, etc.)? You may see lists like this and think: "Is this candidate really proficient in all these technologies?" You may also ask: "Why does he think I care that he knows about technologies that were discontinued a long time ago?"

◆ **Notice factual claims.** Résumé padding is rampant. (In 2006, the CEO of Radio Shack resigned after it was discovered that he misrepresented his educational credentials.) Don't be afraid to ask direct questions about a candidate's claims. ("Were there other people working on these Web sites you designed, or was it all your doing?" "Did you write most of the code for that billing system or were you a member of a team?")

Résumés are rarely read from top to bottom. Typically, they are glanced over quickly (various studies show that the average résumé gets well under a minute's attention). This glancing process allows the manager to hunt for things that he's looking for, as well as to see what else jumps out at him. These are reasons why a well-formatted and carefully crafted résumé is so key.

Telephone Screening

After screening résumés, but prior to face-to-face interviews, some managers like to do telephone interviews to narrow down the list of candidates. A quick 5- to 10-minute telephone conversation can reveal quite a bit. For the more hands-on and technical positions, you can use a few technical questions to gauge a candidate's level of expertise. Telephone screening is ideally suited for customer service representatives like Help Desk analysts, since it gives you some insight into their telephone manner, their communication skills, and how they might be at interacting with customers and users.

For the less technical and more supervisory positions, you still might be able to use a brief telephone interview as a gauge to their interpersonal skills — especially if these skills are a critical part of the job requirement. Of course, telephone screening just helps you narrow down the field, you still need to meet with those candidates that do well on the phone.

At What Level Should I Interview?

If the position reports to one of your managers, consider having that manager do the first rounds of interviewing. This saves your time and empowers your manager. If you have several levels of staff reporting to you, you may not feel the need to be involved in the interviews for every position in your organization. However, you should be involved in interviewing for:

✦ Positions that report directly to you

✦ Positions that report to your direct reports

✦ Positions in your organization that are highly visible or very critical

Even if you feel you don't need to be involved in interviewing for a lower-level position, you may want to at least briefly meet with finalists before offers are extended.

Narrowing Down the List

Like many information-based activities the Internet has streamlined, searching for a job has been radically simplified. For just a few dollars, a job seeker can send out thousands of résumés. As such, hiring managers like you are deluged with résumés. The pendulum swings back and forth from not enough candidates to too many candidates. Having too many options may seem like a desirable problem to have, but it's a difficult issue in its own right.

How to Choose from Hundreds of Candidates

First of all, get help. Ads posted on job sites often generate hundreds of responses. Of course, many are completely mismatched to your posting, but someone has to weed through the electronic stack of files (many named "resume.doc," of course) to glean the real candidates from the wannabees. Sophisticated résumé-scanning software (your HR department may already use this) can quickly scan hundreds of résumés for specific keywords.

Get help from HR — fast. See the section, HR Department's Role (page 44) for details. Some companies have résumé-screening software, coded P.O. Box numbers, and third-party answering services to handle the first wave of responses. Give HR a list of specific requirements for the position you're looking for and a specific number of résumés you want to read: "I would like to see thirty résumés of qualified candidate — no more." If you receive fewer than five qualified candidates in a hot market, then this is a problem that points to an issue with your advertising. Did you use the right terms? Did you look in the right places? See the section, Advertising Options (page 58) for more details about advertising.

If you receive several hundred résumés, you simply won't have the time to give each one appropriate consideration. To narrow down the pile you may have to select a few criteria. You may want to eliminate those résumés that don't have a cover letter, or drop those that are outside your geographic area (especially if you don't plan on paying to relocate someone), or toss out those that show a history of job hopping.

How to Choose from 30 Qualified Candidates

Having narrowed the initial number of résumés from the hundreds down to 30, now you must use a different set of skills to move from 30 to 5. (These numbers are approximate; decide which numbers work for you.) Your goal is to winnow the number of résumés you are reading down to a manageable number of candidates you can interview in person. As discussed before, sometimes a phone interview is an ideal method for prescreening candidates.

While grateful for help from HR, you'll probably review their selections next. You may have 30 "qualified" choices but 5–10 can be eliminated right away. You may not have specified it to HR, for example, but the person can't be entry-level, or must have hands-on programming experience (not just classroom time). Whatever the reason, about one-third of your candidates will probably fall to the side.

That still leaves you with 20 qualified candidates. In a hot market, it's good to remember that many candidates could fit the bill. Give yourself some room when making this decision: you aren't trying to find the *perfect* candidate (there may be five perfect candidates, or more likely, there won't be any), you're trying to hire a person who fits your requirements and your team well.

Choose five candidates to talk to in person, but keep the remaining 15 on hand just in case the first round doesn't work out.

Should You Hire an Overqualified Candidate?

The two simple answers are:

1. Yes, because in a hot market (for employers) you'll get more for your money.

2. No, because in a hot market (for employees) they'll jump as soon as they get an offer that matches their skill set better.

Ask your HR department and fellow managers what their take is on the short-term prospects for the hiring market.

Young managers (that is, recently appointed managers, not youthful managers) should be very careful about hiring overly qualified candidates. These individuals are often more challenging to manage; that doesn't mean they're more difficult, it means they require special attention. They didn't acquire all these skills by accident; they're probably very aware of career paths, training programs, and openings in other departments — things an employee with less experience might not know (or care) about. They may also be fully aware that they're taking a job they're over-qualified for, and could easily turn into an attitude problem for you and everyone else.

General Interview Guidelines

Some guidelines for conducting interviews include the following:

✦ The candidate may be nervous or tired (especially if he's met with several others before meeting with you, or he's anxious to get back to his current job before his extended lunch hour is noticed). Try to make him feel comfortable with a few light comments (for example, "I hate interviews, don't you?") or by asking a few easy questions (e.g., "How are you? Did you have any difficulty finding the office?").

✦ After you get started, see if you can get the interview away from the Q&A format and into more of a conversation or discussion. Both you and the candidate will benefit from a more relaxed exchange of information. Not every person can relax in an interview, however, and there are other factors (such as the chemistry between the two of you) that may influence the tone of the meeting. Don't overemphasize this aspect of the interview, especially for individuals whose interpersonal skills aren't as critical to their success on the job as, say, their technical skills.

✦ Don't do all the talking! Many interviewers spend a great deal of the first interview talking, as opposed to listening. Don't tell the candidate too much about what you're looking for (at least not until you've heard what the candidate has to say). If you do, the smart interviewee will simply regurgitate what you said back to you. It's the candidates who should do all the talking, but they can't do so unless they are given a chance. You are there to evaluate them first; all your other responsibilities (like presenting the position, representing the company, and so on) come second.

✦ Avoid asking yes/no or other short-answer questions. You really want the interview to become a "discussion." Use questions that force the candidate to give descriptive answers. Questions that start with "how" or "why" are great for this. Make them think on their feet.

✦ Toward the end of the interview, always give the recruit a chance to ask her own questions. Most candidates are usually armed with a couple of standard questions for this opportunity. The smart candidate might ask you a question about something discussed in the interview to demonstrate that she was listening or is interested.

Prepare a List of Questions

Always prepare a list of questions that you can refer to during the conversation. You can, and should, ask both technical and non-technical questions (performing a technical interview is discussed later in this chapter). The balance of questions will depend on the position you are recruiting for. If you're recruiting for a project manager, for example, you might be more concerned about the candidate's leadership and management skills than you would be if you were interviewing a programmer. However, if you're involved in interviewing a programmer who reports to one of your project managers, you may not have the expertise to ask meaningful technical questions. Still, your interview in this situation can be just to evaluate the individual's background, professionalism, maturity, and personality.

Once prepared, ask the candidate what they think the key issues in their field are and how well they know them. Also ask them if they can provide a specific example that can confirm what they just said about themselves.

Non-Technical Questions

Some non-technical questions that you can ask include:

- ✦ "How was this position described to you?" (This is a great way to find out how the people the candidate met prior to you, like the hiring manager and HR, view the position.)

- ✦ "What were your responsibilities at your last job?"

- ✦ "Describe a crisis that you were involved in, and how you dealt with it."

- ✦ "Describe an assignment or role you really didn't like, and why you didn't like it."

- ✦ "Describe the pace and culture at your previous jobs, and which ones were good and bad matches for you."

- ✦ "What did you like/dislike at your last/current job?"

- ✦ "Tell me about the relationship you have with your current manager. Do you work well together? What would she say about you? Is she a good manager?" (Be careful not to tread into personal waters here. A person can be a great manager and a difficult person and vice versa, but for the purposes of this conversation, make sure to keep the conversation on a business level. If the candidate starts making personal comments, change the topic.)

- ✦ "Which industry trade journals do you read?"

- ✦ "What do you know about this company?"

- ✦ "Did you go to our Web site? What did you think of it?"

- ✦ "Why are you interested in this job, or working for this organization?"

✦ "What doesn't your résumé tell me about you?"

✦ "What motivates you?"

✦ "What do you like, and not like, about working in IT?"

✦ "What do you want/expect to do on a daily basis at work?"

✦ "Do you mind if I ask what do you like to do when you're not at work?"

You can also have them walk you through their job history. They can tell you why they took certain jobs, why they later left them, and what they took away from each job (regarding learned experiences).

Remember, you're listening to *how* they answer, as well as to *what* they answer. You may not agree with everything they say, but if they can convey their answers clearly, with confidence, and back them up with sound reasoning, it demonstrates a certain level of professionalism, maturity, communication skills, analytic thinking, etc.

It's good idea to have a set of questions that you ask all candidates. This allows you to have a common frame of reference. And, take plenty of notes during the interview. After just a few candidates, you'll have difficulty remembering who is who. Good notes can come in very handy a few days later when you're trying to decide who to bring back for a second interview, or when you're trying to explain to a recruiter why their candidate isn't qualified.

What Not to Ask

Court decisions and legislative statutes have placed some topics off limits in interviews: race, gender, marital status, age, handicap, sexual orientation, and religion, among others, are topics to be avoided. Not only should these items never be discussed in an interview, or any other job-related discussion, you can't use them as factors in making decisions.

For example, if a petite woman applies to be a PC technician, you may doubt her ability to do the lifting of equipment that the job requires. However, you cannot dismiss her out of hand. What you *may* be able to do is say to her that "the job requires you to unpack, move, and lift PC equipment that weighs up to 50 pounds; are you able to perform these tasks?" Similarly, if the same small woman applies for an operations position in the computer room, you may be concerned about her ability to reach the tape cartridges stored on the top shelves. If she is otherwise qualified, the courts would probably tell you to hire her and to make "reasonable accommodation" like investing in a step stool. *These are all very sensitive areas. Before asking any list of questions, consult with your HR or Legal department. You may be putting your company and yourself at risk of litigation.*

Some interviewers like to ask particularly tough questions and conduct interviews more aggressively. Sometimes this is for sound reasons (e.g., you want a sales rep that can handle all kinds of customers and prospects and difficult situations). Other times it could be because the hiring manager has a large ego, and seeing others squirm reinforces his status (at least to himself). If candidates are wiping their forehead and saying "whew" when they finish an interview, you may want to ask what value you get from that interview style.

Who Else Should Interview a Candidate?

Allow others to interview the candidate, whether it's for technical reasons or to compare personalities and demeanor.

+ You can have your own peers interview the candidate.

+ You can also ask individuals who are at peer level to the open position.

+ You may want to have your boss meet the recruit.

+ If the position requires interaction with other departments, they may want to have a representative involved in the interviewing process.

+ The HR department, if they haven't done the initial screening, will also be able to provide an alternative view.

+ If you're interviewing someone who will have management or supervisory responsibility, it isn't unheard of for them to meet with some of the people who will be their direct reports.

Including other interviewers makes the process more complicated and adds more time. But it's well worth it. You'll find that multiple interviewers, collectively, are more selective than any one of you individually. That's a positive thing. It increases the chances that when you do agree on a candidate, it will turn out to be a good one. Also, allowing other members of the department to participate in the interviewing process demonstrates to your team that you respect their opinions and that you're interested in hiring someone who will fit well into the team.

You may not want to bring other people (or be directly involved yourself) until a certain stage in the process; some job postings generate hundreds of responses and require an aggressive filtering process before the first interview is held. If you are going to have people help you with interviewing, plan *when* you want their help before you contact them.

A Different Perspective on the Same Data

One of the co-authors was interviewing a candidate who seemed to be a good fit for a position. The candidate was brought back to meet several of his peers-to-be for interviews. On this second round, all the male interviewers thought favorably of this candidate, but the one female interviewer had misgivings and thought that something was amiss. She suggested that the candidate may have a problem working with women. The candidate was brought back to meet with another female interviewer who took an instant dislike to the candidate. It will never be known if the candidate did indeed have a problem with women and/or that "woman's intuition" detected it. But, the important thing here is that different people do have different perceptions and insights. Consider that an asset and tool at your disposal. The candidate was rejected.

Key Concepts for a Good Technical Interview

Technical interviews are needed to help judge if a candidate has the appropriate skill level for the job. However, it's quite common for IT Managers to lack the knowledge base for conducting in-depth technical interviews. This is most frustrating if you're interviewing for a position that reports directly to you. In some cases, you can have others within the IT organization conduct technical interviews. And it's common to hire a consultant to conduct technical interviews with candidates you're interested in.

Don't be ashamed that you don't have detailed technical expertise. You're *never* going to have all the expertise that your employees do — the IT world is changing too fast. And, since you're a manager, you may no longer be spending your days doing the hands-on work you did just a few months or years ago. Find out what the key issues are for the technical area that you're interviewing for. Talk to some of your other employees, they may know some of the key topics.

Do Some Preliminary Reading

Research particular topics of concern on the Web or in print materials. Even if you don't ask specific technical questions, you can ask a candidate about important issues associated with his area of expertise. What does he think of a particular vendor's support, or quality assurance? What does she think of competing products? What about open source? What did he think of the various antitrust actions in the United States and overseas against Microsoft? What is her prediction of the future of Linux?

Let Them Explain Technologies to You

A clever way to hide your ignorance, as well as get an education, is to ask candidates to explain certain technologies to you. "What is a subnet mask? What is meant by object-oriented programming? What does RAID mean? What are the pros and cons of Java versus C++?" Of course, you may not know if the candidate's answers are correct, but you'll probably be able to judge if he's just "winging it" or really has an understanding of the matter at hand. And you'll also be able to determine what type of interpersonal skills he has: Can he articulate complex thoughts clearly? Does he come across as condescending? Are his opinions so strong that you worry he may prove to be inflexible?

Testing Candidates

You may also consider giving the employee a formal test. This could be one you develop yourself or done with the assistance of testing software. Of course, many candidates may not like taking a test as they realize that it may show particular skill deficiencies, or they may be poor test takers.

But more important, testing may create an impersonal atmosphere that places more value on specific knowledge than on the individual person and their ability to contribute, accomplish, and succeed on a team. Also, testing only evaluates the mechanics of a skill. It doesn't evaluate the employee's aptitude with it. Nor does it evaluate the employee's other qualities such as dedication, ability to juggle multiple priorities, and interpersonal skills.

Nonetheless, testing can be an effective technique for some positions. Jobs that have very specific and easily quantified requirements (specific software application experience, for example, or words-per-minute typing skills) are good candidates for screening tests. In addition, many jobs now get many "qualified" candidates and many of those candidates are willing to "fudge" their abilities; testing can level that playing field.

You should have a standard test with an answer key. If you have a very small department or company and you can't develop your own test, call in a consultant to help you craft one. Having the test results readily available can also give your technical staff something concrete to discuss with the candidate — it forges an instant bond if the chemistry is there.

Are "Profile" or "Personality" Tests Useful?

"I have found these tests — which we call 'Profile tests,' by the way, because 'Personality tests' are *not* what they are — to be an extremely useful hiring and management tool.

Here are some things to consider if you are going to try them:

- ✦ The "softer" aspects of a person can be difficult to evaluate in a two-hour interview process. These tests often reveal information that we would not have figured out until later, after the person was hired.

- ✦ While these tests are very accurate about some items, *the final decision is still up to you* on how to use the information they provide. They measure raw intelligence power well, for example. However, not every job needs to be performed by a very intelligent person; at the same time, some jobs are complex, analysis-driven positions that require high IQ power just to understand. These tests can help you make that determination.

- ✦ When we decided to use these tests, we tried them on *everyone* in the company first. We found them to be very good predictors of corporate behavior.

- ✦ We use them on the *second interview*; the first interview is a general one, where we try to keep our commitment level and the candidates' to a reasonable level. Sometimes, despite all the paper, it only takes a few minutes for a person and a company to figure out they are not a good match. Profile tests (which take about 45 minutes and are administered by an outside firm) are done once the first hurdle has been passed."

—Cathy Thompson
Co-founder and Principal
Thompson, Doyle, Hennessey & Everest, a commercial
real estate firm in Boston, Massachusetts

One final note of caution: some companies have strict guidelines against testing candidates. The legal implications of testing are unclear; be sure to verify with your HR department what your company allows you to do.

The Right Skill Set for the Job

Have a well-defined list of criteria before you start. Use this list to weed out résumés, and then use a fine-tuned version of that list to interview candidates.

Bring the list to the interview itself — you are running the show, so worry more about being thorough and complete and less about appearances. Keep in mind there are two skill sets that you're interviewing for. One is *technical* skills, and the other is *everything else*: their attitude toward work, ability to juggle multiple priorities, ability to work with others, general intelligence, resourcefulness, potential for growth, dedication and commitment, professionalism, and maturity. You may also be looking for project management skills, supervisory skills, and interpersonal skills, as well as the ability to write reports or give presentations.

When to Accept "Similar" Experience

Should you accept "similar" experience? It all depends on how similar the experience is to what you're looking for. It also depends on your needs. If you need to put someone to work on the first day, to be productive on a critical project, your definition of similar might be quite narrow. However, if you can afford to invest time to bring an individual up to speed, then your definition of similar may be more forgiving.

If you like a candidate, but have concerns that his experience isn't similar enough, share your thoughts with him directly. "I like your background, Patrick, you have excellent experience, you'd be perfect for the job, but I'm concerned that you don't have enough experience with X technology." At the very least, by doing this, you're being honest with the candidate and letting them know why there is a chance they won't get the job. More important, you're giving the candidate an opportunity to respond. For all you know, Patrick may have something in his background that wasn't mentioned on his résumé that will make you feel a lot more comfortable about his experience or about his ability to compensate for the gap.

With your responsibility as an IT Manager revolving around technology, it's easy to get caught up in specific technology experience when recruiting— hardware model numbers or software version numbers. Of course, these skills are important, but the technical skill set is only a portion of the qualifications. Softer skills like interpersonal interaction, writing, attention to detail, and ability to function in a team environment can be just as vital.

Rank Criteria

Have a well-defined list of criteria for a job established *before* you go into the interview. As part of the definition process, you can rank each criterion in terms of importance. These rankings will vary from department to department and company to company. Some organizations rank teamwork way ahead of technical skills; others place a much higher value on technical competence than they do on the ability to work well with others.

You may find that an interviewee is a bit weaker in one area than you would like, but significantly stronger in another area. And, more than likely, you'll see résumés and candidates who have similar experience to what you're looking for. You may find that a candidate's technical expertise is weaker than you would like, but they strike you as someone who is very bright, picks up new skills quickly on their own, and is a very hard worker.

It is pretty common for a manager to value softer skills (personality, intelligence, interpersonal, resourcefulness, etc.) over specific technical skills. The idea behind this is that technical skills can always be learned (and in the ever-changing field of IT, picking up a new skills is an ongoing requirement for success), but teaching someone how to be responsible, likeable, or intelligent isn't as easy.

And, the priority you assign to these skills will vary on the job in question; many technical jobs require relatively little personal interaction, so a candidate's ability to "work well on a team" may not be of much value.

In the end, as you weigh all of these issues to make your choice, don't be surprised if you feel you're making a judgment call — you are.

Other Requirements That You Might Be Flexible About

+ **Years of experience**. What's more important than the number of years is what the candidate *did* in those years.

+ **College degree**. Perhaps this is more important for a manager, but it's less so for a technologist. And the more years *since* that college degree, the less it adds value as opposed to experience.

+ **Training**. Pertinent training? Fundamentals or advanced? How long since the classes were taken? Have the skills been used out in the real world?

+ **Specific hardware and software technology**. Is a dot version or two behind in software truly a disqualifier? These days, *everything* gets outdated quickly.

+ **Environment size**. This can be measured in MIPS, users, number of applications or servers, or number of locations — whatever is appropriate for your needs.

+ **Certification**. It may not show anything more than they can cram and memorize to pass an exam. See below for a separate discussion of this issue.

+ **Industry experience.** Frequently, IT workers don't see enough of their company's business environment to really have a legitimate feel for the industry they're in. While similar industry experience is nice, you may want to broaden it to a more macro level like manufacturing or services, for example.

Ability to Learn

When considering prerequisite technical skills, remember that virtually everyone in IT must be at least smart enough to master new skills and adapt to changes in technologies and products on a regular basis. If you have faith that a person is smart enough to learn new skills, you may want to consider trusting that faith with someone who might have to take some time to come up to speed on the specific technology set in your environment.

Example

For example, if you're looking for an HP-UX administrator, you might consider someone with skills in IBM's AIX to be close enough. You may figure that if they mastered the IBM product, they could certainly master the HP product in short order. On the flip side, if the ideal candidate doesn't have any Unix skills, but is a genius with IBM's mainframe MVS software, you might be concerned about investing the time and training to bring this individual up to speed in mastering Unix. Then again, there's no reason to suspect that an MVS genius couldn't become a Unix genius. It all depends on your needs and your ability to provide the opportunity (time, exposure) to allow those skills to develop.

The Value of Certification

The IT world has gone a little crazy with certification. Chances are that if you've heard of a particular hardware or software product, the vendor is offering some type of certification for it. There's an alphabet soup of available certifications including: CCNA, CNE, CNA, MCSA, MCSE, CCIE, CCNP, A+, CCIP, MCAD, MCT, CISSP, PMI, MCSD, MCP, MCDST, MCDBA, OCA, OCP, OCM, CLS, and CLP, just to name a few.

Certification really hit the front pages with Novell's Certified Netware Engineer (CNE). In the late 1980s and early 1990s, everyone wanted to be a CNE. To many it seemed like the passkey to dream jobs. However, by the mid- to late 1990s, a new term was coined: "paper CNE." This term referred to people who took crash courses, studied intensively, and passed the CNE exams, but had virtually no experience to go with the new accreditation on their résumé. Novell's restructuring of their certification program helped to deal with this. It's an interesting commentary that 10–15 years later, having a CNE was considered of minimal value since Novell had lost so much mind- and market-share.

Vendors must monitor their certification programs like the Federal Reserve monitors interest rates to balance between too much and too little growth.

Vendors don't want their certification program to be so easy that it has no value or prestige, but at the same time, they don't want the programs to be so hard and elitist that too few people are able to pass the tests.

Test-Taking Skills

Whether it was in high school, technical school, or at the Department of Motor Vehicles, we all learned that a passed exam only represents knowledge at that particular moment — which may only in itself represent the ability to study prior to the exam. The same can be said of technical certification. If someone is certified, you know what their knowledge set was at the moment they were tested, which could mean they have the ability to study very hard, have a steel-trap memory, or they have information that was ingrained during years of experience. While many IT Managers recognize this, many also look for certifications on résumés. Similarly, many managers looking for programmers prefer individuals with four-year college degrees, even though a college degree may add no value to a programmer's skill set.

Value of Commitment

One aspect of accreditation that's often overlooked is its representation of commitment and persistence. Getting certified usually means passing a series of exams. For many, it also means taking a series of classes. Doing this takes time, energy, and motivation. When you see someone who has been certified, perhaps the first thought you should have is "here's someone who can stick with something, and see it through to the end." Not a bad trait for someone who will be managing projects. The same can be said about college degrees, especially if they've obtained it while working full time.

When you see a candidate with certification, be sure to consider how long it's been since that accreditation was obtained and to what degree those skills have been used since. If required, ask them if they have kept their certification current with continuing classes and exams.

Checking the Value of a Certification

There are a number of steps you can take to check the value of a certification:

- ✦ Talk to your own network of contacts.
- ✦ Contact the technical area's association (if there is one). Ask them about the value of certification; they might be also able to point you to a source that can either verify or deny their claims.

✦ Contact the product manufacturer. Companies like Cisco, IBM, and Micro-soft have extensive certification programs and local contacts. Again, they will tout their own benefits, but they might also be able to point you to specific individuals who benefited from or are looking for those skills.

✦ Scan the classifieds and the Web. Are other employers asking for this in their ads? If the certification appears often, that is a good sign.

Education

The value of an education has changed radically in the last twenty years. Online paper mills, rock-hard certification courses, $200K tuition bills — the simple criteria of yesterday ("A four-year education is invaluable these days") has changed.

Bill Gates is chairman of one of the world's largest and most successful companies, yet he never finished college. Neither did Steve Jobs. On the other hand, Larry Page and Sergey Brin, co-founders of Google, met while they were pursuing doctorates at Stanford. College graduates earn over $18K more a year than their high-school graduate counterparts (*www-hoover.stanford.edu/publications/books/fulltext/ed21st/25.pdf*).

When looking at the value of an education for a new hire for your company, consider three things:

1. Type of education

2. Direct value to the job

3. Indirect value to the job

There is no argument to be made against education, or more education. However, as a hiring manager, you have to determine if particular educational accomplishments, like degrees, are important to the position you're trying to fill. Or, if setting those requirements is needlessly narrowing your field of candidates.

Direct Value to the Job

As a rule, the more hands-on and technical a position, the less *direct* value a typical four-year degree has for you as the employer. This is even truer for a graduate degree. Is a Java programmer with an MBA a better programmer than a Java programmer who only finished high school? Some might argue that the programmer with only a high-school degree might be better since all those years went toward actual experience, rather than the more theoretical academic experience. Notice the emphasis on the word "direct." Of course the MBA may serve the programmer well as he moves up in his career (perhaps at your company).

While "Nearly 76 percent of those with a four-year college education in America hold jobs, the Bureau of Labor Statistics reports, compared with only 60 percent of high school graduates," that isn't the whole story. This *New York Times* article also points out: "the median weekly pay of the high-school educated is up 3.6 percent since 2000, adjusted for inflation, a rate of increase four times as great as the rise in pay for the college-educated." In other words, people without college degrees are getting hired more frequently. A college degree, or any certification for that matter, is no longer an automatic ticket to employment (*http://www.nytimes.com/2005/10/02/jobs/02Uchitelle.html*).

A college education is of more value to a position that involves supervisory or management responsibilities. And, a college degree is often a prerequisite to getting a supervisory or management role. As a general rule, actual experience and skill should always carry more weight than any educational requirements. And even for someone who has significant educational credentials, the value of that education generally decreases with time. The most important point here is: How easily can the candidate learn new things? The world and the marketplace we work in change quickly and significantly. Has this candidate shown the ability and interest to learn new tools and skills as they become the new standards? Lifelong learners are often the most productive employees in an organization.

A four-year degree will also sharpen skills for writing, analytic thinking, reading comprehension, etc. Sometimes the value of those skill sets are often overlooked until you see that first horribly written e-mail from a staffer.

Indirect Value to the Job

On the other hand, a college-educated employee can provide several important *indirect* benefits to a position. Pursuing a four-year degree can be a difficult and complex task; it can show the individual's willingness to make a commitment and follow through. It can be a financial challenge; many people have to earn a portion of their college education themselves. It can be intellectually challenging; a person may be pursuing a programming career now, but 10 years ago chose biochemistry as a major in college.

At the minimum, you should seek a high-school degree for virtually all positions. This should at least give you an indication (although no guarantee) that the individual has the fundamental skills to operate in a job (reading, writing, basic math, etc.). As you move up the education ladder (two- and four-year degrees, graduate degrees, etc.), look to it as an indication not necessarily of a higher degree of technical skill, but of more skilled analysis, comprehension, and verbal skills.

Business-Related Degrees

If their degree is in a business-related discipline, it may indicate that they've been exposed to many ideas and concepts that they'll encounter to various extents within IT. This exposure may be valuable for someone who does systems analysis or is involved with management.

Hard Sciences-Related Degrees

If their degree is in one of the hard sciences (physics, mathematics, chemistry), it may show that they have a stronger ability for logical and analytical thinking. Candidates from these fields may also have greater focus on detail, documentation, procedure, etc. Start with this assumption and verify it with further questioning.

Soft Sciences-Related Degrees

If the person has a degree in one of the social sciences (e.g., psychology), they may have greater skills in user-oriented activities (support, training, process improvement, designing interfaces, etc.). They may have a greater ability to see things from a different perspective and not be limited by the idea of "only one right answer." Start with this assumption and verify it with further questioning.

Famous Schools

A well-recognized and prestigious school is nice, but don't let the reputation overwhelm you. Pay careful attention to the questions you brought to the interview and focus on the candidate's answers. If a candidate seems to be namedropping his well-known school frequently, it may indicate that reputation is important to him, and he has high status expectations of the job and the company — issues that may be at odds with your environment. He may also be relying more on reputation than actual experience in his background. Ask pointed questions to see if it's all show, or real meat, that he's bringing to the table.

Technical Courses

Many candidates now list on their résumé individual technical courses they have taken, even if they haven't received any certification. If the skill in question is one you are interested in, ask about the courses, how far into the course had the candidate gone, and why did he stop?

Checking References

References are too often overlooked. Some employers ask for them (especially on the application) but never check them. Some employers check them after the candidate starts, and some check them before the offer is made. Most HR departments handle the reference checking aspects of hiring; confirm with your HR department to see how your company handles this process.

There are two types of references to check, background checks and professional references.

Background Checks

This is the validation of the accuracy of what the candidate says on the application or résumé. This usually includes contacting schools to see if the person did attend and received the degrees and certificates he claims. This is also for confirming his past employment to see if he did indeed work at the companies he claims for the time frames he claims. The background check may also including a review for any criminal record.

Doing background checks can be tedious and time-consuming, and many companies outsource it to firms who are experienced at doing it. Some organizations that are contacted for this information may first ask for authorization from the individual (such authorization is usually included in the fine print of many employment applications). Some organizations (particularly former employers) may only give out limited information. They will typically confirm the dates of employment, but won't provide title, salary, or any comment (good or bad) about their performance.

Professional References

This is the opportunity to speak to individuals that the candidate has worked for and with to get some more insight into the candidate. It's quite common to ask for three references. If the candidate can't provide them, an immediate red flag should go up.

You should assume that any references the candidate gives you will only have positive things to say — he'd be crazy to put you in touch with people who thought otherwise about him. It's for this reasoning that some people place little value in calling these references, or simply think of it as clerical work that HR can do.

However, there is still some value to be gained by making these calls, and making them yourself. While you're unlikely to hear anything negative about the candidate, you should ask open-ended questions to see what the references say about the candidate. Are they using similar adjectives, describing the same traits and characteristics, etc.? Does the information provided by the references match what the candidate said?

Some questions you can ask include:

+ "When, and for how long, did you work with John?"

+ "What was his role?"

+ "How would you describe him as a worker?"

+ "Why did he leave your company?"

+ "What types of work does he enjoy" (What types does he excel at)?

+ "How would you describe his relationships with co-workers and his manager?"

+ "What types of work does he enjoy least?"

+ "Is there anything else you'd like me to tell you about him?"

+ "Would you want to work with him again?"

With luck, the references will give you feedback that matches your own perception of the candidate (and validate what he's told you and put on his résumé). If there is a disconnect, you have to try to gauge how big a gap there is, and what that might mean.

Common Hiring Mistakes

At some time or another you'll probably discover that you misjudged a candidate. You may discover that someone you thought would be fine doing program-maintenance is a stellar performer and has great potential. Or, you may find that the candidate you thought was ideal turns out to be a dud. Hopefully, your errors in judgment will be more of the former than the latter. To avoid out-and-out mistakes, be on the lookout for:

+ **A poorly defined position**. If you don't describe the position accurately (the good *and* the bad), you may end up getting bad résumés and selecting a candidate that doesn't fit.

+ **Hiring for the wrong reasons**. You dislike the entire hiring process, so you only meet with two people and pick one quickly.

+ **Not getting enough input**. As suggested earlier, it's a good idea to have other people meeting with strong candidates. Every interviewer has a different approach and perspective and asks different questions. It's entirely possible that someone else may have discovered something that you didn't.

✦ **Talking too much (or too little) during a job interview**. The best interviews occur when both the candidate and the interviewer have a chance to learn about each other. If one party does all the talking, there will be a large information gap when it is over.

✦ **No reference checks**. Not every company does these (because the responses are often so rote), but if your company does do them, have HR follow up with the candidate you choose. Many companies are now outsourcing this function, so it might be worthwhile to alert your candidate to the fact that their references will be receiving a call.

Offering the Correct Amount for an IT Position

When you start to recruit for an opening, you should have a salary range in mind. This range can come from several key sources of salary data:

✦ The HR department of your company

✦ Recruiters

✦ Classified ads

✦ Web and computer magazine salary surveys (e.g., *salary.com*, *payscale. com*, *wageweb.com*, and *salaryexpert.com*)

✦ Other individuals in your company doing similar work

✦ Salary levels that you're seeing from candidates who apply

✦ Salary of the previous individual in that job

✦ Salaries of the staff members, if any, that report to this position

Before Making the Offer

Make sure that HR and whatever other upper management individual(s) need to approve the final offer are in agreement on the specified range. You'll know if your range is too low based on the response you get to your recruiting efforts. If only a handful of people apply, you're probably offering too little. Although it is not uncommon for someone to change jobs for the same salary, most people expect at least a 10% increase. This increase compensates them for the risk that is inherent whenever someone changes a job, but it also entices them to take your job. Nonetheless, you can't offer more than you, or your company, can afford to pay. And you're probably not the only person who decides that figure. If the last individual in the position was a poor performer, that might be justification to convince yourself, HR, and the powers-that-be that you need to offer more money to attract better talent. An extended search that doesn't find any reasonable candidates can also be a justification for reviewing the salary range.

Using Agencies

Be careful when you share the salary range with any agencies you use. Since their commission is based on the annual salary, they have a vested interest in placing someone at the highest possible salary. It makes their job easier to find good candidates if the salary you are offering is competitive. If the recruiter winces when you tell her the approved salary range, don't take it too personally — she's just doing her job.

Because the agent's commission is based on the salary of the person you hire, they may be tempted to inflate the salary of the candidates they send you. As a check, ask the candidate themselves about their salary. The written application that the candidate fills out (with the usual legalese about misinformation being grounds for immediate dismissal) can also help you get a true sense of what their current compensation is.

Other Ideas Besides More Money

Invariably, the candidate you like the most will be the one that stretches the envelope of your salary range. If you don't think you'll be able to attract this person with your salary offer, there are a few things you can try:

✦ Consider promising a salary review (not a guaranteed *increase*, but a *review*) six months after the person starts. Don't commit to a specific increase amount (after all, the candidate may not work out, or the company may change its salary ceiling). But the chance of an increase in six months may be just what you need to attract the person. (Make sure to get approval from HR/management before you promise anything.)

✦ Make the position and environment sound as exciting and attractive as possible. Naturally, remain truthful about it. Making something exciting doesn't mean lying about it. You want the person to be as motivated to take the job as you are in offering it to him; that will make finding a middle ground much easier.

✦ Get the candidate to look at the entire package. Today's competitive IT environment has spawned a wide range of non-cash incentives that can be far more lucrative than "mere money." Emphasize those to the candidate.

Does the position have *bonus potential?* Make sure the candidate includes that figure in her consideration. Does your company offer a stock purchase plan? A profit-sharing plan? A matching 401(k) plan?

✦ Also, make sure that the candidate is fully aware of your company's benefits programs; health and insurance benefits can have very important positive tax benefits. Stock options should also be clearly specified if you are making them part of your offer. Originally a benefit only for the upper reaches of a corporation, stock options have now become a part of many workers' pay plans throughout the ranks of an organization. Companies are offering employees a more direct participation in the profits of the organization as a whole. Is it a good working environment, with little demands for overtime and beepers? If so, it could be a key selling point. What about flextime? Or telecommuting? Or the on-site gym?

✦ Don't forget to talk about vacation time. With today's society, particularly in the IT world, it sometimes feels like the workday never ends. It's not uncommon for people to leave the office, go home for dinner and time with the family, and then log on to the office to answer e-mails and get more work done. Many people take their laptops and Blackberry devices on vacation to keep up with what's going on in the world. If the position you're hiring for doesn't require as much off-hours attention, or allows for some working at home, or your company has specific policies or practices in place to minimize overwork, be sure you mention that as part of the overall package — they can be very attractive to individuals.

3.5 Outsourcing and Offshore Outsourcing

Managing your staff and your resources is a major task of an IT Manager. Outsourcing in all of its forms can be a very effective tool for helping you accomplish that task. But as you can imagine, outsourcing is not without its own associated costs. See Table 3.5 for definitions.

There are many tasks that you and your department perform. There are some that you perform because you *have* to, but you would gladly assign them to someone else given the opportunity. Perhaps doing these tasks chews up valuable skilled resources that you could use better somewhere else; perhaps your department doesn't do them well because they fall outside your core competencies, or perhaps no one likes doing them for other reasons.

Companies outsource a wide range of tasks; some send their Help Desk departments or their entire accounting functions outside. *SearchCIO.com* says that IBM manages Xerox's entire IT services.

Table 3.5   Outsourcing definitions

Term	Definition
Outsourcing	When one company makes an agreement with a second company to provide services that the first could provide, but chooses not to. IT companies often outsource portions of their software development, for example. They might do this for various reasons (see the discussion below), but the important point is that they could perform that task if they chose to. Using a third party to perform a task your company doesn't normally do — say you develop software but need your new offices wired for electricity, so you hire an electrical contractor — is *not* outsourcing. The distinction between the two types of hiring matters a great deal and one that you will need to understand. It's discussed in the section below.
Offshore Outsourcing	Arranging with a second company to provide services that the first company could provide but chose not to — and the second company isn't located in your own country. A common example of offshore outsourcing is a company in, say, Redmond, Washington, USA, contracting with another company in, say, Hyderabad, India, to help it with its software development.

One way to think about outsourcing is to think of one company with one kind of expertise — building software, for example — hooking up with a company that has a different kind of expertise such as accounting. Could the first company build its own billing system if it wanted? Yes. But it might be cheaper, get better results, and have fewer headaches if it contracted to have another company do it.

There are entire companies dedicated to the process of helping you outsource your tasks. Before you make that call, though, contact your HR department as they probably already have agreements set up with third parties that do some of the work you need done.

Offshore Outsourcing Overview

Sending work overseas is a much more drastic method of outsourcing. "Drastic" both in a good and bad sense. We'll outline the positives and negatives of doing this (see Table 3.6), but keep in mind that offshoring outsourcing is a *very* hot topic and likely to remain one for some time. The decision whether to contract with an offshore company ("send local jobs overseas") isn't likely to be made at the IT level. But here are some things to think about if you are called in and asked for your recommendations.

Table 3.6   Pros and cons of offshore outsourcing

PRO	CON
Many of the tasks that Americans have traditionally performed, especially in IT, can be done for less money in other countries. Americans have a high standard of living compared to the rest of the world, and programmers overseas aren't paid at near the same rate. This is also true for Help Desk workers, data center employees, and software testers (among others).	The first negative is publicity: If word gets out that you are replacing local jobs with overseas work, there will be a significant public relations issue to be dealt with. Not everyone agrees that globalization is inevitable and that the march of jobs to the lowest paying corporation (wherever they may be) is the most efficient, let alone the most moral course to take. Many companies now go out of their way to hide their offshore outsourcing agreements.
In addition to cost, another often cited benefit of outsourcing work overseas (to India and Russia in particular) is that your company gets the benefit of a 24-hour work cycle. Once developers are finished with their workday in the United States, for example, they then send the code to the second company located in India or Russia. Since these countries are virtually on the other side of the world, their workday is only beginning. The continuous work cycle can have very positive effects on development time lines.	Secondly, the overhead costs involved in establishing a smooth relationship overseas are significant. It still may eventually be worth your company's while to do this, but there will be a steep cost curve at first.

(Cont.)

Table 3.6 Pros and cons of offshore outsourcing (continued)

PRO	CON
It's common now: "Microsoft Chairman Bill Gates recently announced that the software giant will nearly double its workforce in India, to 7,000 and invest $1.7 billion there. IBM has added at least 10,000 Indian workers this year and could employ more than 50,000 Indians by the end of 2006. Accenture, EDS, and other consulting firms are following close behind. By 2015, 3.3 million jobs will have been sent overseas, according to Forrester Research. As the offshoring trend matures, U.S. firms will contract out increasing amounts of white-collar work like accounting, drug research, technical R&D, and even cartoon animation."	There will also be cultural considerations. While many IT workers overseas speak some English, for example, and many are trained in the United States, many workers are not. And different cultures have different laws about hiring, about contracting workers, recommended work weeks, different holiday schedules, etc. There will be some learning involved before both companies are comfortable with the arrangement.
	Lastly, with the focus on security on compliance issues (see Chapter 8, IT Compliance and Controls, page 201), many companies have concerns about exposing sensitive data to third parties in another country.

Outsourcing and offshoring can be very challenging, and while it can save money, companies have to be careful about what it means to the quality of work and impact on customers and operations. In 2003, Dell shifted its support operations to India. However, after being deluged with complaints, Dell decided to return to U.S.-based call centers for its corporate customers (*http://homepage.mac.com/techedgeezine/112603_dells_service_dehli.htm*).

In 2005, Sears, Roebuck and Co. ended a $1.6 billion/10-year outsourcing agreement it had signed with CSC Corporation just a year earlier for "failure to perform certain of its obligations" (*http://www.computerworld.com/industrytopics/retail/story/0,10801,101774,00.html*).

3.6 Additional Resources

Web Sites

- ✦ *searchcio.techtarget.com* (product technical information)
- ✦ *www.bangaloreit.in/index.asp* (India offshoring resources)
- ✦ *www.cheatingculture.com/resumepadding.htm* (resume cheating info)
- ✦ *www.destinationcrm.com/articles/default.asp?ArticleID=4354* (outsourcing discussion)
- ✦ *www.hireright.com* (background checking company)
- ✦ *www.LinkedIn.com* (professional networking site)
- ✦ *www.microsoft.com/india/indiadev* (Microsoft development in India)
- ✦ *www.naceweb.org/press/display.asp?year=2005&prid=216* (National Association of Colleges and Employers)
- ✦ *www.payscale.com* (salary survey information)
- ✦ *www.salary.com* (salary survey information)
- ✦ *www.wageweb.com* (salary survey information)
- ✦ *www.zoominfo.com* (professional networking site)

Books and Articles

- ✦ [No Author Identified], "Hiring and Keeping the Best People," *Harvard Business School Press*, 2003.
- ✦ Berglas, Dr. Steve, "Serenity Found: How to inoculate yourself against stress and burnout (once you understand the difference)," *CIO Magazine*, December 1, 2005, p. 42.
- ✦ Coffee, Peter, "Set Expectations for Outsourcing," *eWeek*, September 26, 2005, p. D1.
- ✦ Computerworld Special Report, "Knowledge Center Outsourcing," *Computerworld*, November 14, 2005, p. 61.

✦ Erlanger, Leon, "Business Process Outsourcing: Putting IT in the Director's Chair," *InfoWorld*, February 27, 2006, p. 23.

✦ Gladwell, Malcolm, "Getting In: The Social Logic of Ivy League Admissions," *The New Yorker*, October 10, 2005, p. 80.

✦ Gomes-Casseres, Ben, "Outsource, Don't Abdicate," *CIO Magazine*, October 1, 2005, p. 36.

✦ Hoffman, Thomas, and Thibodeau, Patrick, "Working through the Pain, After Rocky Starts, Some US Clients are Learning How to Get Better Results Offshore," *Computerworld*, December 5, 2005, p. 46.

✦ Margulius, David L., "10 Ways to Get Offshoring Right," *InfoWorld*, August 28, 2005, p. 33.

✦ Mornell, Pierre, Hinrichs, Kit, *45 Effective Ways for Hiring Smart: How to Predict Winners and Losers in the Incredibly Expensive People-Reading Game*, Ten Speed Press, 2003.

✦ Overby, Stephanie, "Simple Successful Outsourcing," *CIO Magazine*, October 1, 2005, p. 51.

✦ Uchitelle, Louis, "College Still Counts, Though Not as Much," *New York Times*, October 2, 2005.

✦ Wendover, Robert, *Smart Hiring at the Next Level*, Sourcebooks, Inc, 2006.

✦ Yate, Martin, *Hiring the Best: Manager's Guide to Effective Interviewing and Recruiting*, Adams Media Corporation, 2005.

Project Management

We must all hang together, or assuredly we shall all hang separately.

—BENJAMIN FRANKLIN, AT THE SIGNING OF THE DECLARATION OF INDEPENDENCE

As an IT Manager, your life will revolve around projects — some small, some enormous. Projects are an integral part of corporate life; this chapter discusses how they are conceived, organized, funded, tracked, and executed.

CHAPTER FOUR

Project management is a complex and formal management science (although it is often more art than science). While you probably won't need all that complexity and formality to run most successful IT projects, it's essential to your success as a manager to understand not only the basic principles but a few of the advanced concepts of project management.

If you have been assigned the "project" of installing an e-mail upgrade for the company, and you are working for a 400-person company, you need to carefully plan how you're going to accomplish this task, who is going to help you, how much it's going to cost, and when is it going to be done. While it may appear a simple task to someone outside the department, anyone with much experience in IT knows an upgrade project like that can take an enormous amount of time, planning, money, and effort. Careful project management can be the key to successfully accomplishing this task.

4.1   Projects and "Project Management": A Quick Overview

You won't go too long as an IT Manager without hearing the word "project" — you probably heard it a lot even before you became a manager. "Project" is a catchall word.

Different Kinds of Projects

The range of activities defined as projects is very wide:

+ It could be a relatively simple activity like getting new PCs for all the building's receptionists. It might be a more complicated venture, like deploying a system-wide software or an operating system upgrade. Or it could be a monumental task, like implementing an Enterprise Resource Planning (ERP) application throughout the company.

+ It might be highly complex and involved (ERP applications are notoriously difficult to implement) in nature, or not at all (getting a new color Blackberry for all the executives).

+ It might be staffed by a single person in your office or a team of 75 people from 5 different organizations in 3 different countries.

+ Simple projects may require little planning, and all the key information is maintained in someone's head. A complicated project may need special project management software, along with group calendaring and scheduling to keep it all on track.

✦ It might have a very tight and immovable deadline (e.g., installing a new tax package before the start of the fiscal year), or the time frame may be much more forgiving (e.g., "as long as it gets done sometime this year").

Your ability to manage a project so that it meets its goals, within the defined time frame, and within the approved budget, will be one of the single most important skills you can develop as an IT Manager.

The Value of Project Management

Project Management has become a formal discipline and a widely practiced part of today's corporate life. While it isn't necessary for you to become an official "project manager" (PM) and get certified by the Project Management Institute (PMI), it's useful for you to know some of the important principles of project management to help you in your role as a manager. Every manager has some PM responsibilities, regardless of how those needs are defined; it can be critical to your success to not only accept, but embrace these responsibilities. Take control of the projects in your business life and manage them well — it will be well worth your effort.

Five Key Phases to a Project

Starting with Section 4.2 on page 99, the five key phases of a project are discussed.

1. Scope the project

2. Develop a project plan

3. Launch the project

4. Track the project's progress

5. Close out the project

Various companies and organizations define these phases of projects differently. However, these particular five stages are taken from the PMI's *Project Management Body of Knowledge* (PMBOK), the standard text for project managers. The PMBOK is the PM community's bible; according to the preface, it's "the sum of knowledge within the profession of project management."

Do You Have to be a Certified Project Manager to Run a Project?

No. Being a certified PM is definitely an advantage when running large and complex projects, but it isn't a requirement — this issue is not too different from the discussion on technical certifications in Chapter 3, Staffing Your IT Team in the section The Value of Certification (page 80).

There are many pitfalls that face anyone running a project and we'll discuss some of them in this chapter. One common problem, for example, is that most project managers may be tasked with managing the project but don't have formal authority over project team members that are from other departments. This issue can make managing individuals a difficult challenge. But that particular difficulty isn't solved by certification of the project manager.

The Project Management Institute (PMI)

The PMI (*www.pmi.org*) is the international organization that trains and certifies project managers. Unlike many certification organizations, PMI is the real deal. Its main certification, a Project Management Professional ("PMP"), requires "7,500 hours in a position of responsibility leading and directing specific tasks"

Why I Chose PMI

I have been a project manager for many different companies in many industries all over the world for over 40 years. A long time ago I decided to get certified as a PM and, after careful study, I chose the Project Management Institute.

I picked PMI because:

+ They are by far the largest organization of its kind in the world.

+ They are truly a world wide group; there are many PM groups, but they are recognized more by the countries where they are located. Their requirements for certification are very rigorous.

+ You must pass a thorough exam.

+ There is a significant cost involved.

+ And it requires a demonstrated depth of experience.

George Puziak
Area Project Manager
Alutiiq, LLC

---

as well as "35 hours of Project Management Education." If you see a PMP certification on a resume, it means the individual has spent a lot of time and effort achieving these goals.

IT Managers may or may not need all the experience that a certificate from the PMI implies. (Although some IT Managers now have, and more are pursuing, a PMP. The organization now has over 100,000 members.) However, it's important for you to know that the science (and art) of project management has become much more formalized in the last 10 years and that the PMI has been at the center of that change.

The PMI and its PMP certification are certainly well regarded in the industry. But, like other certifications and educational backgrounds, the story doesn't end there. It all depends on how these skills are put to use.

4.2 Phase One: Scope the Project

A project generally starts as an idea — either yours or someone else's. At the very beginning, a project is usually short on specifics. There's no framework for costs, time frames, or the resources required. In fact, as these areas begin to get quantified, potential projects often get killed because they take too long, cost too much, require too many staff members to implement, the benefits just aren't worth the cost or risk, or they are too elusive.

How a Typical Project Can Start

Once you have a project to manage, whether you gave it to yourself or someone else gave it to you, it's your job to manage it properly. Obviously, projects of different sizes aren't all managed the same way. As mentioned above, the size and complexity of projects can vary tremendously; the approach you take to implement a 3-year, 75-person project will vary greatly from the way you give a single subordinate an assignment to accomplish in a week.

Clearly Define the Project's Objective and Scope to Avoid "Scope Creep"

First and foremost, the project needs a clearly defined objective. Objectives can take all kinds of shapes. But one effective way to think of the objective is to ask yourself: "What is the achievement that will most clearly show that this project is completed and successful?"

A project objective must have several important characteristics. It must be:

+ Clearly defined

+ Agreed upon by the important people related to the project (see the discussion of "stakeholders" below)

+ Documented

+ Measurable

There are other issues that need to be considered, but you must first define your objective, get it agreed to, and put in on paper. Document not only goals but decisions, so you won't hear "I never agreed to that" or "We decided to only allow 50 users into the system." You want to be able to reply: "No, actually, the number was 150 and I have the notes to prove it."

PMI's definition of "scope creep" is right to the point: "adding features and functionality (project scope) without addressing the effects on time, costs, and resources, or without customer approval." Hallway conversations, quick notes in a mid-status report review, and meeting asides are ways that new responsibilities can sneak into your project without you realizing it. If your objective is clear, agreed upon, and documented you will go a long way toward avoiding scope creep.

Very often, when a project's scope is documented, there is a section identifying what areas are considered out of scope. For example, a project team may be formed to implement a new application, but the team will only be implementing the core modules and not other ancillary modules. Similarly, the scope may only be for domestic use, and international use is out of scope for the project.

Also, be prepared for radical changes in project direction — projects seldom progress as planned. It is important to plan — you need an intelligently designed structure to work within — but be ready when the plan needs to be changed. In addition, be ready with a rough cost/benefit analysis if new features are suddenly required.

Department versus Company Objectives

Carefully match your project's objectives to the company's overall objectives. It's better not to think of yourself or your department as an island, but instead think and act as if you are part of a dynamic, constantly changing organization. As a consequence, define your project's objective within the company's overall goals. This step may sound obvious, but it often isn't done.

Sometimes the connection between your project and the company's overall direction is not obvious: it is then your job as the manager of the project to formulate this connection and state it clearly. If your company is an auto parts dealer and you are installing a new upgrade for the phone system, many people in the company might wonder why they have to help and how that activity helps them. You need to have the answers to those questions ready.

Get Proper Sponsorship for the Project

Along with clearly defining the project's goals, you need to carefully define the sponsors of your project.

A project sponsor is someone who can:

- ✦ Champion the project at higher levels

- ✦ Clear away organizational obstructions

- ✦ Provide resources (people, budget, software, hardware)

- ✦ Communicate with key stakeholders

- ✦ Keep the project alive by providing funding, authority, and influence

- ✦ Protect the project from enemies/turf wars

Very often, a project sponsor will send a communication out to everyone involved as the project gets launched. Typically, this communication identifies the overall objectives, the importance to the company, and thanks everyone for their cooperation. A simple communication like this can help pave the way to success for the project and can eliminate the chance of someone saying "this project is news to me."

Other types of sponsors can include:

- ✦ Perhaps your boss handed you the project; make sure that you clearly inform her that you will need her support soon.

- ✦ Maybe your boss's boss came up with this clever idea, and it was passed down to you. If that happens, find out as quickly as possible from the source of the idea how much help you're going to get when it comes to issues like funding, personnel, and so on.

- ✦ If you created the project yourself, after clearly outlining its goals, set about finding out how much help you're going to get from others in the company.

You almost assuredly need help from people outside your department, and you'll probably need help from people higher up than you on the corporate ladder. Find out how much help there is going to be before you start making any significant decisions or commitments. Your project may actually be a pet project of the company president or some other high executive. If so, having this type of sponsorship and backing can be enormously helpful to you in eliminating roadblocks, particularly as you try to make use of resources from other parts of the company. If somebody "upstairs" wants everyone to have access to all business applications from their homes, you're going to need a lot of personnel, time, effort, and money to make it happen.

Identify the Stakeholders

"Project stakeholders are individuals and organizations that are actively involved in the project, or whose interests may be affected as a result of project execution or completion" (PMBOK, p. 24). The key word here is "or." Obviously, people and groups working on a project will be affected by its outcome. But stakeholders are also individuals who don't work on the project but who are directly affected by it. You need to identify *all* the stakeholders in a project. Sometimes this task is a difficult one.

Examples of potential stakeholders in IT projects include:

+ **The departments and end users that will be directly impacted by the system**. An example of stakeholders would be the Accounting and Finance users when the new General Ledger system is put in.

+ **Those that will be indirectly impacted by the system**. Although the warehouse may be the primary beneficiary of the new inventory system, the way it improves efficiency may also have an impact on Shipping and Receiving, as well as the Procurement Group. Further down the chain it could impact Accounts Receivable and Payables.

+ **Oversight groups**. Some departments like HR and Legal oversee activities of the entire company. A project to scan old paper records into a new document management system is generally a good idea. However, HR may be concerned about who gets assigned to that task and who gets proper training, while Legal may have thoughts about what it means for records retention policies.

+ **Direct and Indirect sources of funding**. Those that are paying for the project have a vested interest in it. Maybe your department is paying for the required hardware, but other departments are picking up other project costs (software, consultants, training, etc.).

✦ **Outside vendors**. Maybe your company's adoption of this new software is a bigger deal to the vendor than you realize. You might be able to wrangle better maintenance agreements as a result.

✦ **Government agencies**. Your company's expansion into a new country may trigger all kinds of regulatory issues that will have to be addressed.

✦ **Those further up the corporate ladder**. Your bosses' superior may be using the success of this project as part of a means of evaluating your boss. So the reviews of both you and your boss may be on the line.

Identify the Constraints, Interdependencies, and Risks

Projects aren't easy to manage. If they were, everyone would do it. There are a lot of factors to consider, many of which are discussed in this section. But note that some of these factors are under your control, and many are not.

Potential Variables

Going into a project, make sure that all the issues and variables that aren't certain are known to all members of the team. Examples of these include:

✦ Approval of associated costs such as travel expenses for contractors from out of town

✦ Availability of identified required resources

✦ Risks such as uncertainty of vendor deliveries, or implementation of new technology

✦ Interdependencies such as the inability to move to a new data center until the construction is complete

✦ Constraints such as the unavailability of resources from Accounting at the end of the year because of the priority of year-end closing activities

Possible Solutions

You'll also want to indicate how you're dealing with those issues.

✦ Associated costs might be shared with other departments that stand to benefit directly from the project but who aren't formal members of the team.

- ✦ Resource availability might be less of an issue if multiple resources for the same task can be identified. It sounds easier to do than it is, but sometimes you can find duplicate personnel to cover your bases.

- ✦ The risk of implementing new technology can sometimes be mitigated with adequate training and testing time.

- ✦ Interdependencies can sometimes be addressed by simply alerting the various parties that they are part of a larger schedule.

- ✦ The constraint of resources during the year-end closing can sometimes be addressed via juggling the scheduling in ways that don't affect the final deadline.

The Project Charter

The project charter is usually the document that really launches a project and covers everything addressed in the section above:

- ✦ Scope

- ✦ Objectives

- ✦ Sponsors and stakeholders

- ✦ Constraints, interdependencies, and risks

The project charter also sometimes has a formal signature line for signoff. In addition, the project charter often provides estimates of the items discussed later in this chapter:

- ✦ Time frame estimates

- ✦ Resource estimates

- ✦ Cost estimates

- ✦ Roles and responsibilities

Depending on the project, it may warrant investing some time to determine these so that the estimates listed above are more than educated best guesses.

As mentioned earlier, in addition to identifying what's in scope in the Project Charter, it could be very valuable to also identify in this document those areas that are out of scope.

When complete, the Project Charter is virtually the "bible" for the project. It's the document that everyone sees and agrees to before signing on to the project.

When there are issues of scope creep, the Project Charter can serve as a reference to determine what's in and out of bounds for team members to work on.

Get Historical Perspective

Some projects are brand new events with no precedent. But these are the exceptions. Most projects have some history to them, some kind of background that can help you put the entire venture into a framework.

✦ Was a project similar to this one undertaken by the company before? If you are installing the servers for the new office in London, see if the notes and personnel for the expansion across the street that was finished last year are still available.

✦ Do some of your team members have legacy experience you can leverage? If the two techs who installed the phone system last month are still with the company, can you get them on this team to help with the network installation?

✦ Does the executive management of the company remember similar work? Does your boss recall the two previous laptop upgrade projects? If he doesn't, remind him that in 2003 (and way back in 1999) it took twice as long as anticipated to get machines in from the field.

See the Time Estimates section below (page 107) for further discussion of the value of historical perspectives for projects.

4.3   Phase Two: Develop a Project Plan

Three Critical Components to Any Project

Every project has three critical components: time, money, and resources. You will also see this concept displayed as a triangle (see Figure 4.1)

The point of this graphic is that the *interplay* of the three characteristics of a project — time, money, resources, and how each relates to the other — directly affects the quality of a project.

For example:

◆ You might have plenty of *time* to install a new server (the hardware isn't even arriving for another month), but if you don't have enough money (your boss doesn't want to pay for the configuration you recommend) or the resources (both technicians who routinely do this work are gone — one has left the company and the other has been reassigned), *the quality of the project will suffer.*

◆ *Money* may not be an issue ("Spend whatever you need" was the instruction you heard from your boss on the new "mission critical" Blackberry deployment), but if it's only one person doing all of the work for 125 units and the work must be done "yesterday," *the quality of the project will suffer.*

◆ You might have all the *resources* you need (you have five people of your own plus two from the vendor for the installation of a state-of-the-art video conferencing facility), but you haven't been given enough money (the whole budget for the set up only included the cost of the hardware and didn't consider the cost of installing it) or enough time (people are moving in on Monday — *this* Monday), *the quality of the project will suffer.*

Think about each critical component of a project carefully when developing a project plan.

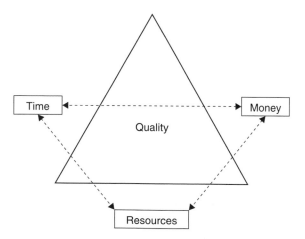

Figure 4.1 Three Key Components of a Project

Write the Project Plan with the Closeout Report in Mind

It sounds contradictory to plan the beginning with the end in mind, but in fact, that's exactly what you should do to achieve maximum project success. Everything you do, from the first planning meeting to the final celebration party, should be executed with the final result in mind. If you plan this way, the end result will force you to constantly act in certain ways, making decisions based on certain criteria. And that way of working will result in a better outcome.

Specifically, write your Project Plan with what you want to say in the Closeout Report. A Closeout Report is the report written at the end of a project. It can be a brief, 3-page document, or a 50-page, detailed report. For more on Closeout Reports, see the section Writing a Closeout Report in this chapter (page 119).

Now that you know what you'll say at the end of the project, prepare to be ready to say it at the beginning. Be as specific, actionable, and quantifiable as possible. "Make the Sales department happy" isn't actionable, specific, or quantifiable; you may (or may not!) make them happy by executing this project. Regardless, it will be hard to quantify. In your plan write a goal such as "install, upgrade, or refurbish all laptops in the Sales Department by January 1." When the new year rolls around, you will be able to say you have achieved the goal of that project.

Another useful suggestion is to include how much money you will save the company: "upgrading the Web-hosting facilities will cost the company $10,000 a quarter, but initial estimates are that faster processing time, more availability, and larger storage capacity will save the company a minimum of $25,000 per quarter for the first year alone."

Time Estimates

Next, determine how much time this project will take. Determining how much money and how many people you'll need is hard, but figuring out how long a particular project will take is even harder. Most people don't estimate time well. Some people are excellent at determining the approximate length of a project, but keep in mind that estimating is a poorly-practiced art. Knowing this fact in advance will help you to better estimate time.

The best place to start with time estimating is to find out if there is history: Has a project like this been done before? If so, how long did it take? That doesn't mean that if it took two months to install a previous version of the operating system across the company, it will take two months this time. (OS upgrades have gotten much more efficient and people are much more familiar with the process. Some people, of course, refuse to cooperate, but that is another problem.)

It may not take you the same amount of time as before, but it gives you a framework to operate under. You have a general idea of how much time this will take. And when you present your project plan, you can add that historical data to your report. ("In 2003, it took us two months to get everyone up and running with Windows XP. We propose to do this new Windows version in three weeks maximum.")

Many times, however, you won't have a historical record to work from. You will be executing a project for the first time. In that case, be sure to do two things:

1. Have some basis for your estimate. If you're essentially guessing that something will take two years, it should be based on estimates of the time required for the component tasks.

2. Overestimate. You're working with the unknown and you should estimate accordingly. Most people usually plan for things to go well. You also have to try to account for unforeseen problems, conflicting priorities, and "unreasonable" demands.

A helpful way to estimate a project is to get all the key participants in a room to talk about all the things that have to be done, the order in which they have to be, and how long they take. Ask questions like: "And after that will we be done?" or "What *exactly* do we have to do to get that done?" Continue to drive things to a finer level of detail and help get all the requirements and tasks out for discussion.

It's common to come up with a time estimate as a group — members of your project team (see the section Decision-Making Techniques in this chapter on page 120) will all have opinions about how long a project will take. Some managers take the number proposed and double it. That may sound devious, but as mentioned before, time estimation is a notoriously difficult thing to do. You'll be much happier overestimating than you will underestimating. It seldom occurs that more time is given to an IT project than is required. It happens, of course; but not very often.

Also remember that when time is estimated, everyone has to factor in that all team members are seldom working on only one thing. They are usually working on this project, along with several others, as well as everything else that they have to deal with on a day-to-day basis.

Resources Required: Employees (From Internal and External to IT)

For team members that report to you, it's easy enough to assign them to the project. But you can't simply go into other departments and assign individuals to your project. You need to meet with their department heads and explain your project to them and what resources you're coming to them for. This may take a great deal of diplomacy, especially if the various department heads don't have much of an interest in your project. It is at times like this that you'll need to call on your well-defined objectives, explain how those objectives fit in with the overall company goals, and be ready with an explanation of how your project positively affects the person you are talking with. When the objectives don't convince them, you can either re-evaluate your project and objectives, or call on your project sponsor to place a phone call or write a quick memo to help dilute the resistance.

Full-Time versus Consultant Employees

See Chapter 3, Staffing Your IT Team, section Should You Hire a Full-time Employee or Consultant (page 49), for a fuller discussion of the reasons to hire a full-time employee or a consultant. The short story is that each has its advantages and disadvantages, depending on the circumstances and need. The nature of the work also helps you determine which kind of worker is your best choice. One of the advantages of consultants for projects is that they will usually be dedicated solely to the project, while full-time employees usually have many other responsibilities in addition to your project. And, if a consultant is only needed for the duration of the project, their assignment can be easily terminated when the project wraps up.

Vendors and Service Providers

You may have vendors involved in this project, perhaps on a consulting basis, to implement a new application or at least on a support basis. You may also have service providers, such as telecom carriers, that are critical for getting certain components implemented.

It's important that you identify all the resources required and identify constraints and parameters of their involvement. In some cases you may have a resource completely under your direction (such as an employee or consultant), or you may have limited authority (such as a vendor's technician only being available to you for two weeks). In some cases you may feel almost helpless regarding certain resources, like waiting for your ISP to deliver a new circuit or a hardware vendor to ship a particularly constrained item.

Money

Chapter 6, Budgeting (page 161), offers a fuller discussion on what you need to know as an IT Manager about budgeting. But for project management, you want to be able to identify different types of costs:

+ One-time costs
+ Ongoing costs

- ✦ Hidden costs
- ✦ Consultants
- ✦ Internal resources
- ✦ Capital versus operating expenses

One-Time Costs

As the name implies, one-time costs are incurred for those items that require a single outlay of money. For example, new hardware and software licenses generally represent a one-time cost. Of course, if the hardware is leased (and there are monthly payments), then it wouldn't be considered a one-time cost.

Ongoing Costs

Ongoing, or recurring, costs pertain to those items that are paid for continuously. For example, the monthly cost for a new telecom circuit is an ongoing cost and so are the maintenance and support costs related to hardware and software (even though the hardware and software themselves are a one-time cost).

Hidden Costs

Besides the visible costs of a project, there are many "invisible" costs that it will serve you well to consider. This chapter discusses "hidden" items such as unnecessary meeting attendance, but there are others. Consider the loss of productivity the company suffers when an employee is suddenly transferred to a new project and can no longer work on the tasks and assignments he had been doing.

Consultants

The cost for consultants is often broken out separately for accounting purposes. As with the above, consultants may be a one-time cost (e.g., 6 months of time during implementation), or perhaps an ongoing cost (e.g., for ongoing support, training, etc.).

Costs of Internal Resources

In many companies, the costs of internal resources, primarily staff salaries, are factored into the total cost of the project. The decision to do this is essentially a policy set by the Finance department. You should check with them to see if they want these costs included. If so, you need to determine how far these costs go (e.g., in addition to salary do they include benefits and cost of overhead such as office space?). Generally, if you have to account for these costs in your project, there are rules of thumb available from Finance for calculating them.

Capital versus Operating Expense

As a general rule, one-time costs are considered capital expenses, while ongoing costs are considered operating expenses. There may be exceptions to this, for example, one-time costs under a certain threshold aren't capitalized. In addition, there may be gray areas as to whether or not certain costs should be capitalized. For example, Finance may elect to capitalize the cost of training if it's exclusively needed for the project. But, if it's training that would've been taken anyway, it may get treated differently.

Work with Finance on these issues. You won't be the first one to ask these questions, and they'll understand that they are new issues to you in your new role. Get a good understanding of these policies the first time, and you'll make everyone's life easier.

For a further discussion of capital versus operating expenses see Chapter 6, Budgeting (page 161).

Roles and Responsibilities

A critical element to the success of any project is the clear definition of roles and responsibilities from the outset. In as much detail as possible at the start, work with everyone on the team to define all the roles.

Note that defining everyone's roles doesn't mean *dictating* to people what those roles will be. There will be times where power plays occur, or where one person doesn't want to assume the role that he should. Plan for the more common occurrence — every player on the team wants to know exactly what their role is and what they are responsible for accomplishing.

Confusion about roles is a real project killer. The question "Who is in charge of the project?" is a common source of problems as well as "I thought I was doing testing," etc. You won't be able to answer every question at the beginning of the project, but you should spend as much time as possible trying to anticipate any potential trouble areas.

Multiple Projects

To further complicate the issue, it's entirely likely that you, and many others on your team, will be involved with several projects simultaneously, each of a different size, each at a different point in its life cycle, and each competing for resources. Not only will you be coordinating the company-wide upgrade to a new accounting system, for example, you may also be overseeing the new operating system installation for a server, be involved in the purchase of a new phone system for the organization, and serve on a cross-functional team evaluating the corporation's new health benefits package. And every member of the various projects you're working on is also working on other multiple projects themselves.

Not only should you be identifying everyone's roles, but you should also be estimating what portion of their time will be expected on the project. In some cases their involvement in the project may come in batches. One example might have one person with virtually no involvement for the first three months, but then they will have to give 50% of their time for four weeks.

4.4   Phase Three: Launch the Project

You have scoped the project and developed a formal project plan; now it's time to get the project off the ground.

Range of Launch Options

The range of options for launching a project is quite varied. Some projects start off with a brief memo passed down from your boss: "We are starting a project to upgrade our Web site to allow online shopping." Not an easy task, but a project has been initiated.

The other extreme might be one of Microsoft's product launches. Microsoft announced it would spend over $100 million on marketing Vista, the successor to Windows XP. Launching a new operating system is no easy task, but in a similar way, a formal project has been initiated.

Most of your projects will fit somewhere in the middle: you will get more formal notification of its beginnings ("Let's meet Friday to discuss the request from Accounting to upgrade their database"), and a little less than Microsoft's billions ("We have to keep this project under budget, too, so let's make sure the $15,000 number is kept on everyone's minds").

Stage a "Kick-Off Meeting"

It may be wise to enlist your boss when trying to demonstrate the value and importance of your project to other department heads. Often the senior-most executive who is "sponsoring" the project will call for a meeting, along with various department heads, at the beginning of a project. The purpose of a meeting like this is to make sure that all the various department managers are aware of the importance of the project, and to encourage them to commit resources to it as needed. A meeting like this, often called a "kick-off meeting," can be a critical success factor in a project.

A good kick-off meeting will have every member of the team in attendance. The roles and responsibilities can then be defined — ideally in front of the sponsors. Goals, schedules, budgets, etc., can also be presented to everyone — in front of everyone. This public accountability (if appropriate for your project) can be a very effective method to solidify your team's goals.

Goals of Your Kick-Off Meeting

At your kick-off meeting set some ground rules, establish some administrative procedures, and make sure that everyone is on the same page. Make sure everyone is very clear about the project's objective and scope. This is the perfect time to discuss the project's goals. You have already written them down, and this first meeting is the place for you to distribute them and make sure everyone buys into them.

At this same meeting you may want to establish how often and where the project team is going to meet. A regular schedule of a weekly meeting at the same time, in the same room, is helpful — it sets a valuable routine.

4.5 Phase Four: Track the Project's Progress

The bigger your project, the harder it is to keep track of who is doing what, how long different tasks will take, and so on. Several techniques for project management (project meetings, minutes, etc.) are discussed throughout this book. But these techniques provide more snapshot-type information and fall short of giving any perspective about the "big picture." Although there are many software tools available for project management, one in particular, Microsoft Project, has become the predominant choice. It has become very popular for managing projects of almost any size.

Microsoft Project

There are many project management software tools but Microsoft Project is the most popular. It has legions of users who would never dream of using any other product. And they can't imagine why you would consider using anything else, either. In some companies, using Microsoft Project has achieved a

---

How Formal Do I Have to Get?

"Focus your time, energy, and money tightly. You don't have to be very formal about it — not every good project manager uses Gantt charts, for example. But you have to manage your project carefully, regardless of how formally you do that.

Whether you are installing a new phone system, taking over the management of a building, or deploying a fleet of brokers to evaluate a potential new marketplace, you have to *systematically schedule your efforts and the team members'*.

By managing your time lines, you can anticipate when your resources will be slack or overdrawn, when the project will slow down or intensify, and when you need to step in and rearrange things. You need this kind of information, or the project will overwhelm you."

—Peter Hansen
Principal, Hansen Realty, Berkeley, CA

---

near-religious status. If you're working for one of those companies, get used to receiving .MPP files.

Simply entering your project's information into Microsoft Project is a valuable exercise in itself. It forces you to think of the specific tasks needed, their dependencies on other tasks, and the times and resources needed. As you do this, Microsoft Project will alert you when the left hand doesn't know what the right hand is doing. For example, if you've over allocated resources, or if time constraints are exceeded, Microsoft Project will let you know.

By defining to Microsoft Project which tasks can occur simultaneously, and which must be done sequentially, it's easy to make changes to any portion of the project and have all the dates and resource allocations updated automatically and see what the impact is.

Microsoft Project also allows you to integrate your data with other time tracking and office productivity tools relatively seamlessly.

Remember, however, all the power that Microsoft Project provides can overwhelm you and you can forget that *you* are running your project, not Microsoft Project.

Other Project Management Tools

One reason you might consider using a different tool is that Microsoft Project is a sophisticated product. It has many features and capabilities, many more than the average (that is, non-professional) person managing projects would ever use.

In addition, there are many companies that use enterprise project management tools and require their project managers to use that tool. Enterprise project management tools track multiple projects and resources assignments across all of them. These tools can provide the manager with a high-level view of the status of all projects and identify opportunities to re-assign resources among different projects. Examples of enterprise project management tools include:

- Primavera
- Planview
- Niku
- Oracle Projects
- Microsoft Project EPM
- IBM Rational Portfolio Manager
- Mercury Project Management

Also, Web-based project management tools are gaining popularity. Rather than e-mail files back and forth, users are making changes to a single file stored on a server. It's more efficient and often more correct.

Gantt Charts and Time Lines

A Gantt chart tracks time along the horizontal axis. The vertical axis lists all the tasks associated with the project, their start and end dates, and the resources required.

See Figure 4.2 below for an example of a Gantt chart that can be generated from Microsoft Project. When you print out the Gantt chart for a particular project, you and every member of the project team (along with anyone else who is interested) can see the real scope of it, the time frames, tasks, dependencies, resource assignments, etc. Gantt charts rarely fit on a single page, by the way, so it is common for the entire report to require a whole wall to view when all the pages are taped together.

PERT Charts and Critical Paths

Program Evaluation and Review Technique (PERT) charts or PERT diagrams are graphic representations of the dependencies between tasks in a project.

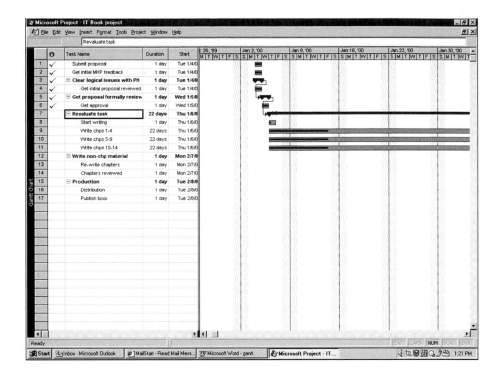

Figure 4.2   Sample Gantt Chart

"PERT is basically a method for analyzing the tasks involved in completing a given project, especially the time needed to complete each task, and identifying the minimum time needed to complete the total project" (Wikipedia: *http://en.wikipedia.org/wiki/Program_Evaluation_and_Review_Technique*).

In Figure 4.3 below, a circle represents a task start and/or end and a line between two circles represents the actual tasks and how they're related.

Critical Path

One of the more helpful pieces of information from a PERT chart identifies the "critical path." The critical path is the series of tasks or events that determine the project's total duration. In other words, if any of the tasks on the critical path take longer than expected then the entire project will be delayed by that amount of time. Tasks that aren't on the critical path won't have the same influence on the overall project for various reasons (perhaps because they're done in parallel, as opposed to sequentially).

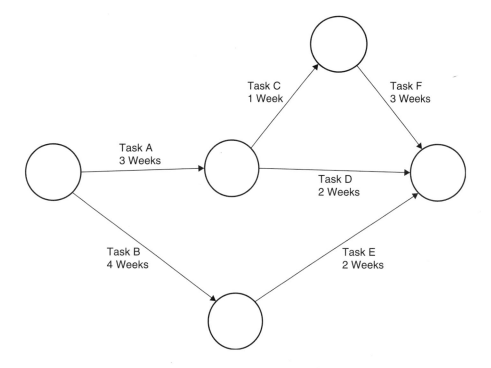

Figure 4.3   PERT Chart

In Figure 4.3, the critical path consists of tasks A, C, F. If either of these tasks takes longer than expected, it will delay the project as a whole. Activities outside the critical path can change (up to a point) without impacting the entire project. "Slack time" is the term used to indicate how much a non-critical-path task can be delayed without impacting the project as a whole.

Project Milestones

Both Gantt and PERT charts allow you to identify and track your tasks. Creating a milestone in your Gantt chart allows you to add a very useful level of functionality to your project tracking.

A milestone is a major event in the life of a project. A large project can have many milestones: Moving your company's offices from New York to Raleigh won't only have many individual tasks, but it will have many milestones. When the decision is officially made, for example (it might have been bandied around for years), is a milestone. But that will be only the first milestone; when the new site is selected, when the lease for the new building is signed, when the phones and wiring are complete, when the data center is ready, when the telecommunication lines are turned up, when office construction is done, when the first people started working in the new building are all milestones.

Think specifically about what needs to be accomplished to reach your project goal. Begin by breaking the objective down into a few milestones. You don't need a lot of detail here, but divide the project down into a few chunks so that you can begin thinking about the kinds of people you want on the project team, and maybe begin to develop some perspective on time frames, costs, and other resources. You may have enough knowledge about the project to do this on your own, or you may want to chat with some colleagues, your boss, or seek outside resources (books, Web sites, classes, and consultants).

Updates to Management and the Team

One of the things that everyone wants to know about a project is: "How is it going?" Certainly your boss and the project sponsor want to know this, and the project team needs to be told as well. Oftentimes a project is so big that team members are only familiar with their own piece, and aren't aware of the overall project as a whole.

Regular project meetings (discussed in the section Productive Project Meetings below on page 128) can be helpful for keeping members of the team up to date. But these meetings may not be sufficient for everyone; some people are only involved in the project during certain periods, for example, and therefore don't attend every meeting. Sending out project status reports (see below) and posting meeting agendas and minutes, as well as current version of project plans, etc., are two ways of making sure that everyone has access to the data they need.

Summary Updates

Gantt charts, PERT charts, critical paths, etc., are useful tools, but the chances are that your manager, the project sponsors, and the stakeholders may not want to see that level of detail. Even your own team members may not want to wade through all of that just to see if things are on track or not. Providing regular updates that summarize progress can be valuable to all. These summaries can include topics like:

✦ Accomplishments since the last update

✦ Mention of those items in progress and whether they're going faster or slower than expected

✦ Upcoming activities

✦ Issues and concerns (perhaps vendor deliveries are taking longer than expected, or a key member of the team recently resigned)

✦ Overall status; this is the opportunity to identify if things are going as planned, or whether you're anticipating delays, cost overruns, etc.

Determining the appropriate content, who sees it, and how often these updates go out is a matter of judgment. For example, a daily report for a two-year long project may be overkill. It may make more sense to do it monthly for the first 18 months, and then switch to bi-weekly and weekly as the projects gets closer to implementation. Similarly, the summary above may be sufficient for your boss, but perhaps an even briefer summary is appropriate for her boss.

Red, Yellow, Green Indicators

Another technique used to keep everyone informed about project status is to use red, yellow, and green status indicators for key items. Stealing from the traffic light paradigm (everyone is familiar with what the colors mean), they are a simple and effective way of communicating the status that might otherwise get lost in a verbose explanation. These indicators are usually included as part of other status reports, and are associated with key tasks and milestones.

4.6　Phase Five: Close Out the Project

Writing a Closeout Report

A Closeout Report is the report written at the end of a project. It can be a brief, 3-page document, or a 50-page, detailed report. It should contain, at minimum, the purpose of the project and how well the team executed that purpose. Additional components of a Closeout Report can include: a brief history of the project, specific goals accomplished and/or missed, resources used, which aspects went well, and what lessons were learned from things that didn't go well.

One simple method of generating a Closeout Report is to take the initial Project Plan — the document you worked so hard to create at the beginning of the project — and compare it directly to what you accomplished during the project. Earlier in this chapter we discussed developing a plan with a Closeout Report in mind. For example, say your plan called for the purchase and installation of six new servers in less than two weeks; you accomplished that, so identify the goal, the steps, and the accomplishment. Name names, specify how much money and time you saved, and pat your team on the back.

Additional Accomplishments

If pertinent, add the new uses or new procedures that your project uncovered. Maybe the new system you installed caught the attention of another department, and it's now serving two purposes. Maybe the automating of the sales process saved more money than expected, as well as reduced errors. Point these successes out.

Dealing with Bad News

If your Closeout Report contains bad news, be clear about it. Compare it to the Project Plan and try to identify how things could have been different. Were the goals set too unrealistically? ("Purchase and install six servers by COB Friday.") Were you given enough resources? ("You can use one person from Accounting, but that's it.") Don't name names, and try and learn from the problems: What can the company learn from this failure? ("In the future, changes to the time reporting software need the involvement of someone from HR.")

The Need for Follow-up Activities

It's pretty rare that a project finishes with every loose end tied up. There are often a number of items that require follow-up. These could be items like making sure ongoing maintenance is done, the contractors complete all the documentation they promised, etc.

The completion of projects — the installation of a new billing system, for example — often generates the need for more training. And this training can be identified either while the project is being worked on or as it's completed. If the project completion is going to get a critical function working (such as a billing system), training should be scheduled well in advance to have users ready.

4.7 Decision-Making Techniques

One way to think about the decisions you'll have to make in your role as a PM is to think about the four types of decision-making mechanisms you can use. These mechanisms are, naturally, only one of many ways to approach the issue. How and why people make decisions is now a giant field of research. But these approaches are fairly common methods used to look at the issue.

Four Types of Decision-Making Methods

1. **The Majority Wins**. You take a vote and whichever side of the issue gets the most votes, wins. This is certainly the most democratic method, it

makes team members feel the most involved, and is often the perfect solution to some clearly defined, black-or-white types of problems. On the other hand, it can lead to strange decisions (Do you really want the team to meet off site every week?), and is often not the right method for solving very complex problems. And, commonly, the *favored* approach may not be the *best* one. Some people may opt for it because it's the simplest, quickest, or cheapest.

2. **An appointed subcommittee decides or recommends.** This technique is good because the committee can gather and analyze detailed facts and present a recommendation to the group as a whole. It is bad because not everyone is involved in the decision and because even small committees can get locked up. This approach is excellent for problems that have many components that need to be researched before a decision is made, or for issues that need to be decided quickly and outside of the large group. The U. S. Senate, for example, has many committees and subcommittees whose function is to do the often critical preliminary work before presenting a bill or a nominee to the Senate as a whole.

3. **You decide with help from your team.** This is often the most efficient and most popular method. Many decisions on a project don't lend themselves to group dynamics; there is either not enough time, or the issue isn't all that important to the group (Does everyone really have to vote on which conference room to use?). But you can solicit opinions from team members that you know care about the issue and then decide. It's not 100% democracy, but it's not 100% dictatorship, either.

4. **You make the decision by yourself.** A manager will make plenty of decisions all by himself and no one will care. To keep a project moving along, sometimes it's critical simply to make a decision and move on. (The team lost two programmers on Friday, for example; you decide to contact HR that afternoon to begin to fill those positions. You know other people in the group feel the positions should be filled with analysts, but you don't, and time is ticking away. Make the decision and go.)

Some decisions made unilaterally won't be popularly received, of course, by team members who perceive these as decisions "imposed upon them." When that happens, you'll be well served to have a history of democratic decision making behind you, as well as an explanation about how this particular decision was made with the project's ultimate goals in mind. You may not make everyone happy, but if you do it well, you will be respected.

With the difficult decisions, you may not be sure that the right decision was made, but you can be sure it was a good decision if:

✦ All views, concerns, and issues were voiced and discussed

✦ All alternatives were considered

✦ You can explain (when questioned in the future) the factors and reasoning that led to you deciding the way you did

Once a decision is made, you shouldn't feel compelled to revisit it unless some of the key factors related to it have changed.

4.8 What to Do If/When the Project Gets Off Track

Managing time and money are your biggest opportunities to succeed in project management — and your largest possibilities for failure. Watch them both carefully. This section provides suggestions for how to deal with the inevitable problems associated with managing time and money.

Regardless of how or why your project is taking more time or money than expected, it's imperative to keep the stakeholders (particularly the sponsor and your boss) informed. If you try to cover up the problem, it will almost assuredly come back to haunt you. Invariably, the problem will eventually surface, and you'll not only be faulted for the original problem, but also for the attempting to cover it up (which could do more damage to your reputation than simply being late or going over budget).

Some Issues Out of Your Control

There will be events in every project that are out of anyone's control:

✦ People get sick

✦ Family emergencies come up

✦ Long-planned vacations arise

✦ Calls from other departments come in for "your" resources

✦ Personnel get promoted and move on to other responsibilities

✦ Team members move on to other positions

✦ Vendors fail to meet their commitments

✦ A corporate downsizing is announced

✦ Severe weather events occur

✦ Changes in the organizational/management landscape suddenly take place

---

Four Tongue-in-Cheek "Laws" of Project Management

Managing projects can be a complex task and most projects run into some difficulty before they are completed. Before discussing how to handle some of these difficulties, it seems appropriate to let you know about the following four "laws" of project management. They are often presented in a tongue-in-cheek way. However, they prove true more often than not:

1. No major project is ever installed on time, within budget, or with the same staff that started it.

2. Projects progress quickly until they become 95% complete, and then remain 95% complete forever.

3. When things are going well, something will go wrong.
    a. Corollary: When things can't get any worse, they will.
    b. Corollary: When things are going well, it's because you have overlooked something.

4. The "80/20 Rule" (in software development): The first 20% of a project schedule completes 80% of a project's goals, but the remaining 20% of the project's goals takes 80% of the project schedule.

When a Project Gets Behind Schedule

If your project falls behind schedule, don't panic. Consider the following ideas when you see a project slipping:

✦ Determine exactly how far behind you are. If you're using a Gantt chart, for example, you can track which tasks are behind schedule. (Microsoft Project calls them "variances.")

✦ Try to isolate the problem. Are you behind on one small, relatively isolated part of the project? Or is the entire mission going to be late?

✦ Try to recalibrate. Can the schedule be changed easily? If the task involves one person working on a single piece of the project, can you work with him to reset the timetable?

✦ Gain perspective. You may not be able to reset the schedule for the offending task and the entire project may be delayed, but how big a problem is that? If you promised a completion date for a three-month project of Friday, will having things finished on Monday really matter?

✦ Be open to all your team members and stakeholders. If time is slipping away, you have a responsibility to everyone to let them know the status of the project. In particular, people below you (team members) need to know what's really happening. And people above you (your bosses) need to be kept informed.

✦ Lead, don't just manage. Here is a chance for you to shine as a leader. When you have to let people know about a problem with the project, make it less about assigning blame ("We'd be fine if Jack pulled his weight") and more about showing your skills as a leader ("We are two weeks behind schedule but here is my plan for how we can catch up").

✦ Involve others. When someone alerts you to a problem or delay, ask them for their recommendations and suggestions on how to deal with it. Of course, you have to be careful with this technique. Individuals may shy away with identifying problems if they have a sense they're going to be stuck with the ownership of resolving it.

✦ Do some research on the reasons for the delay. The schedule might have been unrealistically set (by you or someone else) at the beginning; if you look into delays as they occur, and you carefully track them, you will be able to better anticipate problems in the future.

✦ Be aggressive in solving the problem. If you need more time to complete a project, tell people and get more time. Hoping no one will notice isn't a strategy for continued success.

Perils of Adding Staff

Consider, but don't automatically decide, to add resources. Some projects are either understaffed from the outset or suddenly develop a need for further resources in mid-project; adding staff to these tasks often results in a speed up of the project. Consider how long it will take a person to get up to speed and productive on this project.

Other types of projects, however, aren't well suited to the additional-staff fix. Software development, famously, rarely benefits from adding developers. Fredrick Brooks, in his groundbreaking book *The Mythical Man-Month*, states his famous law: "Adding manpower to a late software project makes it later." Keep in mind that some tasks can't be sped up by adding staff. For example, no matter how many women you assign to the task, it will still take nine months to produce a baby.

Your Project is Costing More than Expected

Projects run over budget all the time. How *far* over budget is often the most important issue.

Consider these solutions:

✦ Determine exactly how far over budget you are. $500 over on a $300K project is meaningless; $5,000 on a $15,000 project is a problem you have to address immediately.

✦ Do some research on the reasons for the budget overage. The budget might have been unrealistically set (by you or someone else) at the beginning; if you look into the overages as they occur, and you carefully track them, you'll be able to better anticipate problems in the future.

✦ Be clear to your boss (and other stakeholders involved in the money side of the project) that there is a problem. A 5% variance on dollars can be trivial or critical (depending on the size of the budget), but most bosses will want to know about that discrepancy.

✦ Adjust the project deliverables. Many projects are redefined halfway through: If your initial project goal called for all 14 satellite offices to get individual servers, and installation costs on the first 5 sent you over budget already, it is time to re-evaluate your project goals. All the offices may get their own servers, but that may not happen until next year, instead of this year.

✦ Find "hidden money." Your project budget may have a contingency budget, or your boss may have money from another project you can use.

✦ Avoid falling into the trap of thinking that you'll save money later in the project and in the end you'll be OK.

4.9 Useful Project Management Techniques

Project Teams

Formalizing a group of individuals working loosely together toward a common goal can have tremendous benefits. Calling these people a special group, or telling them they are all now members of a "project team," can solidify a project's goals and make progress toward those goals much more evident. When people feel identified with a project, they are much more likely to feel responsible and accountable for it.

The size and complexity of your project will determine how formal you need to be with assigning teams: getting three new sales people up and running with laptops, for example, may take a day or two and involvement from several different people in IT at various times, but the task probably doesn't need a formal team.

Moving your company's offices, on the other hand, is a classic project that benefits from formalizing a team. Each member has specific tasks, and everyone can have a clear idea of what the goal is and how they can help with that goal.

Candidates for the Project Team

Who are candidates for your project team? Individuals' involvement on the team can be quite varied. Some people may be dedicated nearly 100% to the project throughout its life. Others may spend only a small portion of their time on the project. Still others may only be involved with the project during certain phases. In addition, a project team will probably consist mostly of employees, but there may also be outside consultants if special expertise is needed.

The first people you'll include on the team are the ones you think it will take to achieve the project's goal. As you talk with these people, they will offer up suggestions of others that need to be involved. They will also offer you different perspectives on what it will take to make the project succeed. Some of the project's team members may be on your staff. Others that you'd like to include might be your peers, direct reports of your peers, and individuals from other departments — perhaps some that are senior to you.

While it's tempting to pick the best and brightest for your project, you may want to temper that instinct. Projects are great mechanisms to allow others on your staff to shine, and to give them the opportunity to show what they can do. Since the best and brightest are always in high demand, give careful consideration to balancing your project team with a mix of people from the A-list as well as those that deserve the opportunity to show they can be a member.

Create a "War Room"

For some projects, it has become trendy to have a project room or war room. (A movie about President Clinton's 1992 presidential campaign — a project that used a project room to great effect — is called *The War Room*.)

This room provides team members a place to work on the project that is separate from their regular work area. The idea of the war room is to keep members from being distracted from the project by their regular duties, and to increase communication (and hopefully productivity, quality, etc.) by having the team members near each other. Lately, war rooms aren't complete unless they also include a whole host of toys (Koosh balls, hacky sacks, Nerf games, etc.), a whiteboard, an endless supply of munchies and soft drinks, and "open" seating, so that team members can easily communicate.

Formalized Project Frameworks

Chapter 8, IT Compliance and Controls, has a section called Methodologies and Frameworks (page 216). A number of these, such as IT Infrastructure Library (ITIL), ISO 9000, Six Sigma, and Capability Maturity Model Integration (CMMI), have aspects and techniques you can apply to your projects to help ensure quality and that goals are met, and for managing/tracking the progress.

Participate in the Project Yourself

Consider participating in the project yourself — give yourself tasks to do besides managing the project. While managing the project is often a full-time job, if team members see you working on the project, it inspires them. Plus, it gives you greater insight to the project, as well as your staff's activities. Until the late 1990s, Bill Gates contributed directly to Excel's code.

Offer Project Perks

Brown bag lunches, team T-shirts, coffee mugs, milestone achievement awards — think of ideas to keep your team active and involved. Consider small rewards along the project time line (weekly team meeting small prize drawings, for example), instead of awards at the end. Company-paid doughnuts have a very attractive cost-in-exchange-for-information ratio, and often get people to meetings.

The Flying Pig Award

At our company, we have a challenging project — one that some people say we will complete "only when pigs fly."

Every month we have an all-hands meeting where we present a "Flying Pig" award and certificate. The flying pig is a ceramic pig that the winner is allowed to keep for a month — until someone else "wins" (earns) it. Team members nominate potential awardees. People post the certificate in their cubes and sign and decorate the pig when their month is up.

Karen Hitchcock
System Engineer

Give Your Project a Code Name

"Operation First Falcon" sounds a lot more exciting and important than "Operation General Ledger." For projects that are large enough, create a code name and a project logo, put them on polo shirts, and you'll be flooded with requests for people to join your project. (Not necessarily the people you want on the project, but that's a different problem.) Use the logo and name on documents pertaining to the project.

Productive Project Meetings

Okay, now you have the project team, or at least the first cut at the project team. The next thing you want is to get all the team members together.

Keys to Successful Project Meetings

Work to make sure every one of your meetings is as effective as it can be. Information should be shared, issues discussed, decisions made, and action items determined.

+ Set clear goals in your first project meeting: document the objective and scope of the project, how frequently meetings will be held, have minutes taken, and so on.

+ Holding a successful project team meeting involves several simple but effective meeting techniques. These methods are discussed below; use them to increase the productivity of your meetings and your team.

+ Don't forget that you're in control, and therefore responsible, for the success of both the meetings and the overall project. Watch both carefully.

Meeting Agendas

Typically, each project meeting will follow a consistent format. Develop one that seems to work well for you and your team and that everyone is comfortable with. Typical areas for a project meeting agenda might include:

+ Review status of open items and action items from previous meeting

+ Re-state decisions and agreements from previous meeting

+ Review overall status of project, and discuss any major issues

+ Updates from each sub-team, or team member

+ Accomplishments of note

+ Key tasks and milestones coming up

You will also want to use the meetings for special events. For example, it may be an opportunity to demo a recently completed application component. Or, it may be the right place for a vendor to demo a product that may be appropriate for the solution. Alternatively, if the project hits a snag, or a particularly important decision needs to be made, the agenda can set aside time for an in-depth discussion of the issues.

Minutes of the Meetings

Have minutes taken so that there is no disagreement on items that were decided, tasks that were assigned, etc. Minutes should also include accomplishments, areas of concern and problems, updates on time frames, and so on. The minutes should be distributed to all team members and project sponsors as soon as possible after the meeting occurs — and certainly before the next meeting. Taking and distributing minutes can be painful tasks that can be easily forgotten or ignored; they can also be critical to the long-term success of the project.

As manager of the project, it's your job to make sure these tasks get done. You may get volunteers to take minutes, or you may not get any. A popular technique is to rotate this assignment each meeting. Or decide that the person who shows up *last* for the meeting is the one assigned to take minutes. This is a clever way of making sure people arrive on time. Among other things, the minutes ensure that everyone is aware of how the project is progressing.

The minutes may also give senior executives an idea of when they need to get involved; they may decide to rally the troops, motivate, or buy lunch for everyone because a milestone is met. Minutes can chart the progress of activities and tasks from week to week and serve as a reminder of things that need to be done. The minutes can also document who is responsible for each item. Too often, especially in large project teams, it's too easy for everyone to think "someone else" will take care of it. Although several people may be working on an item, it's important to identify a single person as the one to take the lead.

The minutes should reflect the key items of the meetings such as decisions, issues, project status, etc. Consider using the ideas discussed in this chapter in the section Updates to Management and the Team (see page 118), for the meeting minutes. Each meeting's minutes should follow the same format so that people know where to look to find the information they need.

The Hidden Cost of Meetings

There are, of course, the small costs of meetings: booking the rooms, the dough-nuts, video-conferencing, maybe you all will have to fly to a common city to meet, the cost of setting up and training on Web conferences, etc.

But the largest cost of meetings isn't often calculated. One way to think about meetings is to total up the hourly wage of every person attending the meeting. This cost is seldom considered, but it should be computed every time. If it were done each time there was a meeting, far fewer meetings would be held and far fewer attendees would be invited. Right now, you are inviting the VP from Sales because she is a stakeholder and you want to do the correct political thing; she may be attending because it allows her to meet with your boss before the meeting. In fact, perhaps she shouldn't be invited and wouldn't miss attending; if properly informed, she can get the status of your project from your weekly update e-mail and you can get more done with fewer (non-contributing) people in the room.

Next time, run the numbers and see how much the company is paying for everyone to be in that room. If the meeting has to be held out of town, these calculations are now (in these more ROI-conscious times) commonly done. But "at the office," way too many meetings with too many non-essential personnel are still held.

Project Meeting Options

There are now a variety of ways for your entire project team to meet:

+ **Face to face**. While this is still the most common and often the best option, it is sometimes completely impractical. Even people down the hall from you can't always attend meetings in person, much less the Help Desk team in India (and your group is in New York).

+ **Video-conferencing**. The price for this option has plummeted. Many companies now have Web cameras and speaker phones available for employees. Even an occasional video-conference at a rental facility (many Kinko's have this capability) can save radical money over airfare and hotels for all participants.

+ **Teleconferencing**. This is now a very common and more accepted alter-native to other types of meetings. Cell phones now come equipped with "Conference" buttons. But teleconferences have two drawbacks: they tend to drag on, and because people aren't being watched, they can do other things while in the meeting. "Do other things" often means check-ing e-mail, but it can mean other, more distracting things, too. Some tele-conference participants are 100% there; some aren't even 25% engaged.

✦ **Web-based tools**. There are a variety of simple, cheap (often free) tools that can facilitate remote meetings.

✦ **Video-conferencing via Instant Messaging (IM)**. IM tools (like Yahoo, AIM, and MSN) allow you to do simple video-conferencing using inexpensive Webcams. The IM tools are free, so the only cost is connecting the Internet and the Webcam.

✦ **Online Meeting Services**. Tools like WebEx and Microsoft's LiveMeeting, used in conjunction with a conference call, can help facilitate online meetings and training, allowing you to do presentations, demo applications, poll attendees, chalkboard, etc. These tools allow you to do real-time collaboration, so that you can pass a document (or control of your desktop) over to another user on the call. These services are available from many resellers, so you don't need to build your own infrastructure to host them.

Useful Meeting Techniques

At each meeting, review the minutes of the previous meeting. It's a good way to remind everyone about accomplishments, and to re-review any items that were still pending (commonly called "action items") or unresolved at the end of last week's meeting. In addition, stating the desired length of the meeting up front can be an effective technique for getting people to participate. If everyone knows that the goal is to finish the meeting in one hour, people will make more of an effort to get to the point (and will try to force those who don't to cut things short). Meetings held early in the day are more productive than those when people are tired after a full day's work; on the other hand, many critical project meetings are held at the end of the day to have a daily project meeting update.

4.10 Funding Projects

In general, when it comes to IT projects, the concerns are primarily about "hard" dollars. Hard and soft money are economic and budgeting concepts. The definitions may vary from organization to organization, but for the most part, "hard" costs are those that the company has to write a check for (hardware, software, outside consultants, etc.). "Soft" costs refer to costs that are less concrete (office space, use of existing staff, time, etc.). When corporate management wants to know how much a project is going to cost, they often only care about hard costs. However, at times, it may be advantageous to add in the soft costs (for example, when you're trying to make a project look more impressive in a press release or on your resume). In addition, referring to the soft costs will demonstrate to management that you're aware that the use of existing resources costs the company money as well.

Your best source for determining a project's costs might be the members of the project team, or it might not. It was their expertise that led you to select them for the team; tap this same expertise to evaluate costs. However, it's very possible that team members may only be able to provide you with information about the technologies that will be required, but not the costs of these technologies. This isn't unusual. Many technical personnel aren't interested in, or aren't exposed to, the business side of the technology. When you face this situation, you may have to contact the vendors and manufacturers directly to get estimates on the products your team members identified. In some cases, a project team may include someone solely dedicated to tracking the project's budget, and other administrative activities.

Estimating Costs: Go High

As a general rule, projects always exceed their initial cost estimates. As a result, it's common for project managers to inflate their cost estimates by factors of 10% or more, sometimes a lot more. There are several reasons for this.

When estimating costs, it's not unusual for smaller, "miscellaneous" items to be overlooked as everyone focuses on the big expenses. However, these miscellaneous items can add up to a significant amount.

+ If management balks at the total cost, the inflation factor provides you with some room to revise the estimate downward without (in theory) impacting the success of the project.

+ If the cost estimate is going to be wrong, err on the side of too high than have it be too low. If it were too low, you would end up in the embarrassing position of having to admit your poor planning and shortsightedness, and ask for more money.

The inflation factor gives a PM an opportunity to look like a hero if he can complete the project for less than was estimated. Then again, wildly padding your estimate simply to ensure you come in under budget can negatively impact your credibility in the eyes of management, as well as the credibility of the IT department.

Projects Always Cost More Than Estimated

There are many costs to include within any IT project. Besides the obvious costs of hardware and software, others common costs to consider include vendor support costs, travel, installation costs, annual licenses and maintenance, physical plant expenses (raised floor, air conditioning), training, telecommunications, books and manuals, user group fees, trade shows, software utilities, test equipment and environments, parallel testing, integration costs, incentives for project team members, consultants, and so on. And don't forget some money for the Nerf balls, munchies, sodas, and pizzas for working during lunch or late into the night.

Capital Expenditures and Expense Items

The last consideration when estimating project costs are the differences between capital expenditures and expense items. A capital expenditure is for an item that will have a useful life of several years — like a piece of hardware. Some companies consider software to be a capital expenditure. An expense item is something whose value is gone almost immediately. (See Chapter 6 for a more thorough discussion of this and other budgeting topics.)

Exactly Who Is Going to Pay for It?

If the company is going to pay for all the costs you've estimated for this project, someone has to figure out where the money is going to come from. More than likely, the company's budget as well as your department's budget have already been set. And unless someone built enough padding into either of these to cover your new project's expenses, it's likely that your project may cause your department, as well as others, to go over budget.

This dilemma may not be the problem it initially seems. If corporate management approves your project and costs, then the various department heads will have your project as a ready justification when they have to explain their overruns. If the project is sponsored or initiated by a very high-level executive, she may direct you to charge all of the project's costs to a special department code that she is responsible for, which alleviates everyone else's concerns about their own budgets.

Chargeback Codes

Some companies may choose to set up special "chargeback codes" for projects so that it's easier to track the total costs. This is especially true for very large projects. For smaller projects, individual departments may be instructed to "eat" the costs as part of their regular budget. It's important that you know how upper management wants to pay for the costs associated with your project so that there are no surprises, and that your project doesn't make enemies among other department heads at the same time you're trying to develop allies.

In larger corporations, certain projects may be assigned accounting codes of their own. This means that other departmental budgets aren't impacted by the project, and it also presents a convenient way to track the project's costs. Then again, when such a special code exists (sometimes jokingly referred to as a "slush fund"), it can be awfully tempting to use it for items that have a barely tangential relationship to the project.

Justifying the Costs

No matter who initiated the project, sooner or later you're going to have to defend the costs. If you're the one who initiated the idea for the project, you may have to justify the project even before you know the costs. The most efficient means of justifying your costs is to try to show a clear Return on Investment (ROI) for your project. For example, if you wanted to implement a pool of shared printers, you could easily justify the costs by demonstrating that the company will no longer have to pay for individual printers at each desk and workstation.

However, project cost justification is rarely so cut-and-dried. More often, the justification consists of a variety of intangibles that are hard to quantify. In the printer pool example used above, you could also cite that it would simplify the inventorying of toner and spare replacements parts.

First, here is a list of the more tangible benefits:

✦ Improved productivity and efficiencies (faster and/or cheaper)

✦ Reduced costs (fewer dollars/resources needed to accomplish the same task)

✦ Meeting changing demands of the marketplace (e.g., the introduction of the Euro)

✦ Less waste (materials, time, resources)

✦ Reduced head count (in these more politically correct times, it's better to phrase this in more sensitive terms: "reallocation of existing staff to other company areas" or "eliminate the need to add to staff")

✦ Compliance with legislative regulations (tax laws, environmental issues, safety regulations, etc.)

Next is a list of the more nebulous intangible benefits:

✦ Increased advantage over competition

✦ Improved customer relations

✦ Better company/product/brand awareness

✦ Higher quality

- ✦ Improved staff morale
- ✦ Greater convenience (for staff, customers, business partners)

Both of these lists can come in handy when defining your project charter. Think of the project's justification as the answer you give to people when they ask, "Why should we do this?" and later when they ask "Why are we doing this?"

4.11 Multiple Projects: How to Juggle Well

You **Will** *have Multiple Projects*

There are some IT Managers who work on a single project 40 hours a week, but they are the exception. Almost every manager, and certainly almost everyone in IT doing project management, has to juggle multiple projects. Some may be small, some may be due later in the year, but almost everyone is juggling more than one project. You may decide that an enterprise project management tool (discussed on page 115 of this chapter) is the sort of thing you need to help manage multiple projects.

Prioritize by Time and Money

Some projects are huge. "Huge" depends on the size of your organization, of course, but if they need 75% of your time, be clear to yourself and others that this is where you'll be spending most of your time and effort.

Sorting tasks by time is a common technique: if you have a relatively low priority task that is due tomorrow but a high-value task that is due in two months, you can accomplish both by doing the lower priority one first. But that is the simple case. More often the problem is juggling two competing projects, both "due yesterday." You'll become a radically better manager of projects if you can take situations like this and convert them to your advantage: evaluate each project and determine which one has the highest priority. Make that determination and act clearly upon it.

Prioritize by Politics

Why kid around? Some projects are simply more important because they are *politically* more important. If your boss wants all executives to have flat-screens installed, you are going to do this before you install the new network printer downstairs. Be clear about your tasks and tell your boss about your other priorities; often, they won't care, but often they'll rearrange their needs when informed of your conflicts — the new network printer required downstairs may be for a department he's trying to appease.

4.12 Dealing with Non-IT Departments on a Project

It's important to remember that IT is a service organization: it exists not to test out the latest hardware and software (although that is definitely a perk), but to provide computing capabilities to other groups within the company.

Working with other groups in the company is inevitably going to mean having non-IT members on a project. In that situation, three basic issues will arise: how to motivate individuals you aren't managing, which department is in charge, and how do we charge our time?

Motivating Employees Outside Your Department

This situation isn't always a problem: most project members are willing and capable performers. Many see the task defined, see their roles as part of the bigger picture, and perform admirably.

Others, however, do not. And employees that don't play well with others are hardly unique to IT-managed projects. There are two actions you can take in this situation: emphasize the company's overall goals to that individual ("when this project wins, we all win") and, if more drastic measures are required, speak privately with the person's manager. If more direct managerial actions are required to get the desired employee performance, let the correct manager handle the situation. You wouldn't want some other manager "handling" your employees.

Who Is In Charge?

Some projects will never resolve this issue, but most will. And you can save everyone a lot of headaches by addressing this issue as quickly as possible. Bring the point up in the introductory meetings, at the funding meetings, and at the kick-off meeting. Get the issue settled as fast as possible.

One common scenario is one department (say IT) is working with another (say Sales). Both departments have vested interests in the success of the project and the time and money investments are the same. But one of the department heads has a much more domineering personality; this individual is very vocal about his needs and those of his department.

If you find yourself in this situation, *from the beginning* you must be clear to your team members, his team members, and the two or three people up the ladder that you both report to, that this will be a 50-50 project in terms of decisions. When you're clear to everyone about that, be clear that you will "go upstairs" as required, and the people upstairs know it and everyone on the team knows it.

4.13   Additional Resources

Web Sites

- ✦ *software.isixsigma.com/newsletter* (Six Sigma — quality control implementation methodology)

- ✦ *www.mercury.com/us/products/it-governance-center/project-management* (enterprise project manager tool vendor)

- ✦ *www.microsoft.com/office/project/prodinfo/epm/overview.mspx* (enterprise project manager tool vendor)

- ✦ *www.niku.com* (enterprise project manager tool vendor)

- ✦ *www.oracle.com/applications/projects/intro.html* (enterprise project manager tool vendor)

- ✦ *www.planview.com* (enterprise project management tool vendor)

- ✦ *www.pmi.org* (Project Management Institute)

- ✦ *www.primavera.com* (enterprise project manager tool vendor)

- ✦ *www.wisegeek.com/what-is-six-sigma.htm* (brief article about Six Sigma)

- ✦ *www-306.ibm.com/software/awdtools/portfolio* (enterprise project manager tool vendor)

Books and Articles

- ✦ *A Guide To The Project Management Body Of Knowledge* (PMBOK Guides), Project Management Institute, 2004.

- Bender, Stephen A., *Managing Projects Well*, Butterworth-Heinemann, 1998.

- Bradbary, Dan, and Garrett, David, *Herding Chickens: Innovative Techniques for Project Management*, Jossey-Bass, 2005.

- Brooks, Frederic, *The Mythical Man-Month*, Addison-Wesley Professional, 1995.

- Garton, Coleen, and McCulloch, Erika, *Fundamentals of Technology Project Management*, Mc Press, 2005.

- Geer, David, "Measuring Project Risk," *ComputerWorld*, January 9, 2006, p. 38.

- Gibson, Stan, "IT 101 Switches Gears," *eWeek*, September 26, 2005.

- Rapoza, Jim, "The Game of IT Management: How to Avoid Hearing 'You Sank My Project,'" *eWeek*, October 3, 2005, p. 43.

- Snedaker, Susan, and Hoenig, Nels, *How to Cheat at IT Project Management*, Syngress Publishing, 2005.

- Tynan, Dan, "Proving Your Project's Worth," *InfoWorld*, November 21, 2005, p. 25.

- Wideman, R. Max, *A Management Framework for Project, Program and Portfolio Integration*, Traddford, 2004.

Changing Companies

CHAPTER FIVE

*Just because everything is different
doesn't mean anything has changed.*

—IRENE PETER

Taking on new responsibility is always a little scary. But if your company promotes you to a manager's role, you can take comfort in the familiar surroundings. You know the staff, you know the organization, you know the technical environment, and you know how things operate.

However, changing jobs is a whole different animal. It immerses you in unfamiliar surroundings. Aside from the people that interviewed you, the only familiar things may be the technology product names being used (and even some of those may not be too familiar).

As you first get settled, your boss will be looking for signs to confirm to him that he hired the right person. And you'll be trying to determine if you made the right decision in accepting the job offer.

5.1 The First Day

Even if you went through an extensive interview process, you probably spent less than eight hours talking with people at your new company, and most of that time was spent for them to learn about *you*. There was only a limited opportunity for you to learn about *them*. You're hoping that your gut instinct about the company and its people have led you to the right choice. Your boss is hoping that the person he met on the interview, and to whom he extended the offer, is the same person that shows up for work.

Don't be nervous. The first day at a new job isn't all that different from the first day at a new school and trying to figure out the lay of the land. (Remember the tension of those days?) You've got every reason to be nervous, but keep it to yourself. You want to demonstrate confidence. In fact, in a manner not too different from the interview, you want to show a combination of confidence (but not cockiness), experience (but not a know-it-all attitude), enthusiasm (but not giddiness), etc. In short, it's a good idea to try and maintain your interview persona, perhaps relaxed just a notch, when you first start a new job.

Meeting the New Staff

Unless you were told otherwise, it's probably safe to assume that your staff is like many other IT staffs with a healthy cross-section of technically brilliant people, socially challenged people, hard-working people, under-performers, and various combinations in between. To make things more complicated, your boss (demonstrating his professionalism) didn't give you his thoughts on individuals, because he thought you should form your own opinions. (And he's right.)

Unless it was made clear to you at the outset that your staff is a serious problem, you can probably assume that you have not been hired just to "kick some butts" — although you may determine later that some kicking is called for. Most likely you were hired to demonstrate leadership, professional maturity, management, and to provide direction.

On that first day, you'll be introduced to everyone, and in short order you'll forget their names, their faces, what they do, and where they sit. That's OK, that's normal. Hopefully, you were provided with the department's organizational chart; it can be a handy map to help you become familiar with your new surroundings.

Those first days will give you a chance to talk to your staff, perhaps as a group. They'll be judging what you say, and how you say it.

A Few Ideas for What to Say to Break the Ice

When you first talk to your staff, here are a few things you might bring up:

✦ A little bit about your background (last company and position you held, areas of IT you've worked in, different industries you've worked in)

✦ Some recent projects the group has completed (hopefully you got this info from your new boss)

✦ Upcoming projects and challenges facing the group (again, information your new boss provided)

✦ What goals you have, and what areas are important to you (e.g., customer service, reliability of systems, documentation, etc.)

✦ Why you're excited to be part of this company

✦ "My door is always open" (but don't say it if it isn't true)

Some Don'ts

As much as you want to get those first days off to a good start, you also want to avoid doing anything that leaves a bad taste in anyone's mouth:

✦ Don't talk too much about yourself and your accomplishments. You're not trying to impress them, just give them a sense of who you are.

✦ Don't try to make them afraid of you or to make them love you. You want their respect.

✦ Don't say things you're not reasonably certain you can do. For example, don't say you want to get everyone trained, and then discover that you have virtually no training budget.

One-On-One Meetings

More important than the small talk on the first days, however, is having one-on-one meetings with your staff. Even if you have a very large organization that has several layers below you, you should try to meet everyone on the staff. You'll benefit from hearing everyone's perspective, and they'll be pleased that you took the time and effort to talk to them. In many cases, simply having a chat can be of more value than anything specific that's discussed.

Of course, some of those one-on-ones may prove to be challenging. Your direct reports are probably seasoned enough to have a "conversation." But those from the lower ranks may be uncomfortable, scared, or just not great at holding a business conversation with the big boss (especially one they just met). Then again, some may really bend your ear.

If warranted, especially if you have a large team, you may want to meet some of the lower level staff in small groups. This may dilute the pressure that some of the quieter ones may feel.

Some Topics to Get the Conversational Ball Rolling

- ✦ How long have you been working here?
- ✦ Where were you before?
- ✦ What do you like best/least?
- ✦ What projects are you currently on, and what's your involvement?
- ✦ What are the best and worst things about the department/company?
- ✦ What's your function? Have you always been doing that?
- ✦ What areas, projects, type of work would you like to get involved with?
- ✦ What do you think of the department?
- ✦ What needs to get done?
- ✦ Is there anything you'd like to ask me? Or tell me?
- ✦ What are your concerns?
- ✦ What are the areas that you think need improving?
- ✦ Do you have any ideas for those improvements?
- ✦ Do you have any advice for me?

The last question may elicit some surprise that you asked for advice, and you may be surprised by some of the things that you hear. But it will probably buy you some goodwill as it's an indirect way of saying that you don't have all the answers, and that you are eager for other people's input and help. Since no one is going to expect you to remember everything, it's OK to take notes during these conversations. Not only will the notes help you later when you're trying to remember who said what, but it shows the staff that you care enough about what they say to write it down.

Remember to treat everyone with respect and professionalism.

What to Say to Those That Wanted Your Job and Didn't Get It

It's almost certain that someone on your staff (maybe even a peer) wanted your job — some may have even actively campaigned for it. For those that didn't get the job, they may not have really wanted it (and just applied as an opportunity to gain some visibility and face time with decision makers), and may even feel relieved they didn't get it. For others, though, the emotions may still be strong.

Unfortunately, you may not learn until later who wanted your job, why they were denied the opportunity, and most important, what (and how) they were told about why they didn't get it. In a worst-case scenario, they only learned that they didn't get it when they heard you were showing up to take that spot.

If you do know who applied for your job, you probably are better off not mentioning it to them directly. They may feel like you're rubbing salt in the wound. And, even if you try to be sensitive, they may resent the sympathetic posture from the person who took the job they wanted — you certainly don't want to appear condescending or patronizing.

The emotions from these individuals can be a combination of resentment, depression, disappointment, and indifference. The best thing you can do is to treat everyone equally with respect and professionalism. Over time, they'll come to terms with their disappointment and focus on their jobs. If they don't, that will be a signal that it's time for a heart-to-heart conversation with them. This conversation doesn't need to be any different from any conversation a manager may need to have with an employee demonstrating performance or outlook problems.

There is also a chance, hopefully very small, that one of the individuals may be so bitter that they are actually working against you. The smart person, although disappointed, should realize that their best approach is to align themselves with you, so that they become your indispensable right-hand man. Invariably, anyone who tries to sabotage their new manager will end up losing in a number of ways:

1. Squandering the opportunity to look good to the new manager;

2. Losing the confidence and trust of the new manager; and

3. Showing that they aren't a team player.

In some cases, one of these individuals may have been unofficially filling your role while the position was vacant. It might be a very good move for you to allow them to continue doing some of the tasks that they had taken on — running some meetings, leading some projects, etc. If you let them know that you respect and value what they do, that you want to work with them, and that you're not going to take things away from them just because you're the new big boss, you'll be sending a very strong message about the type of person you are.

How you deal with individuals and individual circumstances is often a tough judgment call. But exercising judgment is pretty much what your job is about. How you deal with people who applied for the job you have now might be one of your first big challenges, and one of your first big opportunities, as a new manager.

Establish a Relationship with Your Manager and Your Peers

There are two key factors that can insure a successful relationship with your new boss:

1. Knowing what she expects from you, and

2. Earning her trust that those expectations will be met.

Both take time, and you can expect occasional missed signals, or miscommunications along the way. Things to look out for include:

- ✦ Does she prefer e-mail, telephone, or in-person communications?

- ✦ What are her priorities: projects, technologies, certain applications or specific user groups?

- ✦ Does she prefer constant updates on details, or just periodic status reports on the big picture?

- ✦ Does she like to get right down to business, or does she enjoy a little casual conversation?

- ✦ Is she more impressed with form or function?

- ✦ Is she focused on process? Or metrics?

- ✦ Is she involved with her staff, the mood of the department, etc.?

- ✦ Is she focused on building an empire? Or her own status and growth?

- ✦ Are her decisions based on raw data, judgment calls, or input from her staff?

- ✦ Is she a consensus builder?

- ✦ Does she make snap decisions and judgments? Or does she form these over time?

✦ Does she have a very formalized project management methodology, or does she prefer the "let's just get it done" approach?

✦ What is her own boss like? What is her relationship with her management — do you know what they expect of her?

Keep in mind that while you're figuring out how to deal with a new manager, your new staff is doing exactly the same thing with you. This frame of mind can help you keep some perspective about the dynamics of the situation.

Remember, your new manager wants you to succeed. When you succeed, it makes her life easier by having a winner working for her. And, it makes her look good that she hired a good manager. You have a built-in ally.

In a similar vein, your peers (your fellow managers) also want you to succeed. They might have been frustrated that your team hasn't had much management prior to your arrival, and might have atrophied during that time. They may also be a little bit more forthcoming about the weaknesses they see in your team's members and operations. They can also give you some insight into the culture of the department and the company, hot-button projects, and issues.

Just like you do with your boss, you'll want to build relationships with your peers, demonstrate that they can count on you, and that you're eager for their guidance and input as you get settled. You don't have to take all their guidance and input at face value, but there can be great value in listening to it.

Learning the Landscape: Key Users and Key Applications

There's a lot you don't know about your new environment, and the sooner you start closing the gap, the better off you'll be.

The first thing you may want to know is who your key users are, and what the key applications/systems are. Depending on the industry you're in, the answers could differ considerably. If you're working for a law firm, the key applications may be the document management system and the system for recording billable hours. In a manufacturing plant, the key applications probably revolve around the supply chain.

You also want to learn some basic information about the environment, some of which may have come out when you were interviewed.

✦ How many locations does the company have?

✦ How many users are there at each location?

✦ How large is the technical environment (number of servers, amount of storage, number of applications)?

✦ Is it staffed 24/7? If not, how is after-hours support handled?

- Is IT distributed or centralized?

- What do the wide- and local-area network topologies look like?

- Historically, where have the major problem spots been?

- Who are the key vendors and partners?

- Is there any documentation about policies and procedures and current projects?

- What are the high-level technology standards (messaging, development tools, database, storage, operating systems, etc.)?

Chapter 9, Getting Started with the Technical Environment (page 231), further discusses the issue of learning about the environment for which you're now responsible.

Find the Key Meetings

Invariably, IT is involved in numerous regularly scheduled meetings — weekly, bi-weekly, monthly, etc. Some may strictly be for ITers, some may be with the users or other department heads, and some may be situations where IT is simply an invited guest.

Start asking around about these meetings and joining in. It sounds strange to ask around for meetings to attend (many people prefer to go to as few meetings as they can), but many meetings are critical. You'll find that some you'll want to attend regularly, some occasionally, and some not at all. Some you'll be invited to and some you'll have to wangle your way in.

If meeting minutes and agendas are available (a worthwhile idea that is often overlooked), it can help you determine which meetings you need to be involved in.

Be Realistic about Timetables for Fixing Problems

Chances are that you'll notice problems more than you'll notice things that are going well. That's OK, it's just human nature. The important thing is to not feel overwhelmed by the problems. No one is expecting you to fix the world in your first week, or even your first month.

When starting a new job, it's very tempting to refer to the way things were done at your last job — especially if you're proposing it as some sort of example for your new company. Co-workers will quickly get tired of hearing it, and they'll invariably think "if your last job was so great, why did you leave?" You can propose the same ideas, but be careful about referring to your old job too often.

Some First-Day-at-Work War Stories

Below are true stories from various employees' first days on the job:

The Employee Got Surprised

✦ "A senior level technical director joined our company and had four direct reports and 10 more indirects. He assumed his job was to manage his team. However, the culture of our company was such that *every* engineer was expected to write code, including the CTO on occasion. It was a huge source of tension in the company and eventually the CTO asked the new director to leave. It never occurred to him to ask in the interview if he needed to code, since he had not done that in years."

✦ "A senior level, reports-to-the-CEO type, took a job after a series of interviews at the swanky downtown office. When he showed up for the work the first day, he was informed his office was located down the street at one of the manufacturing plants. The job went downhill from there."

✦ "Shortly after starting a new job I learned that my predecessor had quit after six weeks. Had I known that, I might not have taken the job to begin with. I kept wondering what he had uncovered in those first few weeks that made him decide to leave so abruptly. I was there for six years."

✦ "I reported for work on Monday morning and the manager who had hired me had been fired between the time I last spoke with him and when I started work! Fortunately, my new boss turned out to be a great guy, and everything worked out, but I was very surprised that first day."

The Company Got Surprised

✦ "Back when ITers ruled the day (pre-computer industry crash), an engineer left her job and joined our company because the distance between her house and our company was exactly the distance she wanted to ride a bike every day. She had several other offers, but our 'roundtrip' distance fit the bill."

✦ "We made an offer to an engineer and he accepted. We then sent him the employee agreement to sign and he refused the job. He did a lot of coding on the side and was concerned that the employee agreement was worded in such a way that the company might be able to lay claim to his work in the future. (We tried to convince him otherwise but he didn't want to take the chance.)"

(Cont.)

Everyone Came Out Ahead

✦ "A very good friend of mine took a job with a company because they said they would help finance his green card. And they did: they paid thousands of dollars and many man hours getting it done. In return, he stayed with them for 15 years and was a very loyal employee."

—Michele Robinson (and others)
Account Manager, 14 years

5.2 The First Month

No Organization Is Perfect

In the first few weeks (and perhaps months) on the job, you'll start to learn about things that might seem a little unusual. There could be strange reporting relationships (inside and outside of IT), odd standards, inconsistencies in centralized/decentralized policies, unusual job descriptions, people with titles that don't match their jobs (like the programmer with 20+ years of service with a manager's title, yet doesn't manage anything), overlaps of some areas, and gaps in others, some things are overly complicated while others are overly simplified, and some divisions are wholly owned while some are only partially owned.

People who have worked there for a while will probably admit that certain things don't make complete sense. Certain corporate peculiarities may have a long and imbedded history. Other situations may be the result of an errant decision made by an executive who won't admit the mistake, and as soon as she leaves, it'll be put back to "normal." Other conditions may warrant changing, but the hurdles (effort, time, political, cost) aren't worth it right now. But, take note so that you don't lose sight of them and begin developing a plan.

Chances are there are reasons for everything that seems odd or strange. They may not be very good reasons, but those are the reasons nonetheless. The important thing is to show flexibility and adaptability. If these are the way things are, then you simply have to work within that framework (at least at the start). You won't be judged for what you inherited, but you will be judged by how you deal with it.

The oddities you want to focus on are the ones in your department, the ones you have control over. But don't feel you need to correct everything your first week, or first month. They've probably been that way for years, and things will survive a little longer as you investigate why they're that way, and the risk and impact of changing things.

Quietly Advertising What You Bring To the Table

It's not good form to try and impress people right away — showing up on the job with a know-it-all attitude, and boasting about what you've done before and what you'll do next. Let your results and actions speak for you.

Still, there are subtle things you can do when you first get started to give people the sense that the company hired the right person. Professional courtesies and maturity can go along way.

- ✦ Speak the language of your company and users, and not of IT (i.e., talk in business terms, not technical jargon)
- ✦ Maintain a positive attitude
- ✦ Maintain open and effective communications
- ✦ Show up to appointments on time
- ✦ Recognize the difference between moving mountains, and molehills
- ✦ Ask insightful questions (and be sure to *listen* to the responses)
- ✦ Try to convey a sense of perspective about time; which issues need to be addressed now, and which ones would be better to be looked into later
- ✦ Return e-mail and voice-mail messages promptly
- ✦ Write professional and succinct e-mails and memos
- ✦ Take notes during meetings
- ✦ Deal with assigned tasks quick and effectively

Do Some Preliminary Research Before You Start

You can also show that you've done your homework. During the interview process you've probably learned some things about the IT department: which vendors they use, which project they're working on, projects coming up, etc. Doing some research on those things (as well as your new company itself) can be worthwhile. Check out vendor Web sites and trade journals. You'll never know when you might have the opportunity to subtly drop a nugget of information into a conversation that will let people know that you have some knowledge to share.

Bring a Fresh Perspective

In addition to your skills and experience, you bring something to the job that no one else at your new company can — the objectivity that comes with a fresh set of eyes. Take advantage of that. Of course, you don't want to use it to question the wisdom and reason of *everything* at your new job, but you may see things in a way others haven't before. There may be very good reasons (which a newcomer would have no idea about) for things being the way they are, but learning about them will give you a better understanding of the environment.

Be on the lookout for areas and activities that seem to be ignored or overlooked because no one wants to do them. Those are great opportunities to volunteer and show what you can do, especially if they are in an area you excel at or enjoy. For example, if cost/benefit analysis needs to be done, volunteering to do it is a great way to force yourself to become immersed in something. Similarly, if you're a wiz at Microsoft Project, and everyone else hates doing project plans, your expertise will be appreciated, you'll become fully versed on the project, and it's a great opportunity for you to begin to take on the project's management (which is probably what you were hired to do).

Ask and Listen

Don't forget that you can earn a lot of respect by asking good questions, and that asking insightful questions usually comes from effective listening. By asking the right questions, you can show that you're astute, that you've got the right perspective on things, and that you have some sort of understanding of the topic at hand.

The challenge is in knowing which questions are the right ones to ask. Asking how much the company reimburses for meals in a discussion about an important team trip to a remote site shows your priorities aren't right. Questioning the value of user-acceptance testing on a project shows you're not really interested in quality, and like to take shortcuts whenever you can. On the other hand, asking about a back-out plan if a proposed change fails shows that you consider all contingencies. Asking about security, especially in today's environment, and performance are always safe bets.

Projects in Progress, and Projects on the Horizon

Projects will probably be a big part of your life (which is why we dedicated Chapter 4 to them). Every job has projects mixed in with all the day-to-day activities. Some projects are so small it's barely worth calling them projects, others so large that you think a new term might be needed.

One of your first priorities should be to learn about existing projects and those coming up in the very near future. You should be asking every one you meet (staff, boss, peers, department heads, etc.) about their particular projects. There's a good chance that in one way or another, you'll be involved in them soon.

Projects exist for a variety of reasons, and most of all because they are important to someone. Maybe they're important to you or your boss, maybe they're important to the CTO. Either way, by learning about the project activity, you get a sense of where the priorities are for individuals as well as the department and company.

Some of these projects may fall squarely on your shoulders, and you'll find that you're the Project Leader. Some of your staff may be leading projects, and your involvement can vary depending on how well you determine they're being run. Other projects may just have you as a team-member, perhaps playing a very large role, or perhaps a very small role.

Whether you're forced to take ownership of a project, or simply sit in some meetings, projects are an excellent way to quickly become knowledgeable about what's going on, meet others in the organization, be involved, and allow others to see why you were hired.

Is The Status Quo Good Enough?

Just because there aren't any complaints doesn't mean that things are "good enough." You, and your department, should always strive to be better. Of course, "better" may have different meanings:

- ✦ Better Service Level Agreements (SLAs)
- ✦ Faster transactions
- ✦ More thorough documentation
- ✦ More up-time
- ✦ Better reliability
- ✦ Improved morale
- ✦ Fewer errors
- ✦ Processes with fewer steps
- ✦ Better communication with the user community

You certainly weren't hired to make things worse, and they probably wouldn't have hired you if all they needed was someone to keep things as they are. It's important to remember that making things better is somewhat of an iterative process, where each of a few changes contributes a little bit to the entire solution.

For example, there are a number of things you can do to increase the up-time of a database:

- ✦ Keep the database software up to date with vendor patches and fixes
- ✦ Run periodic database maintenance

✦ Stay abreast of suggestions and guidelines from the vendors (hardware, database, OS), on best practices

✦ Keep the server's operating system up to date with vendor patches and fixes

Each of the above can improve the reliability of the database to various degrees. Taken together, they may significantly improve the up-time statistics.

You may find a similar approach works best in improving the overall performance of your department. While there may be a small number of things that can be changed to have a big impact, your focus should also be on the continual process of small improvements that chip away at problem areas. From your perspective as a manager, it's sometimes very difficult to see changes on a day-to-day, or week-to-week basis. You frequently have to look back over a period of months, or sometimes a year, and ask "remember when we used to. . . .?"

People to Meet and Know

At this point you're busy developing relationships with your staff, your peers, and your boss. But, it doesn't end there. There are lots of people you have to establish relationships with. It's a good idea to start collecting names and setting up introductory meetings with key people you'll be working with. Your boss, your peers, and even your staff can offer up some names.

Some areas you'll want to be sure to connect with include:

✦ **Key User Areas.** You'll want to find out which areas are most dependent upon IT and the services IT provides. Meet with those department heads, learn how they use IT, when they have their busiest periods, etc. (Examples may include the Marketing and Sales, Accounting, HR, and the Manufacturing departments.)

✦ **Senior executives.** It's always a good idea to have a strong relationship with upper management. Learn which ones are big proponents of IT, and which have the worst experiences with IT. In addition to building a good rapport with executives, you should do the same with their assistants.

✦ **Human resources.** As described later in this chapter (page 154), you'll probably quickly discover a lot of HR issues. Find out who in HR you can work with to review different situations.

✦ **Finance and Accounting.** IT often has one of the largest departmental budgets. You'll want to have someone to partner with in Accounting to help you deal with budgeting issues, chargebacks, forecasting, tracking spending, etc. IT budgeting is discussed in depth in Chapter 6 (page 161).

✦ **Procurement.** IT has a large budget because it buys a lot, and all that buying goes through a procurement process. In some organizations, IT purchases go through the company's general Procurement group. In other organizations, IT purchases may be done directly by the IT team. If the former, you'll want to form a strong relationship with the Procurement group to make sure your orders are handled quickly and accurately. If the latter, find out how your own procurement process operates.

✦ **Legal.** With that large budget and all that purchasing comes an awful lot of paperwork, with an awful lot of legalese. Whether it's a maintenance contract or a volume agreement with a vendor, you'll be working with the company's Legal department to wade through it all.

✦ **Audit.** In all likelihood, especially if yours is a publicly traded company, or you work in a heavily regulated industry (e.g., finance, healthcare), you'll be doing a lot of work with your internal audit team. This is a result of the ever-increasing scrutiny and demand for integrity in the IT professional in recent times. Chapter 8, IT Compliance and Controls (page 201), details some of the topics that may have you working very closely with your Audit team.

Quick Hello Meetings

Introductory meetings can be as short as 10 minutes, or as long as an hour (usually it's dependent on how much either of you enjoys talking). You can start off by saying up front that you don't have a particular agenda, and that you're simply in the process of meeting key people in the company to establish relationships. Ideally, it's best if you can go into these meetings with some background; perhaps recent experiences (either good or bad) that this individual or department has had with IT, or upcoming projects you know you'll be working on together, etc.

Section 9.2, Understanding the User Environment (page 240), covers discussion topics for meeting with various user groups and department heads. More than likely, the people you meet with will ask you about which company you came from, how you like the new job so far, etc. They'll probably be reasonably honest, but polite, about their opinions of IT. As you meet with all the different people, you may begin to see a pattern emerge telling you what kind of reputation your department has in the organization. This information can prove to be very valuable in figuring out where the strong and weak spots are.

HR Issues

In short order, you'll start to learn about the HR problems that you'll be facing. Some you may sense by intuition, but in all likelihood most of them will be brought directly to you; perhaps by your staff, the HR department, your boss and peers, and maybe even from the user community.

Some of your staff will be delighted to bring their pet issues to you, in hopes that a new manager will finally take care of things.

Some things to be on the lookout for:

✦ Staff who are unhappy with their job, title, or salary

✦ Those who are unhappy with their cubicle or office

✦ Employees who think they are being treated unfairly compared to others

✦ Issues of racial or sexual discrimination

✦ Staff who think some of their co-workers aren't pulling their weight

✦ Individuals who feel their contributions aren't being recognized

✦ Employees who feel that they should be much further along in their career given their experience, education, certifications, etc.

✦ Co-workers who simply can't get along

As you become aware of these issues, it's important that you listen objectively and effectively (repeating what someone has said in your own words works well), ask questions about the situation, and take good notes about what you're being told.

Soon, Later, and Tomorrow: When Should You Address Issues

Some issues may not require much follow-up aside from continued observation. For example, if an employee says he didn't get the rating he deserved on his last review, there's not much you can do about that as a new manager. But, you can promise the employee that you will judge everyone fairly and objectively when you do performance reviews.

Other issues may require some follow-up. For example, if an employee says that he should have an office instead of cubicle, you can check with HR to see what the policy is. Maybe they're in a position that doesn't merit an office, and you can explain the company policy. Perhaps they do merit an office, but there may not be one available right now. You can promise that offices will go to eligible employees, in order of seniority, when the space is available.

And some issues will require a longer term effort to deal with. If there are complaints about inequities in titles and salaries, for example, you may find that you agree with the people raising the issue. But correcting things of this nature will take time, careful planning, and perhaps some organizational upheaval.

Regardless of What Happens, Let Them Know You've Heard Them

The important things to remember as HR issues come your way is that each person deserves to know they have your attention, and they each deserve a response. It may not always be a response that they like, but they each deserve a response. You certainly don't want to earn a reputation in your first weeks that you ignore things.

Budgeting

One of the less exciting and less interesting parts of your job, but important enough to get its own chapter (see Chapter 6, page 161), is IT budgeting. Few departments will spend more money than IT, and it's important that you become knowledgeable about your department budget. Since you aren't likely to be held responsible for a budget you didn't create, you don't have to start sweating over it right off.

The easiest way to get started is to get a copy of your department's current budget. Then you'll want to ask Accounting for a report that indicates how much money your department is actually spending. By glancing at these reports you can quickly see which categories are the largest portions of the IT budget (and perhaps require the most scrutiny), and see where the biggest differences are between the actual spending history, and what was budgeted. Make sure Accounting knows that you want to get all the Accounting reports for your department.

In general, you won't be expected to explain every dollar. However, you will want to learn about those items that have the biggest impact on IT budgets, and especially significant changes from year to year.

As you learn about the budget you inherited, you should be thinking about next year's budget — the one you'll be responsible for preparing, presenting, defending, and adhering to. As is typical, each year's budget is compared to the previous year's. It's important that you make note of which items might go up, so that you can explain them.

Making Those First Decisions

There's a saying that 20% of life is what happens to you, and that 80% is how you deal with it. Another way to look at it is that your success is not much more than the cumulative results of the decisions you make.

Some decisions may be easy: "Can I leave a little early today?" Others could be more difficult: "Accounting is working on closing the books and won't allow any downtime, but we need to take their database off line to run a maintenance routine to prevent it from getting corrupted."

Anytime you make a decision, you want to make sure that it's based on sound reasoning that you can later defend if necessary. You may get faulted for making a bad decision, but if it's based on reasoned thinking, you can hold your head up with pride.

The first thing you need to do is make sure that you fully understand what the problem is, what the implications are, and the impact of the various alternatives. Those who bring the problem to you may provide some options, and you may have some of your own. You may want to run the issue by other people on your team to see if they have a different perspective.

Depending on what's involved, you may want to alert key people outside of IT, either to make them aware of the situation (like the users), or involve them in the resolution (like the head of Accounting in the above example).

Sometimes, the decision-making process is easier if you think about having to explain/defend the worst-case scenarios for each alternative — if it should happen. For example:

+ Your database server crashed, and it's taken seven hours to restore. To be certain that the restored database is 100%, you should run an integrity check utility, but that will take another three hours. Do you run the integrity check and sentence the users to another three hours of downtime, or just hope for the best and bring the database online as soon as it's restored?

+ If you don't run the integrity check, you risk the database being down for an additional 10 hours (7 hours to restore again, and 3 hours to run the integrity check you decided against the first time). If you do run the integrity check, you have to explain why you decided against bringing it online as soon as possible.

+ Many people might be willing to take the risk by rolling the dice and not running the integrity check, especially if they have reason to believe it may prove to be unnecessary. However, many of those people will also change their mind when asked if they are ready to explain their decision to senior management if they end up being wrong.

You want to appear confident and calm as you approach key decisions. These traits are important because they are contagious. If others see you keeping your cool, they'll probably do the same.

5.3 Two IT Departments — What Happens If Your Company Merges with Another?

Mergers and acquisitions are pretty common events in the business sector. They come in all shapes and sizes from mutually agreed upon merger plans to hostile takeover scenarios.

Any sort of organization merger or acquisition can have an enormous impact on the IT department, and you as its manager. Until it is complete, there are two IT teams — each with its own processes, standards, vendors, technologies, and culture.

With luck, your company has included you in the high-level planning for the merger. This lets you, as the IT Manager, learn about the other company's IT department. You'll then be able to report to your management and advise them as to what type of effort might be involved to join two teams, systems, and environments into one.

From an IT perspective, there are generally three ways to go about merging an acquired company's IT environment. The path you choose may depend on your company's management style (centralized vs. decentralized), available resources, timetables, etc.

1. **Brute force.** This amounts to re-building everything at one company that isn't compatible with the other. This approach usually results in a shock to the system of the acquired company and its IT department. It's pretty painful, but is often the fastest way of getting the two companies integrated and operating as one. Usually, the first technology addressed is e-mail, followed by business applications, OS platforms, WANs, etc. This process also includes evaluating procedures and vendors. The brute-force approach won't be successful unless the appropriate authority and mandate from senior management is in place to see it through, along with the necessary budget and staffing resources. Expect a bumpy ride, culture clashes, and some staff turnover.

2. **Leave them alone.** The opposite extreme would be to just leave the other company as is. Your company may have a culture of decentralization or divisional autonomy that supports this kind of posture. Or perhaps your company bought this other organization because they are lean, fast-paced, and profitable, and may not want to tamper with success. In fact, your management may hope that the parent becomes more like the adopted child, and not vice versa. In a case like this you may not need to do much more than add the acquired company's addresses into your e-mail system, and establish some basic connectivity. Regardless, make sure you contact the other company's IT Manager to establish and maintain a relationship. Share with her

information about resources your organization may have (e.g., staff expertise, volume purchase agreements) that she may want to take advantage of. The more you share with her, the more she's likely to share with you.

3. **Phased integration.** This is the obvious compromise path. In a case like this, you work with the IT Manager of the other company to set future milestone targets — each of which brings you closer to full integration. Depending on the circumstances of the two companies, they may set common (and integrated) goals, but take different paths to get there.

No matter what the situation, it's vital to remember that what may have been the right choices for one of the companies in the past, may not be the right choices for the unified organization. Equally important is that just because the acquired company is in the subordinate position doesn't mean they have nothing to offer — each can learn from the other. An emotional attachment to a technology or product limits your perspective, and can backfire. At times like this, those who can demonstrate an ability to adapt to change will be the most successful.

5.4 Additional Resources

Web Sites

+ *careerplanning.about.com/cs/firstjob/a/new_job.htm* (first-day tips from about.com)

+ *www.asktheheadhunter.com/hastartjob.htm* (tips from a headhunter)

+ *www.raycomm.com/techwhirl/employmentarticles/contractorsuptospeed.html* (tips for getting contractors up to speed in their new job)

+ *www.raycomm.com/techwhirl/magazine/gettingstarted/tipsforstartinganewjob.html* (tips for starting your new job)

+ *www.workopolis.com/servlet/Content/tprinter/20001014/TS27929* (tips from Canada's biggest job site)

Books and Articles

+ Blitzer, Roy J., Reynolds-Rush, Jacquie, *Find the Bathrooms First!: Starting Your New Job on the Right Foot*, Crisp Learning, Inc., 1999.

◆ Ciampa, Dan, and Watkins, Michael, *Right from the Start: Taking Charge in a New Leadership Role*, Harvard Business School Press, 1999.

◆ Duncan, Les, *They Made You the Boss, Now What?: A Practical Guide for New Leaders*, Publish America, 2004.

◆ Holton, Ed, and Naquin, Sharon, *So You're New Again: How to Succeed When You Change Jobs*, Berrett-Koehler Publishers, 2001.

◆ Robinson, William, *Your First 90 Days In A New Job (How To Make An Impact)*, Lulu, Inc., 2004.

◆ Watkins, Michael, *The First 90 Days: Critical Success Strategies for New Leaders at All Levels*, Harvard Business School Press, 2003.

Budgeting

Money Makes the World Go 'Round.

— R. KELLY

As a manager, one of the things you have to manage is money and how your department spends it. And, because IT departments usually have one of the largest budgets in the organization, many eyes will be on yours. This chapter will help you minimize, and deal with, the raised eyebrows over all those eyes. In the pages that follow, we discuss the general issues behind a variety of topics such as how and when a budget is generated, capital versus operating expenses, leasing versus buying, and key factors you need to watch out for when developing your department's budget.

CHAPTER SIX

6.1 The Budgeting Process

The budgeting process assigns specific amounts of money to specific departments within a company for a single period of time called a "fiscal year." Sometimes a company's fiscal year is not the January–December calendar year. The year that the budget tracks can be any 12-month period, although it generally begins on January 1, April 1, July 1, or October 1 (the beginning of a quarter).

Regardless, the 12-month period for your budget is called the fiscal year. If the fiscal year isn't the same as the calendar year, you identify the fiscal years by the year in which it ends. For example, if your fiscal years go from July 1 to June 30, you would refer to the budget that covers July 1, 2007 through June 30, 2008 as the 2008 budget, or sometimes as "fiscal 2008."

In general, the budgeting process begins 2 to 3 months before the start of the fiscal year. At this point, you begin to develop your first draft of the budget, estimating the amount of money you plan to spend during the upcoming 12 months. You prepare this budget based on the past year's spending as well as factoring in future growth. You will also include projects that you know your department is likely to undertake.

Ideally, you should have discussions with other department managers to see if you can learn about their upcoming needs and projects that might impact your department's spending. Depending on your company and the business that it's in, you may want to also include discussions with key partners, clients, suppliers, and customers. Similarly, it couldn't hurt to take a closer look at your company's chief competitors to try to learn about their use and plans for IT.

If you are new to management, you will quickly discover that the budget process and all its associated processes are critical to you and your department's success. Regardless of how important your role in the company is deemed to be, unless that importance is backed up with financial support specified in the budget process, you will find getting anything done to be a very difficult task.

Possible Budget Items

One of the best ways to get started with a budget is to review the previous years' budgets for your department. Budgets are historical records and are (in most cases) carefully tracked — somebody in your company is always watching the money.

Every company keeps track of budgets and spending a bit differently and may use different names, categories, and groupings from the ones below. Find out how your company budgets and then customize the concepts and techniques described here to meet your needs.

Which Items to Track

Below is a list of potential items for your department's budget. Check each item to see if you are tracking it in your department and if not, why not.

Personnel

- ✦ Staff compensation (salaries, overtime, bonuses, etc.)
- ✦ Benefits
- ✦ Recruiting (agencies, ads, etc.)
- ✦ Bonuses/overtime
- ✦ Education/training
- ✦ Consultants/temporary help

Hardware

- ✦ Upgrades
- ✦ Maintenance and support
- ✦ New equipment
- ✦ Leases/rentals
- ✦ Replacement components

Software

- ✦ New software (applications, operating system, utilities, etc.)
- ✦ Maintenance and support
- ✦ Upgrades
- ✦ License renewals

Telecommunication Services

- ✦ Dial-up services
- ✦ Service fees for handheld devices and cell phones
- ✦ Leased lines
- ✦ Frame relay
- ✦ ISP services

Supplies

- ✦ Printer consumables (paper, toner)
- ✦ Backup tapes

- Miscellaneous cables
- Basic office supplies

Travel and Entertainment

- Conferences
- Off-site travel to branch offices and new sites

Miscellaneous

- Books and subscriptions
- Membership dues for professional organizations
- Postage
- Duplication

Depreciation

- Hardware
- Software

Physical Plant

- Data center services (cabinets, raised-floor, HVAC, electrical)
- Cabling (fiber and copper)
- Furniture

Outside Services

- Disaster recovery
- Off-site tape storage
- Service bureaus
- Consultants

Overhead

- Telephone
- Rent
- Utilities

Reviewers for Your Budget

Most likely you'll be reviewing the first drafts of your budget with your director or vice president. In general, it's a good idea to get as many eyes and minds involved with your budget as possible. You don't want to overlook anything. It's also a good idea for you to get your direct reports involved in the process. Solicit them for ideas about projects they know about, things they'd like to get done, and so on.

In all likelihood, involving your staff in the budget process will benefit both of you — not only will they appreciate the opportunity, they will most likely offer up some items that you had neglected to think about. At the same time you're collecting the expected dollar amounts for your budget, you want to make sure you're collecting the associated explanations and justifications. You will have to refer to this information when it comes time to explain, justify, and defend your budget. See the section below, Getting Approval and Defending Your Budget.

Estimating (and Overestimating) Your Numbers

It's general practice to overestimate your budget to a certain degree. While this style sounds questionable from a practical (and ethical) perspective, it's so widely practiced and accepted that you need to address the issue directly when you present your budget. Most experienced managers are expecting an overestimation.

It's important to understand that the practice of overestimating is very common and well understood by both sides. If you consciously do *not* overestimate (and many managers don't), make a point of bringing this up during budget discussions with your supervisors.

There are several benefits to overestimating:

+ It gives you room to cut if upper management asks to reduce spending.

+ It gives you room for those unanticipated expenses that invariably crop up.

+ It increases the likelihood that you'll be within budget for the year, which could be a critical factor in determining your bonus or merit increase.

In either case, you need to thoroughly understand and know your material before making a formal presentation. You need to be fully versed in how you came up with your numbers, what assumptions were used, etc. Many managers, IT and non-IT alike, don't do their homework before making a formal budget presentation. This lack of preparation clearly shows during the meetings.

Of course, the downside of overestimating your budget is that if you don't use all the money allocated to your department, you may not get approval for such a large budget in future years. Very often, the end of the budget year has department managers either shifting some of next year's purchases into this year's budget (trying to use up unspent funds), or shifting some of this year's purchases into next year's budget (trying to avoid going over their budget).

In general, the budget may be approved by your CFO or executive committee around the start of the fiscal year. However, it's not unheard of for the final approval to be delayed until a month or two into the new fiscal year.

Getting Approval and Defending Your Budget

As you work to develop your budget, it is likely that you'll have to present it or defend it in some manner. While there may be great temptation to review each item line by line, this isn't a common practice. Summaries are generally the expected norm.

You'll probably have to give a high-level overview of your budget to your superiors — using more words than numbers. You may end up presenting this to your manager, to Accounting, or to some sort of company budgeting committee. You'll be better off to couch these explanations in business terms, as opposed to IT terms. Don't try to explain why three programmers are needed for the e-commerce project. Instead, explain the value of the e-commerce project to the company, and that the cost of the programmers is the means to that end.

Also, be prepared to explain how budget reductions will impact various goals and projects. For example, time frames may be extended, or functionality will be sacrificed. It may be appropriate to make references to last year's budget and projects as a comparison.

When presenting your budget, not only are you providing information and letting your audience see what they're getting for their money, but you're also trying to make them feel confident, so that they feel like you know what you're doing.

Don't be surprised if your budget goes through several iterations. The powers-that-be may kick it back and ask for reductions or more explanation. You may be asked to eliminate certain projects so that those costs can be recovered, or you may simply be asked to reduce it by a fixed amount or percentage. If so, be sure that you explain the consequences of those reductions.

During the Year: Tracking and Revising Your Budget

During the year, your Accounting department will probably furnish monthly reports of your department's year-to-date spending. You should look closely at these reports. It's not uncommon for data entry errors to occur where another department's purchase is charged to your cost center or for one of your own purchases to be charged to the wrong category.

The report you get from Accounting will probably have several columns for each category:

+ Budgeted amount

+ Actual amount for the month

+ Actual amount year-to-date

+ Variance against budget (an over/under amount indicating how well you are doing compared to the expected amount based on your original budget)

+ Variance against last year (an over/under amount indicating if you are spending more or less for the same items as last year)

Your Accounting department may be able to give you reports with different formats based on your needs. Detailed reports can usually be requested if you have questions about information in summary reports.

Revising Your Budget

During the year, you may have one or two opportunities to revise your budget. These revisions are often referred to as forecasts, re-forecasts, or updates. These revisions can be used to:

+ Include projects that weren't expected during the initial budgeting process.

+ Eliminate or reduce costs for projects that were canceled or scaled down since the initial budget was proposed.

+ Update estimates based on other changes (e.g., vendor pricing, expansion, size of projects).

+ Demonstrate anticipated cost reduction as a result of (management-ordered) belt tightening.

Each opportunity to revise the budget is a chance to deliver a more accurate estimate. Your initial budget is essentially a 12-month projection. However, a midyear revision is 6 months of actual costs and only 6 months of projection.

6.2   The Difference between Capital Expenditures versus Operating Expense Items

Often a budget consists of two sets of numbers: one for capital and one for operating expenses. Typically, these are considered separately, with different amounts of scrutiny. IT is a bit of an odd duck department in the budgeting process in that it usually has a significant capital budget. After all, most of the traditional corporate departments (Marketing, Finance, HR, etc.) usually don't have much need for acquiring assets.

Whenever you spend money on something, you'll have to consider if an item is a capitalized or operating expense so that it can be treated accordingly in the Accounting process.

Capital Expenditure Definition

A *capital expenditure* is for an item that will have a useful life of several years, such as a piece of hardware. Examples of capital expenses would include most hardware, software, Enterprise Resource Planning (ERP) solutions, furniture, physical plant items (e.g., cabling, data center cabinets, etc.) and so on.

Operating Expense Item Definition

Alternatively, an *operating expense* item is something whose value is gone in a shorter period of time. Operating expenses are the cost of resources used to support the ongoing operations of a business. They often recur, in that they have to be paid each month or quarter (e.g., the electric bill or salaries). Operating expenses are for items that last for a short time, and have no residual value after that period. Examples of operating expenses would include salaries, telecom lines, software and hardware maintenance agreements, equipment rentals, etc. A software support agreement, for example, is an operating expense item. The value of the money spent each year only lasts for the 12 months of the agreement.

Capital Expenditure Details

If the useful life of a $10,000 router is expected to be five years, accounting principles of capital depreciation allow you to spread the cost over the life of the equipment — in this case five years. So, even though the company may have to write a check for the full amount when it buys the equipment, the impact of this purchase on the company's books may only be $2,000 that first year and in each of the subsequent four years of the device's expected life.

Because there is more paperwork involved in tracking a capitalized expense for each year of its useful life, there is generally a minimum dollar amount for capitalizing items. For example, a computer cable might be useful for 10 years, but since it only costs $25, it would not be capitalized. The minimum amount for capitalizing varies from company to company. Figures of $500, $1,000, or $1,500 are common — check with your Accounting department.

Although the useful life of a connection to the Internet might seem to be quite long, in reality its useful life is only as long as your last payment to the carrier. Stop paying the carrier, and its life drops to zero. Since you're really just renting it from the carrier, it can't be considered an asset on the books of your organization.

Check with Your Company's Policies

You'll do yourself a big favor by checking with your Accounting and Finance departments to get an understanding of your company's policies regarding capital expenditures, depreciation schedules, and so on. Armed with this, it's within your best interest to group projects' costs into three categories: capital expenditures, expense items, and any recurring costs that will continue after the project is completed (e.g., maintenance contracts, telecommunication costs, etc.).

Gray Areas

There are several gray areas with capital and expense items. Typically, assets are tangible items. However, software and applications aren't things you can touch. There used to be a lot of variance in the treatment of software costs (see the box below). Some organizations will capitalize a vendor's consulting services if they're bundled with the sale of hardware. Similarly, there may be justification to capitalizing the staff salaries associated with a particular project.

Interpreting accounting regulations can be as difficult as interpreting any other legalese. You're always best to check with the experts. And for accounting issues, the experts are your Accounting department.

Another issue related to the consideration of capital versus operating expense is your company's sensitivity to each. Some companies are particularly sensitive to capital expenditures, while others are more sensitive to operating costs. You probably won't find any official statement or policy about this, but you're likely to get a sense of it fairly quickly.

Software: Capital or Operating Expense?

In 1999, the American Institute of Certified Public Accountants adopted a new set of accounting rules regarding software. These rules became part of the Generally Accepted Accounting Principles (GAAP), which all public corporations must comply with. Specifically, the new rules, called SOP-98-1, specified that:

✦ "Purchased off-the-shelf software, systems development and systems integration costs are to be treated as assets capitalized."

✦ "Planning, operations, and implementation costs for all internally developed software may be expenses as a current holding cost and need not be capitalized."

Paul A. Strassman
"GAAP Helps Whom?," *Computerworld*, December 6, 1999

Items to Watch Out For

For items that are capitalized, you will see the cost for each year of the item's useful life charged to your budget (usually in a category called "depreciation"). The Accounting department has software called a "fixed assets application" to track the cost and depreciation of capitalized items.

The example above said that a $25 cable wouldn't be capitalized because the cost was too low, even though it had a long useful life. If you place an order for 1,000 cables, you still wouldn't capitalize the cables (even though the order totaled $25,000) because individually they cost so little. However, some companies may still choose to look at the total order so that it can be capitalized. Taken to an extreme, this philosophy would mean that a very large order of paper clips would be capitalized — even though this is clearly inappropriate.

6.3 Lease versus Buy: Which One Is Better?

One of the discussions you're likely to have about acquiring hardware is "lease versus buy." Leasing computer equipment carries with it essentially the same pros and cons as leasing a car (see Table 6.1 below).

When you lease something, you're essentially renting it for a specified period of time. In general, you make arrangements to purchase a piece of hardware, but the leasing company makes the actual purchase. The leasing company is then the owner, and they lease it to you. Over the period of the lease, the total lease payments will total higher than the purchase cost. This difference is a result of the rate charged by the leasing company (essentially interest).

During the term of the lease (which is generally several years), you're responsible for the hardware, its maintenance, upkeep, and so on — just as if you owned it. You will generally make monthly or quarterly lease payments. It's important to note that lease payments are generally treated as an expense item, not as a capital asset. The reason is simple: you don't own the leased equipment. See the box below.

At the end of the lease, you have several choices:

✦ Terminate the lease by sending the equipment back to the leasing company.

Operating versus Capital Lease

Some leases are essentially rentals, while others are really purchases that happen over a long term. For example, if you rent office space for a year, the space is worth nearly as much at the end of the year as when you started; you're simply using it for a period of time. This is an operating lease. If you lease a server for five years, at the end of the lease the computer is worth a lot less than it was when the lease started. The leasing company doesn't want the unit back at the end of the lease, because it's highly unlikely to find a customer that will be interested in a five-year old device. The company you leased it from has to account for this, and charges you a payment that will recover all of the lease's costs, along with their margin for profit. At the end of the lease, ownership of the unit transfers to you. This type of lease is referred to as a capital lease, and is really a purchase with a built-in loan. According to Financial Accounting Standards Board (FASB) Statement 13, a lease is considered a capital lease if it meets any one of the following criteria:

✦ The lease transfers ownership of the property to the lessee by the end of the lease term.

✦ The lease contains an option to purchase the leased property at a bargain price.

✦ The lease term is equal to or greater than 75% of the estimated life of the leased property (for example, the lease term is 6 years and the estimated life is 8 years).

✦ The present value of rental and other minimum lease payments equals or exceeds 90% of the fair value of the leased property less any investment tax credit retained by the lessor (for example, the present value of the rental and other minimum lease payments equals $9,000 and the fair value is $10,000).

✦ Extend the lease (although you should be careful that the new lease payments are based on the unit's current market value, not the original purchase price).

✦ Buy the equipment. Often you can do this for a very low cost ($1.00) or for its current market value.

Keep in mind you generally have to inform the leasing company of your plans 90 days prior to the end of the lease.

Leasing

Should you lease an item or buy it? As Table 6.1 shows, there are pros and cons to each choice.

Table 6.1 Pros and cons of leasing

PRO		CON	
	Predictable payments for the life of the lease could ease budget projection and administration.		Extra effort during purchasing to coordinate activities between leasing company and equipment vendor. During the life of the lease there is ongoing administrative work to process the invoices and payments. (Although some leasing companies take care of this issue.)
	Allows companies with limited cash flows, or lines of credit, to obtain expensive equipment.		Complications arise if equipment is upgraded during the life of the lease: Should the upgrade be leased or purchased? If leased, it needs to be co-terminus with the original lease. If purchased, you have to remember not to send the upgrade back to the leasing company at the lease's end. Also, some leases have provisions in them that stipulate that any upgrade will invalidate the lease.

(*Cont.*)

Table 6.1   Pros and cons of leasing (continued)

PRO		CON	
	Allows for predictable and planned turnover of equipment that's regularly replaced (e.g., PCs).		If you're leasing a high volume of equipment (like PCs in a large environment), there is an additional effort to track inventory precisely so that equipment can be located at the end of the lease to be returned.
	Many businesses have discovered they don't need to own the equipment they use.		The packing and shipping of equipment returned at the end of a lease could be burdensome.
	Depreciation and interest on debt may produce potential tax benefits.		If you charge equipment to the department where it's used, it could require extra effort to properly code each lease invoice.

Who Makes This Decision?

Lease versus buy isn't a decision that IT should make alone. In fact, it's a decision usually made by the financial departments with input from IT. Very often, the decision will be based on whether or not the company can better accommodate the costs as a capital expense or an operational expense.

6.4   Other Budgeting Factors to Consider

There are a number of key factors that you should consider when budgeting:

✦ Growth of your department's workload

✦ Technological change

✦ Staff

✦ Software maintenance

✦ Hardware maintenance

Growth of Your Department's Workload

In general, the IT workload grows each year. Even if the company's growth is flat, and the general cost of technology continues to decline, it's very likely that the need for IT resources will continue to grow. This growth could include items like faster line speeds, more server horsepower, greater redundancies, and more disk space.

It's hard to determine an exact figure for each year's growth. Often it's no more than a best guess. Before making your guess, however, you should examine how the IT workload has grown in the past, and learn about upcoming activities and projects that the company has planned that might impact the demand on IT.

Technological Change

Technology changes. This is a fact of life that makes this industry so fascinating and frustrating at the same time. When you buy a new piece of equipment, (a server, for example), it's safe to say that you'll need to upgrade it over time to get more out of it as growth demands. You'll need to add memory, disk space, and perhaps additional processors. Eventually, there will come a time when it really doesn't pay to invest more money into this device, either because the technology has changed (e.g., new generations of processors) or the cost of new equipment is relatively inexpensive.

Regardless of the specific reason, you need to anticipate this fact. While technology does change fast, you need to be able to forecast the need to upgrade it and its eventual obsolescence and replacement. As equipment gets replaced, you're likely to be questioned for the need of the replacement. Be prepared to explain to users who have little understanding of technology why you're buying a new piece of equipment to do the same job as the piece of equipment you bought three years ago.

Staff

Growth of staff salaries (annual merit increases, promotions, spot bonuses, etc.) should be routinely factored into each year's budget. A more significant budget factor is staff turnover.

The turnover rates of IT personnel vary tremendously. Those individuals that enjoy always working with the latest and greatest technologies may not last more than a year or two before they're off to greener pastures. PC technicians may also last a short time as they seek to find opportunities beyond the Help Desk. Your company, salary and benefits, each employee's goals and objectives, and their overall happiness with the company — and with you as their manager — are all factors that will influence your staff members' decisions to stay with the company.

Even though your staff may seem quite content, you should assume that there will be some turnover. You may not be able to predict who and when, but you can probably estimate the number of people that will leave. As you try to best guess the turnover, you need to estimate what it will cost to recruit their replacements: headhunters, newspaper ads, Web postings, and so on. And when you're thinking that some employees may actually leave you, you might want to also throw some money into your consulting budget to provide for interim staffing while you recruit new employees. Lastly, the new staff may need some training to bring them up to speed on some of the technology solutions you're using. As a manager it's always best to remember that it is generally less expensive to retain staff than to recruit them.

Software Maintenance

No one knows everything there is to know about technology, and that's why vendors offer maintenance agreements. This can be a significant factor for software — annual fees of 20% of the purchase price are not unheard of. Some packages are so critical to your environment that you can't even consider forgoing support. Other packages will be not be as important.

Keep in mind that sometimes software vendors differentiate between *maintenance* and *support*. Maintenance may be limited to your ability to get upgrades for the product. Support, on the other hand, generally refers to your ability to get assistance (phone, Web-based, etc.) when you have a problem or question regarding the use of the software. Make sure you understand what your vendor means by maintenance and support.

Hardware Maintenance

Like software, some critical hardware (e.g., a production server) may have very high levels of formal maintenance arrangements, while other devices (e.g., a printer) may go without formal support for a variety of reasons (it may be just as easy, or cheap enough, to simply keep a spare around).

While software support and maintenance are often only provided by the original manufacturer, there are numerous sources for hardware maintenance. Factors to consider when looking at maintenance agreements for hardware include:

✦ Days and hours of coverage required (9–5 Monday–Friday, 24/7, etc.)

✦ Response time guarantees (keep in mind that frequently the "response" time refers to how long before the vendor calls you back, not how long it takes for a technician to arrive on site, and certainly not how long it takes to repair the device)

✦ Plans for spare parts (some vendors you contract with may offer to keep a locked cabinet of parts in your computer room so that they are always available to them)

✦ Whether the vendor and/or its technicians are certified

✦ Pricing: standard versus premium for extended coverage, or escalated response times

✦ Financial penalties if the vendor fails to meet promised service levels

Time-and-Material Contracts

Alternatives to maintenance contracts are Time-and-Material (T&M) arrangements. With these arrangements, when you place a service call for a piece of hardware, the vendor will bill you for the technician's time and the parts that are needed — similar to a repair on your car. Because of the high degree of reliability of today's technology, it's entirely possible you'll save money by forgoing hardware maintenance contracts and rolling the dice on T&M.

Risks with T&M.   There are two risks associated with T&M:

1. The repairs could be costly, and it's likely that the cost of a single site visit for a repair will be more than the cost of an annual contract.

2. Vendors usually give greater priority to calls placed by customers with contracts than to calls for T&M service.

If you go with T&M, make sure you set up the account with the vendors you'll use. By establishing a relationship in advance (knowing your customer number and site number, and having the right phone number to call), you will expedite the process when you need to make a call.

Vendors' T&M Policies.   To make sure you fully understand what you're entering into with a T&M policy, be sure to inquire about the vendor's policies regarding

✦ Hourly rates, overtime

✦ Minimum time charges

   ✦ Charges for travel

   ✦ Credit for defective parts that are swapped out

   ✦ Availability of parts

Warranties

The last choice for hardware support is the warranty that comes with new equipment. Warranties of up to three years are common. However, sometimes the warranty requires that you send the unit back to the manufacturer or bring it to an authorized repair center (although some equipment does come with an on-site warranty). But it's important to realize that most on-site warranties generally provide for a "best effort" for a "next business-day" response. Generally, vendors and/or their resellers offer upgrades for new equipment warranties to provide for higher levels of response.

When you're thinking about skipping a maintenance contract on a piece of hardware because the price seems too high, be sure to think about the cost to your environment and its impact on customers, users, clients, and business partners if that unit should go down.

And consider a situation where a piece of equipment fails after business hours on a Friday. Your call may not even be handled until the following Monday, and a next business-day response would get you a technician on Tuesday. She may diagnose a faulty part, and its replacement has to be overnighted from the warehouse for delivery on Wednesday. In this case, you've been down for five days. Throw a few wrinkles into the situation — a technician who doesn't show, a misdiagnosis, out-of-stock parts, a holiday, delayed deliveries — and your downtime could easily be a week.

6.5 **Additional Resources**

Web Sites

   ✦ *hbswk.hbs.edu/item.jhtml?id = 2647&t = finance* (a Harvard Business School article on corporate budget problems, specifically tying budgeting to compensation)

   ✦ *www.informationweek.com/805/budget.htm* (article on budgeting software)

   ✦ *www.wisegeek.com/what-is-budgeting.htm* (article on budgeting)

Books and Articles

- Droms, William G., *Finance And Accounting For Nonfinancial Managers: All The Basics You Need to Know*, Perseus Publishing, 2003.

- Fields, Ed, *The Essentials of Finance and Accounting for Nonfinancial Managers*, American Management Association, 2002.

- Finney, Robert G., *Office Finances Made Easy: A Get-Started Guide to Budgets, Purchasing, and Financial Statements*, Amacom, 1999.

- Kemp, Sid, and Dunbar, Eric, *Budgeting for Managers*, McGraw-Hill, 2003.

- Siciliano, Gene, *Finance for Non-Financial Managers*, McGraw-Hill, 2003.

- Strassman, Paul A., "GAAP Helps Whom?," *Computerworld*, December 6, 1999.

- Thibodeau, Patrick, "Gov't IT Execs Seek Software Accountability," *Computerworld*, October 18, 1999.

Managing Vendors

Everything is negotiable.

—ANONYMOUS

Purchasing IT equipment has become more complicated as time has passed. The players have changed (software salesmen now know something about their products), the metrics have changed ("Is it under $1000?" is no longer a very useful criteria), the information changes so quickly (new versions no longer come out only once a year), and the sources for purchasing items have changed (nobody sends you floppies in the mail anymore).

This chapter discusses how to deal with vendors, how to create useful matrices for evaluating products, how to get current information, and where to buy IT products.

7.1 Dealing with Vendors

As an IT Manager, you will be buying a lot of hardware and software. You have a complex matrix of responsibilities that includes saving money for your company, getting the right resources to make the projects work, giving your

CHAPTER SEVEN

179

employees the right tools, and meeting a series of overlapping deadlines that occasionally seem hopeless. Try to balance all these needs with some perspective: there will be other projects, other deadlines, and other issues.

Establish a Relationship

Relationships between IT buyers and their vendors have now reached the level of maturity that buyers from other well-established industries — clothing, merchandise, food, etc — have enjoyed and suffered from for a long time. Gone are the days of "get-me-the-latest-as-fast-as-you can." Very few companies automatically upgrade to every version a vendor releases. Companies now make a determination if this upgrade is worth the expense and effort, and may choose to skip this version, and wait for the next.

As a consequence, IT buyers get to enjoy, and suffer from, all the aspects of a more "well-defined" experience with their vendors. Companies don't buy as quickly or as blindly, nor do vendors come out with major upgrades or change sales people quite as frequently. New versions are released as frequently, but the "real" functionality change isn't as great as it once was. Security and anti-virus patches are notable exceptions.

Add to the mix that the amount of money involved is exponentially higher than it ever was (and budgets on both sides of the table are tighter than they ever were), and you have the elements of a combustible experience. Your job is to make sure that if anyone gets burned, it ain't you.

Finally, be careful not to get locked into long-term contracts (outsourcing or supplier) with vendors. Vendors need to provide the lowest price and highest quality — all of the time. Contracts that specify "sole source" are usually based on bad IT business decisions. Flexibility is the key.

Past Experience

Past Organization Experience

Your company and your department most likely already have extensive experience, good and bad, with a long list of vendors. If you've just joined your company, one of the first things you should do is find out who the company's informal historian is. If you're lucky, this person will be either in your department or at least near it.

Members of your staff remember the department's experience with certain vendors and have experiences of their own. Consider this information; don't accept it all as absolute fact, but don't throw it away, either. For certain product categories and technology solutions, you may not always have viable alternatives.

Past Personal Experience

If you've been in the computer industry any length of time, you will have direct experiences with all kinds of vendors. Use these experiences. But remember that the computer industry in particular, and the corporate world in general, changes very quickly. If you had a negative experience with a particular vendor two years ago, factor it into your decision on which products to use, but don't eliminate this vendor from the consideration list. The product has changed, but most likely, the company, the rep, and your needs have changed. The marketplace in IT is constantly changing. Although new companies and products are being introduced all the time, existing companies are merging and being acquired. The merger of Compaq and Hewlett-Packard is a classic example. Computer Associates and Symantec are two companies that have grown tremendously as a result of acquisitions.

Negotiate

Everything is negotiable. The point we're making by including this quote isn't to suggest you try and wheedle every penny out of a sale that you can. The key point is that when you enter into a purchasing conversation with a vendor, remember that every aspect of the purchase should be carefully considered. You are certainly aware that your new router costs X and comes with a three-year service contract. You may be aware that the vendor will install it for you for free if you simply ask. But you're probably not aware that his competitor is in talks to buy his company out and that he may be out of a job in a couple of weeks, so the price may not be as competitive as you think. Depending on the size of your purchase, put some time and effort into researching the product world you're about to enter.

Help Your Vendors

There is a second principle at work here: Put yourself in the vendor's shoes. In any conversation, trying to imagine what the other person is thinking can help your thinking. In buying situations, try to imagine what the vendor is thinking. Sometimes it can be obvious; he is trying to "nickel-and-dime" you and that's all there is to it. But sometimes you can guess his next move; if he drops his initial asking price, for example, he may have chopped a year or two off of the length of the service contract.

Along those lines, make sure your vendors get paid. Track big invoices through your Accounting department so that you know your vendors are happy. Some day you'll need to ask them a favor — like needing immediate delivery on an item that usually has a long lead time.

Think Long Term

Remember that a vendor/client relationship is a two-way street. It may appear to be one-way, but it is in fact two-way. There will be times when you will be able to make or break a vendor's monthly quota, but there will also be times when you will need a server delivered over the weekend or a copy of a new piece of software the day it is announced. In both situations, it helps both parties to view the relationship as one that can help each other, rather than an adversarial one where only one wins at the expense of the other.

Use words to this effect the first couple of times you speak to vendors; for those people who are just job hopping this speech will mean nothing. But to those people looking for business not only this quarter but also next year, you will quickly get their attention.

Also, often you have a choice of paying for a service contract either monthly or yearly with a discount when paying yearly. If the contract is with a vendor with whom you have an established relationship and have had good experiences with in the past, then the yearly option might make sense. However, if you have no experience with the vendor, "locking in" by paying for several years up front may not make not be a good idea yet.

Get Multiple Bids

Many IT products have become commoditized. "Commoditized" means undifferentiated: There is little or no difference between Product A and Product B. Toothpaste, for example, is a product that most would agree has been commoditized. Marketing departments everywhere are constantly battling against this problem. What should you do if your product, your market, your entire company, gets commoditized?

Companies selling in the IT world commonly face many problems, but two of the most common are:

1. What do you do if the 800-pound gorilla from Redmond enters your market?

2. What do you do if your product becomes commoditized?

On the other side, as an IT product buyer, you rejoice at these problems. If a product category suddenly offers an entry from Microsoft, you can be sure that the category now has some legitimacy. You now have other problems, but now at least there will be some other (big) players in the market.

If the product you're evaluating to buy has multiple competitors, you should always get multiple bids. Some organizations — government agencies, for example — are *required* to get multiple bids. But in most cases there may not be a legal requirement, but there is certainly a budgetary or performance imperative.

Be warned if a vendor reacts negatively when you talk about getting multiple bids. It's a common sales technique to try and get the customer not to look at other options; any vendor worth their salt is going to understand you're shopping around. They will tailor their sales approach to your actions, not over-react when you bring it up.

Set Up a Trial Experience

Buy something small, make your needs clear and realistic, and note how well the vendor performs. Tell a salesman that you need three units on site and installed by Friday. If they're delivered as promised, the decision is easy. If the machines never arrive, and he never shows or calls, the decision is also easy. But if he calls on Thursday and says they won't be available until Monday, you get a feel for how he might respond to future requests.

In some cases, you may not want to make the purchasing decision until you've had hands-on experience with the product so that you can do a thorough evaluation. Many software vendors allow you to download 30-day evaluation versions of their product right off their Web site. Hardware vendors are also eager to deliver a device for you to try for yourself. In some cases, the vendor will work with you to set up the product or service. This works to your benefit as well as his — it reduces the learning curve and setup time, and the vendor is sure that the product is performing optimally for you.

How Well Does Each Vendor Meet Each Criterion?

For important purchase decisions, set up a simple matrix that allows you to compare all of your options. An evaluation matrix doesn't make the decision for you, but it clearly outlines your options and locates them conveniently next to each other. A formal matrix is not required for every buying decision, and the cost and the importance of the purchase will naturally dictate how much effort you want to put into analyzing things before actually buying.

But seeing all the criteria and the items listed right next to each other can be of tremendous value when trying to determine how important the issue is for you, which vendor to use, and which equipment to buy. (Some buyers then share that matrix with the winning vendor.)

With larger purchases, an evaluation matrix can help document (perhaps to your boss or to Finance) why a particular item was purchased instead of a competing item.

Spending Limits

Many companies have formal standards designed to determine which level of personnel can sign for how much. If your company doesn't have these standards in place, they should consider setting them up. And if they have them set up, find out what they are. This shouldn't be very difficult; the first time you sign a purchase order for a million or two over your limit, you'll hear about it. Instead of embarrassing yourself and your company, find out in advance what your limits are.

And if they're too restrictive for your responsibilities — if you are required to keep the company's road warriors outfitted with the latest machines and you have a signing limit of $500 — work aggressively with your boss to correct the situation quickly so you can make the purchase process work for you.

Reviewing Contracts with Vendors

Depending on the size of your organization and the size of the contracts (in monetary terms), getting formal legal help can be of great assistance in this situation.

If your company isn't big enough to have an in-house lawyer, have the contracts reviewed by a legal consultant. Regardless, you should read the contract and be able to understand the following:

+ What exactly am I agreeing to?

+ How much am I actually paying?

+ What exactly are my liability and rights?

+ What exactly are the vendor's liability and rights?

In many contracts, the up-front portion contains some standard legalese that may go on for pages: issues of confidentiality, warranty, liability, applicable laws, and so on. This is the part you really want the legal experts to look at. They know if anything here is putting the company at risk.

They will alert you to:

+ Any wording that they're virtually forbidding you (i.e., the company) to agree to

+ Terms that they're uncomfortable with (for these they should suggest alternatives)

+ Terms that they're uncomfortable with, but recognize you're unlikely to get changed (although they will suggest you at least ask)

You need to turn your attention to the section called Terms and Conditions (also called "Ts and Cs"). As an IT Manager, this section of the contract deals with items that you're concerned about.

This section might have terms like:

◆ Service level guarantees

◆ Specifications of hardware and software

◆ Support, maintenance, upgrade terms

◆ Automatic renewals

◆ Ability to return/cancel if not satisfied

◆ Specific deliverables

◆ Associated costs, time frames, and so on

Everything is negotiable. Don't feel that just because it is on a form that you have to accept it. You may end up accepting it, but at least know that you can ask for changes. Remember that whatever promises your representative told you are of no value unless they're in writing. If it is important to you, ask to have it included in the Terms and Conditions. Also, remember that by the time you get to the negotiating, your representative can virtually taste the commission he's making from this sale. He will do essentially anything to get you to sign: at this point he almost becomes an advocate for you to his own Legal department. Take advantage of this ally.

Direct Company Reps

This, too, can be a very effective means of getting the equipment you need. The advantages are obvious. Most company reps are better informed about their product than a Value Added Reseller's (VAR) salespeople with multiple product lines; the company rep has a better sense of how their product works, how many items they have and, if they don't have one themselves, have an idea where one might be. The disadvantages are clear, too. If you need multiple items from multiple manufacturers (which you will much of the time, since there are so many things you need and so many manufacturers), you're going to have to make multiple phone calls. Also, company reps move through that job quickly, so talking to the same person over the course of a year isn't a guarantee. Company reps are usually very well versed in their products and associated technologies, and they can also tell you how others use their products.

Many manufacturers prefer to sell their products through the "channel" (VARs, retailers) and simply don't have the resources to sell directly. It's common for manufacturers like this to have sales reps to keep you informed and educated about the product, but who really can't sell you the equipment.

VARs

For many IT Managers, VARs are the preferred means for purchasing many products. As the name implies, VARs resell other manufacturers' products. Because they have a very high volume, VARs often can provide excellent pricing and have enough stock to meet your delivery needs. "Value-added" refers to additional services that the VAR can perform for you (for a fee, of course). The VAR can preload software onto the PCs they ship to you. They can install the additional memory in the printer before it ships, so that you're only receiving one item and don't have to do the install yourself. If you buy all your software through your VAR, they can help you keep track of your licenses. VARs usually have excellent contacts with the manufacturers, which may enable you to get detailed information you need before making a purchase decision, or when you need support. If your organization is small, a VAR can help provide you with manufacturer contacts and perks that might only be available to larger customers.

If you have an order that consists of components from multiple manufacturers, the VAR can hold all the items until the entire order is complete. This saves you from receiving and storing multiple deliveries. A VAR is usually able to service virtually all the products they sell, which means you have fewer support channels to deal with. And, as indicated above, a VAR can usually augment a manufacturer's warranty/service offerings customized to your needs.

7.2 Key Evaluation Metrics

Today's technology environment is so complex and so charged with money that the number one rule of buying any technology product has to be: "Be Prepared." Products have gotten so complex — and systems they are designed for have gotten so complex — that a simple "Yeah, this server can handle 1000 e-mail users at the same time" kind of statement no longer flies. You need benchmarks, you want other clients' stories, you have to have objective data; in other words, when it comes to functionality, you have to do your homework.

Throughout this chapter we discuss where to get other information and sources you can use to do that "homework."

Set Up a Matrix

There is a relatively standard set of metrics you can use to evaluate most technology products. At the end of this section we show you a sample matrix. Typical evaluation matrices include:

- ✦ Functionality
- ✦ Price
- ✦ Performance
- ✦ Vendor viability: Is this a vendor that will be around for a while?
- ✦ Training required
- ✦ Vendor services
- ✦ Scalability
- ✦ Support and service
- ✦ Interoperability
- ✦ Speed of delivery and availability

Functionality

The most obvious question is: "Does this product do exactly what you need it to do?" These days, you need to ask that question of a vendor several times. Yes, the data sheet on the router claims it can handle speeds of up to X, but is that in the vendor's perfectly controlled test environment? Is that performance available "out of the box" or is it only available with some upgrades to the base model? How fast can it handle traffic in the real world, i.e., your data center?

If it's something for your end-user community, they may be the key players in determining if the product does what it needs to do, does it well, is easy to use, etc.

Price

While important, often this shouldn't generally be your only criterion. Rank the other criteria below for each purchasing decision. This is good information to have on hand when someone from Accounting asks why you purchased brand X over Y, or used vendor Z.

There are two components when evaluating a technology product on price:

1. Capital Investment
2. Total Cost of Ownership (TCO)

Capital Investment   The short term, up-front cost of an item. It includes the hardware and/or software and all the associated components to make it do what you need it to do. There are other considerations about up-front price that we will discuss later, but for the purpose of this section, it's the price you pay up front. For hardware, you may want to consider volume discounts. For software, in addition to volume discounts, you want to consider how the product is licensed.

TCO   In addition to the up-front capital investment, think of the costs for ongoing support and maintenance, implementation, training, prerequisite hardware/software, conversion/migration, and so on. TCO has become a much more popular method of evaluating products in the IT world. Competing platforms vendors, for example, try to justify higher initial prices by claiming their TCO is lower.

There are products where TCO isn't relevant. If you are buying a server rack, there isn't going to be much maintenance, training, etc., required. But most other products you buy in IT *do* require some TCO evaluation. See page 231 in Chapter 9, Getting Started with the Technical Environment, for further discussion of TCO.

TCO analysis is a large and complex field, filled with vendors, consulting companies, and competing theories. Depending on the size of your purchase, you may want to create your own TCO analysis sheet. Include costs for capital investment, maintenance, support, training, installation, and any other either company- or product-specific costs. For example, your company may be virtual, in which case your installation costs may include not only getting the software installed but location-specific fees. Or you may be installing a new server but you have to consolidate the two older ones first; the costs associated with consolidating the two should be factored into the TCO of buying the new one.

See the discussion on hardware and software maintenance on page 175 in Chapter 6, Budgeting, for additional information.

Vendor Viability

Is this vendor one that is likely to be around for a while? Are they at risk of going under because they're a fledgling startup? Or are they ripe for acquisition or merger? Depending on the type of purchase you're considering, this may be a key issue.

Training Required

Will your staff need to be trained on this new product? Or is it something they can pick up on their own? If training is required then this cost has to be considered. Is training readily available, or is it only offered twice a year, and only in one location? Can the training be done at your site?

Vendor's Services

Do you need, or will you want, professional services from the vendor to customize the product, or help with its installation or integration into your environment? This could be an important factor to help ensure the success, but it could also be a considerable cost factor. The use of a vendor's professional services can raise the cost of an implementation considerably.

On the other hand, the vendor may be so eager to make the sale that he is willing to offer assistance at no charge. Similarly, will the vendor provide you with an opportunity to evaluate the product at no charge?

Performance

Not all computer hardware performs at the same level of quality, of course, but your needs may not always be to purchase "the best," either. Everyone wants the most for the money, but sometimes in the frenetic IT world, the "fastest right now," or the "one I can get installed tomorrow," instead of the best, is the preferred option. IT Managers tend to have an attitude of bravado toward hardware performance: "The bigger, the faster, the better performing, the more I want it." Take careful stock of yourself if that sounds like you — that attitude may be costing more *in the long term*.

On the other hand, hardware performance is often easily quantifiable. In addition to processor speed there are a variety of other issues that can impact performance: type and amount of memory, number of processors, bus speed, amount of level-2 cache, etc. Performance benchmark standards are common. And if a vendor starts touting the performance of his equipment using standards other than those used in the industry, take it as a sign that his equipment may not perform as well. If everyone knows throughput is the standard and you start hearing about duration, be wary. Ask about the machine's throughput and be ready for a quasi-explanation about why that standard may not be correct. Standards aren't inviolate, of course, but they mostly exist for very good reasons — a lot of people tested various methods and arrived at the same conclusion.

Scalability

Will the product *scale* to meet the size of your environment? When considering an enterprise-wide application (e.g., e-mail), your test bed will probably be quite small. However, the results may be very different when the product is deployed throughout your organization. Does the vendor know of another company your size using this product? What does the rest of the market think of the product? Is this one considered a leader, an up-and-comer, a has-been, or a never-will-be?

Support and Service

These can be valuable components of an IT purchase. Products are getting more complex and their maintenance requirements are getting larger. Treat the item and the service options or contract as equally important elements in the buying decision. One may appear to cost more than the other, and be more important in the short term, but over time, the value of each can even out.

Also consider serviceability. Are parts easy to get? Does one vendor have long hold times on their support line? (This can be easy to verify with a call from your office.) Will you be able to find staff or training that can help maintain this item? Are technicians and parts available 24/7? How is the quality of their tech support?

These issues relate directly to the long-term vendor relationship discussed earlier in the chapter.

Interoperability

Does the product *integrate well* into your environment, or will it require specialized interfaces? Does the product adhere to industry standards, or is it based on proprietary technology?

Speed of Delivery and Availability

As often, or more so, than price, this item can be the deciding factor in important hardware decisions. The IT world moves very quickly, and a vendor's ability to move with it — and along with your schedule — is a critical factor. Like cost, you should carefully evaluate the importance of this issue on every buying decision.

Naturally, you want everything ASAP — who doesn't? But how much are you willing, and how much should you be willing, to pay for that speed? If you don't need something tomorrow, don't have it sent overnight; use cheaper delivery options.

Train your vendors to think the same way. You need things delivered *on your schedule*. Sometimes that's this afternoon by courier, but sometimes that can be tomorrow, or after the weekend. Yelling about wanting everything as soon as possible dilutes your message and makes those times when you really do need things ASAP more difficult to deal with.

Finally, availability is a major factor in the speed of delivery. You may want the latest PDA the very afternoon it arrives at the reseller's warehouse, but so do all her other clients. Keep in mind that getting that hard-to-find item will be influenced by traditional speed variables such as distance, shipping method, and so on; item availability also matters, as well as the relationship you've carefully developed with the vendor.

If you purchase a large volume of certain products, you want to make sure that your vendor keeps adequate stock in his warehouse to meet your needs. You don't want to continually hear that they are back-ordered. Using FedEx won't help if there is no product available to be delivered.

On the other hand, anything you buy you'll probably have to live with for a few years. So, be careful about making a short-term issue (delivery time) a factor that leads to a long-term decision.

Sample Evaluation Matrix

Figure 7.1 is a simple example of an evaluation matrix that can be used for comparing alternatives. Depending on the particular solution you're evaluating, you could have many categories to consider, with varying degrees of granularity.

You may want to use a matrix to do a weighted comparison of each vendor. Because each of the factors are rarely a yes/no issue, you can weigh the importance of each category, and then rate each vendor's ability/offering/response for that category on a scale of 1 to 10. After the math is done, you can see how all the pros and cons for each vendor net out against each other.

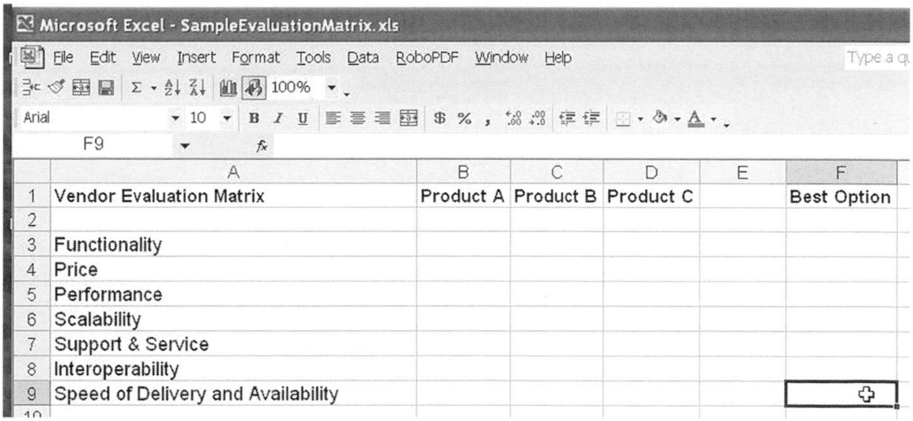

Figure 7.1   Blank Evaluation Matrix

7.3 Getting Current Information

At the rate companies are formed, acquired, and merged, and the rate that new products are introduced, developed, enhanced, and discontinued, it's impossible for any single person to be fully aware of all that is available in the marketplace. IT trade journals may help, vendor Web sites can help, but even they can't keep up with every nuance and niche area. Hence, the need for sites and journals that specialize in various segments of the market (LANs, communications, mobile services, e-mail, Windows Server, Unix, etc.).

There are a variety of resources you can use to keep up with all the changes. In addition to the Web, there are trade journals, trade shows, vendor representatives, e-mail, and consultants. Generally, you'll have little trouble getting data. The effort will be in trying to filter it, digest it, and turning it into information that you can use effectively.

It's a full-time job trying to stay on top of industry developments. But you already have a full-time job managing your IT department — staying abreast of industry events should take only a fraction of your time.

But also remember that you are not in this alone. Your staff should contribute a great deal to this effort. They're the ones who will be working with the technology, hands on, day to day. They should be the ones most in tune with what's going on in the marketplace.

Options for staying current include:

✦ The Web

✦ Vendor representative

✦ Trade journals (electronic and print)

✦ Trade shows

✦ Brown bag lunches

The Web

The Web can be a great resource — if you know what you're looking for. Otherwise, it's likely to overwhelm you with information. Use the Web to visit vendor Web sites for product information, announcements, and so on. Most IT trade journals have Web sites with current information, and a variety of newsletters to which you can subscribe. And, there are outlets that are publishing IT news for the Web only, like *www.cnet.com*, *www.itmanagersjournal.com*, and the very popular *www.slashdot.org*. In addition to news and product information, the Web can be an incredible resource tool. Organizations that are responsible for technology standards (e.g., ANSI at *www.ansi.org* and IEEE at *www.ieee.org*) have sites. And there are sites that offer valuable reference information (e.g., *www.whatis.com*, *about.com*, *wikipedia.com*, and *www.webopedia. com*). You may also use the Web to subscribe to e-mail-based mailings, or join newsgroup discussion threads.

Vendor Representatives

In general, you should invite key vendors to come in and meet with you once or twice a year. You set the time and the schedule. This could be specific product vendors, system integrators, or resellers. Have them tell you of new product announcements, changes in product lines, what their other customers are doing with technology, and so on. You can share with them your upcoming plans for the department, the company, and your customers.

These meetings can be in your office, perhaps with key members of your staff, or some vendors may whisk you away to their "executive briefing center" for the full dog-and-pony show complete with smoke and mirrors. While you may not get any specific useful information from these meetings, you can use them to establish and reinforce a relationship. You never know when some tidbit of information that's shared today is just the nugget that's needed to help resolve an issue six months from now. Invite your vendors to put you on a mailing list so that you're kept aware of any key announcements, seminars, demos, and so on.

Trade Journals (Electronic and Print)

There are hundreds of sources of journals and newsletters in the IT industry. Many are free, others are very expensive. Start with some free ones. Publishing groups like Ziff-Davis (*www.ziffdavis.com*), CMP (*www.cmp.com*), and IDG (*www.idg.com*) produce some of the most popular journals in the industry. They have offerings to address the various disciplines of IT from the very technical up through issues that are important to CIOs. You can usually apply for the free ones right on the Web.

You probably won't have time to read any trade journal in full, but at least glance at the headlines. It will help to keep you aware of what is going on, and you never know when you'll spot an article that addresses a problem you've been struggling with. Avoid getting bogged down in journals that don't match your level of responsibility (e.g., too technical, or not technical enough) or about topics that have no relevance to your department's functions. If you spot an article that you think one of your staff should read, rip it out and send it to them. Not only will you be sharing information, but you'll be letting them know that you're involved.

Many trade publications have e-mail services that send out regular, often daily, e-mails. Sometimes these contain the latest news reports; other times they offer brief synopses of full articles that appear in print. Sign up for those that work best for you.

Trade Shows

Just as there are trade journals dedicated to specific segments of IT, there are trade shows that cater to similarly specific areas. Between vendor representatives, junk mail, and trade journals, you'll probably learn about the ones that are pertinent to you. Unfortunately, trade shows are usually only held in large metropolitan areas, and often the travel expense prohibits many IT professionals from attending.

For the most part, trade shows are all identical in structure: most prominent is the exhibition hall where vendors pay large amounts of money for booths that have more square footage than many homes. The prominence of the exhibition hall is followed by the speeches — usually by major figures in the industry. Then there are the seminars, conferences, and panel discussions. And lastly, there are the vendor hospitality suites.

The various speeches, usually including a handful of "keynote" speeches, often get the most coverage, which usually means they need little of your time. While they might be entertaining, especially with a particularly dynamic speaker, it's unlikely that they offer any groundbreaking news.

Visitors to the exhibition hall usually enjoy the opportunity to talk directly with vendor product developers, executives, and technical staff. The exhibition hall usually offers an opportunity to touch and feel — especially nice for recently announced products — and often to try out a product. However, some exhibit visitors find that some of the products they see demonstrated never actually make it to market. While the exhibits of the larger vendors may be the most alluring, you may actually find that the smaller vendors' booths (often tucked away in the back of the hall or on another floor) are of greater value. After all, there are lots of ways to get information about the large vendors, but your radar may not otherwise detect the smaller vendors and their products. And you never know when a small vendor has just the utility software or hardware item that is the perfect solution for your needs.

The seminars, conferences, and panel discussions can be very valuable. A trade show may have several of these going at one time. Very often, the people who host these and participate in them are IT practitioners just like you. The topics may be about a recently completed project, management strategies, or the pros and cons of different technologies. The attendance at these sessions is usually small (less than 100 people), and they frequently conclude with a question-and-answer session. This up close and personal format in a session of interest to you can be very valuable.

When evaluating products, be it hardware or software, the first thing you want to be sure of is that the product does what you need it to do. With most products, you usually arrange for the opportunity to evaluate the product in your environment. Thirty-day evaluation periods are quite common, and they are often extended to 90 days just by asking. Sometimes, you can even arrange for the vendor to provide some on-site expertise to help you. If you're offered this kind of help, grab it! It usually speeds up the evaluation process since you can speed by all those bumps in the road that usually arise when you try a new product for the first time.

Brown Bag Lunches

Brown bag lunches are informal get-togethers where attendees bring their own food — hence the name — and listen to speeches, presentations, workshops, stories, etc., from a presenter. The setting is casual. No one is paying the speaker nor is lunch typically provided. But the exchange of information can be invaluable.

Your team is brimming with technical expertise — some of it you know about, and some of it is buried. Trading technical data has been a long standing tradition in IT, so have your department continue it. Sometimes it can be a formal reason — in Chapter 2, Managing Your IT Team, in the Section Maximizing the Value of Training on page 30, we discuss employees returning from training classes and sharing their knowledge at a brown bag lunch. But sometimes it can simply mean one of your team is assigned ("volunteered") to present briefly on a technical topic of their choice. You, and your entire team, can thereby catch up on the latest trends in a corner of technology.

7.4 Purchasing Sources

IT products can be purchased from a wide range of sources (besides the vendors themselves):

✦ Web (and catalogs)

✦ Retail stores

✦ Gray markets

✦ VARs

See Table 7.1 below for some pros and cons of purchasing sources on the Web.

Table 7.1 Pros and cons of buying on the Web

PRO		CON	
	It's generally easier to get more detail about the product.		You may not have an opportunity to establish a relationship.
	You don't have to buy something from a site to get information about it.		Online vendors may insist on a credit card payment, as opposed to the corporate purchase order you prefer to use.
	It's generally easier to find comments (pro and con) from other users/purchasers of the product.		It may be difficult to assess your delivery, warranty, and service options and rights.
	Most important, items sold online are sometimes (though certainly not exclusively) less expensive.		
	You can often buy directly from the manufacturer, as well as from various resellers.		

Web and Catalogs

If you need two routers by next Friday, and you have ordered 10 routers from this catalog company before and they delivered them on time for a great price, many IT Managers won't go online to see if they can save 1% in price or shave off a day — they will go with what works. On the other hand, if you need three laptops for new employees starting next month, you might go to the Web to see if you can beat the price. Your company and your department have hardware standards, so you're probably not going to experiment here: You know the machines you want, and the Web will let you search for the best price and the fastest turnaround.

Catalogs are useful for three reasons:

+ You can quickly scan them to get informed about product categories. (Just how many speech recognition software packages are there, anyway?)

+ You can quickly scan them to get price information. (How much is a new router going to cost me? I paid X last year.)

◆ You can access them even if you aren't connected or near your machine. This situation occurs more often than you would think — you have the time or the need to evaluate different products and you aren't connected to a network.

You might be stuck in a cab in a traffic jam or searching for something to look at on the plane. If you have paper catalogs ready to read at these common non-electronic moments, you can get some useful work done.

Retail Computer Stores

Retail stores can simultaneously be the most convenient and most inconvenient source for computer products. If they have what you want, it may be the quickest place to get something in an emergency. However, they certainly lack the flexibility and motivation that your VAR's dedicated rep has. This is the most unreliable, and often the fastest, method of buying hardware. Selling computer equipment through retail channels has been tried many times in many places, and much money has been spent trying to make the concept work. But most people would agree that the system still needs work (see Table 7.2 below).

Table 7.2 Pros and cons of buying from a retail store

PRO		CON	
	It's fast. If they have it, you can walk out with it.		**Its inventory is limited.** They may not have what you're looking for in stock.
	It's tactile. That means you can touch it. This feature isn't as important for something like a router or a hub, which looks like a stereo receiver, which looks like a server, which looks like a firewall appliance ... but it can matter if you're buying flat panel screens, keyboards, mice, etc.		**It's a retail operation.** Which means it has the trappings of traditional retail operations, e.g., it's open only certain hours, there can be lines at the checkout counter, it can be populated with uninformed individuals trying to sell you things you don't want, and it can be difficult to find what you're looking for.
			It's primarily targeted for the consumer market and may not carry the brand or item you are looking for.

Most corporate IT purchases are not made in retail stores. Professional organizations have sophisticated hardware needs that most stores aren't prepared to meet. In addition, most corporation employees don't have the time to go shopping at a store for company purchases. However, there are few IT Managers today who haven't ducked into a CompUSA with a credit card to buy a part or component in an emergency.

Stores have recognized these shortcomings, and they have begun to offer sophisticated alternatives to the "come-into-the-store-and-buy-the-item" options. As a corporate customer, you can call someone like CompUSA, and you'll be given the choice of contacting an individual store or talking to a CompUSA sales rep. This rep will then be able to determine if the item you're looking for is in stock at your local store.

The Famous "Gray Market"

Gray market goods are not counterfeits. (The dangers of using unauthorized copies of software are well documented.) Gray market goods are brand name items sold outside of the producer's official distribution channels. Most importantly, gray market goods don't include the company's warranty, service, and support. If something goes wrong with it, you have to go back to the people who sold it to you, not the manufacturer. PCs from Taiwan aren't necessarily gray market goods — a company may have a manufacturing plant there. But brand name PCs bought from the back of a catalog are most probably gray market items.

Dollar Costs

The costs associated with purchasing these items are much higher than they initially appear. Say you buy three PCs from a gray market company and save a few hundred dollars. Now you have three machines on a "services and support island"; that is, they have no maintenance structure attached. If one of those machines breaks (and PCs, in case you haven't heard, do break down), you'll easily pay back the money you saved on the initial cost by having the item repaired at out-of-maintenance-contract rates.

See the section TCO above on page 188. The numbers seldom add up to buy items outside of normal distribution channels.

Legal Costs

A seldom understood, but nonetheless serious, consequence of purchasing goods from the gray market is "legal exposure." You may be putting your company at significant legal risk. Many small technology companies don't have the resources to pursue legal actions against gray market vendors, but the number of companies who can do this is growing quickly. And large and small companies alike are banding together to form groups like Alliance for Gray Market and Counterfeit Abatement (AGMA). AGMA has "small" corporate members like HP and Cisco.

VARs

VARs can be your best avenue for purchasing hardware and software provided you know *exactly* what you want.

A VAR combines various components — hardware, software, services or a combination of all three — to provide a custom solution. So VARs have a vested interest in selling you their particular solutions, whether those solutions are a suite of software applications or the integration services you'll need to get those applications up and running in your shop.

Nonetheless, your environment may be so complex, or your needs so well defined, that the added value and cost that a VAR brings to the table may be exactly what you need. Just remember that they're bringing a very specific agenda to the table; you want to make sure that agenda matches up well with your particular needs.

7.5 Additional Resources

Web Sites

+ *www.agmaglobal.org* (gray market alliance)

+ *www.answers.com* (general information source)

+ *www.cmp.com* (consulting vendor)

+ *www.computerworld.com* (IT technical journal)

+ *www.dobetterdeals.com* (Web site for Joe Auer, who has written frequently for *Computerworld* on the issue of IT vendors and contracts)

+ *www.eweek.com* (IT technical journal)

+ *www.idg.com* (IT technical journal)

+ *www.infoworld.com* (IT technical journal)

+ *www.itmanagersjournal.com* (IT technical site)

✦ *www.techrepublic.com* (IT technical site)

✦ *www.theregister.co.uk* (IT technical site)

✦ *www.ziffdavis.com* (IT technical journal)

Books and Articles

✦ Gallegos, Senft, and Manson, Gonzales, *Information Technology Control and Audit*, Auerbach Publications, CRC Press, Boca Raton, FL, 2004.

✦ Thompson, Robert Bruce, and Thompson, Barbara Fritchman, *PC Hardware in a Nutshell*, 3rd Edition, by R. O'Reilly & Associates, Sebastopol, CA, 2003.

IT Compliance and Controls

For duty, duty must be done; The rule applies to everyone.

—GILBERT & SULLIVAN, RUDDIGORE

Certainly one of the biggest changes to affect the IT industry over the past few years has been the concern for compliance of a variety of regulations and legislation. Spurred by events like the financial scandals of Enron, Worldcom, HealthSouth, Adelphia, Tyco, Qwest Communications, and Global Crossing (to name a few), attention has been drawn to the integrity of financial reporting and controls. In these cases, senior management was allegedly aware of events and activities that led to the misstatement of the financials and the deception of investors.

Following this series of scandals, there was renewed interest in ensuring that there were sufficient controls in place to make sure that this couldn't happen again. Most

CHAPTER EIGHT

well known is the Sarbanes-Oxley Act of 2002, which was passed by the U. S. Congress. Of course, while Sarbanes-Oxley is the best known, it isn't, by far, the only set of regulations that makes sure that data, financials, etc., are being handled properly.

8.1 The Importance of Compliance to IT

"Compliance" is a broad term that can carry a lot of meanings. Is the entrance to your building ADA (Americans with Disabilities Act) compliant? Is your television HD (high definition) compliant? Is your healthcare provider HIPAA compliant?

Overview

In this chapter we'll present some important compliancy regulations. You may have heard of some of these and are wondering if they pertain to your group or company. The goal is to provide you with a brief overview of the rule or regulation; you can then either pursue further information or decide the issue does not pertain to your company.

For example, the HIPAA *privacy* provision took effect in 2003, but the *security* provision of HIPAA didn't take effect until 2005. You may be working for a healthcare provider and heard the term "HIPAA compliant" for years but not understood what that meant. For ITers, the biggest impact of the rules and regulations of compliance generally relates to controlling, securing, and managing data. This is no small issue: making data flow from one place to another is hard, and making it flow only to certain places and *not* to others is even harder. In 2006, the FTC imposed a $10 million fine on ChoicePoint for failing to comply with the data protection obligations of the Fair Credit Report Act when a security breach resulted in the potential exposure of financial records for over 100,000 individuals.

The Victims of Non-Compliance

There is a perception that the victims of non-compliance are the employees of the companies themselves. And that is in fact true: Global Crossing's excesses affected 10,000 employees and WorldCom's 12,800. Many people lost their entire 401k savings in addition to their jobs.

But many more people are affected by corporate perfidy than is generally understood. In HealthSouth's case, not only did the company's employees suffer, it radically affected the financial well-being of its hometown, Birmingham, Alabama. When corporate scandals took their toll on companies based in New York, the state suffered a $1 billion reduction in tax revenues (*www.osc.state. ny.us/press/releases/aug03/082003.htm*).

The situation can easily snowball well beyond a single company or state. A failing company impacts its suppliers and partners, and in some cases it may have an impact on the financial markets as a whole. Non-compliance can lead to media attention; lack of trust by employees, customers, suppliers, and partners; individual and organizational financial loss; and in some cases, bankruptcy.

8.2 The Rules

The sections below aren't meant to be comprehensive, but they do represent some of the more impactful guidelines under which many organizations and IT departments have to operate. This chapter isn't intended to be a how-to guide for ensuring compliance, but to make the new IT Manager aware of the various issues and their importance.

Sarbanes-Oxley

Named for its two sponsors, Senator Paul S. Sarbanes (D-Maryland) and Representative Michael G. Oxley (R-Ohio), and frequently called by a variety of nicknames (Sarbanes, SOX, Sarb-Ox), it's formally called the Public Company Accounting Reform and Investor Protection Act of 2002 and is considered to be the most significant change to U. S. Securities Law since the 1930s.

The primary objective of SOX is to ensure the integrity of financial statements. It's interesting to note that SOX doesn't directly regulate Information Technology, but since IT systems are usually at the core of how a company manages and reports its finances, it is no surprise that IT is significantly impacted by it.

Although less than 200 words long, Section 404 of Sarbanes-Oxley has the most impact on IT. Of particular note is the requirement for companies to annually

(1) state the responsibility of management for establishing and maintaining an adequate internal control structure and procedures for financial reporting; and (2) contain an assessment, as of the end of the most recent

fiscal year of the issuer, of the effectiveness of the internal control structure and procedures of the issuer for financial reporting.

In addition, Section 404 requires the auditors to "attest to, and report on, the assessment made by the management."

Those few lines of requirements have had an enormous trickle-down effect throughout companies, with a great deal of it being felt in IT. In fact, SOX has placed such an enormous burden on IT that an online poll in the latter half of 2005 by Share, an independent IBM user group, showed Sarbanes-Oxley compliance was considered the biggest waste of IT staff's time (*http://www.share.org/ news/details.cfm?id=*151).

However, that doesn't mean it should be taken lightly. Misstatement of financials under Sarbanes-Oxley can lead to jail time, fines, or both for executives.

HIPAA

HIPAA, the Health Insurance Portability and Accountability Act, has regulations promoting the privacy and security of medical records. These regulations are primarily related to the healthcare industry. HIPAA's regulations directly cover three basic groups of individual or corporate entities:

+ Health plans (e.g., public and private insurance carriers, employee medical plans, etc.)

+ Healthcare providers (e.g., doctors, hospitals, or any provider of health or medical services)

+ Healthcare clearinghouses (e.g., a processor of health information, such as a billing service)

While HIPAA primarily impacts those in the medical industry, it can indirectly impact organizations outside of the field. For example, non-medical companies would want to make sure that the process of dealing with and administering employee medical benefits complies with the act.

The Security Rule of HIPAA is designed to assure the confidentiality and integrity of Protected Health Information (PHI). Protected health information under HIPAA includes any individually-identifiable health information. This refers not only to data that is explicitly linked to a particular individual, but also includes health information with data items that reasonably could be expected to allow individual identification.

The Privacy Rule of HIPAA is intended to protect the privacy of all Individually Identifiable Health Information (IIHI) in the custody of covered entities, regardless of whether the information is or has been in electronic form.

Basel II

Basel II is an updated version of the Basel Accord·that was adopted in 1988 in Basel, Switzerland. Basel II, formally known as the International Convergence of Capital Measurement and Capital Standards, was endorsed in 2004 by the central bank governors and the heads of bank supervisory authorities in the Group of Ten (G10). G10 refers to the 10-member countries of the International Monetary Fund (the United States, UK, Germany, France, Belgium, The Netherlands, Italy, Sweden, Canada, and Japan) plus Switzerland.

The Basel Committee on Banking Supervision (BCBS) drafted the text of Basel II. The Basel II Framework sets out the details for adopting more risk-sensitive minimum capital requirements for banking organizations. The new framework reinforces these risk-sensitive requirements by laying out principles for banks to assess the adequacy of their capital to ensure that banks have sufficient capital to support the risks that they undertake. Like Sarbanes-Oxley, it also seeks to strengthen the transparency and integrity of banks' financial reporting.

The Basel II Accord is built around "three pillars":

+ **Pillar 1** of the new capital framework revises the 1988 Accord's guidelines by aligning the minimum capital requirements more closely to each bank's actual risk of economic loss.

+ **Pillar 2** of the new capital framework recognizes the necessity of exercising effective supervisory review of banks' internal assessments of their overall risks to ensure that bank management is exercising sound judgment and has set aside adequate capital for these risks.

+ **Pillar 3** leverages the ability of market discipline to motivate prudent management by enhancing the degree of transparency in banks' public reporting. It sets out the public disclosures that banks must make that lend greater insight into the adequacy of their capitalization. (Source: Bank of International Settlements, *www.bis.org*).

In the United States, adoption and implementation of Basel II is managed by the four Federal banking agencies (the Office of the Comptroller of the Currency, the Board of Governors of the Federal Reserve System, the Federal Deposit Insurance Corporation, and the Office of Thrift Supervision). So far, these agencies have only recommended that the largest banks be required to implement Basel II. Currently, ten banks meet these size requirements, and another ten banks have chosen to adopt the advanced approaches of Basel II. It's expected that over time other large banking and non-bank institutions will also choose to adopt advanced capital calculations.

SB-1386

California's Security Breach Information Act (SB-1386) is a state law requiring organizations that maintain personal information about individuals to inform those individuals if the security of their information is compromised. This Act stipulates that if there's a security breach of a database containing personal data, the responsible organization must notify each individual for whom it maintained information. The Act, which went into effect July 1, 2003, was created to help stem the increasing incidences of identity theft. Essentially, it requires an agency, person, or business that conducts business in California and owns or licenses computerized "personal identifying information" to disclose any breach of security to any resident whose unencrypted data is believed to have been disclosed.

SB-1386 defines Personal Identifying Information (PII) as an individual's unencrypted first and last name in conjunction with at least one other piece of information, such as:

+ Social Security number

+ Debit or credit card number

+ Driver's license number or California ID card number

+ Account number in conjunction with a PIN or access code

Because of the reference to unencrypted data, many organizations have taken to encrypting data that leaves their custody. Interestingly enough, the law doesn't set any minimum requirements, or make any statement about the strength of the encryption.

Although it's a California state law, it doesn't mean that companies located outside of California are exempt. If your company does business anywhere in California, you are affected. As California has the largest population of any state, it's highly likely that SB-1386 has an impact on your business.

When data is compromised, SB-1386 outlines specific courses of action that an affected company must follow.

FACTA

The Fair and Accurate Credit Transactions Act (FACTA) of 2003 is a consumer rights bill that became fully effective June 1, 2005, and is an extension of the Fair Credit Reporting Act (FCRA). The rule says that in regard to consumer information (such as name, Social Security number, address, etc.) you must "take reasonable measures to protect against unauthorized access or use of the information." FACTA is designed to cut down on the incidences of identity theft as a result of valuable consumer information contained in business records. FACTA also discusses destruction methods such as shredding of paper documents and destroying/erasing electronic media.

While you might think that this Act only applies to organizations like credit bureaus, banks, and retailers, its reach is actually far greater. You could easily have FACTA-covered data if you've done background checks on your employees and job applicants.

Gramm-Leach-Bliley

The Financial Modernization Act of 1999, also known as the Gramm-Leach-Bliley Act (named for it's Republican Party sponsors Phil Gramm, Jim Leach, and Thomas Bliley), or GLB Act, has provisions to protect consumers' personal financial information held by financial institutions. The Act is enforced by multiple federal agencies as well as states. It affects not only banks, insurance companies, and security firms, but also brokers, lenders, tax preparers, and real estate settlement companies, among others.

The GLB Act consists of three sections:

1. The Financial Privacy Rule, which regulates the collection and disclosure of private financial information

2. The Safeguards Rule, which stipulates that financial institutions must implement security programs to protect such information

3. The Pretexting provisions, which prohibit the practice of pretexting (accessing private information using false pretenses)

For IT, it's important to note the Act provides that:

each agency or authority described in Section 6805(a) of this title shall establish appropriate standards for the financial institutions subject to their jurisdiction relating to administrative, technical, and physical safeguards
1. to insure the security and confidentiality of customer records and information;
2. to protect against any anticipated threats or hazards to the security or integrity of such records; and
3. to protect against unauthorized access to or use of such records or information which could result in substantial harm or inconvenience to any customer.

GLB also requires the safeguarding of "non-public personal information," which includes nonpublic "personally identifiable financial information" such as any information. . .:

+ a consumer provides to obtain a financial product or service

+ about a consumer resulting from any transaction involving a financial product or service otherwise obtained about a consumer in connection with providing a financial product or service (Source: *www.ftc.gov/ privacy/glbact/glboutline.pdf*).

The Act also requires financial institutions to give customers written privacy notices that explain their information-sharing practices.

U. S. Securities

+ **Rule 342 of the New York Stock Exchange (NYSE)** states that member organizations shall have "internal supervision and control of the organization and compliance with securities' laws and regulations." The rule also provides that member organizations have "reasonable procedures for review of registered representatives' communications with the public."

+ **Rule 440 of the New York Stock Exchange (NYSE)** requires that: "every member organization shall make and preserve books and records as the Exchange may prescribe and as prescribed by [SEC] Rule 17a-3. The record keeping format, medium and retention period shall comply with Rule 17a-4 under the Securities Exchange Act of 1934."

+ **Rule 17a-3 of the Securities and Exchange Act of 1934** defines the requirement to keep various types of records.

+ **Rule 17a-4 of the Securities and Exchange Act of 1934** provides that "broker and dealer shall preserve for a period of not less than 3 years, the first two years in an accessible place . . . originals of all communications received and copies of all communications sent by such member, broker, or dealer (including inter-office memoranda and communications) relating to his business as such."

+ **Rule 3010 of the National Association of Securities Dealers (NASD)** requires that member firms establish and maintain a system to "supervise" the activities of each registered representative, including transactions and correspondence (which includes e-mail) with the public. In addition, NASD 3110 requires that member firms implement a retention program for all correspondence involving registered representatives.

Patriot Act

The USA Patriot Act (formally called Uniting and Strengthening America by Providing Appropriate Tools Required to Intercept and Obstruct Terrorism Act of 2001) was passed in the wake of the terrorist attacks of September 11, 2001. While the act primarily provides for giving greater latitude to the U. S. government, it does have its impact on the private sector.

The Act has a number of requirements for financial institutions in regard to verifying customers' identities, and determining whether the customer appears on any list of known or suspected terrorists or terrorist organizations (*http://thomas.loc.gov/cgi-bin/bdquery/z?d107:h.r.03162:*).

OFAC

The Office of Foreign Assets Control (OFAC) is part of the U. S. Department of Treasury and administers and enforces economic sanctions programs primarily against countries and groups of individuals, such as terrorists and narcotics traffickers. OFAC regulations prohibit individuals and businesses from transacting business with specific individuals, organizations, and countries. Compliance with the OFAC regulations requires checking the names of customers against the OFAC list.

CLERP-9 (Australia)

The Australian Corporate Law Economic Reform Program (Audit Reform and Corporate Disclosure) Act 2004 (more commonly known as CLERP-9) came into effect on July 1, 2004, and is designed to restore confidence in the market after a number of high-profile corporate collapses.

CLERP-9 is a substantial piece of legislation that in many ways is comparable to the Sarbanes-Oxley legislation in that it includes reforms relating to:

✦ Disclosure of directors' remuneration

✦ Financial reporting

✦ Auditors independence

✦ Continuous disclosure

✦ Enhanced penalty provisions

And, like SOX, misstatement of financials under CLERP can lead to jail time, fines, or both for executives.

PIPEDA (Canada)

The Personal Information Protection and Electronic Documents Act (PIPEDA) is a Canadian law that regulates the collection, use, and disclosure of personally identifiable information.

Under PIPEDA, information has to be collected with the individual's consent (and only for reasonable purposes), used only for the purpose for which it was collected, correct, properly safeguarded, and available for inspection and correction. Organizations, including corporations, individuals, associations, etc., are generally subject to the privacy requirements of PIPEDA if they collect, use, or disclose personal information in the course of a commercial activity.

Privacy and Electronic Communications Directive (European Union)

This legislation covers many aspects of electronic communications. Some of the significant provisions that focus on security of data and networks and guaranteeing the privacy of communications cover:

+ Security of networks and services
+ Confidentiality of communications
+ Spyware and cookies
+ Traffic data (information about a person's electronic activities such as web-sites visited)
+ Location data (data that identify individuals' whereabouts)
+ Public directories
+ Unsolicited commercial communication (i.e., SPAM)
+ Caller ID
+ Nuisance calls
+ Emergency calls
+ Automatic call forwarding

8.3 How to Comply with the Rules

The last few pages touched the surface of some of the rules and regulations that exist for corporations in general, and IT in particular. There are many more, and if you're in a heavily regulated industry (e.g., healthcare, pharmaceuticals, financials) there is often yet other layers to deal with.

Obviously, it's beyond the scope of this book to provide step-by-step guidance for ensuring compliance. In fact, even among the experts there is considerable debate as to what is the appropriate way to address the requirements. When regulations are replete with words like "adequate" and "sufficient," and "reasonable" they're clearly open to some interpretation.

However, there are some common practices that can help get you where you need to be:

+ Document the policies

+ Identify control mechanism(s)

+ Educate your employees

+ Maintain evidence

Each practice is discussed in more detail in the sections below.

It can also be difficult to know when enough is enough. When it comes to security and controls, there's always more that can be done. And, sometimes it's easy to lose sight of the fact that the regulations are usually focused on specific areas. For example, Sarbanes-Oxley is focused on the integrity of financial reporting. Yet, in many organizations it's often used as the impetus for change in things that have only the remotest relationship to financial reporting.

Document the Policies

Unfortunately for all those ITers who hate writing, documentation is becoming more and more a fact-of-life requirement in IT. Happily, many of the IT policies that are required for compliance are often rather short. As the name implies, they simply require that you state the policy; they are *not* how-to-manuals.

For example, the backup policy would address items like:

+ How often backup is run

+ What types of backup are executed (e.g., full, incremental, differential)

+ What is being backed up (e.g., servers, databases, e-mail, workstations, remote sites)

✦ What process is employed to ensure that the backup tapes were successfully created

✦ What tools are used (e.g., backup software, tape library, tape-drive format)

✦ What happens to the tapes after backup is complete (e.g., sent to off-site storage facility)

✦ Any special encryption that might be used

✦ How long the backup tapes are retained before being recycled or destroyed.

✦ What records are kept (e.g., logs from the backup software)

A document like this might just be a few pages long.

Before publishing the document, get as much input and comment as possible. Oftentimes that input and comment will only be from other ITers. In other cases, you may want to review with Legal or HR.

There are some key items that every policy document should have:

✦ Date it was published

✦ Name(s) of the author(s) and approver(s)

✦ Some sort of revision history

As a general rule, it's good idea to review all policies at least once a year. Even if there aren't any changes, you're at least showing your auditors that it's periodically checked and updated as needed.

Lastly, the policy should be publicly available to everyone who needs to know. An intranet site, or shared network folder, can be ideal.

Identify Control Mechanism(s)

Too often, policies are created and then universally ignored. With compliance, you want to have processes to confirm that the defined policies and procedures are actually used. This control mechanism provides the appropriate check and balance.

For example,

✦ If your policy defines that only duly authorized individuals are allowed to have access to the data center, you could periodically review the access-card logs to the data center to see if any unauthorized individuals have entered.

+ Similarly, in the backup example above, a process of regularly review-ing the backup logs to ensure that they were executed and completed without errors can serve as a control mechanism.

+ If you have a policy that unused network accounts should be disabled after a defined period, you could regularly run reports to identify when accounts were last used, and whether or not they are disabled.

Not only do the control mechanism(s) help you make sure that policies are being adhered to, but they are also convenient for your auditors.

Educate Employees

With your policies and control mechanisms defined, you want to make sure that everyone is aware of them.

Your department intranet or shared network drive is an ideal place for centralizing the storage of these documents. For simpler policies it may be sufficient to simply e-mail a link to the documents, not only when they are first published, but when they are changed, updated, or when annually reviewed (as discussed above).

For more complex policies, it may be warranted to hold meetings or small classes so that the policy can be discussed, demos conducted, and questions can be answered.

Maintain Evidence

Perhaps the most critical item in your compliance regimen is to make sure that you're keeping evidence of your activities.

Examples of evidence include:

+ In the example above about access to the computer room, a simple e-mail indicating that the access-logs have been reviewed.

+ In the example of notifying employees about a new policy, a copy of the e-mail would serve. In the case of the class for more complex policies, a record of who attended the class and the class outline show that the class was held.

+ In the example about disabling unused accounts, e-mails indicating that the report was run and reviewed and directing which accounts to disable.

When the auditors come knocking, they'll be looking to see that you have policies that comply with the various rules and regulations and that you're actually following those policies. The steps defined above can put you on the right track.

8.4 Hidden Benefits of Complying with the Rules

In terms of effort, compliance is at best a burden, and at worst an enormous use of time and resources. You have employees to manage, a department to run, service levels to meet, systems to keep operating, and a company to help keep profitable. All these rules can be seen as just more obstacles to be overcome to accomplish your goal.

Nonetheless, like Chapter 20, Disaster Recovery (see page 515), compliance activities provide a major hidden benefit: You can do important, but potentially overlooked, portions of your job *at the same time*. You can comply with regulations while simultaneously getting your "real work" done. The following sections explain how you can pull this off.

The Hidden Benefit of Documentation

The first method of compliance, "Document the Policies," is a perfect example. Sure, some policies you need to document are obscure, but most are policies that you want a record of in order to do your job better. You should have a clearly documented backup policy. Not only for compliance reasons, and not only for disaster recovery reasons, but for backup plan efficiency reasons.

If you (or one of your employees) has the entire backup plan in his head (or just as bad, has the "real" plan as opposed to the written outdated plan or the plan no one can understand), the future of your entire company's data depends on the reliability of one person. Becoming compliant may wake you up to that scary fact and cause you do something about it.

The Hidden Benefit of Control Mechanisms

The benefit to the second method of compliance, "Identify Control Mechanism(s)," is similar to the first: Your policies shouldn't be abstract documents in a file somewhere, but living items that positively affect and reflect your department's behavior. Your security policies are an excellent example. Regardless of the legal requirements, you should be aggressively monitoring your security procedures.

Control mechanisms will give you (as well as the auditors) the confidence that the policies you worked so hard to define are indeed being applied.

Depending on the level of security at your company, that monitoring can be a daily affair. There are many companies where even access to other departments is carefully restricted. If your company isn't one of these, do you need to become one? And how did you answer that question? Off the top of your head or by understanding the latest version (not the one put together last year) of your company's security policy?

The Hidden Benefit of Educating Your Employees

Keeping your employees informed isn't only a required component of some regulations, but it's simply good business practice. It's much easier for employees to comply with the policies if they know what they are.

Many employees were hurt by the recent accounting scandals. Employees — and that includes you — as well as investors, now want to know much more about what their company is doing. And it's your responsibility, as well as the responsibility of your superiors and colleagues, to provide that information proactively. Like most problems, if you aggressively approach the issue before it becomes a problem, you can turn it into an opportunity.

A timely example of keeping employees informed is to let them know the exact financial health of their company. This information, if you work for a publicly-held corporation, is clearly available in many locations. As a proactive, concerned manager you can provide that data to your employees. And you can provide it in an abbreviated form. Few people want to read the entire 10-K and 10-Q forms; but most people would want to read a paragraph or two about the financial health of the company and where to get more information if they want to do further research. Your Finance department can either provide you with that data or, more likely, point you to where that data already exists.

If the financial news for your company isn't good that quarter, you'll have happier and more confident employees if you tell them, instead of them first hearing it from CNN.

Hidden Benefits of Maintaining Evidence

Maintaining evidence might be considered a polite euphemism for the popular CYA acronym. But, in truth, the evidence proves to anyone who might ask (regulators, Legal, auditors, etc.) that you're actually operating by the established policies. Maintaining evidence is essentially good record keeping, and is a good habit for all to have — especially in the business world. And record keeping just might get people in the habit of doing more careful documentation.

8.5 **Methodologies and Frameworks**

In light of all the activity surrounding compliance, you should be aware of a number of methodologies, frameworks, and processes developed by third parties. Although these weren't specifically designed for compliance activities, many organizations have adopted them to help provide increased structure to monitor and maintain their activities. Oftentimes, these methodologies, processes, and frameworks are adopted and incorporated into all projects and activities by your organization's Project Management Office (PMO).

COSO

From its own Web site, the Committee of Sponsoring Organizations (COSO) "is a private sector organization dedicated to improving the quality of financial reporting through business ethics, effective internal controls, and corporate governance."

COSO has developed a framework to help organizations evaluate and improve their risk management.

The COSO framework for internal controls has several components:

+ Internal environment
+ Objective setting
+ Event identification
+ Risk assessment
+ Risk response
+ Control activities
+ Information and communication
+ Monitoring

The COSO framework has been adopted by thousands of organizations to help address their compliance activities.

COBIT

Control Objectives for Information and related Technology (COBIT) was developed by the Information Systems Audit and Control Association and the IT Governance Institute and is essentially a set of documents that provide guidance for computer security. Much of COBIT is available at no cost.

COBIT breaks down the control structure into four major areas:

1. Planning and Organization

2. Acquisition and Implementation

3. Delivery and Support

4. Monitoring

These are then broken down even further into 34 subcategories.

ITIL

The IT Infrastructure Library (ITIL) is published by the Office of Government Commerce in Great Britain. It focuses on IT services, and is often used to complement the COBIT framework.

ITIL consists of 6 sets:

1. Service Support

2. Service Delivery

3. Planning to Implement Service Management

4. ICT (Information and Communication Technology) Infrastructure Management

5. Applications Management

6. The Business Perspective

Within these, a number of very specific disciplines are described.

A 2005 survey by Forrester Research estimated that about 12% of $1 billion-plus companies had adopted some portion of ITIL, and one-third said they were getting started on it, or were considering it.

Although ITIL was originally created by a UK government agency, it's now being adopted and used across the world for best practices in the provision of IT service. The main focus of ITIL is IT service management. While not specifically designed for compliance, the ITIL is often mentioned in the same sentences as COBIT and COSO.

CMMI

Capability Maturity Model Integration (CMMI) is a framework for process improvement, developed at Carnegie Mellon University's Software Engineering

Institute. CMMI is designed to achieve process improvement across a project, a department, or the whole organization. CMMI can help bring together functions that are often done separately, set goals and priorities, and be a mechanism for appraising current processes.

The CMMI is probably best known for its five maturity levels:

1. Initial

2. Managed

3. Defined

4. Quantitatively Managed

5. Optimizing

Each level represents the next step toward full process maturity, and is characterized by several of the 25 defined "process areas." Organizations can have their maturity level determined by using a Standard CMMI Appraisal Method for Process Improvement (SCAMPI) Appraiser. CMMI appraisal results at the higher levels are coveted by many organizations, and are a point of pride. Many organizations will do press releases after getting a particularly good appraisal result.

ISO 9000

The International Organization for Standards (known globally as ISO – which is not an acronym) is the world's largest developer of standards. ISO standards address everything from standardization of paper sizes, credit card sizes, public information signs, performance and safety, technology connections and interfaces, etc. ISO isn't a government organization, it's essentially a network of standards organizations from over 100 countries. ISO standards are voluntary; however, they often become requirements dictated by the marketplace.

The ISO 9000 standard, originally developed in 1987 and revised every few years since, provides a framework for quality management throughout the processes of producing and delivering products and services. ISO 9000 really consists of the three components:

1. ISO 9000:2000 Quality management systems – Fundamentals and vocabulary

2. ISO 9001 Quality management systems – Requirements

3. ISO 9004 Quality management systems – Guidelines for performance improvements

ISO 9000 has 5 main sections:

1. Quality Management System — Covers ensuring that an organization has established what its processes are, how they interact with each other, what resources are required, and how processes are measured and improved.

2. Management Responsibility — It's management's responsibility to set policies, objectives, and review the systems, as well as communication to the organization about processes.

3. Resource Management — Covers a wide range of specific resources, including the human resources (such as numbers of competent workers, training, etc.), infrastructure, suppliers and partners, financial resources, and the work environment.

4. Product Realization — Covers the processes that are needed to provide the product/service.

5. Measurement Analysis and Improvement — Collecting metrics about the products, customer satisfaction, and the management systems and ensuring continual improvement.

The continuous improvement cycle of ISO 9000 can be summed up with the popular acronym of PDCA — Plan, Do, Check, Act. PDCA was originally developed by Walter Shewhart, in the 1930s, and is sometimes called "the Shewhart Cycle." It was popularized by W. Edwards Deming, and some have come to refer to it as the "the Deming Wheel."

Six Sigma

Six Sigma was originally developed as a process for measuring defects in manufacturing, and a way to work toward the elimination of those defects. Since its original incarnation for manufacturing, it has been adopted by many organizations across a wide range of industries.

At the core of Six Sigma are two methodologies:

1. DMAIC

2. DMADV

The DMAIC methodology has five phases and is for the refinement of existing processes:

✦ **Define** the project goals and customer (internal and external) deliverables

✦ **Measure** the process to determine current performance

✦ **Analyze** and determine the root cause(s) of the defects

✦ **Improve** the process by eliminating defects

✦ **Control** future process performance

The DMADV methodology also has five phases and is for the creation of new processes:

✦ **Define** the project goals and customer (internal and external) deliverables

✦ **Measure** and determine customer needs and specifications

✦ **Analyze** the process options to meet customer needs

✦ **Design** (detailed) the process to meet customer needs

✦ **Verify** the design performance and ability to meet customer needs

The Six Sigma methodology also has roles and certifications that go by names like Green Belt, Black Belt, Master Black Belt, Champion, etc.

8.6 It's Not Just Regulatory Compliance

While this chapter provides a taste of the world of IT compliance, as required by various legislation, there are other "compliance" activities outside of enacted statutes.

Electronic Discovery

Frequently, IT departments are involved in many of the lawsuits that are brought against an organization. It's becoming more and more common for lawsuits to require a search for e-mail, documents, and system logs.

✦ Class action lawsuits against a company (perhaps by investors or customers)

✦ Disgruntled employees (often claiming wrongful termination) may bring action against an organization

✦ Allegations by current employees of discrimination or harassment

- ✦ Invasion of privacy concerns (e.g., one employee claiming that another has had unauthorized access to the first employee's documents and e-mails)

- ✦ Lawsuits brought by partners, suppliers, customers, vendors, etc.

IT has found itself working with increasing frequency with the company's Legal department to provide information about IT operations (e.g., e-mail archiving policy, availability of backup tapes, response to subpoenas, etc.). As such, it's becoming increasingly common for IT to review policies and procedures with in-house lawyers before considering them "approved."

Working with Auditors

It's usually not sufficient for IT to simply establish their own procedures to meet regulatory compliance. Very often, they need to "prove" their compliance to internal as well as external auditors. The discussion earlier in the chapter about maintaining evidence goes a long way to help you prove you're doing what you're claiming.

While these audits can take a toll on IT resources, they do serve to help ensure that defined procedures are followed. And, if something is overlooked, it's better to find them during an audit than as a result of an interruption of service or loss of data.

Incident Response

Whether a security breach, a major service disruption, or a virus infestation, IT frequently has to bring all resources to bear to react to immediate need. A professional and successful response can be a major point of pride for you and your team across the organization.

However, such incidents also often provide marvelous learning opportunities. Many organizations will prepare a "postmortem" after a significant event in an attempt to document and analyze what happened.

Such a postmortem will usually contain:

- ✦ A chronology of events, from first sign of the problem to resolution

- ✦ Identification of what procedures, tools, resources, etc., worked well

- ✦ Identification of what items didn't work as expected

- ✦ An analysis of the root cause of the problem

✦ A plan to address and correct the problems and issues identified as a result of this problem

A summary of the postmortem, usually without too much IT jargon, is often provided to management. This summary is usually welcomed by the upper management, since it documents the how and why of what happened and an action plan to ensure that a similar event doesn't occur again. These are very helpful in furthering upper management's perception of IT.

Disaster Recovery and Business Continuity

While disaster recovery and business continuity may also be the subject of some regulatory compliance, most organizations are concerned about it more for their own interests. Both of these subjects are covered in Chapter 20, Disaster Recovery (on page 515).

Definition of Policies and Procedures

The compliance legislation discussed previously is sufficient reason for establishing policies and procedures. However, even without being compelled by law, it's always wise to define and document policies and procedures for the IT department, as well as the user community.

For example, there may be an informal policy that has determined when personal printers (as opposed to shared-network printers) are permitted. However, if this policy is documented and posted, it helps to ensure that all employees (both IT and users) are aware and that it can be applied consistently. Other examples of policies that can be defined include:

✦ Password requirements (length, frequency of changes, etc.)

✦ Limits on the size of e-mail messages and mailboxes

✦ Retention period for files and messages

✦ Resources and rules in place for spam and virus defense (e.g., the blocking of certain attachment types)

✦ Rules and approvals needed for non-standard equipment requests (laptops, flat-screen monitors, equipment at home)

✦ Requirements for password-protected screen savers

✦ Process for installation of non-standard software

✦ Policies for disabling/deleting unused accounts

✦ Policies pertaining to IDs and access for non-employees (temps, consultants, partners, suppliers, etc.)

✦ Provisions for requesting a restore of files

✦ Approval required for accessing the files of a former or unreachable employee

✦ Employee reimbursement for special services (cell phones, broadband connections at home)

✦ Proper use of IT resources (e.g., no personal use of computer equipment)

✦ Limitations of support for company equipment at home

Of course, many of these policies should include comment and approval beyond IT before being considered official. In some cases (e.g., file and message retention), Legal should be involved. In other cases (e.g., company equipment at home), it would be wise to involve HR and Finance. Involving other departments not only helps IT establish partnerships with these groups, but it ensures that IT isn't determining policies in a vacuum.

Outsourcing

Over the past few years, outsourcing and offshoring have become very attractive solutions. However, it's important to remember that when you outsource certain business activities, your organization is still responsible for ethical and compliance activities. While outsourcing is adding value to your organization's services, products, and bottom-line, you want to make sure that you're not risking the company's reputation or compliance responsibilities as a result (*http:// www.organicconsumers.org/clothes/nike041505.cfm*).

One example of the difficulties with outsourcing is the issue of "sweatshops." While it doesn't directly affect IT, it illustrates the serious problems that a company can get into when outsourcing. Nike, for example, outsourced the manufacture of shoes to lower paying workers overseas for years. When this practice was discovered and the harsh spotlight of international publicity shone on them, the company found itself reading headlines like: "Nike Acknowledges Massive Labor Exploitation in its Overseas Sweatshops." Wal-Mart faced similar negative publicity for importing goods made in China (*http://www.fastcompany. com/magazine/77/walmart.html*).

But what about outsourcing IT? How could sending code to India be a problem? Forget legal compliance issues or trade barriers — what about sending dear old American jobs overseas? There are all kinds of opinions about the correctness of shipping prime programming jobs overseas (*http://news.com.com/Offshoring+U.S.+needs+reforms,+not+rhetoric/2009-1070_3-5198156.html, http://www.ecommercetimes.com/story/42781.html,* and *http://knowledge.wharton.upenn.edu/index.cfm?fa=*viewfeature&id=693). One thing, however, is for certain: It's a very controversial tactic. If your company is planning to do it, make sure it's a decision that all the key players know about. You don't want to be surprised with a news channel microphone in your face as you leave the office one afternoon.

For more on the pluses and minuses of outsourcing see Chapter 3, Staffing Your IT Team, Section 3.5, Outsourcing and Offshore Outsourcing, on page 89.

8.7 Additional Resources

Web Sites

+ *knowledge.wharton.upenn.edu/index.cfm?fa=viewfeature&id=693* (article on outsourcing back-office functions)

+ *www.compliancepipeline.com* (online journal for IT compliance-related issues)

+ *www.discover6sigma.org* (information about Six Sigma)

+ *www.ecommercetimes.com/story/42781.html* (article about India's offshore outsourcing)

+ *www.fastcompany.com/magazine/77/walmart.html* (article about Wal-Mart's offshore practices)

+ *www.ftc.gov/privacy/glbact/glboutline.pdf* (Gramm-Leach-Bliley Act)

+ *www.isaca.org* (trade association for IT governance professionals)

+ *www.isixsigma.com* (information about Six Sigma)

+ *www.iso.org* (information about the International Organization for Standards, and ISO 9000)

+ *www.itgi.org* (trade association for IT governance professionals)

+ *www.itil.co.uk* (information about ITIL)

+ *www.organicconsumers.org/clothes/nike041505.cfm* (article about Nike's offshore practices)

+ *www.sei.cmu.edu/cmmi* (information about CMMI)

SOX

✦ *aicpa.org/sarbanes/index.asp*

✦ *news.findlaw.com/hdocs/docs/gwbush/sarbanesoxley072302.pdf*

HIPAA

✦ *www.hhs.gov/ocr/hipaa*

✦ *www.hipaacomply.com*

Basel II

✦ *www.bis.org/bcbs/index.htm*

✦ *www.federalreserve.gov/generalinfo/basel2/default.htm*

SB-1386

✦ *info.sen.ca.gov/pub/01-02/bill/sen/sb_1351-1400/sb_1386_bill_20020926_chaptered.html*

✦ *www.theiia.org/itaudit/index.cfm?fuseaction*=forum&fid=5501

FACTA

✦ *www.epic.org/privacy/fcra*

✦ *www.ftc.gov/os/statutes/fcrajump.htm*

Gramm-Leach-Bliley

✦ *www.epic.org/privacy/glba*

✦ *www.ftc.gov/privacy/privacyinitiatives/glbact.html*

U. S. Securities

✦ *nasd.complinet.com/nasd/display/display.html?rbid*=1189&element_id=1159000466

✦ *rules.nyse.com/NYSE/Help/Map/rules-sys454.html*

✦ *rules.nyse.com/NYSE/Help/Map/rules-sys552.html*

✦ *www.sec.gov/rules/final/34-44992a.htm*

Patriot Act

✦ *thomas.loc.gov/cgi-bin/bdquery/z?d107:h.r.03162:*

✦ *en.wikipedia.org/wiki/Patriot_Act*

✦ *www.epic.org/privacy/terrorism/hr3162.html*

OFAC

✦ *www.treas.gov/offices/enforcement/ofac*

✦ *www.treas.gov/offices/enforcement/ofac/articles/abamag.pdf*

CLERP-9

✦ *www.asic.gov.au/asic/asic_polprac.nsf/byheadline/CLERP+9?* openDocument

✦ *www.treasury.gov.au/contentitem.asp?NavId*=013&ContentID=403

PIPEDA

✦ *www.pipedainfo.com*

✦ *www.privcom.gc.ca/legislation/02_06_01_e.asp*

Privacy and Electronic Communications Directive

✦ *europa.eu.int/information_society/policy/ecomm/site_services/faq/* *index_en.htm*

✦ *register.consilium.eu.int/pdf/en/02/st03/03636en2.pdf*

Books and Articles

- Anthes, Gary H., "ITIL Catches On: British-Bred Quality Framework is Becoming the Tool of Choice in US Data Centers," *Computerworld*, October 31, 2005, p. 39.

- Flynn, Nancy, and Kahn, Randolph, *E-Mail Rules: A Business Guide to Managing Policies, Security, and Legal Issues for E-Mail and Digital Communication*, American Management Association, 2003.

- Gincel, Richard, "The Awful Truth About Compliance," *Infoworld*, December 12, 2005, p. 29.

- Gomes-Cassere, Ben, "Outsource, Don't abdicate," *CIO Magazine*, October 1, 2005, p. 36.

- Hoffman, Thomas, "Double Dipping on Sarb-Ox," *Computerworld*, November 7, 2005, p. 42.

- Hoffman, Thomas, "New Obstacles Dogging Outsourcing Customers," *Computerworld*, October 24, 2005, p. 10.

- Lynch, C. G., "Most Companies Adopting ITIL Practices," *CIO Magazine*, March 1, 2006, p. 18.

- Surowiecki, James, "Sarboxed In," *The New Yorker*, December 12, 2005, p. 46.

- Thibodeau, Patrick, "Sarbanes-Oxley Adds to IT Costs But Pushes Companies to Prepare," *Computerworld*, October 24, 2005.

- Worthen, Ben, "ITIL Power," *CIO Magazine*," September 1, 2005, p. 47.

The Technology of Being an IT Manager

Getting Started with the Technical Environment

The secret of getting ahead is getting started. The secret of getting started is breaking your complex overwhelming tasks into small manageable tasks, and then starting on the first one.

—MARK TWAIN

CHAPTER TABLE OF CONTENTS

In IT, it's too easy to be distracted by the exciting developments in hardware, security, networking, software, etc. However, as a manager, you also have to keep your eyes on those areas that aren't quite as alluring. While activities like tracking your Total Cost of Ownership (TCO) and inventorying your environment may be items you will be tempted to put off, you must not do this. In fact, taking a formal inventory can be one of the activities that gives you an excellent under-standing of how your environment operates. A first-hand knowledge of your IT environment, its history, users, and operations can help you to better define needs and future plans, as well as avoid repeating past mistakes.

9.1   The Technical Environment

You probably have more technology in your environment than you realize. And it can be very difficult to get a handle on it all — especially if you're new to a job. The value of carefully determining everything you're responsible for, how-ever, cannot be overestimated. Not only does it help you figure out your role, but it helps you understand the amount of resources you have. In addition, an inventory gives you a sense of scale about the environment as well as a feeling for whether resources are under- or over-utilized — although you're likely to find it's a combination of both.

Completing an inventory not only provides you with a frame of reference for what you've become responsible for, but it is excellent information to include in a disaster recovery plan. (For more on disaster recovery, see Chapter 20, Disaster Recovery, on page 515).

What Do We Have Here?

Don't be surprised if the existing infrastructure documentation is out of date (or non-existent), with the latest version only in the minds of your staff. Your promotion or entry into this job is as good a reason as any for getting current with documentation.

Making sure there's a complete inventory can be a very valuable tool for a wide range of different projects. For example, when it's time to do budgeting, and you need to determine how much to budget for support and maintenance, a complete inventory can be very valuable. Similarly, when it's time to do something like an upgrade of an operating system, an inventory will let you see what items you need to test it with.

Define Your Scope

To avoid being overwhelmed with information, you should start at the highest levels and work your way down to the detail you think you'll need. The level of detail you need as a manager varies and generally depends on the size of your organization and the size of your staff. As a manager, you probably don't need to be tracking nitty-gritty inventory details like serial numbers, firmware versions, room and rack locations, etc., but you want to make sure that someone on your staff is doing that.

An excellent way to determine the scope of your inventory is to think about a disaster recovery scenario in which you have to bring the entire IT infrastructure back up after a major failure (such as a fire, earthquake, or hurricane; see Chapter 20 on page 515). If you can walk your way through the entire recovery scenario, then your scope is complete. If you find yourself guessing at some of the elements of your IT infrastructure, then your scope needs refinement.

In this situation, a picture can be worth a thousand words. Very often the easiest way to get a clear view of an environment is with a schematic diagram. Not only does it convey a great deal of information, but your technical staff will probably find a diagram easier to create (and maintain) than the equivalent material in text.

Key Elements to Include

Make sure that your inventory includes a number of key areas:

- ✦ Wide Area Network Environment
- ✦ Local Area Network Environment
- ✦ Carrier Connections
- ✦ Server and Storage Environment
- ✦ Workstations
- ✦ Application and Software Inventory
- ✦ Vendors

Wide Area Network Environment

A Wide Area Network (WAN) schematic (see Figure 9.1 below for an example) can include information like site locations (differentiating between remote offices and disaster recovery facilities), types of connections (VPN, leased-line, frame relay, Internet), backup communication facilities, carriers, bandwidth, firewalls, DMZs, etc. You may also want to include types and number of servers, number of users, IP addressing, key contacts, and street addresses. In many cases, you may have connections to third parties such as service providers

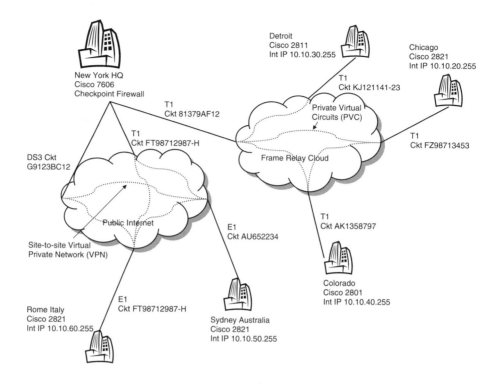

Figure 9.1 An Example of WAN Environment

(e.g., payroll) or partners (e.g., suppliers or distributors). Not only do you want to make note of the connections, but you probably want to indicate who is primarily responsible for the connections and the hardware: sometimes you are, sometimes the third party is.

The WAN schematic should be updated regularly and distributed to members of the IT department. It should be posted on the wall of the data center for easy reference. The network manager should have it posted by his desk. It takes work to create one of these, and more work to keep it current. But it's an invaluable aid to the entire department. If you don't have one, go make one.

Local Area Network Environment

The Local Area Network (LAN) schematic is the next level of detail. A typical LAN schematic (Figure 9.2, below) drills down into some of the detail of a particular site. It should include the topology, location, and connectivity of switches, routers, and hubs. It should identify different types of cabling (copper, fiber). It can also include room locations for various network equipment,

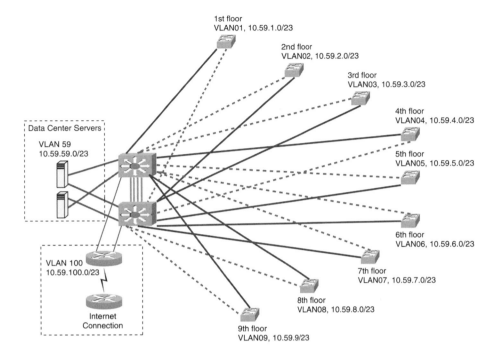

Figure 9.2   LAN Schematic

model numbers for key components, IP addresses, wireless capabilities, and so on. Like the WAN schematic, the LAN schematic should be regularly updated so that it's always current, and distributed widely so it's available for easy reference to all that need it.

If your responsibility also includes the phone system, it may be appropriate to include information about the voice environment on the LAN schematic — especially if you use voice-over IP (VoIP). This data will include information about the switch, the voice-mail environment, trunks, etc.

Carrier Connections

The carrier connections inventory goes into the details of the WAN connections that were defined in the WAN and LAN schematics. Items to track here include circuit numbers, circuit endpoints (including building and room numbers), carriers, type/speed of line (T-1, analog, ISDN, etc.), and phone numbers for reporting problems. Although telecommunications in the United States are very reliable, problems still come up. When a line goes down, you don't want to find yourself asking, "Which line?" and scrambling to find the circuit number or who you have to call to report the problem.

In larger environments, there are so many lines and so much activity in regard to adding, changing, and canceling them, that it's quite easy to lose track. It isn't unheard of for large IT environments to discover that they've been paying the bill on a line that they didn't know they had and had stopped using years ago.

Server and Storage Environment

The documentation for the server environment drills down further and starts to give insight into how the applications work. In many cases, you may not be able to get all the detail you need into a single diagram. For example, you may find that you need one diagram just to indicate the basics, and others to talk about how key architectures (e-mail, active directory, storage area networks, etc.) are set up.

Workstations

Keeping track of workstations can be an enormous headache because there are so many of them and there is a lot of activity in regard to refreshing, upgrading, and physical movement. As a manager, you should really only be keeping track of summary information (and leaving the details of the inventory to your staff). Important summary information can include:

+ Total number of workstations

+ Workstations broken down by Operating System platform and version (Mac, Windows, Unix)

+ Average age

+ Current standard configuration(s) (make, model, disk, memory, etc.)

+ Type and duration of warranty/support (desktop vs. laptop)

You may also want this information broken down by department or location.

An often forgotten portion of the total number of workstations are the ones that are remote: users that travel, users that have company equipment at home, etc. These often fall into the out-of-sight, out-of-mind category. It's important that these devices be treated like any other company workstation so that they can be tracked, maintained, and updated properly. And when an employee leaves the company, you can expect HR to ask IT if that employee has any computer equipment at home.

Application and Software Inventory

Applications are pretty much IT's reason for existing — all the technology doesn't do much good unless it serves a purpose. For some of the previous items we suggested using a diagram for getting an understanding of how the environment operates. For the applications, it may be best to resort to a good old fashioned list. (Although for complex applications with lots of data flowing in and out, a diagram can be very helpful.)

When thinking of applications, we generally think of the big business applications (such as supply chain, HRIS, payroll, accounting, e-mail, etc.). But as long as you're developing an inventory, you should also include all the tools in use: application development tools, desktop tools (e.g., word processing, browsers, etc.), and infrastructure tools (e.g., backup and monitoring utilities, etc.).

An application inventory can include items such as:

+ Application name

+ Brief description

+ User community (departments, number of users)

+ Current version number

+ Vendor

+ Database environment

+ OS environment(s)

+ Any interfaces to other applications

+ Support/maintenance arrangements in place (and expiration)

+ Whether the application is considered "critical"

+ Which server(s) the application runs on

+ Which IT team is responsible for that particular application

+ Where to find a copy of the current version

+ Installation instructions

+ Special considerations

+ Special backup requirements

+ Peak periods of use

+ Executive usage

+ Who needs to be notified when scheduling downtime, or when there is an unexpected outage.

Vendors

You're going to deal with lots of vendors, and each will have several contacts for sales, billing, technical support, and so on. It's important to keep track of who you're dealing with and any special arrangements you have. Some vendors you will call so often that you'll have the phone number memorized, but they still need to be documented. For others, like vendors of legacy environments that you only speak with once a year or so, this inventory will be very helpful.

This vendor inventory should also include information about your support arrangements with the vendor. When there's a problem you should know immediately where to turn to find out how to call for service, including phone number and account number, and what levels of coverage you're entitled to, when your support contract expires, etc.

It's particularly important that the information be current and available to everyone who needs it. You don't want to wait until there's a component failure to learn that the support provider's phone number changed, or that your contract expired.

Tools for Tracking the Technical Environment

There are a variety of tools out there that can help you (and your team) track what's in your environment. Hardware vendors in particular have tools available to help you track and manage their devices. In some cases, the tools will also integrate with other vendors' products. Some tools can track and inventory, some can do management and alerting, others will do configuration management.

The vendors listed below have management tools available to help you manage your environment:

- ✦ Cisco
- ✦ Hewlett-Packard
- ✦ Dell
- ✦ IBM
- ✦ Altiris
- ✦ Microsoft
- ✦ NetIQ
- ✦ LANDesk
- ✦ NetSupport

✦ Peregrine

✦ Computer Associates

✦ Remedy

✦ Opsware

✦ Sunflower Systems

✦ Novell

✦ Ipswitch

The cost and licensing of these tools can vary widely. In some cases, the product (or a "lite" version) may be included when you buy the vendor's hardware. In some cases they may have to be licensed on a per-seat or per-device basis. Some of these tools for gathering information about the environment are stand-alone, and others are part of larger suites. Many of these tools can integrate with some of the others, while some are more proprietary.

Most of these tools are really designed for your staff to use, but they can be a great start for assembling the information you need. You probably won't find the exact tools to assemble the information together in the exact format you'd like (particularly those schematics), but you can use tools like Microsoft Excel, Access, PowerPoint, and Visio for massaging and diagramming.

In some cases (e.g., the vendor list or application and software inventory mentioned earlier) the best route may be developing your own simple tool for keeping track. Whether a small spreadsheet or database, it may prove to be the best, quickest and cheapest way, and allows you to set it up in a way that works best for you.

The Value of Good Infrastructure Documentation

The documentation about the environment should be in an easily readable format. The use of diagrams, charts, schematics, and so on, is very effective. Infrastructure documentation should be updated and available to all (ideally in a shared directory on a server, or better yet, on your IT intranet). Although this type of documentation is considered valuable, many environments don't have it because IT workers often have little interest or enthusiasm for creating documentation. However, not only is the documentation important, but the process of having your staff collect the information and create the documentation can be of great value in itself. Naturally, you should work toward making the process of collecting this information as efficient and as natural to your organization as possible.

In addition to putting this documentation on your IT intranet, there will be other valuable places for them. Hard copies (at home and the office) can come in handy for disaster recovery; your engineers will probably appreciate some of the schematics being posted in the computer room. Your Help Desk staff may value some of the information being posted on their cubicle walls for immediate reference.

Show your staff that you use this information and rely on it. Use the materials in your memos and presentations to corporate management. And when your staff is discussing various plans and issues with you, bring out the documentation and refer to it. Ask them to explain what they're talking about using the documentation they've given you.

What You May Find

An inventory can uncover under- or over-utilized resources, potential problem and risk areas, and resources and facilities that were assumed to be working but may not be. It may uncover technology that's outdated and no longer needed, or that needs to be upgraded. Or it may uncover resources providing similar or identical functionality that can be combined. It can also help you to feel comfortable that your staff has a good perspective on their environment.

9.2   Understanding the User Environment

Even though they don't pay you a fee (internal chargebacks aside), your users are also your customers, and you should treat them that way. Find out who they are, how they use your services, what additional services they may be able to use, etc.

One of the most important things you can do as an IT Manager is to establish and maintain a good relationship with your users. They should see you as available, reliable, dedicated to service, and having their best interest at heart. For the most part, they don't care about your other customers, your bosses, the vendors, the technology issues — they care about their own needs. Prior to becoming a manager, you had exposure to only a portion of your users, and only a portion of their IT needs. Now that you're managing the department, all of the users, and all of their IT needs, rest squarely on your shoulders.

Determine Who Your Users Are

IT departments have all kinds of users that represent a cross-section of the company: executives, assistants, local users, remote users, finance, marketing, warehouse, HR, facilities, and users that love technology and users that hate technology.

It's important to note that some organizations don't like the term "user." Because IT is a service-focused organization, many organizations prefer "customer" or "client" instead. In an organization like a law firm, the term "client" could cause confusion, just as in other organizations the term "customer" might cause confusion. Find out what your company prefers to call the people to whom IT provides services.

Regardless of what they're called, users' needs are best addressed in a careful, planned manner. Everyone knows what the results of knee-jerk reactions to problems are; the problem may eventually get solved, but much more money and time is spent than should have been. Spend some time in advance planning to address your users' needs.

Find Out Who Your Department Thinks Its Users Are

Don't quibble, keep focused: Who are the people your department is trying to serve? This can be a simple inquiry; bring everyone together and ask your people while you're discussing other matters with them. Keep it informal. They may say that their users are a small subset of the company; they may reply that their users are mostly in Legal or "Tom S., who calls me all the time." While these are true, they aren't the entire story. Your users may also include customers or business partners of the company; find out who they are, where they are, and how they function within their company, and what their relationship is with your department and what they want out of the relationship. You'll want to make sure that your entire department has the same view as to who the users are.

Find Out Who Your Boss Thinks Your Users Are

This is an important perspective for a few reasons. First, it gives you some insight into how your boss views the organization's world. Secondly, it will probably alert you to where some of the challenges are. Those challenges might include some political minefields, or perhaps information on areas that have been particularly critical of IT's services.

If your boss's perception of who your users are varies significantly from yours, you need to learn why the difference exists, and which one of you is right. (It's a safe bet that you're both right, though.) If your boss always mentions the shipping department's needs and problems, ask why he never mentions the Sales department.

Having spoken to your team and your boss, now canvass the rest of the organization. Contact the leads of the major departments of the company. Obviously, size matters. If you work for a 10-person start-up, talking to all the key players won't take long, nor will it be a major effort. You still need to prepare, but you can do it fairly quickly. On the other hand, if you work for a Fortune 500 corporation with divisions around the globe, canvassing your users is going to require some careful sampling.

Meet the Users

Once you've started to assemble a list of who your users are (either by name, group, or function) you need to meet with them, establish a relationship, and ask them some questions about their needs. Tell them that the more candid they are, the better it is for you.

These questions can help to get the discussion started:

✦ What services do you currently get from the IT department?

✦ How well does IT satisfy your needs?

✦ Have we fallen short in any areas? Or surpassed expectations in others?

✦ Which services do you need, or would you like, that you aren't currently getting?

✦ How do you view the use of IT in your department?

✦ Who else would be worth speaking to?

✦ What are your short- and long-term goals and needs?

✦ Have you read, or heard, about any technology solutions, perhaps used by competitors, that you'd like to explore?

Ask these questions of the key department managers in your company. Tell them you're trying to align your department's functions with their needs. They may look at you funny — especially if they haven't seen this level of interest before from IT — but then they will usually be happy to chat.

Use meetings like this to establish a continuing dialog and relationship with key users and departments. This might be an ongoing process, or it might be facilitated through periodic meetings, perhaps a few times a year.

And remember that these discussions shouldn't be one way. You have as much information to share as your users do:

✦ Alert them to projects that you're working on.

✦ Tell them about IT projects that other departments are exploring.

✦ Tell them that when it's time to prepare annual budgets, you can be proactive in giving them some general cost estimates for common items such as workstations, laptops, printers, telephone costs, etc. Invite them to contact you to review costs for special projects they're considering for the upcoming year.

✦ If you've read any trade journal articles that you think might be of interest to them, pass them along.

Although much of the discussion may be at a high level, you may get one or two detail items (e.g., "this printer always jams with legal paper," or "whenever I login from home I always have to enter my password twice"). In some cases, these minor problems may actually be symptomatic of a larger issue. Whatever the cause, these are great opportunities to demonstrate what they can expect from you as the new IT Manager. You should investigate these problems, and make sure that they're resolved. Then, just as important, follow up with that department head to tell him you looked into the problem(s) he reported and provide an explanation of what was found and how it was addressed. Even though they're small problems, you'll be showing that you listened to what was said, cared about it, took action, and followed up. You will never be faulted for demonstrating those traits.

These initial discussions are also a good opportunity for you to let department heads know how your organization is set up, what your processes are for support, evaluation of deployment of new solutions, etc.

What you're trying to do is establish a relationship. Relationships are always the key to success. Remember that in the beginning, the most important asset you may bring to these discussions will probably be a set of ears.

9.3 TCO and Asset Management

Two phrases that have garnered a lot of attention for IT Managers over the past few years are Asset Management and TCO. Many people use these phrases synonymously; while they're similar, they aren't identical.

Both of these phrases are most often used in reference to laptops and desktops. IT people certainly realize that with a population of several hundred or several thousand desktop computers in a company, it takes an enormous amount of resources to support, manage, and track them. On the one hand, there are many hidden costs associated with these devices, their use, and their support. On the other hand, there can be significant savings in effectively managing these devices.

Although TCO and asset management are most frequently used in conjunction with devices like desktops and laptops, the concepts are readily applicable to other equipment types, like servers.

TCO

TCO is a term used for the sum of all the costs associated with a computer, in addition to the obvious costs of hardware and software. There are many published studies about the true cost of a personal computer; annual TCO figures range from $3,000 to $12,000. There is endless debate over what the true number is and, of course, the figure can vary significantly from company to company.

The discussions around TCO are usually very controversial. While it can be easy to total the hard costs of the hardware and software, the "softer" costs are much more difficult to calculate.

In addition to the cost of the hardware and software, items that factor into the TCO include:

◆ Cost of support (staff, consultants, vendors)

◆ Network facilities (servers, applications, cabling, routers, hubs, etc.)

◆ Training

◆ Administrative (purchasing, inventory, auditing, etc.)

◆ Money costs (capital, depreciation, etc.)

Some analyses have taken TCO to a very detailed level and have included:

◆ Consumables (diskettes, toner, paper, etc.)

◆ Wasted user time (playing games, changing settings of fonts, colors, screen savers, etc.) — referred to as "futzing" among those that study TCO.

◆ Downtime from problems like viruses, crashes, etc.

◆ Co-workers' time (when user A has to stop doing his job because user B asks him a question)

Calculating the TCO

At some point, someone may ask you about your organization's TCO. Calculating it isn't for the faint of heart.

First, you have to calculate the current TCO — if you don't, you'll never know if cost was reduced. Capturing these costs isn't easy because you frequently have to make assumptions, define rules-of-thumb, and do some educated guessing. For example, if your Help Desk also takes calls about problems with the phone system, you may need to subtract that portion of their time for calculating the support costs for your computers.

Once you know what the costs are, you have to evaluate which ones can be reduced, and how much effort is required to reduce them, and ironically, how much it costs to reduce those costs. For example, you may be able to reduce the hardware costs by negotiating better pricing, or finding a new vendor. You may be able to reduce Help Desk costs by providing better training for the users. But how much will that additional training cost?

Once you've decided where you want to reduce costs and the steps to do so, you then have to implement them. But things are seldom as simple as they seem. You may find that the new hardware vendor's equipment is cheaper, but the quality isn't as good, necessitating a lot of returns and calls for services. Or, it turns out that you can't get users to show up for the training classes because they are busy with other activities.

After doing all that, you now have to go back and re-measure your TCO. Having done it once, it should be easier the second time. The most important consideration is to be sure to measure it using the same sets of assumptions, educated guesses, and rules-of-thumb that you used the first time; otherwise, you're not comparing apples with apples.

The whole TCO process can be quite arduous and tedious and easily take a year. However, the findings can be eye-opening. There are many consultants willing to help you with the process, of course. How these consultants' fees enter into the TCO equation (not to mention the cost of your time on the project) also raises some interesting discussions.

The important thing to take away from this is that there are a lot of costs and factors that are associated with information technology. As such, there are opportunities for tremendous savings by managing these costs well, enter — asset management.

Asset Management

With all the cost variables mentioned in the discussion above of TCO, it's critical for an IT Manager to keep a careful watch on costs. If TCO is the cost associated with computers, then "asset management" refers to what you do to keep those costs down. These actions can include everything from policies and procedures to technology issues. Like TCO, asset management usually focuses on desktop and laptops. However, many of the same principles are used with other resources. Some of the most popular asset management techniques include the following:

- ✦ Maintaining hardware and software standards (see Section 9.4 on page 247). The fewer the number of technology products in your environment, the easier it will be to support, maintain, and administer.

✦ Outsourcing functions that can be done less expensively, or more effectively, to others.

✦ Using tools to automate repetitive procedures.

✦ Investing in software distribution tools so that the technical staff doesn't have to visit each workstation to deploy software and/or upgrades.

✦ Employing disk cloning technology so that newly purchased computers don't have to be loaded manually with software.

✦ Proactively checking for problems (e.g., virus checking, system monitoring, etc.) and performing preventive maintenance (e.g., disk defragmenting).

✦ Having your hardware reseller preload your standard disk image on your workstations when they ship, so that they can be deployed to users right out of the box.

✦ Using inventory tracking software.

✦ Implementing restrictions so that users can't change system configurations and cause adverse impacts.

✦ Proactively deciding on upgrades, and replacements, as opposed to waiting for the unit to fail, or the vendor to discontinue support.

✦ Defining and setting appropriate hardware and software defaults.

✦ Providing support personnel with resources (reference materials, vendors' support lines, etc.) to help them do their jobs.

✦ Tracking software usage, frequently referred to as license metering, to ensure that you're not paying for more licenses than you need, nor risking being under licensed.

✦ Performing upgrades only when they are deemed necessary and you've tested them to be reliable, instead of installing them every time the vendor announces one.

As you can see, most of these techniques and ideas are designed to reduce the demands on the support staff and/or the number of interruptions that users encounter. This is because the most expensive factor related to desktop computers is the labor — whether it's the cost of the support team, or the cost of the user's time when system problems prevent them from working.

Of course, if you're going to be implementing asset management techniques to reduce your TCO, you'll want to know if you're having any success or not. Most of the asset management techniques listed earlier have an implementation cost, either in terms of hardware/software or staff time, and so on. At some point you'll have to make some value judgments to decide which to implement — figuring out which might be the most worthwhile for your needs for the least cost.

9.4   Standards

One of the classic jokes in this industry is the IT Manager who says "Yes, we're a firm believer in standardizing — that's why we have so many standards."

The benefits of standardizing your technology are many-fold. It eases the support burden if the technicians have to know fewer products and their idiosyncrasies. It also means that you don't have to keep spares for as many product types. For devices like printers, it means your inventory of consumables is simplified. And, it eases things for your procurement team and shortens your vendor list. Those features can lead to shorter delivery times and better opportunities for volume discounts.

As the discussion below will show, there has to be some flexibility in standards, particularly where users are concerned. And, it's important to periodically review standards — perhaps annually — to address changing costs, vendor offerings, requirements, industry directions, etc.

Standards for Users

When personal computing technology first started to become popular, it was quite common for organizational users to ask for specific products like an "IBM AT," "IBM Model 80," a "Pentium processor," or a "laser printer." When Apple introduced their candy-colored iMacs, users were generally more concerned about which color they got than the technical specifications.

Perhaps because of the ubiquity of technology, or the difficulty in keeping up with the constant stream of new products and technologies, those days are mostly gone. Technology that users can see has changed so quickly that users are now much less specific about what they ask for. There are so many new products coming out so quickly, it takes a professional (that is, someone in IT) to keep up. In addition, many products have become commoditized. IBM's selling off their PC division to Lenovo, a Chinese company, was a shock to people outside of the industry; people within the IT world knew for a long time that an IBM laptop was just like an HP, or a Dell, or one of the other major names. And, most of those computers were built and assembled, using many of the same components, by third parties in foreign countries anyway.

Issues That Users Care About

That isn't to say that users are completely uninterested in what they use. Of course performance is an issue, but it isn't uncommon for end-users to be more concerned about things that may or may not impact performance, and are often related to "technology envy" — the phenomenon of making sure your technology keeps up with the Joneses (or co-workers). Similarly, issues related to how the product impacts on their daily life, as opposed to pure performance, are also important to users.

Items that may fall into these categories include:

◆ Cordless mice and keyboards (to eliminate some wires)

◆ The coolest looking cell phone/handheld device (regardless of its capabilities)

◆ Flat-panel monitors (the larger the better)

◆ The lightest and smallest laptops (for ease of travel)

◆ Tower units to go under the desk (so that the valuable desktop real estate isn't taken up)

◆ Desktop units (so that the user doesn't keep banging their knee into it)

◆ Privacy and anti-glare screens (especially in cubicle farms)

◆ Leather laptop carrying case vs. canvas

◆ Preference for devices in certain colors

For situations like these, IT can have standards and still provide some flexibility for users. For example, instead of insisting that all users use the exact same model laptop, two choices can be made available. One option is relatively small and light, easy to carry, and functional enough for the user who just wants to do e-mail, word processing, spreadsheets, etc., when traveling; the alternative is perhaps larger with a bigger screen for those who never work outside of the office and do not worry about the weight of their machines.

Similarly, if a user asks for a flat-panel screen (a more common request now that the prices have dropped so dramatically), virtually any flat-panel will do — regardless of the meaningful specifications (dot pitch, viewing angles, etc.).

For issues like ergonomic devices and anti-glare screens, the IT department should readily provide whatever the user asks for. No one wants an employee going to the HR department complaining of carpal tunnel syndrome or eye strain because IT's standards prohibit these relief-offering devices.

Regardless of the standards you set, you can count on exceptions as a fact of life. No matter how carefully you selected your standards, it's only a matter of time before some executive asks for something that isn't a standard. Rank has its privilege, and it would be unwise for you to say no (if you do, expect to hear from your boss informing you that he reconsidered your answer for you). However, before you say no, you can certainly have a discussion with that executive asking him what features of that device are attractive to him, and showing him that those same features are available on the device that is part of your standards. He may not care all that much because yours isn't as cool looking as the one he wants. But, it's a small sacrifice to keep an executive happy — customer service is what IT is all about. (See Chapter 17, User Support Services, on page 451.)

Issues that IT Cares About

While IT needs to offer greater flexibility to accommodate the individual needs and preferences of users, it has greater latitude in defining the technical standards that are generally beyond a user's interest or concern.

Because technology products have a limited life span (generally 5 years or less), and product offerings are changing so fast, it's unlikely you'll ever have a 100% standardized environment. But that doesn't mean you should just throw in the towel. In fact, the opposite is true: This is an important issue that you will be working on continuously.

IT should standardize on:

✦ **Hardware configurations (memory, disk, etc.):** Most of these items are now pretty modest in cost. Choose configurations that should last the life of the machine. The cost of an additional 512 MB of RAM is miniscule compared with the effort to do an upgrade after the fact (order, receive, payment, installation, interruption to user, etc.).

✦ **OS and application software (vendor and version):** The more consistency in your software set the greater the chances of full compatibility of files among users, and the easier the support and training burden is on your staff.

✦ **Software configuration (options, settings, directory and menu location, etc.):** It's not uncommon for application software to have over a hundred various settings (e.g., where to store files, how often to do an automatic backup, etc.). Users are unlikely to ever know about these, and less likely to deal with them. Let IT set standards so that software operates identically for all users. Again, it will pay dividends in the future in terms of support effort.

Non-Standard Requests

While the request for a non-standard mouse or monitor may be a relatively minor issue, the situation changes dramatically for non-standard desktops, laptops, applications, etc. If a user asks for a contact management package, IT has to determine what its ability is to support this tool. In some cases, the users are content to deal with the vendor directly for support as long as IT can install the package and get it running. In other cases, depending on the scope of the request, the business need, etc., IT may have to adjust its model to include these non-standard items as part of the supported suite of products. However, these conversations have to be had with the user community as the products are considered, not after they've already been purchased.

Standards for IT

In addition to technology put into the hands of the users, there are technology products that users are unlikely to ever see (although they may hear them referenced by IT). These include products like servers, routers, switches, storage solutions, gateways, network operating systems, etc.

ITers may have strong feelings about certain products in these categories, but they are unlikely to be swayed by secondary issues such as color or packaging. Perhaps that's because ITers deal with so much technology that some issues seem unimportant while others are paramount. Non-technical people are often surprised by the IT department's standards for using technological products, but they forget that people in IT not only have a deeper understanding of the core technology of the product, they generally have a longer history with the issue in general. IT people know what it means to purchase and install a new product from Microsoft versus one from a startup. The startup's product may have many more bells and whistles, but will the young company offer tech support, volume discounts, maintenance upgrades, and will it even be around two years from now? And, how well does that startup's product integrate with everything else in the environment?

It's generally easier to define these behind-the-scenes standards by finding agreement among some of your more senior engineers. If you have consensus at the top, the rest of the team will probably go along. Some may disagree (making a case that choice X is a far better solution that choice Y), but unless they feel quite strongly about it, they will readily participate in adopting uniform standards.

And, just like workstations for users, infrastructure technology should have standards for configuration, setup, etc. In an environment that has a large volume of servers, for example, engineers should not have to "hunt" for the location of log files. They should know that all servers are set up identically (including naming conventions) so that when there is problem, they can spend their time examining the log file, not looking for it. A comparable analogy can be applied to virtually all technology platforms and makes the case for standardization pretty evident.

9.5 Technology Refreshing

Different types of technologies have different lifetime expectations. Workstations may have a useful life of 3–4 years, as do servers. Networking equipment, like switches and routers, may easily last 5 years, printers may last even longer. On the other hand, laptops and handheld devices are on the shorter end of the spectrum simply because they physically take more abuse, are subject to being lost or stolen, and the technology for these products is evolving rapidly.

Some organizations may set defined refresh cycles, while others may choose to use things until they simply won't operate any more.

Deciding which path to take depends on a few factors:

+ **The cost of vendor warranties after a certain point:** A new server may come with a three-year warranty and service contract, but getting a contract for a four-year-old server may be cost prohibitive. To make this decision, you have to factor in how critical the device is to the environment as well as the cost of the service contract compared to the cost of a new device.

+ **How easy it is to replace a device that fails:** If a printer fails, it's generally not that difficult to press another one into service. Replacing a server could require considerable effort and (down)time before the new one is up and running.

+ **How Accounting depreciates IT assets:** Length of depreciation policies vary widely from company to company; work with your Accounting department to determine what these particular procedures are.

+ **How your company views IT spending:** Some organizations see IT as critical and strategic to their operation and fully endorse appropriate spending so that it remains current. Other organizations see IT spending as merely a cost of doing business (like paying the electric bill), or a necessary evil.

The most important consideration for refreshing a piece of technology often comes when the organization can no longer bear the cost of it:

+ Vendor support is unavailable, or cost prohibitive.

+ The technology is no longer meeting your needs.

✦ The technology presents risks to the environment (reliability, security, etc.)

✦ The technology is holding up other IT projects (e.g., the latest software from your database vendor won't run on your aged server)

As you can see, the "costs" are not always dollars and cents. It will be your job to assess these costs and move to refresh the technology *before* the cost of the not refreshing becomes too high.

9.6 Additional Resources

Web Sites

✦ *www.altiris.com* (technology management solution vendor)

✦ *www.ca.com* (technology management solution vendor)

✦ *www.cisco.com* (technology management solution vendor)

✦ *www.dell.com* (technology management solution vendor)

✦ *www.hp.com* (technology management solution vendor)

✦ *www.ibm.com* (technology management solution vendor)

✦ *www.intel.com/standards/execqa/qa0904.htm* (Craig Barrett on the Importance of Global Standards)

✦ *www.ipswitch.com* (technology management solution vendor)

✦ *www.landesk.com* (technology management solution vendor)

✦ *www.microsoft.com* (technology management solution vendor)

✦ *www.netiq.com* (technology management solution vendor)

✦ *www.netsupport-inc.com* (technology management solution vendor)

✦ *www.novell.com* (technology management solution vendor)

✦ *www.opsware.com* (technology management solution vendor)

✦ *www.peregrine.com* (technology management solution vendor)

✦ *www.remedy.com* (technology management solution vendor)

✦ *www.sunflowersystems.com* (technology management solution vendor)

Books and Articles

✦ McAllister, Neil, "You Can't Kill TCO," *Infoworld*, August 29, 2005, p. 40.

✦ Meyers, Michael, *Mike Meyers' Network+ Guide To Managing and Troubleshooting Networks* (Mike Meyers' Guides), McGraw-Hill/Irwin, 2004.

✦ Pratt, Mary K., "Finding the T in TCO," *Computerworld*, November 11, 2002.

✦ Schiesser, Rob, *IT Systems Management: Designing, Implementing, and Managing World-Class Infrastructures*, Prentice-Hall PTR, 2001.

✦ Stallings, William, *Data and Computer Communications*, Prentice Hall, 2003.

Operations

Nothing endures but change.

—HERACLITUS

For the user community to benefit from the applications and systems they use, a lot of work goes on behind the scenes to make sure that those systems are functioning properly, working reliably, and are readily available.

In this chapter we'll cover some of the fundamentals of the various areas of Operations.

10.1 Operations Center

Depending on the needs of your organization, the Operations Center may be more of a concept than a physical place. Either way, the Operations Center (which might also be called "Systems Operations Center," "Ops," "Network Operations," etc.) performs a number of key duties to help ensure things run smoothly.

CHAPTER TEN

Backup and Restore

Backup is perhaps the simplest and most effective step any environment can take to act as a safety net for recovering from a variety of events from simple human error (e.g., accidental deletions) to disaster (e.g., fire).

In addition to making sure that the backups are performed, your Operations team has a number of responsibilities concerning the backup environment:

- ✦ Checking the logs to make sure that backups are completed successfully and without errors

- ✦ Keeping accurate records so that the correct tapes can be quickly and easily retrieved when data need to be restored

- ✦ Performing tests to confirm data that are backed up can be successfully restored

- ✦ Scheduling the backup jobs to ensure that they don't interfere with application, processing, and transaction jobs

- ✦ Monitoring the amount of time required for backups and alerting the appropriate teams when it appears that the defined backup window isn't long enough

- ✦ Ensuring that newly installed systems are added to the backup cycle

- ✦ Making sure that the tapes in the tape drives, libraries, and changers are replaced on schedule

The subject of backups is covered in more detail in Chapter 16, Storage and Backup (page 433).

Monitoring

As discussed in the first section of Chapter 9, Getting Started with the Technical Environment (page 231), there are a wide variety of tools available for monitoring and managing systems. But like all other tools, simply having them isn't sufficient; they have to be set up, and they have to be used effectively.

The Operations team will be responsible for:

- ✦ Making sure that all scheduled jobs run, and run successfully

- ✦ Correcting basic errors and restarting jobs when they fail

- ✦ Knowing which jobs must run in a certain sequence, and which can run in parallel, as well as the priorities of different jobs

- ✦ Keeping an eye on the monitoring tools, and responding to notifications and alerts

- ✦ Identifying and differentiating among various types of notifications and severities, and taking appropriate action (an indication that disk space has reached the 80% threshold justifies a less urgent response than one indicating it has reached the 98% threshold, or a server crash in the production environment requires a different response than a server crash in the test environment)

- ✦ Knowing the on-call schedule for the IT team, how to reach them, and which team members are responsible for which systems

- ✦ Having procedures for dealing with common warnings, errors, and alerts

- ✦ Doing basic troubleshooting and testing before escalating a problem

- ✦ Having contact information for key vendors (phone numbers, required IDs, etc.)

System Thresholds

Part of the job of the Operations staff and the tools they use include monitoring for different thresholds or parameters. Essentially, these thresholds are the specifications or parameters for normal operations, and if they're exceeded, it could be the indication of a problem. Different types of thresholds may include:

- ✦ CPU utilization

- ✦ Disk space usage

- ✦ Network throughput

- ✦ Application performance

- ✦ Data center facilities (electrical loads, cooling)

- ✦ Number of errors or warnings generated

- ✦ Security alerts

The specifics of the threshold are usually set by representatives from different teams (networking, security, server support, systems development, etc.). In addition, there are different ways to monitor thresholds violations. For example, you may want to set a threshold to receive an alert if the CPU utilization of a server goes above 90%. However, since CPU utilization often has intermittent spikes, you may want to configure the monitoring so that you're only alerted if there's a sustained violation of the threshold (perhaps over 90% for more than two minutes) or if the spike violates the threshold a certain number of times in a given time period.

Similarly, the thresholds may vary by time periods. Since the heavy-duty batch processing mostly happens during the late shift, you may want to relax the thresholds during that period.

After Hours Support

Murphy's Law usually ensures that the worst problems happen when the fewest support people are around. The corollary to this is that when needed, the support people are in transit, at home asleep in bed, or enjoying their weekend or vacations.

Most IT environments are assumed to be 24/7 operations, even though the on-site staff is only there during business hours. Part of the reason for this is because most systems can easily run 24/7, and part of this is because the technology now exists for the support staff to deal with many problems remotely and at any time of day.

Minimizing After Hours Demands

In today's world, everyone who works in IT is usually well aware that their job doesn't end at 5:00 p.m. But the need for after-hours support has to be balanced against the intrusion into the lives of your staff. Put another way, you should set up processes and procedures so that the demands for after-hours support are minimized.

✦ Set up a rotating schedule so that after-hours support responsibility is shared equally among team members. Make sure everyone is aware of the schedule, and have procedures in place if someone needs to make a change.

✦ The on-call schedule should include a backup and primary, as well as a path for escalation.

✦ Define the responsibilities of the backup and primary individuals on call. This could include time frames for responding to alerts, lists of critical and non-critical systems and issues, when to escalate to management, when and how to alert others, etc.

✦ If an on-site Operations staff is available at all times, they should be able to do basic testing, diagnostic, and resolution procedures for routine issues before escalating to the on-call team.

✦ Schedules can be defined (either for monitoring tools, or the Operations Center staff) for different levels of problems. For example, a "critical" problem is called out to the on-call person regardless of the time of day. But, you might decide that "warnings" can wait if they occur between 11 p.m. and 5 a.m.

✦ Provide the on-call staff with the appropriate tools (handheld e-mail devices, cell phones, laptops at home, etc.) to facilitate remote after-hours support.

✦ Make sure that procedures and tools are in place and available for the Operations and Support personnel to record after-hours activities. If a crisis happens during the night, perhaps only the operator and on-call technician are aware of what happened and what steps were taken. If neither is available the next morning, the rest of your staff will need to have a way of learning what took place. Call tracking software (discussed below, as well as in Chapter 17, User Support Services, page 451) is one way of addressing this.

For Companies Without a Full 24/7 Staff

If you don't have the luxury of a 24/7 Operations staff, and are relying on your monitoring tools to notify the after-hours team with pages and e-mails, you should take steps to make sure that these tools are configured to be as effective as possible.

✦ If the tools are sending out alerts for every minor warning, your staff may quickly come to ignore notifications. Of course, this has to be balanced with the need to make sure that critical notifications are sent.

✦ If possible and appropriate, configure the software so that notifications for lower level problems are only sent during certain hours, while more critical notifications are sent regardless of the time.

✦ It may be possible to group alerts. For example, a network problem may cause an alert to be sent for every server on the LAN saying it's not responding. Instead of one alert for each server, you maybe able to configure your management tool to recognize when similar alerts are detected in a short time-frame, and to only send one notification instead of 100. Similarly, a serious of unrelated alerts in a short time frame could be indicative of a larger problem.

✦ Your management tools may be configurable to send repeat alerts at predetermined intervals if no one has logged in to "acknowledge" the event. Similarly, it may be configured to send alerts to other individuals if the event isn't "acknowledged" in a set time frame.

Call Tracking

In Chapter 17, User Support Services (page 451), call tracking is discussed in more detail. While the IT department and the Operations Center will use a variety of tools to track what's going on, the call tracking system is usually at the center of it all. Many of the monitoring tools used by IT integrate directly with popular call tracking software packages. For example, an alert detected by the network monitoring tool automatically creates a ticket in the call tracking software. ("Tickets" or "incidents" are call tracking software mechanisms for tracking problems and their resolutions. At one time, a ticket was a literal item on a piece of paper, but it's now a reference to an entry in a tracking system.)

One of the most important aspects of call tracking software is its ability to serve as the audit trail for what happens with a ticket; that is, keeping track of when the ticket is re-assigned to an individual or a queue, when it is escalated or resolved, recording notes from the technicians, etc.

Because call tracking serves such a critical role to the ongoing operations of the environment, it's vital that the Operations staff be diligent in the use of the tool: that new incidents generate new tickets, that open tickets are monitored and worked on, and that tickets are closed when the issue is resolved.

Key Items to Document in Tracking Tickets

Although most ITers aren't big fans of writing (hence, the uphill battle to get appropriate documentation), it's important that the Operations Center staff develop habits for entering appropriate detail into a ticket. Tickets with descriptions like "system not working" or resolution notes with "problem fixed" are virtually meaningless and will only infuriate anyone else that has to refer to that ticket.

The staff must be diligent in logging details like:

✦ E-mails (and responses) to others about the item

✦ Details of error messages, and other system responses (many call tracking applications allow you to attach external files, such as log files)

✦ Attempts to reach others by phone, or pager, including unsuccessful attempts (like leaving a voice mail, or no answer), and what was discussed and agreed to

✦ Details related to discussions with vendor support (number called, name of the representative spoken to, vendor incident number assigned, summary of discussion, on-site visits, etc.)

✦ Details in regard to problem symptoms such as error messages, slow performance, improper results, etc.

✦ Specific steps taken to resolve the issue, and the results of those steps

Value of Well-Documented Problems

Good detail in the ticket is a value for several reasons:

✦ It provides the necessary detail for discussions with vendors about repetitive problems, poor support, etc.

✦ It allows you to slowly build an in-house knowledge base so that other technicians have the benefit of seeing what was done in the past, when a similar problem comes up

✦ It can be used to validate or refute those who claim that when they reported a problem, nothing was done or they were never contacted

✦ The metrics available from a properly-used call tracking system can be invaluable to you as a manager to help you manage your staff and support your need for additional resources

Most call tracking packages include the ability to attach files to the tickets and automatic date and time stamping of activities, providing an effective trail of what happened.

Ideally, all calls start at the Help Desk, or with the Operations Center, where the ticket is created. But too often, when an issue is brought directly to the attention of an engineer (perhaps by a user, or by the monitoring software), the problem is addressed without any ticket being created, and no documentation is kept. In today's culture of accountability and auditability, all staffers should know that they must create tickets for the work that they do. Not only does this create the proper audit trail, but it also ensures that management can see and monitor the volume of work being done.

Like so many other tools, there are many ways to configure call tracking software so that it is customized for your needs. But, as is always the case, the tools must be used to be effective.

10.2 Multiple Environments

The IT world is in a constant state of flux. The obvious reason is because science marches on to offer new technologies. But that's only part of the reason.
In addition:

✦ User requirements change

✦ Vendors are regularly providing updates, patches, and fixes to existing products

✦ Security threats force the department to adjust

+ New uses are found for existing technologies, requiring new expectations for operations and performance

+ The growth of some applications exceeds expectations. (e-mail is an excellent example)

+ Regulatory compliance requirements impact solutions and procedures

Trying to maintain a stable world as things are constantly changing requires several disciplines to manage how those changes are introduced. One of the most popular of these disciplines is the idea of multiple environments.

By establishing multiple environments, you can test changes prior to their introduction into the production environment that the users access to do what they need.

Types of Environments

Typically, there are three main environments that are known by various names:

1. **Production**: This environment has the live data and the live applications. Changes to this environment are only made after they have been successfully tested in the Test environment. The Production environment has the strictest controls to ensure its integrity.

2. **Test** (sometimes called "stage" or "QA" – "Quality Assurance"): This environment is a virtual duplication of the Production environment (usually both software and hardware). It's where changes are tested to see if they work, as well as to determine what kind of impact they will have on the Production environment.

3. **Sandbox** (sometimes called a "playground" or "Development" environment): The term "sandbox" is appropriate for this environment, because this environment allows the development staff to "play" with various changes. A developer can make a change in the Sandbox to gauge its impact on other portions of the code.

For some organizations, or sometimes even for certain specific applications, there may be a need for additional environments (again, the names may vary):

+ **Demo:** This environment is reserved for the Sales team to demo products to clients and prospects. This is usually a scaled-down replica of the production environment that is loaded with false data. It exists for two reasons: so that sales reps aren't embarrassed during demos by discovering that the system failed because a programmer was testing a change and so that certain data (such as actual names and SSNs) can be stripped off.

✦ **Training:** Similar to the Demo environment, it's a small replica of the Production environment (again, with false data) for training users. In some cases, the training environment may be upgraded before production in order to train users on new enhancements that are going to be implemented in the near future.

✦ **Beta:** In some cases, the user community may have a need for a test environment of their own. This environment is similar to the test environment defined above, but users would be less impacted by the tests that IT is conducting (which might interfere with the users' own testing).

The number of environments required can vary due to a number of factors. You may not have a need for the Training and Demo environments. In smaller organizations, the Sandbox and Test environments may be combined into a single one. For especially critical or sensitive applications, the three main environments can be called for. For less vital applications, you may be able to get away with just one environment by arranging for changes and testing by coordinating a schedule with the user community (and having a back-out plan).

Issues to Consider

There are a number of factors to consider when you have multiple environments:

✦ **Data sensitivity:** Data from the Production environment is often replicated to other environments in order to perform comprehensive testing. However, if the data is sensitive (e.g., salaries, etc.) or considered "personal identifying" (e.g., Social Security numbers and dates of birth) you have to make sure you have a script or utility that changes some of the data, and strips out or alters certain fields and identifiers. This eliminates the risk of the data being available to unauthorized users.

✦ **Frequency of replication:** The Test environment should be a virtual replica of the Production environment in order to ensure effective testing. But if it is updated continuously, it does not allow for anyone to get their testing done. If it was only refreshed quarterly, however, it could be too far out of synch with production to be considered an appropriate test environment. Your final development schedule will best determine how frequently you should update your secondary environments.

✦ **Separation of environments:** Access to the Production environment is carefully controlled to maintain its integrity. The hardware for production is usually dedicated to production. But how far can you afford (in dollars, time, effort, or in risk) to take that concept? In some cases, the Production environment may warrant its own network. For some of the other environments, they may actually reside on the same devices.

✦ **Movement between environments:** How changes are moved between environments (especially production), and who moves them is the subject of change management. (See Section 10.4 on page 270). Typically, developers aren't allowed to move changes (particularly their own) into the Production environment. Very often there may be a small team, usually within the IT Operations group, that is responsible for moving code into production. Alternatively, there may be an automated system used for moving code. The purpose is to make sure that there is an audit trail for changes in production, and to eliminate the risk of a developer making a surreptitious change on their own.

✦ **Cost of multiple environments:** Having more than one of anything is going to cost money — software licenses, hardware, bandwidth, etc. Some software vendors have taken this into consideration and have provisions for licensing their products for developers' use only. Some hardware configurations may warrant duplication in the Test environment (e.g., if production consists of clustered servers, you probably want to also test things on a cluster), while others may not (e.g., monitoring tools). The cost of the "lesser" environments might be mitigated by using server virtualization software, which is discussed in Chapter 14, Software and Operating Systems (on page 383), to have multiple environments on one box, or by using older hardware for them. The redundancies that you have in production (e.g., redundant power supplies, mirroring of data) may not be warranted in the other environments.

✦ **Some things may not warrant replicating:** Again, depending on your specific circumstances, you may not have the need to replicate your entire production environment. For example, the organization's connections to the Internet are often shared by all environments. Similarly, a full-size SAN (storage area network) or dedicated backup library may not be warranted (or affordable) in the test environment. Similarly, production will have the highest SLAs, while the other environments are more relaxed.

Test Environment

After the Production environment, the most important is probably the Test environment, because of the value it brings to your team while helping ensure the stability and reliability of all systems.

A good Test environment offers many benefits:

✦ It allows for testing of the new software and getting exposure to it before it's made available to all the end users in the live production environment

✦ It allows you to assess the impact on performance

✦ It allows you to test back-out procedures

✦ It allows you to test the new features of the software to see if they work as the vendor promised

In general, a Test environment allows you the luxury to evaluate and test the impact of new software on your environment, without disrupting your Production environment. Of course, even the best Test environment is of little value if not used effectively.

Too often, a Test environment is cobbled together with unlicensed software and outdated equipment that's just laying around. In some cases, that system may be entirely adequate for the immediate needs. However, as your company grows, and the organization's dependence on IT grows, it becomes increasingly more important to have a more rigorous Test environment.

The Test environment should essentially have similar class hardware (similarly configured), copies of databases, current versions of software and utilities, and so on. If your shop does a significant amount of in-house development, the Test environment will be regularly used by the programming staff before new applications are moved into production. Each time a problem is found in Production that could have been detected earlier in the Test environment, but was actually missed, it brings further scrutiny to your testing techniques.

In an organization that uses its Test environment effectively, this scrutiny can serve as an iterative self-correcting process to keep the Test environment current and useful.

Finally, you may consider redundant environments. These environments are essentially swapped (cut over) and re-pointed during an upgrade. A new software version is loaded on the Test environment. After the testing is considered successful, the data are moved over and the Test environment is now considered production, and the previous Production environment becomes Test. This technique may not be workable for all systems, but can prove useful in some cases.

10.3 Scheduling Downtime

In a perfect world, everything operates the way it should, and nothing ever goes down (or needs to go down). Alas, that's not the world most of us work in.

Even in a 24/7 world, time has to be found to do upgrades, install new software and hardware, testing, migrations, etc.

While downtime can't be entirely avoided, there are steps you can take to minimize its impact:

1. Accurately estimate the impact of the downtime. If you're upgrading a router, perhaps only the users in remote offices will be affected, and the local users can continue unaffected. Or, if you're doing maintenance on your e-mail environment, your users may be able to continue to use the core business applications. If the core business applications are down, perhaps users will be able to continue to work with word processing and spreadsheets and e-mail in the meantime. So, when estimating the impact, you need to consider who will be affected and what functionality will be affected.

2. Consider the duration of the impact. A half hour in the middle of the day may not seem like much to you or your staff given the magnitude of the problem you are facing, but it can be devastating to a sales rep in mid-demo or a VP in the middle of a presentation to the Board.

Estimating and Scheduling Downtime

When you try to estimate how long downtime will last, there are several components to consider:

✦ The amount of time it takes to bring the systems down from production mode to off-line or maintenance mode

✦ The amount of time required to perform the needed work

✦ The time required to test the work

✦ The time required to return the system back into production mode

✦ The time required to back out, or undo, the work if the test results indicate failure and you have to restore to a pre-maintenance state

✦ And, add just a little bit more time for good measure; better to overestimate your downtime and return the system to the users earlier than expected, than to underestimate and have users frustrated that the system wasn't available to them when you said it would be

Sometimes factors outside your control may determine your downtime schedule. Your local electric utility may tell you of its plans to replace the transformer on the corner that interrupts your electrical service, or an upcoming holiday weekend may be the only opportunity that provides you with sufficient time.

Many sites reserve time each month, or each week, for downtime. The details are very dependent on each environment's particular needs and circumstances. In one environment, taking a few hours on a Sunday afternoon may be fine, in another environment it may have to be 2 a.m. Other sites may choose to only schedule time on an ad hoc basis when it's determined there's a need.

Scheduling Factors

Whichever path you choose, there are some things that you need to consider when scheduling down-time:

+ Impact to the users, customer, or partners

+ Impact to the business — even if the users aren't online, there could be important resources and tasks running

+ Availability of vendor support if you need them off hours

+ Scheduling enough time to do the work, and any back-out plans that might be required

+ Availability of staff — sometimes your staff might prefer to work as long as it takes on a Friday night, as opposed to having to interrupt their Saturday

+ Various departments' busy periods, or special projects they may be working on

+ Multiple time zones — if you have users in other time-zones, make sure you're considering the impact of the downtime schedule in all the various local times

When you take all the requirements, constraints, and variables into play, you'll find that in most cases there is no downtime that works well for everyone. In cases like this, you have to make judgment calls as to where the least impact will be.

Regardless of the schedule, proper communications to the user community is essential (see the next section).

Downtime Communications

If you choose to schedule downtime on a recurring basis, such as weekly or monthly, you'll want to make sure that the policy is posted somewhere users are likely to see it, and that users are periodically reminded of the schedule on a regular basis. A weekly e-mail to the effect of "Reminder: the system will be down for maintenance every Wednesday between 7:00 p.m. and 9:00 p.m." will keep everyone on the same page.

If downtime is more on an ad hoc basis, you want to develop an effective process of communicating plans to the users. Some mechanisms include:

- ✦ E-mail to users
- ✦ Voice mail broadcasts to users
- ✦ Messages that display during the network login process (as part of a script)

While communicating to the users is always a good idea, there are a number of factors to consider:

- ✦ Users may quickly get in the habit of deleting messages from IT, especially if they find that they don't understand the content, or if they feel they're overwhelmed by messages from IT
- ✦ Provide too much advance notice, and the users will likely forget about it
- ✦ Provide too little notice (like announcing a weekend of downtime a day in advance) and you may have users angry at you because you're not giving them a chance to adjust for it and work with you if the schedule is a problem
- ✦ During bigger downtime events (such as when you're moving the data center across town) you need to be more aggressive in communicating not only the downtime, but potential unforeseen issues as well

Try to develop short, simple, and meaningful communications for your users. And try to use a consistent format so that they can quickly find the part that might be important to them. See Figure 10.1 for an example.

Sample Downtime Communications

- ✦ Use subject lines that have specific information, such as:
  - ✦ System Downtime: Apr-15, e-mail and print servers
  - ✦ IT Maintenance will occur on Dec-6, affecting Internet access.
- ✦ In the body of the e-mail, be kind to the users. Don't go into technical jargon, or list server names (unless they have meaning for users). Provide a brief summary using phrases and terms that are meaningful to your user community. For example, your users may know what the HRIS system is, but may not be familiar with the name PeopleSoft, or vice versa.

From: **IT Support Center**
Sent: **Thursday, December 6, 2007 8:31 AM**
To: **All Users**
Subject: **PLEASE REVIEW — Important: Scheduled Outage for Dec 11th.**
Importance: **High**

On December 11th from 8:00 PM to 10:00 PM the IT department will be performing system maintenance.

Areas That Will Be Affected:
- Network Printing.
- Network File Access & Sharing.

Areas That Are Not Affected:
- Access to the Internet.
- E-mail connectivity.
- Peoplesoft and Warehouse Inventory System.

If you have any questions regarding this, please contact the IT Support Center at 212-555-1212

Figure 10.1   Downtime Communications Example

+ List which services will be up, and which services will be down

+ Provide the beginning and end time of the outage

+ Let the user know who to contact, or where to call, if they have questions or concerns

The users don't need to know the details of the actual work being done (unless it's a noticeable or important change). The phrase "system maintenance" is oftentimes a sufficiently generic explanation for routine activities like applying patches, upgrading a server's BIOS, doing database maintenance, etc.

You may have a situation where you're unsure if the work being done will actually impact the users, or while the work may take quite a bit of time, the impact to the users will be very limited. In situations like this, instead of blocking out all the downtime, you may want to say that there will be "intermittent interruptions in service" during the specified period.

Downtime Communications Example

Also consider having the messages come from an IT mailbox, as opposed to that of an individual IT staffer.

Communicating to Other Groups within IT

In larger IT departments, there's often a problem with internal communications: One group neglects to notify other groups of what they're doing. For example, the networking team may be frantically working to resolve a problem, but they never advised others in IT. In the meantime, the server team is trying to figure out why their servers aren't responding properly, and the Help Desk is unaware of what's going on aside from the calls coming in from the users. Similarly, when the problem is corrected and the networking team can catch its breath, they may forget to alert the Help Desk that the crisis is over and that users can be advised that everything is now working normally.

While the generally worded e-mail in Figure 10.1 might be appropriate for the user community, ITers need a lot more detail. This topic is discussed further in the next section on change management. But in short, all IT groups should be aware of downtime activities and plans.

Prior to the downtime, notifications should include:

✦ Details of what the change is, and why it's being done (external resources like notes on a vendor Web site may be worth including), and what areas it could impact

✦ The testing that was done in advance to ensure that the change won't have an impact to the environment

✦ What testing will be done to ensure the work was successful

✦ Plans for backing out the work if it doesn't go as planned

Following the work, updates should be sent to indicate if the work went as planned, if it had to be backed out, details on any unexpected findings, etc. Not only is it good for others to have as much information as possible, but it's also your responsibility as a manager to develop a culture of open communications. You always want to avoid having things not go as planned simply because someone on your team didn't know what was going on.

Communicating changes internally to IT is a key aspect of the discussion in the next section.

10.4 Change Management

As discussed earlier in this chapter, IT environments are in a constant state of flux with upgrades, migrations, system changes, etc. Combine all that change with the complexity found in most environments, and it's not surprising to discover that a change made in one place can easily impact many other areas. In larger environments where the IT department may consist of several teams, each focusing on a specific area, the significance of this issue becomes magnified. Not unlike pulling a single thread and seeing how it's integral to the whole tapestry, watching change unfold in IT departments is often a very informative (and scary) activity.

"Change management" (also known as "change control") is the standard process for ensuring that your environment does not suffer as a result of all this change. As the name implies, the intent is to make sure that change is managed as it's introduced into the environment, and managed in such as a way to minimize adverse impact to the others, like the user community, the systems, and the support staff.

Like so many other areas of business, the hallmark of good change management is good communication — making sure that everyone who should know about a change, does know.

The principles of Change Management include making sure that any change to the environment is:

+ Tested

+ Documented

+ Scheduled

+ Properly planned (including a back-out procedure)

+ Communicated

+ Approved

+ Executed

Typically, each change that is put through the process is called a Change Request (CR). Sometimes circumstances dictate immediate action, and some of the above steps need to be severely curtailed or skipped entirely. This is usually the case of an urgent situation, and requires an emergency CR, which is discussed later in this chapter in the section, Emergency Change Requests (ECR) on page 276.

The mechanics of how CRs are managed and tracked will vary from organization to organization. Smaller organizations may find that e-mail and meetings are sufficient. Larger organizations may make use of special software or components of other IT toolsets (e.g., from vendors like Remedy, IBM, Computer Associates, etc.). These tools keep track of CRs with the same rigor that call tracking software is used for tracking calls to the Help Desk.

Which Changes Need CRs?

While few ITers can make a case against change management, the challenge becomes where to draw the line, which changes have to go through the formal change management process, and which changes are considered so routine or minor they don't require it.

For example:

+ Adding a new printer and print queue to the network

+ Changing a switch port from auto-sensing the speed to 100 Mb

+ Updating information on the company's Web site

+ Adding a new field to a database

+ Changing the password on the administrator's account

+ Connecting a new server to the network

It could be argued that each of the above are so routine that unless there is something special about an implementation, it isn't necessary to go through the formalized change management process. On the other hand, with each of the above scenarios, one could imagine circumstances that result in some severe problems or in which these activities would require auditability in the future.

As the IT Manager, you'll have set the guidelines for which changes require the formalized process and which don't. One general rule is that the formal process isn't required if the change is routine and common and there's a virtual certainty that there's no risk and no one else needs to be aware of this particular change. However, in heavily regulated industries (e.g., finance, healthcare) the scope of changes that must be put through the formal change management process may be quite broad.

Change Management Principles

Each IT environment will have to set their own rules, guidelines, and procedures for dealing with changes. But, there are some common themes and principles.

Testing

Changes to the environment should be tested prior to implementation. Depending on the nature of the change, you may be able to test in a separate environment (e.g., a new version of the finance system). Other times you may not have that luxury, or it may not be feasible (e.g., switching ISPs) and you may only be able to do limited testing prior to implementation, and/or the testing has to be done in production during off hours.

It's important that testing be comprehensive and addresses all scenarios. For example, if you're upgrading the backup software on your servers, you'd want to test it with all the different versions of the operating system that you have. Similarly, if you're adding a secondary DNS server, you want to be sure that it's working for users that connect remotely as well as locally. There are many different types of testing to consider, and there's a discussion of these in the later section Types of Testing on page 278.

Testing Before and After Implementation   While testing something before it's implemented gives a good comfort level that it will work in production, it's just as vital to test the change in production after it's implemented. The IT industry is full of war stories of "no-brainer" changes that were implemented with no testing, only to discover that a brain was indeed required.

Documenting

Good documentation is a recurring theme in this book. Good documentation is an important aspect of change management because it will serve as the basis for communicating to others what change is being made. And, like all documentation, it serves as excellent reference material in the future when there's a need to see how something was done before — there is no point re-inventing the wheel. For change requests, a good portion of the documentation may have been done by the associated vendor(s). README files, or pages at the vendor's Web site, can provide excellent information.

The documentation for a change request should include what testing was done, how it was tested and the results, and the high-level steps that will be taken for implementing.

Scheduling

Section 10.3 on page 265 goes into detail about scheduling downtime. However, not every CR requires downtime. For example, a vendor may state quite directly whether or not one of their upgrades requires a re-start or re-boot or if it can be done without interruption.

Still, even if a CR doesn't require downtime, the fact that a CR is done represents that there's at least some concern about impact. As such, it may need to be done during off hours.

As an IT Manager, you may also want to set some guidelines about timing; for example, you may want to say that all changes have to be done on the weekends. Or, you may want to say that at least 48-hours notice has to be given for any change to ensure that all parties have a chance to know about it, raise their questions and concerns, and approve it.

Of course, depending on the same circumstances, some changes may be considered urgent and simply can't wait for the normal cycle.

Planning

The planning aspect of a CR takes into consideration all the steps necessary to make sure that the change is successful. This could include:

+ Taking a backup prior to implementing the change

+ Making sure appropriate resources (both internal and external) are available

+ Coordinating activities with other related change requests

+ Testing post-implementation

+ Determining who needs to be notified

+ Sequencing of events (e.g., upgrading the operating system on the database server can't happen until the database is stopped, and the database can't be stopped until the applications are halted)

+ Determining the impact to other areas. For example, if a server is being replaced, the Operations group will need to make sure that the new device is included in the backup processes; similarly, the server monitoring and management tools will have to be updated so that they are aware of this new device

Communicating

Communicating the change is the most critical aspect of the change management process. For the most part, the communication is a summary of all the pertinent information. The communication mechanism could be an e-mail or a referral to a specific record in a change management tool.

Information that should be included:

+ A summary overview of what the change is, and why it's being done

+ If available, vendor files, or links to Web sites that provide appropriate details about what is being changed, upgraded, implemented, etc.

◆ An indication of who requested the change, and who is implementing the change (including emergency contact information)

◆ What systems, services, or resources will be impacted by the change; this could be users, applications, hardware, etc.

◆ The date and time the change will be implemented, and how much time is allotted for the change

◆ Whether or not user notification is required (this could be the Help Desk's cue to prepare a communication to the affected user community)

◆ What backup steps will be taken prior to implementing the change

◆ What prior testing was done in regard to this change

◆ What testing will be done after the change is implemented to confirm that all things are operating properly

The information listed above is designed for other ITers, and the level of technical jargon and detail should be enough for them to understand the impact of the change. Communication to the users doesn't need to contain this level of detail, as explained earlier in the section Downtime Communications (page 267).

But, like the communications to the users, change request communications should have a consistent format so that everyone becomes accustomed to them and can immediately find the information they need.

Communicating Before and After The previous discusion described what should be communicated about the change, and if everything went as planned, that might be sufficient. However, things sometimes don't always go as planned. Therefore, it's important that a communication go out as follow-up so that everyone will know how things went.

This could include:

◆ An indication of whether the change was successful, partially successful, failed, took longer than expected, canceled, or backed out (along with appropriate explanation)

◆ The results of the testing after the change was implemented

◆ An indication if the back-out process was successful (if it was needed)

Getting Approval

While the previous discussion of communication is the key process to ensure that everyone has a chance to raise questions and concerns about the CR, many environments don't want to take silence as a tacit approval for the CR. It's quite common to have formal change management review and approval procedures.

Many environments have formalized meetings that may occur every week or two (depending on the policy for scheduling changes) to review and approve each CR. These meetings and procedures could include ground rules such as:

✦ Each CR must have the approval from a manager or director of each IT group that it may relate to (e.g., security, infrastructure, desktop, database administrators, systems development, etc.)

✦ A request can be denied if there is insufficient detail

✦ A request can be denied if the requestor fails to show up at the review meeting to answer questions that arise

It's entirely possible that as a result of the review and approval process, a CR may be adjusted slightly, rescheduled, or put on hold because of insufficient testing, or rejected altogether.

Executing

If all the steps described above are taken, the actual implementation of the change should go smoothly. But never take anything for granted.

✦ The planning and testing phases yield useful information — don't ignore it

✦ Make sure appropriate resources (internal and external) are available to ensure a successful implementation, as well as to deal with any emergency that may arise

✦ Test the change after it's made to ensure it's doing what it's supposed to, and that it hasn't had any adverse impacts

✦ Communicating the results of the change

Emergency CRs

The previous discussion assumes that circumstances allow enough time for all CR to go through a defined process. While that may be true for most, it will not be true for all CRs. For those situations when time is of the essence, there is the Emergency Change Request (ECR).

There are plenty of reasons and examples of needs for ECRs:

✦ A critical security flaw is discovered and needs to be patched

✦ A crisis arises (e.g., hardware or line failure)

✦ An approved CR has an unexpected impact elsewhere in the environment and a subsequent change needs to be made (the new server for the Accounting department is bogging down the entire system)

✦ Another environment (supplier, partner, sister company) made a change to their environment without informing you, and you need to make a change to restore interoperability with them

For ECRs, the process is similar but shortened considerably. These requests don't follow the procedures outlined above for requests. Often they are not:

✦ **Tested properly:** It is entirely possible that the nature of this particular change doesn't allow for testing, or only minimal testing.

✦ **Documented in a timely manner:** Due to the urgency of the situation, the documentation is sometimes not done until *after* the change is implemented.

✦ **Well scheduled:** Often emergency changes are implemented "right now!" In other cases, they may be able to wait until the next "quiet" period, which could be as soon as lunch, or 5:01 p.m., or commonly (and unfortunately), 5:00 a.m.

✦ **Properly planned** (including a back-out procedure): By definition, emergency changes don't have the luxury of planning.

✦ **Communicated clearly:** Like the documentation, the urgent nature of the situation may mean that the communication provides minimal advance notice, or may not come until after the change is implemented.

✦ **Properly approved:** Instead of the normal review and approval process, an emergency change might only be approved by one manager or director. In truly urgent situations, the only approval might be the good sense and judgment of the engineer on call at the time.

✦ **Executed well:** Since ECRs can't be put through the normal management and control process, there's a heavy reliance on the skill and expertise of the individual(s) involved at the time.

Enterprise-Wide Changes

In a large environment (with multiple locations and/or multiple servers) it may be possible to perform the upgrade on only a portion of the environment. Most vendors realize that it may not be logistically possible to upgrade an entire environment at once and usually write their software to be compatible with its own earlier versions.

This backward compatibility feature is especially true with software such as operating systems and e-mail. If this is the case for your environment, you should consider selecting a specific site (or server) to be the first candidate to be upgraded. By doing so, you minimize the impact to the entire environment, you gain experience as you upgrade more and more of the environment, and you build the confidence of your users/customers/partners as they see that the initial upgrades went well.

10.5 Types of Testing

Testing can be a whole area of study in itself (several books listed at the end of this chapter are just about the topic of testing). As shown in table 10.1, there are a number of different types of tests that can be used, depending on the circumstances:

Different Approaches to Testing

Just as there are different aspects of systems to test, there are different ways to approach testing. In general, there are two different testing methodologies. Which one is used depends on how much knowledge the tester has of the system.

White Box Testing (Sometimes called "Glass Box," "Clear Box," or "Open Box" Testing)

In White Box testing, the tester has knowledge of the operation of the system being tested and how it's supposed to work. This essentially allows the tester to focus more on those areas known to be particularly complex, problematic, etc.

Black Box Testing (Sometimes called "Opaque Box" or "Closed Box" Testing)

Black Box testing is testing without knowledge of how the system being evaluated operates. One advantage of Black Box testing is that it helps to identify ambiguity or contradiction in the system. More importantly, it can identify problems that occur when the system is used in a way the developer didn't expect (e.g., illegal inputs, performing steps out of sequence, etc.).

Post-Implementation Testing in Production

No test environment will be an exact replica of the production environment. There may be differences in hardware, users' activity, and so on. When you

Table 10.1 Types of testing

Type of Test	Description
Compatibility Testing	This set of tests confirms compatibility of different hardware and software platforms. For example, you might test client software with different operating system versions, or Web pages might be tested with a variety of different browsers.
Function Testing	This set of tests is used to confirm that the item being tested is doing what it's supposed to: that it meets the defined specifications and requirements. This testing can be extensive since all features must be examined using a combination of good and bad data. While developers routinely test for the "expected," the challenge is to test for the "unexpected." This might include erroneous data, doing things out of normal sequence (like logging the receipt of new inventory in the warehouse, before placing the order), etc.
Integration Testing *(passing data)*	This set of tests is used to see how well various components (after they have been individually tested in unit testing) integrate. It is possible that each of the parts may test successfully during unit testing, but problems arise when they are tested with each other.
Performance Testing	This set of tests is used to benchmark (generally in terms of speed) the performance of the item being tested. This not only ensures that the item performs as needed, but to see how it impacts the performance of other parts of the environment. For example, with a new module for transmitting payroll records to the bank, you would want to test that (1) the process completes in a timely manner; and (2) that the process does not have an adverse impact on components like your network, which might in-turn impact the performance of other applications.
Regression Testing	Regression testing is similar to function testing. However, regression testing is focused on ensuring that updates to a program do not introduce new problems or errors at the same time it's attempting to resolve known bugs, or add new functions. It makes sure that the quality of the new version is at least as good as the previous version.

(Cont.)

Table 10.1 Types of testing (continued)

Type of Test	Description
Stress Testing	This set of tests is similar to performance testing. However, it focuses on evaluating how well the item performs under different loads. The results of this testing may show that the performance decreases proportionally with increased loads, or that at a certain point performance deteriorates dramatically, and perhaps even crashes the system.
Unit Testing (sometimes called "Component Testing")	Unit testing is similar to function testing. However, in unit testing, only a specific component (or unit) of the system is tested. Its integration with other components isn't tested; that is done during integration testing.
User Acceptance Testing (sometimes called "UAT")	As the name implies, this set of tests is done by the end-user and is usually the last set of tests done. It's the opportunity to see if the system is operating as they expected, and need, it to.

make a change in your production environment, you want the upgrade process to include some tests for success.

These tests might include:

+ Running programs and procedures (perhaps vendor-supplied) to ensure the upgrade process was complete, and the system status is as it should be

+ Running some production batch jobs

+ Having users test the systems

+ Comparing pre- and post-upgrade statistics and information to ensure the integrity of the system

10.6 Additional Resources

Web Sites

+ *searchwebservices.techtarget.com/gDefinition/0,294236,sid26_gci927714,00.html* (trouble ticket defined)

✦ *www.buzzle.com/editorials/4-10-2005-68350.asp* (White Box testing strategy)

✦ *www.findtech.com/keyword,Problem+*Ticket+Management/search. htm?& (problem ticket management)

✦ *www.scism.sbu.ac.uk/law/Section5/chap3/s5c3p23.html* (Black Box and White Box testing compared)

Books and Articles

✦ Anthes, Gary H., "ITIL Catches On: British-Bred Quality Framework is Becoming the Tool of Choices at US Data Centers," *Computerworld*, October 31, 2005, p. 39.

✦ Black, Rex, *Managing the Testing Process: Practical Tools and Techniques for Managing Hardware and Software Testing*, Wiley, 2002.

✦ Garbaczeski, Paul, "Inside the Software Testing Quagmire," *CIO Magazine*, November 15, 2005, p. 38.

✦ Jayaswal, Kailash, *Administering Data Centers: Servers, Storage, and Voice over IP*, Wiley, 2005.

✦ Levinson, Meredith, "Testing 1, 2, 3. . . ," *CIO Magazine*, November 15, 2005, p. 63.

✦ Lientz, Bennet P., and Rea, Kathryn P., *Breakthrough IT Change Management: How to Get Enduring Change Results*, Butterworth-Heinemann, 2003.

✦ Whittaker, James A., *How to Break Software: A Practical Guide to Testing*, Addison Wesley, 2002.

Physical Plant

I do not fear computers. I fear the lack of them.

—ISAAC ASIMOV

The value of Information Technology is really in the applications. But all those applications require hardware, and all that hardware requires care and feeding, not to mention physical space, electricity, air conditioning, etc.

This chapter covers the physical plant issues related to IT:

✦ **Data Center:** Where all the centralized equipment is kept (servers, routers, switches, telephone systems, communications, lines, storage, etc.)

✦ **Cabling:** The physical issue of connecting all the hardware together, both for items in the computer room, as well as for items that need to connect back to the computer room (like the computers and printers in your department)

The topic of the physical plant is one that requires working close with your company's Building Facilities department. They will most likely be the ones that arrange for the construction, the electrical, and the HVAC experts

CHAPTER ELEVEN

that you'll need. Additionally, there are specialists in the field of data centers who can be enormous help not only in the planning of data centers, but coordinating activities and plans for moving to a new data center.

11.1 Data Center

Often referred to as a "computer room," data centers can vary in size from a few hundred to over 10,000 square feet. Data centers are typically characterized by raised flooring, rows and rows of equipment cabinets, lots of air conditioning, and a fair amount of noise due to the fans on the equipment and the super-sized air conditioning.

Sizing a Data Center

Trying to estimate the size of a new data center presents enormous challenges. You're not only estimating the physical space, and trying to factor in growth, but your estimates will be used to scale the electrical and air conditioning facilities in the data center. And, as you're trying to estimate a reasonable growth factor, you also have to make educated guesses about future changes in technology (such as increased server density) that could impact the data center services.

As you're trying to do this, you may feel pressure from your organization to keep the data center as small as possible. After all, not only is the data center square footage more expensive (construction, ongoing maintenance, etc.) than traditional office-space, but every square foot that you require is another square foot that can't be used for offices, cubicles, conference rooms, etc.

While overestimating the size of a data center does lead to waste, think of the ramifications of underestimating the size. Having to expand a data center is a very large undertaking, and very expensive. The construction involved and the need to re-engineer the environmental facilities, all having to be coordinated so that it doesn't impact the day-to-day operations, is an enormous effort.

Electrical

As technology marches on, most equipment has gotten significantly smaller. Not too long ago, the largest server available from Compaq (now Hewlett-Packard) was the Proliant 7000 and took up 14 U of rack space. (See the section

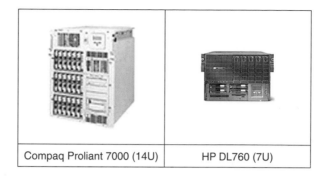

| Compaq Proliant 7000 (14U) | HP DL760 (7U) |

Figure 11.1   Compaq's Largest Server in 1998 (left), and 2006 (right)

later in this chapter about cabinets, page 293, for a definition of "'U.") As of this writing, the largest server available from Hewlett-Packard is 7 U (see Figure 11.1). The most often used servers are frequently 2 U or 4 U, with 1 U servers becoming quite popular. Shrinking server sizes mean greater density, which drives up electrical and cooling needs.

As such, where you used to be able to get just a handful of servers into a typical equipment cabinet, you can now easily get 20, 30, and possibly 40 into a single cabinet. If you're using blade technology for your servers, the number can approach 100. In short, you can now squeeze a lot more processing power into radically less space. In data center parlance, this is called "density."

However, the equipment and cooling requirements for a cabinet holding 5 or 6 servers is very different from that required for a rack holding 20, 40, 60, or 80 servers.

Estimating Power Needs

Back in the IBM mainframe days, a data center may have required about 40 W per square foot. Today, with its significantly higher density of servers, 100 W per square foot is often used as a rule of thumb, 300 W per square foot may be used for particularly high-density environments, and there are those in the field predicting that usage could go easily surpass 500 W per square foot and approach 1000 in 5–10 years.

The per-square-foot measure can lead to some confusion unless it's clarified: Does the square footage include the total data center space, or just the space occupied by IT equipment? Throw in some gray areas (e.g., storage, clearance space for the equipment, space for console operators, space used by cooling and power equipment), and it gets even murkier. As such, it's becoming more common to estimate power in terms of requirements per-cabinet.

Today, it's not unusual to use a rule of thumb of 4.0 kW per cabinet. At the low end of the spectrum, you may have a cabinet that consumes less than 100 W. This would be a cabinet with perhaps just a few pieces of equipment. At the high end, it might be a rack filled with the 1 U servers, and could draw 15–20 kW or more. Today, 4 or 5 kW per cabinet is commonly used for planning purposes.

Scaling the power needs of the data center is more art than science. While it can be a straightforward exercise to determine the power requirements of all the equipment you have today, projecting future growth is less exact. Even more difficult is trying to determine how technology advances, and how much more equipment you'll be able to squeeze into the same amount of space thereby drawing more and more power. And, to make matters more complex, the power estimates that you come up with are the foundations for sizing not only the electrical supply to the data center, but the PDU, UPS, EPS, and the generator's fuel tank as well. (These items are all discussed below.)

Another factor to keep in mind while you're planning is that when equipment is initially turned on and powered up, it generally draws more power than it does when running in a steady state. Typically, this is more of a case for devices that have mechanical components (e.g., disk drives and fans that have to get up to speed).

It's unlikely that you'll have to turn on every device in your computer room simultaneously, so this isn't a significant concern. However, it could come into play on a smaller scale, like powering up every device in a rack at the same time. The problem is generally solved by waiting a few seconds between each device. In fact, some power strips that are installed in equipment cabinets have this intelligence built in: When the power strip is first plugged in, it will automatically provide power to one outlet at a time, in sequence. Some power strips have digital displays to show how much power they're drawing, which can help for monitoring, expansion, and growth planning. Some power strips even have an Ethernet jack so they can be connected to your LAN so that you can monitor and manage them remotely, and have them send alerts when needed.

Uninterruptible Power Supply

Most data centers are equipped with an Uninterruptible Power Supply (UPS) as a way of protecting the equipment and data. A sudden loss, drop, or spike in power can seriously damage hardware. Not only might the hardware be ruined, but the data on the disk drives could be lost. In addition, the ensuing downtime could result in a huge financial impact to the organization.

The UPS is designed to filter the electricity that comes in from "the street" (i.e., your local power company) and to "smooth out" the fluctuations of power that may be present. Just as important is the temporary power that a UPS can provide when the power dips or goes out completely.

Batteries   The batteries in a UPS (which account for the substantial size and weight of UPS devices) are charged during normal operations by the power coming in from the street. In case of a blackout, or even a momentary loss of power, the batteries continue to provide electricity to your computer room.

In the event of a blackout, the UPS will provide electricity for a finite amount of time, which could vary from minutes to hours, depending on the size of the UPS and the electrical load connected to it. When the lights do go out, the UPS batteries are providing you (and the equipment) enough time to either shut down the equipment safely, or switch to another power source (i.e., a generator).

While the UPS batteries may provide enough time for you to go to each device and manually shut it down, they may not provide enough time if the blackout occurs in the middle of the night, and you have to drive to the office and walk up 25 flights of stairs to get to the equipment.

Server Shutdown Software   Fortunately, UPS manufacturers have options that will send a signal to your computers to let them know that they should invoke their shutdown process. This happens by connecting the UPS to your network, and installing special software from the UPS manufacturer on your servers. When the UPS detects that the power has gone out, it sends a signal to your servers, via the UPS unit's interface to your network. The UPS software on your servers detects this signal and then determines what to do, based on how the software is configured. Remember that, because of the electricity provided by the UPS batteries, without this software, your servers wouldn't know anything was wrong, and would continue to hum along until the last ounce of juice was drained from the UPS batteries.

Typically, the software won't direct the servers to do an immediate shutdown. Generally, the software is configured to wait a predetermined time before doing so. The theory (or hope) is that power may be restored relatively soon. If that's the case, the UPS interface to your network will alert your servers that all is well. The UPS software can also log events and send out messages.

The important thing to remember about UPS devices is that over time, the amount of power you get from the batteries can diminish. This is because you typically are adding equipment to your environment. The more equipment you add, the faster it will drain the batteries when there is a blackout, which in turns shrinks the length of time your equipment will have electricity.

It's also important to remember that the batteries in your UPS will eventually have to be replaced, even if you never suffer a blackout. Specifications vary from manufacturer to manufacturer, but the batteries typically have to be replaced every few years. This isn't a cheap process — the batteries themselves are expensive, plus their weight usually means expensive shipping charges, and a fair amount of labor for that heavy lifting. On top of that, environmental regulations generally require specialized handling when disposing of the old batteries.

Power Distribution Units

The Power Distribution Units (PDUs) are akin to the circuit breakers in homes. As the name implies, the PDU distributes electrical power to specific areas or components in a data center. By separating power within the room, power to some devices can be cut off without affecting other devices. This means that one malfunctioning device having some sort of electrical problem (e.g., circuit overload or short circuit) won't affect everything else in the equipment room.

For purposes of load-balancing and redundancies, it's common to have more than one PDU in a computer room (see the section, Equipment Power, below).

Emergency Power Supply

For those operations that require 24/7 up-time, you may need to consider an Emergency Power Supply (EPS), which is usually a diesel-powered generator. The generators are usually outside the building, oftentimes on the roof.

The generators are usually configured to automatically start when needed. Since there is some lag time before the generators come online, the UPS batteries will continue to provide power to your environment to fill the gap between the loss of street power, and the supply of generator power.

While you obviously have to size the generator to provide sufficient power for your environment, you also have to think about the size of the diesel tanks you'll install to provide fuel for the generator. Not only do you have to consider how long a blackout may last, but you'll also have to give thought to what impact an extended blackout may have on fuel deliveries.

Emergency Power Off Switch

Virtually all data centers have a big red switch known as the Emergency Power Off (EPO) switch. The EPO switch is used in only the severest emergencies, where it's necessary to turn off power to the entire data center instantly. Typically, this is only to prevent harm to human life or to prevent major damage to the facility (perhaps in the case of electrocution or fire). When the EPO switch is used, there is no battery power, no smooth shut down. For those who have been in a data center when the EPO switch is pressed, it's instantly recognizable from the deafening silence that occurs.

Since the lights in the data center are generally not connected to the specialized power of the data center, they usually stay on when the EPO switch is pressed.

Veterans of the IT industry can usually share a war story of an EPO switch pressed by accident. Typically, since the EPO switch is near the data center door, someone has mistaken it for the door-release button. That's why you often see the EPO button protected by some sort of Plexiglas door or flap that must be lifted.

Equipment Power

Virtually all the "significant" equipment (i.e., servers, routers, switches, etc.) will either come with two power supplies, or have the option for a second, redundant power supply. It's only smaller devices (e.g., modems, monitors, printers, workstations, etc.) that will have only a single power supply. Some larger devices (like tape libraries, storage area networks, etc.) may have what's called "N + 1" power. In these cases, N is the variable that refers to the number of power-supplies required for the device to operate, and the +1 refers to an additional power supply that acts as a redundant spare.

A redundant power supply in the equipment is a very convenient redundancy as the power supply is one of the components in IT equipment that's more likely to fail. Having a second power supply already built in to the components means the device will keep running when one power supply fails.

A related convenience is that each power supply can be plugged into different circuits (usually referred to as A and B legs), which in turn may be connected to separate PDUs, which are connected to separate UPS units. With a setup like this, any interruption of service that comes through on the A leg (tripped circuit breaker, failed PDU, etc.), will not interfere with the power coming through on the B leg, ensuring that your server stays up. In a scenario like this, it's important to ensure that each leg can handle the full load if its partner fails. For example, if the A leg fails, and all the equipment starts drawing more power from the B leg, the demand can't be so high as to trip the circuit breaker for the B leg. As a result, most planners won't load a circuit to more than 50% of it's amperage capacity. In fact, to provide an extra buffer, it's sometimes limited to 40%.

208 V versus 120 V   One of the issues you'll face with equipment is whether it should run at 208 or 120 V. In general, larger devices like servers, switches, routers, etc., can run at either voltage. Smaller devices (monitors, modems, etc.) will generally only support 120 V.

Certainly, 120 V has the convenience factor in its favor. Virtually all of North America is wired for 120 V, and any outlet you'll run into, whether in the home or office, is 120 V. So why the discussion of 208 V? A device that's running at 208 V will generally draw less power (watts) than it does when running at 120 V. Therefore, everything used to bring power to that device will run cooler, which reduces the risk of eventual failure. And, since a 208 V circuit can deliver more wattage, you can power more from it. Another advantage of 208 V is that the power cords and outlets are twist locks, which means they will be more securely connected, which minimizes the chance of being knocked loose. When you have the choice, you must be sure to order your devices with the correct power cord — it's often overlooked in the process, and more than one project delay has been caused because the hardware arrived, but with the wrong power-cord.

While many devices will run either at 120 V or 208 V, you may undoubtedly have some devices that that will either run only at 120 V or only at 208 V.

Vendor spec sheets (generally always available at their Web site) are full of information about power requirements for their equipment.

HVAC

Once you provide enough electricity for your data center, the environmental control you have to worry about next is the air conditioning. This falls under the rubric of HVAC (heating, ventilation, and air conditioning).

Cooling Requirements

Computer equipment produces value and information and it also produces a lot of heat.

In your home, cooling specifications for air conditioners (such as window units) are usually expressed in British Thermal Units (BTUs). But, in a larger setting, like a data center, air-conditioning capacity is measured in tons.

$$12,000 \text{ BTUs/hour} = 1 \text{ Ton of cooling}$$

To determine how much cooling capacity you need, you can check vendor Web sites. In many cases, specifications are listed for the BTU rating. If not, work with the power specifications to determine how much cooling you need.

$$1 \text{ watt of power} = 3.41 \text{ BTUs/hour}$$

Combining the above formula with the previous formula:

$$\text{One Ton of cooling} = 3.51 \text{ kW of power}$$

The same issues that make it a challenge to decide how much electricity to provide a computer room, also affect figuring out how much air conditioning to provide. These are issues of growth and changes in technology that could mean more densely packed equipment requiring more power and also generating more heat in the same space.

Chillers and Air Handlers

In an air conditioning system, the chiller is the piece of equipment that produces the chilled water. The chiller is usually outside of the computer room, and is usually out of doors — possibly on the roof. The chilled water is then distributed via pipes to the computer room.

In the data center, the chilled water runs through an air-handler unit. The air handlers blow air against the chilled pipes, creating cool air, which then cools the computer room. In a raised-floor data center, the air handlers force the air below the raised floor, which is called "pressurizing the floor," and the air then rises up through perforated tiles, or through the equipment cabinets.

Theory and preferences vary, but data centers are generally kept at about 65 degrees Fahrenheit. Some rooms are kept so cold that a collection of winter jackets is kept in the hallway outside of the room so that they're readily available for technicians to don before entering the data center to do work.

Water Cooling

In some cases, water may be used to cool equipment in a data center. Water is a very efficient means of cooling. In many situations, IT Managers leave equipment cabinets half empty in order to ensure that the temperature in the cabinet doesn't get too high. In short, air conditioning alone cannot always keep up with that much heat being generated in that small a space.

In situations like that, special equipment cabinets are used that essentially have water pipes built into their panels. Chilled water is pumped through these pipes in the cabinet to absorb the heat from the computer equipment. The warmed water is then re-chilled and sent back through the cabinet.

Obviously, bringing water that close to your equipment introduces an element of risk. However, other restrictions and constraints may make it a viable option in certain circumstances.

Humidity

Along with the temperature, humidity is also a concern for data centers. Too much humidity, and there's a chance of condensation on equipment. Too little humidity, and you risk static electricity. Typically, in a data center (which is controlled by the air handlers), it's kept at about 45% relative humidity.

Hot and Cold Rows

One popular technique for cooling a data center is the use of alternating aisles of hot and cold. This is easiest to implement during the planning stages of a new data center. It's much more difficult to implement in a data center that is already filled with equipment.

Prior to the idea of hot and cold rows, equipment cabinets were all facing in the same direction (see Figure 11.2).

When hot and cold rows are alternated, equipment is placed back to back and front to front (see Figure 11.3.).

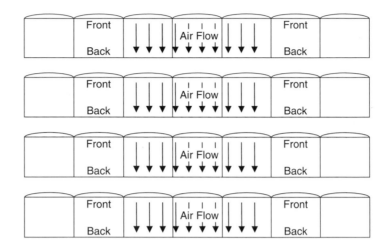

Figure 11.2 Traditional Computer Equipment Layout (Top Down View)

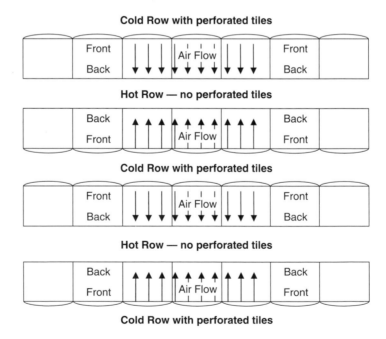

Figure 11.3 Alternate Hot and Cold Rows

A cold aisle has perforated floor tiles that allow cool air to come from under the raised floor, and a hot aisle that has no perforated tiles. In the cold aisle, the cabinets are face to face so the cool air is drawn in through the front of the cabinet and exhausted out the back of the equipment rack into the adjacent hot aisles.

The idea is to keep the cool air separate from the hot air. The thinking being that if the two types of air are mixed, it lowers the overall effectiveness of the cooling system since the cool air is "warmed" before it gets to the equipment, and cool air may also be "wasted" by being returned to the air-cooling units before it's been put to use cooling the computer equipment. Therefore, perforated tiles aren't placed in hot aisles, as this would mix hot and cold air and lower the temperature of the air returning to the cooling units.

The challenge with this system is making sure that all your cabinets and equipment draw air in from the front and exhaust to the rear. Some manufacturers design for bringing cool air in from the sides/bottom, and/or exhausting warm air out the top or sides.

Cooling During a Blackout

A lot of concern when planning a data center goes into keeping the computer equipment running when the power goes out. Typically this means using UPS units and generators. However, if you don't have sufficient air conditioning it really doesn't matter how much electricity you have.

If you halt the air conditioning in a typical data center, it becomes noticeably warmer in about 15–30 minutes. Within 45 minutes to an hour the room is already hot and the equipment is at risk. Wait much longer, and the equipment could start failing or shutting itself down.

When you're planning for emergency power, make sure you're also preparing to provide that emergency power to the cooling facilities so that those components can continue to operate as well.

Cabinets

The simple subject of equipment cabinets sometimes brings out religious fervor in ITers. You would think that a cabinet is a cabinet is a cabinet. However, there are variations that some feel passionately about.

Among the choices:

✦ Height (with 42 U being the most common, one U = 1.75 inches)

✦ Depth

+ Whether the doors (front and or back) should have perforations (or vents) for air-flow

+ Full or split rear doors

+ Use of fans (often at the top) to help with air flow

+ Wire management

+ Power strips

+ Keyboard-Video-Mouse (KVM) solutions

+ Color

+ Access for cables and wires to come in through the top or bottom (see discussion on raised floors in the next section)

Raised Floors

The raised floor has been the iconic symbol of data centers for several decades. They offer significant advantages.

+ They allow the cold air to be distributed under the floor, and perforated tiles allow it to be delivered exactly where it's needed (compared with the difficulty of directing the flow of cold air from overhead ducts)

+ The space under the floor is very convenient for distribution of power and data cables

+ In the event of a water leak, a raised floor would put additional distance between the computer equipment and the water

However, a raised floor brings with it its share of disadvantages.

+ Higher cost

+ With wires and cables running under the floor (and under equipment) it can be more difficult to locate, install, and troubleshoot wiring problems

+ A flood situation has increased risk of immediate exposure to electrical wires

+ Equipment on a raised floor isn't as well "anchored" and could suffer much greater damage in an earthquake

+ Cables and wires under the floor could obstruct air flow. Raising the height of the raised floor to compensate compromises structural integrity (previous bullet), and presents problems with ensuring sufficient head room in the data center

✦ The danger of someone hurting themselves because of a floor tile inadvertently left open

✦ Wasted space needed for the ramp

✦ Dust, dirt, and grit that can collect below a raised floor that's rarely ever cleaned

In computer rooms without a raised floor, all the wiring that's normally done below the floor is done above the equipment, making use of "ladder racks" and cable trays.

Security and Monitoring

The data center protects some very valuable systems, and is at the heart of your IT operations. Although many regulations (see Chapter 8, IT Compliance and Controls, on page 201) compel you to ensure there are adequate controls, the importance of the data center to your organization's operation should be sufficient reason on its own.

Access

Data center doors usually have special access controls. Typically, it might be an access card system, or an electronic key pad. Hand scanners are not uncommon. And, some sites employ more than one access control solution.

At the higher end of access control is a device known as a "man-trap." This could be an entry that's similar in design to a revolving door, or it may be a combination of two doors with a small corridor in between. The idea of the man-trap is to ensure that when access is granted (via access card, keypad, or hand scanner), that only one individual can enter the data center at one time. The purpose is to avoid "tail-gating" where one employee swipes his card, opens the door, and then allows several others to enter with him.

While man-traps are quite popular, they can create logistical headaches for moving equipment in and out of the data center.

Another popular technique is to minimize the number of people who require entry to the data center. Typically, telecommunications lines terminate in the data center. As such, technicians from the carriers have to enter the data center to install these lines and to troubleshoot. Some data centers have chosen to create a special telecommunications room near (or adjacent to) the data center. All telecommunications lines terminate in this so that the carriers' technicians don't get near the computer equipment when doing their work (customer installed cables extend the lines from this room to the equipment in the data center).

Similarly, some sites have tried to move some of the environmental controls (e.g., UPS and PDUs for the electrical service) outside of the computer room, which reduces the need for electricians to be in the data center to work on them.

Fire Suppression

Of course you don't want a fire in your data center. But of equal concern is the impact of water (particularly from a fire suppression system).

Pre-Action Systems   Because IT Managers are fearful of accidental discharge of water from sprinkler systems, a special installation of the sprinkler systems known as a "pre-action" system is frequently used in data centers.

In a pre-action system, the pipes that run to the sprinkler heads have no water in them. Two events have to happen in a pre-action system before water is discharged. First, a special device (which would be activated from the heat of a fire) opens a control valve, which allows water to flow into the pipes of the sprinkler system. Second, the sprinkler heads have to detect sufficient heat in order to open.

The advantage of a pre-action system is that it minimizes the chance of water being discharged from a break in a pipe, or a damaged sprinkler head.

Dry Pipe Systems   A variation of the pre-action sprinkler system is the dry pipe system. Similar to the pre-action, dry pipe systems are free of water. Instead they are charged with pressurized air to hold back the water. However, any break in the system (such as a broken pipe or an open sprinkler head will allow the pressurized air to exit followed by the flow of water).

Gas Suppression   Since water, foam, dry chemicals, and other fire suppression agents can cause extensive equipment damage, some very critical situations employ the use of a gas to extinguish a fire. The gas of choice used to be Halon, and could suppress a fire by essentially "suffocating" it. However, Halon was found to be contributing to depletion of the ozone, and its manufacture in the United States was halted in 1994.

FM 200, Inergen, and Novec 1230 are all replacements for Halon. Each is a clean, non-corrosive gas, which is designed to extinguish fires:

✦ Inergen (Ansul Corporation) is a mixture of three gases (reducing oxygen concentration): 52% nitrogen, 40% argon, and 8% carbonate dioxide.

Inergen extinguishes fire by reducing the oxygen concentration below combustion levels. After Inergen has been discharged, people can still breathe.

✦ FM-200 (Great Lakes Chemical Corporation) extinguishes fires through a combination of chemical and physical heat removal. It doesn't smother flames by removing oxygen. Instead, FM-200 removes heat energy from fire, not oxygen from the environment. FM-200 absorbs heat from the flame zone and interrupts the chemical chain reaction of the combustion process.

✦ Novec 1230 (3M Corporation) is a fluid that looks like water, but oddly enough nothing it touches gets wet. Although stored in a liquid form, Novec turns into a gas when it's discharged and puts out flames without damaging equipment.

Monitoring

Just like you monitor your hardware and software, you want to make sure that you're monitoring your data center environment.

Cameras   It's quite common for surveillance cameras to be positioned so that they capture images of everyone who enters and leaves the data center. Because of the tall equipment cabinets, it's difficult to position a camera inside the data center that captures all the activity that goes on there. One alternative is to position a camera at the end of each cabinet row so that it can capture all activity in that row.

Leak Detection   With air conditioning, sprinkler systems, and possibly water-cooled cabinets, the risk of unwanted water in the data center isn't something that should be ignored. Leak detectors (connected to a monitoring system) can be strategically placed around the data center (particularly under a raised floor where water might not be noticed) to alert you to trouble.

Environmental Controls   With all the investment you made in your data center, it's well worth it to make sure that it (and your equipment) stays healthy. The temperature, humidity, power usage, etc., should all be regularly monitored. Many of the mechanical and environmental devices you put into a computer room (e.g., air handlers, UPS units) can be monitored and controlled through a centralized Building Management System (BMS). These systems can monitor various parameters, report on trends, and send alerts when pre-set thresholds are met.

11.2 The Cable Plant

With the computer room all set up, the next concern of the physical environment is getting connectivity to all the devices you have throughout your building and/or campus. Similar to sizing a data center, running the cabling is something you want to be especially sure to get right the first time. The cost and effort to correct a mistake can be enormous.

If you have always thought that all wires are created equal, managing a cable plant will show you otherwise.

What Is a Cable Plant?

The cable plant refers to the physical wire (be it copper or fiber) used in your facility that physically connects all the network devices (printers, workstations, servers, switches, routers, etc.). In addition to the physical wire, the cable plant refers to the design of the wiring layout and all the components that are used within it (e.g., patch panels, jacks, etc.).

There are special issues related to cabling that make it unique among IT investments. These include the following:

- The cost of cabling is mostly in the installation labor, not the material

- Once the cabling is installed in walls and ceilings, you virtually lose access to it

- It's a capital investment that you can't take with you if you move to another office

- It can't be upgraded, only replaced

- It may be the capital investment that outlasts all other IT capital investments

Unless you're moving into a new facility, you probably already have a cable plant and it was probably installed years ago. Your involvement with cabling may be limited to having new lines installed to accommodate growth; for example, when that corner office that used to support one executive is turned into a bullpen and now needs additional connections to support six programmers.

Designing Your Cable Plant

Designing your cable plant involves many factors:

- LAN technologies used (ATM, Ethernet, Token-Ring, etc.)

- Applications (e.g., video)

✦ Distances involved

✦ Exposure to hazards (Are cables run through public areas where they're more prone to accidental damage, or in secured areas like locked wiring closets? Are they run outdoors?)

✦ Bandwidth (or data transmission speed requirements)

✦ Local building code requirements (e.g., some cable may have to be fire retardant depending on where it's installed)

Whether you're installing a new facility or expanding your existing cabling plant, it's a good idea to get some assistance. Since you probably won't be spending a whole lot of time on cabling issues, it's likely that you won't be current on the latest technologies and product offerings when a cabling project comes your way. There are consultants who specialize in this field and can help you determine the best solution for your needs, which manufacturers offer the most reliable products, selection of components like wall jacks and patch panels, and so on. They can help you implement a system that's easy to maintain and expand, and can offer ideas and solutions to prevent your wiring closets from looking like a room full of spaghetti.

Managing a Cable Plant

As you might imagine, there really isn't much to the care and feeding of a cable plant on an ongoing basis. Unlike other IT resources, you don't have to perform daily backups of a cable plant, or apply bug fixes and patches to them. However, that doesn't necessarily mean you can install it and forget it.

Valuable cable-management tasks include:

✦ **Always maintain wiring diagrams, and keep them current.** Post them where they can be easily referenced. For example, put a copy of each floor's diagram in that floor's wiring closet.

✦ **Get in the habit of labeling both ends of cables.** There are many offerings for this. Everything from label makers to tabs with writable surfaces that can be attached to the cable ends. The label at each end of the cable should identify (1) where this end of the cable connects to and (2) where the other end of the cable is connected to. Depending on what the cable is used for, you may want to identify the room location it's connected to, or perhaps the specific device and port it's connected to.

✦ **Keep wires organized.** This is officially called "wire management." Bundles of wires should be held together. You can use tie wraps for this (some are made of Velcro, which can be reused; others are made of plastic, which generally can't be reused, but provide a more secure wrapping). When bundling wires together, don't make it so tight that there is no any movement at all. Keeping it a little loose ensures that the tie wrap isn't cutting into the cable, and it also makes it easier if you have to trace a particular wire's path.

✦ **Know where your cables are.** Since wires are buried in walls, ceilings, and under raised floors, it can often be impossible to inspect them visually. There are many tools available to help you work without seeing. There are tools to help you trace and test. These can be invaluable in saving hours of guesswork or trial and error. Fluke (*www.fluke.com*) is a popular manufacturer of tools like this. A pair of walkie-talkies (or cell phones) can also help your network analysts communicate when they're troubleshooting a wiring problem.

✦ **Check on your wiring closets periodically.** Your equipment may be generating a lot of heat. There may be a small water leak that is slowly dripping water on your equipment or wires. And it isn't uncommon for mice to gnaw on cables.

Copper or Fiber

The media of choice for computer cabling is either fiber or copper. Both have advantages and disadvantages (see Table 11.1).

Table 11.1 Pros and cons of using fiber

PRO		CON	
	More difficult to tap		More expensive (both for installation labor and material)
	Not susceptible to magnetic and electrical interference		More difficult to install
	Long cable distances		More prone to damage

Copper Cabling

Although the early days of computer connectivity often used twin-axial and coaxial cables, the choice today is twisted pair (see Figures 11.4 through 11.6).

Twisted-pair copper is by far the most popular medium for Ethernet. It's inexpensive, easy to work with, and can support speeds up to 1 GB. Because of its popularity, there are many sources of products and components available for copper-based Ethernet, including network cards, switches, testing equipment, and so on.

Figure 11.4   Twin-Axial Cable

Figure 11.5   Coaxial Cable

Figure 11.6   Twisted Pair Cabling

Twisted pair comes in a variety of flavors, and is classified by categories (generally referred to as CAT, see Table 11.2).

To make matters more confusing, the term "twisted pair" is somewhat generic. It could refer to two pairs or four pairs of wires in the same sheath. And the sheath itself may be shielded (Shielded Twisted Pair, STP) or unshielded (Unshielded Twisted Pair, UTP). The shielding refers to a wrapping that serves as a ground, which reduces the impact of outside interference on the data signal. It should be noted that STP isn't a formally defined spec for Ethernet. STP is primarily used for IBM Token-Ring wiring topologies.

Copper Connectors   For twisted pair, the virtually universal connector is the RJ45 (see Figure 11.7).

For coax connections, choices include BNC, TNC, and F-type (see Figures 11.8 through 11.10).

Table 11.2 Twisted pair cable categories (Source: *www.whatis.com*)

Category	Maximum Data Rate	Usual Application
CAT 1	Up to 1 Mbps (1 MHz)	Analog voice (POTS), Integrated Services Digital Network Basic Rate Interface, Doorbell wiring
CAT 2	4 Mbps	Mainly used in the IBM cabling system for Token-Ring networks
CAT 3	16 Mbps	Voice and data on 10BASE-T Ethernet
CAT 4	20 Mbps	Used in 16 Mbps Token-Ring, otherwise not used much
CAT 5	100 Mbps 1000 Mbps (4 pair)	100 Mbps TPDDI 155 Mbps ATM. No longer supported; replaced by 5E
CAT 5E	1000 Mbps (10000 Mbps prototype)	100 Mbps TPDDI 155 Mbps ATM Gigabit Ethernet. Offers better near-end crosstalk than CAT 5
CAT 6	Up to 400 MHz	Super-fast broadband applications. Most popular cabling for new installs
CAT 6E	Up to 625 MHz (field-tested to 500 MHz)	Support for 10 Gigabit Ethernet (10GBASE-T)
CAT 7 (ISO Class F)	600–700 MHz. 1.2 GHz in pairs with Siemon connector	Full-motion video, Teleradiology, Government and manufacturing environments, Shielded system

Cable Categories

The two most widely installed categories are CAT 3 and CAT 5. While the two cables may look identical, CAT 3 is tested to a lower set of specifications and can cause transmission errors if pushed to faster speeds. CAT 3 cabling is near-end crosstalk certified for only a 16 MHz signal, while CAT 5 cable must pass a 100 MHz test. CAT 5E has recently replaced CAT 5 as the prevalent standard.

The CAT 6 specification is now completed and for some time products have been offered that conform to this specification, which improves on CAT 5E in terms of near-end crosstalk and other ways. According to IEEE, 70% of new installs in 2004 were CAT 6.

A CAT 7 specification exists but isn't yet official.

Source: *www.whatis.com*

Figure 11.7   RJ45 Connector

Figure 11.8   BNC Connector

Figure 11.9   TNC Connector

Figure 11.10   F-type Connector

Fiber Cabling

Fiber's primary advantage is that it can span much greater distances than copper. However, fiber requires more care and skill in installation, and components for fiber are much more expensive.

Fiber cable is more costly, not only for the material, but also for the labor to install it. While tools and hardware are available from a variety of sources and catalogs to allow even a neophyte to work with copper wire connections, it requires special training and expensive equipment to work with fiber. Additionally, fiber is more sensitive and can be degraded by kinks, tight radii, and so on.

There are two primary types of fiber cable: *singlemode* and *multimode*. Multimode fiber is less expensive, and is often used within a building or small campus, since its maximum distance is about 2 km. Singlemode, on the other hand, is more expensive and is used for longer distance runs such as 20 km.

Fiber Connectors   Unlike copper twisted pair, which has one connector type (RJ45), fiber cabling has a variety of connectors (see Figure 11.11). However, very often your choice is made for you based on the connector type available on your hardware.

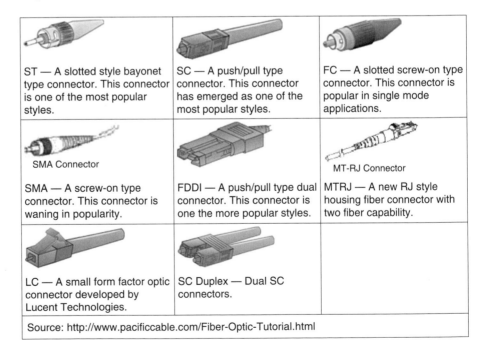

ST — A slotted style bayonet type connector. This connector is one of the most popular styles.	SC — A push/pull type connector. This connector has emerged as one of the most popular styles.	FC — A slotted screw-on type connector. This connector is popular in single mode applications.
SMA Connector		MT-RJ Connector
SMA — A screw-on type connector. This connector is waning in popularity.	FDDI — A push/pull type dual connector. This connector is one the more popular styles.	MTRJ — A new RJ style housing fiber connector with two fiber capability.
LC — A small form factor optic connector developed by Lucent Technologies.	SC Duplex — Dual SC connectors.	
Source: http://www.pacificcable.com/Fiber-Optic-Tutorial.html		

Figure 11.11   Fiber Connectors

Cable Length and Connections

It's important to remember that while cable can be purchased in almost any length, it doesn't mean that it can be used for any length. As a general rule, CAT 5 UTP can carry signals for 100 m (330 feet). Shielded wiring will extend this length (depending on the speed of the data rate). Multimode fiber extends the signal farther, and singlemode fiber even farther.

Connections

When considering your cable plant, it's important to note that although there's a connection from the computer on your desk to the server, it's certainly not one long continuous piece of cable. Typically, the network card in your computer is connected to a patch cable, the other end of which connects to a jack on the wall. On the other side of the wall jack is a cable that probably runs to a wiring closet, where it typically terminates to the back end of a patch panel.

On the front end of the patch panel is another patch cable (typically like the one connected to the computer), which connects to some sort of switch. Coming out of the back of this unit is another cable (perhaps fiber, but oftentimes copper) that travels several floors (or perhaps across a campus) to another switch in the computer room. Also connected to this device, finally, is the server that has the data you need.

Of course, depending on the size and complexity of your environment, a connection from the workstation to the server can be simpler or more complex. What's important to note is that the overall connection is no better than the weakest link. If, for example, all your cabling is CAT 5, except for the patch cable in your office, then you no longer have a CAT 5 connection. And, not only must all the cable conform to the CAT 5 specification, but each jack (including those at patch panels) must also conform to the CAT 5 spec.

Connections to Devices

When installing cabling, it's hard to know what types of devices, how many, and where they'll be needed years from now. As such, it's common practice to overcompensate, and intentionally drop in more connections than are needed. Since the labor cost far outweighs the materials cost when running cable, it makes sense to do as much as you can when you do run cable.

A common practice is to provide two data and two voice connections at each workstation (see Figure 11.12).

Although a typical workstation probably only needs one data and one voice jack, the "quad" solution provides room for expansion for more devices, as well as "backup" connection in case one of the four should fail for some reason.

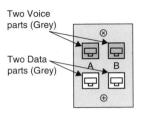

Figure 11.12   Two Data and Two Voice Connections at Each Terminal

In larger rooms (offices, conference rooms, etc.) a few connections may be "sprinkled" about to allow for flexibility should the use of the room change over time. Lastly, connections are usually placed in open areas — again, to allow for flexibility as well as public-use devices (such as shared printers).

Intermediate Distribution Frame/Facility

Typically, because the distance from the computer room to individual devices (workstations, printers, etc.) usually exceeds the maximum distance for copper cabling (generally 100 m), and the cost of running fiber to all those devices is cost-prohibitive, an intermediary facility is used. Your Intermediate Distribution Frame/Facility (IDF) is a term used to refer to what is often called the "wiring closet." As a general rule, there is an IDF on each floor of a facility. In some cases, where the size of the floor is very large, there may be more than one IDF on each floor to ensure that none of the copper cables to the devices exceeds the maximum distance of the specification.

A typical design uses copper cabling to connect the servers to the switches in the data center. Fiber is then used from the network switches in the data center to the network switches in the IDFs, and then the IDFs have copper cables going out to each device.

Because a great deal of connectivity runs through those IDFs, they should be treated as important facilities, frequently similar to the data center by having:

+ Appropriate cooling and electricity

+ Controlled access (e.g., access card)

+ Environmental monitors

+ All items carefully labeled

+ Organization (e.g., good wire management; Figure 11.13 is an example of what a wiring closet should *not* look like)

Figure 11.13   What a Wiring Closet Should *Not* Look Like

◆ Kept clean (i.e., IDFs shouldn't do double duty as storage closets for the building facilities people)

◆ Sufficient redundancies

The last item, sufficient redundancies, is particularly important as the IDF can be a single point of failure for connectivity for as many as a few hundred users and devices. To mitigate this, the IDF usually has redundant connectivity back to the data center (often taking different paths as described below in the section, Redundant Paths). In addition, the IDF may have multiple network devices so that if one fails, only a portion of the users are impacted. Each of the network switches may have redundant power supplies integrated with the UPS facilities, along with the redundant uplinks to the data center.

Redundant Paths

When there's a need to run one cable, it's often wise to run a second cable. Since most of the effort and cost is in the labor, and not the material, there's little downside to a second run. And the second cable can provide redundancy, or be a handy spare if the first one fails.

For even greater redundancy, sometimes two separate paths are chosen so that a mishap that damages the first cable doesn't impact the second one. Within a building, when running cables from the computer room down to one of the floors, you might choose to have two sets of cables installed in separate conduits. In buildings with large floor plates, you may choose conduits in separate risers to further separate the cable runs.

Wires: Can I Do Without Them?

With wireless technology (discussed in further detail in Chapter in 12, Networking, on page 311) becoming so cheap and ubiquitous, it can be tempting to consider eliminating wires altogether. In a new facility, the use of wireless can offer significant savings over the cost of installing a complete cable plant.

Wireless LANs

In general, wireless devices can send and receive data if they're within 300 feet of an antenna. However, that limit can drop significantly if there isn't a direct line of sight to the antenna. Still, by strategically placing antennas so that there are overlapping areas of coverage, the distance limitations can be mitigated. Obviously, careful site planning and installation is a critical success factor to wireless LANs. Wireless LANs are used on college campuses, in hotels, and, of course, neighborhood coffee shops. Many organizations are installing wireless networking so that users can take their laptop from office to meeting room without having to fumble with disconnecting and reconnecting wires.

While wireless technology does not offer the same throughput, security, and reliability as a hard-wired connection, it's entirely possible that the low cost and convenience of it may make wireless a very worthwhile option to consider in certain areas.

11.3 Additional Resources

Web Sites

+ *datacenterdynamics.com* (trade association for data center managers)

+ *ftp://www.apcmedia.com/salestools/NRAN-69ANM9_R0_EN.pdf* (white paper on "Guidelines for Specification of Data Center Power Density")

+ *www.3m.com/novec1230fluid* (vendor Web site about Novec 1230 fire suppression)

+ *www.ansul.com* (vendor Web site about Inergen fire suppression)

+ *www.apcc.com* (vendor of data center power and cooling products)

+ *www.apcc.com/prod_docs/results.cfm?class=wp&allpapers=1* (variety of white papers on data center power and cooling)

✦ *www.cse.mrt.ac.lk/lecnotes/cs5162/08-lan-cabling.ppt* (presentation on LAN cabling)

✦ *www.datacenterdynamics.com/Portals/e5b81c2f-f780-4e59-88fc-068dccab9568/SF04%20Liebert.pdf* (presentation on data center cooling)

✦ *www.e1.greatlakes.com/wfp/product/jsp/faq.jsp* (vendor FAQ about FM-200 fire suppression)

✦ *www.fluke.com* (vendor of cable testing products)

✦ *www.liebert.com* (vendor of data center power and cooling products)

✦ *www.mgeups.com* (vendor of data center power products)

✦ *www.panduit.com/products/WhitePapers/103681.pdf* (white paper on "Facility Considerations for the Data Center")

✦ *www.uptimeinstitute.com* (industry group for data center management)

Books and Articles

✦ Alger, Douglas, *Build the Best Data Center Facility for Your Business*, Cisco Press, 2005.

✦ Barnett, David, Groth, David, and McBee, Jim, *Cabling: The Complete Guide to Network Wiring*, Sybex, 2004.

✦ Hayes, Jim, and Rosenburg, Paul, *Data, Voice, and Video Cabling*, Thomson Delmar Learning, 2004.

✦ Mitchell, Robert L., "Redefining Cool," *Computerworld*, October 31, 2005.

✦ Snevely, Rob, *Enterprise Data Center Design and Methodology*, Prentice Hall PTR, 2002.

✦ Thibodeau, Patrick, "Water Returns to the Data Center," *Computerworld*, August 22, 2005.

✦ Trulove, James, *LAN Wiring*, McGraw-Hill Professional, 2000.

✦ Vacca, John R., *The Cabling Handbook*, Pearson Education, 2000.

Networking

The Network Is The Computer.

—SUN MICROSYSTEMS SLOGAN

"The computer is the network" or "the network is the computer." Either way you say it, the inference is clear — today, without connectivity, the computer is of little use.

In this chapter, we'll cover the basic technologies and concepts involved in networking.

12.1 OSI Model

All networking discussions usually start with the 7-Layer Open System Interconnect (OSI) model. There are many representations and explanations of the various layers available (see Figure 12.1).

CHAPTER TWELVE

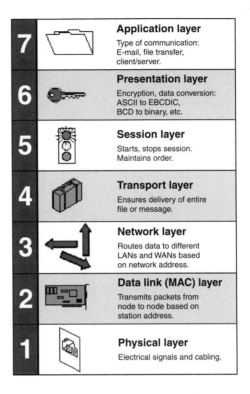

Figure 12.1 OSI Mode (Source: *answers.com*)

Seven OSI Layers

1. The *Physical Layer* is the physical communications media, such as copper, coax, fiber, twisted pair, etc.

2. The *Data Link Layer* is the logical organization of data, such as the framing, addressing and checksum of packets.

3. The *Network Layer* describes the exchanges over various data links between any two nodes in a network, such as the addressing and routing.

4. The *Transport Layer* refers to the quality and nature of the transmission; for example, this layer deals with data retransmissions.

5. The *Session Layer* establishes, maintains, and manages the communication session between computers.

6. The *Presentation Layer* takes the data and converts it into a standard format that the other layers can understand; for example, this is where data is packed or unpacked, encrypted or decrypted. Converting data from one format to another (e.g., EBCDIC to ASCII) also happens at this layer.

Table 12.1 TCP/IP protocols and the OSI model

OSI Model	TCP/IP Protocols
Layer 7 — Application	HTTP, SMTP, SNMP, SMTP, POP3, FTP, Telnet
Layer 6 — Presentation	
Layer 5 — Session	RPC, NetBIOS, Winsock
Layer 4 — Transport	TCP, UDP
Layer 3 — Network	IP, ICMP, BGP, OSPF, RIP, IGRP, EIGRP, ARP, RARP, X.25
Layer 2 — Data Link	Ethernet, Token-Ring, Frame relay, ISDN, ATM, WiFi, FDDI
Layer 1 — Physical	Copper and fiber-optic cabling, radio waves

7. The *Application Layer* is where the user communicates with the computer. Word processing and spreadsheet software isn't considered an application as far as the OSI model is concerned, but tools like Telnet, FTP, browsers, etc., are.

As you'll see, we'll reference various layers as well as the OSI model throughout this chapter. The OSI model has stood the test of time, and some individuals in the networking field define their role as to which layers they work with and are responsible for. The OSI model has proved valuable because:

✦ It provides structure and guidance on how data should be handled and treated as it travels across a network.

✦ It clarifies how software is to interact with the network.

✦ It specifies the boundaries of the layers, the interaction between them, and perhaps most important, that the activity at each layer should be transparent to the other layers.

Internet Protocol Suite

One of the most used terms in IT, particularly in the field of networking, is "protocol." In general, a protocol refers to a set of rules and standards that ease the interconnectivity of devices of different platforms, and from different vendors. The Internet Protocol (IP) suite (or TCP/IP suite, for the most recognized protocols in the suite) is a set of communications protocols that define how the Internet runs.

The IP suite can be described in reference to the 7-Layer OSI model. But, since the OSI model is more theoretical, and the TCP/IP suite is a model in actual use, the TCP/IP protocols don't always map exactly to the OSI layers. Table 12.1 shows how and where some of the TCP/IP protocols are generally accepted to fit into the OSI model.

Table 12.2 Compressed OSI model

TCP/IP Suite Layer	Corresponding OSI Layers	Protocols
Layer 4 — Application	Session (5) Presentation (6) Application (7)	SMTP, Telnet, HTTP, FTP, DNS, DHCP
Layer 3 — Transport	Transport (4) Session (5)	TCP, UDP
Layer 2 — Inter-network	Network (3)	IP
Layer 1 — Link	Physical (1) and Data Link (2)	Ethernet, copper and fiber-optic cabling, wireless

An alternative for looking at the TCP/IP suite in relation to the OSI model is to compress the OSI model into few layers, as in Table 12.2.

12.2 IP Addressing

IP addresses are how devices uniquely identify themselves both on your own local network and on the Internet. Long ago, there were so few devices that it seemed inconceivable that we could ever run out of them. Radically fast progress in IT has proven that preconception to be misguided.

IP Addressing Primer

An IP address is 32-bit string of 0s and 1s like 11001100 01000111 11001010 10100000. This numerical structure yields over 4 billion unique addresses. To make numbers easier to read (and to remember), IP addresses are usually represented as four 8-bit numbers, separated by dots. Each 8-bit number (also called an "octet") can be a value from 0 to 255. The IP address in the first sentence of this paragraph is equivalent to 204.71.202.160.

Each IP address actually has two separate addresses: the network address and the host address. The subnet mask (another 32-bit string) is used to determine which portion of the IP address refers to the network address component, and which portion represents the host (or device) address component. The portion of a network with devices that share a common network address component is referred to as a subnet. Dividing a network into subnets is useful for both security and performance reasons.

Table 12.3   IP address classes

Class	Address Range	# Networks	Octets Used for Network Address	# Device Addresses Available Per Network	Total Unique Combinations
A	1.0.0.1 to 126.255.255.254	127	1st	16,777,214	2,147,483,648
B	128.1.0.1 to 191.255.255.254	16,384	1st and 2nd	65,534	1,073,741,824
C	192.0.1.1 to 223.255.254.254	2,097,152	1st thru 3rd	254	536,870,912

Subnet masks are often expressed like an IP address (e.g., 255.255.255.0). Or, since subnet masks are always a string of 1s followed by a string of 0s, the "slash" format indicates how many 1s are in the subnet mask. If, in our original example, we wanted to indicate that the first three octets referred to the network address, and the last octet was the host address, we would use a subnet mask of 255.255.255.0, or indicate 204.71.202.160/24.

Classes of Addresses

Referring to the class of an address also helps to indicate what portion of the address refers to the network component and what portion refers to the device (see Table 12.3).

Class-A addresses are very rare and quite coveted. They are assigned to some of the world's largest corporations (e.g., GE, IBM, Xerox, Apple Computer, Prudential Securities, etc.).

A Shortage of Addresses

To ensure that addresses are kept unique, the American Registry for Internet Numbers (ARIN) was created in 1997 as a non-profit organization that registers and administers IP numbers for North America. (Other global regions are managed by RIPE NCC, LACNIC, and APNIC.)

However, due to the high demand for network addresses, combined with the fact that organizations were requesting more than they actually needed, the administration of IP addresses became very complex. Organizations requesting addresses were finding that they were being assigned addresses in non-contiguous ranges, or in several smaller classes (as opposed to a single range in a larger class).

Two solutions arose to deal with the shortage of addresses:

1. Network Address Translation

2. IPv6

Network Address Translation

The addresses assigned by ARIN are known as "public" addresses in that they are considered to be (and have to be) unique in the scheme of the public Internet. However, in most cases, you don't need (and probably don't want) the vast majority of your devices to be considered part of the public Internet. In fact, you probably only have a few devices that have this need — your Web site, your mail server, and your connection to the Internet.

With Network Address Translation (NAT), your router and its connection to the Internet can use a single public IP address for all the devices on your internal network. Since all those devices (be it 10, 1,000, or more) essentially share that public address when they need to connect to the Internet, they don't need to have their own ARIN registered address.

As the name implies, NAT translates your internal network addresses into the public address assigned to your Internet connection. (In some cases, you may use a pool of public address with NAT.)

Using NAT frees you from having to register and use assigned IP address ranges from ARIN. In fact, as long as all your internal IP addresses are unique within your network, you can use almost any address you want. However, there are agreed upon standards for private internal networks:

10.0.0.0 — 10.255.255.255 (1 class-A range)

172.16.0.0 — 172.31.255.255 (16 class-B ranges)

192.168.0.0 — 192.168.255.255 (256 class-C ranges)

The first option, usually referred to as 10-dot addresses, is the most widely used for internal networks as it offers the most number of devices and flexibility for subnetting.

IPv6

An alternate approach for dealing with the shortage of IP addresses was to change how IP addressing works. This led to version 6 of IP (the version in use today is version 4), also called IP next generation or IPng.

IPv6 improves on IPv4 by vastly increasing the number of available addresses. While IPv4 allows for approximately 4 billion addresses, IPv6 provides for 340 undecillion (that is 340, followed by 36 zeroes) addresses. The increase comes from changing the address length from 32 bits in version 4 to 128 bits in version 6.

IPng was adopted by the Internet Engineering Task Force in 1994. The use of it has grown slowly, primarily because of the introduction of NAT as an alternative (and some would consider simpler and more convenient) way of dealing with the IP address shortage.

Most vendors have already started incorporating support for IPv6 into their hardware and software, and there are mechanisms for mapping addresses between v4 and v6. IPv6 addresses are written as a string of eight 4-digit hex numbers with a colon between each; for example, FF04:19:5:ABD4:187:2C:754:2B1 (leading zeroes don't have to be expressed). In v6, a string of zeroes can be represented by two colons (::), and a v4 address can easily be expressed in v6 notation by preceding the v4 address with two colons, such as: "::10.5.213.59."

DNS

While IP addressing is effective, long strings of numbers aren't the most convenient, or intuitive, for people. Meaningful names are easier for us gray-mattered beings to remember and deal with. A Domain Name Server (DNS) translates alphanumeric names to IP addresses.

DNS servers are used in two similar ways:

1. Internally, a DNS allows you to name your servers and devices, and translates those names to IP addresses.

2. Externally, the DNS environment of the Internet allows you and your users to use meaningful names (like browser URLs), as opposed to IP addresses.

The two actually work together. In this way, the DNS environment of the Internet is distributed.

As an example (see Figure 12.2), if an application needs to access a Web site, such as *ibm.com*, a series of steps is taken until the address is found:

1. First, the local-cache is checked. If the ibm.com Web site was recently accessed, the IP address may still be in the cache of the device that is trying to access the site. If not . . .

2. A request is then put out to the DNS server (1 in Figure 12.2). The address of the DNS server(s) is provided to each computer when the DHCP server (see the next section) assigns the devices their IP addresses. As with the

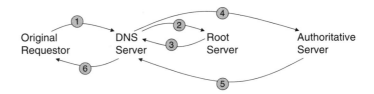

Figure 12.2 DNS Processing

first step, the DNS server may already have the IP address in its cache if there was a previous request for it. If not . . .

3. The DNS server contacts (2 in Figure 12.2) the root-level server for the appropriate top level domain (such as .org, .net, .com, etc.). The root-level server tells (3 in Figure 12.2) the DNS server which server on the Internet is "authoritative" for that domain name (*ibm.com* in this example).

4. Finally, the DNS contacts (4 in Figure 12.2) the authoritative server which returns (5 in Figure 12.2) the IP address for ibm.com and passes it back (6 in Figure 12.2) to the original requestor.

All of this happens within moments, if not sooner.

DHCP

In the days when organizations only had a handful (if that many) of computers, it was easy to administer the IP addresses. But, when a single organization can easily have hundreds or thousands of devices, the challenge becomes that much greater.

Dynamic Host Configuration Protocol (DHCP) is a mechanism for automatically assigning IP addresses. When a computer boots up, it sends a request to the network to find a DHCP server. The DHCP server sees the request, and provides the client with an available address from a pool that has been assigned. The DHCP server can also update the DNS server to create an entry for that computer name having that IP address.

For devices, like printers, which need to always use the same IP address, i.e., "static addresses," the DHCP server can be configured to recognize that device's Media Access Control (MAC) address. The MAC address is a unique code permanently assigned to most forms of networking hardware. For static addressing, the DHCP will recognize the MAC address, always assign it the same IP address, and make sure that no other device is given that address.

In addition to the IP address, the DHCP server will also provide individual devices with other important IP information like the subnet mask, the default gateway, the DNS servers, etc.

DHCP servers greatly ease the burden of IP administration by ensuring that there is no use of duplicate addresses and providing an easy means to track them.

12.3 Local Area Networks

A Local Area Network (LAN) refers to the network that connects the devices in one geographic location, such as a single building, although the local LAN can sometimes be extended to include all the devices in a campus environment. As a general rule, a LAN's boundary is telecommunication facilities (e.g., T-1 lines) and a router (which is used to connect two networks together). These facilities are generally considered to be part of the Wide Area Network (WAN). Designing a LAN is like designing a house. It is dependent on needs, plans for future growth, and changes of use. The definition of a good design can vary with changes and trends in the marketplace and advances in technology.

Not too long ago, there were many LAN technologies to choose from. For example, many organizations were choosing between Token-Ring and Ethernet, among others. The cost difference between a switched concentrator and shared-hub was so significant that switches were generally only used in the data center. Today, Ethernet is the de facto standard, and the cost of switches has dropped so dramatically that shared-hubs are virtually extinct.

LAN Design

The goals of a good LAN design should include the following:

+ **Maximizing the efficiency of network traffic**: The ability to move the data from Point A to Point B as fast as possible.

+ **Reliability**: A LAN is one of those things that no one notices until it fails to function.

+ **Manageability**: So that you can see trends of growth and traffic patterns, as well as identify bottlenecks and problem areas.

✦ **Flexibility**: To be able to adapt to changing environment needs (not the least of which is growth), as well as the introduction of new technologies and applications that require more bandwidth.

Of course, there is no black and white, right or wrong, when it comes to LAN design. Like designing a house, there are many ways to do it, all of which can be right. Sometimes it's a matter of philosophy and personal preferences based on past experiences.

Get as much help as you can, and get as many heads into the process as you can. Tap all the expertise you know. Your VARs and vendors, as well as your staff can help.

Location of Devices

The first consideration in designing a LAN has to be the location of all the devices. This will help you determine the layout of segments, and so on. This will also impact where you put your network switches and Intermediate Distribution Frames (IDFs) since cable runs have distance maximums. Also consider the locations of your centralized resources (e.g., servers and data center). See Chapter 10 on page 255 for a discussion on the physical plant issues regarding data centers, cable types, and IDFs.

Traffic Volume

You then need to consider the volume of traffic. The volume can vary because of the number of devices or the types of data (low-bandwidth requirements for data entry, or high-bandwidth needs for full-motion video). In addition to the volume, consider the traffic patterns. Are most users only sending/receiving data to central servers? Or is there an expectation for a large amount of peer-to-peer sharing? Are these servers located centrally or spread throughout the environment?

The Core Network

Typically, a LAN will have a "core." This is essentially the backbone of the network, and all other devices extend from it.

In a simple network (see Figure 12.3), the core could be a single device, such as the switch in the data center.

In a more complex environment, the core network might be multiple devices like the two switches in the data center in Figure 12.4.

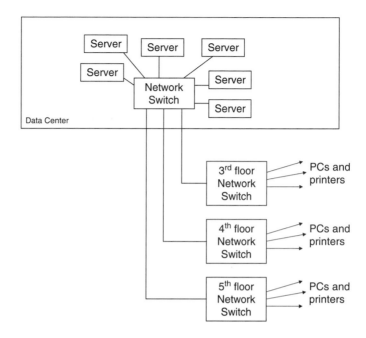

Figure 12.3   A Network with a Single Switch as the Core Network

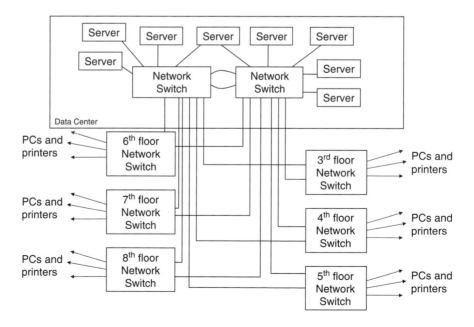

Figure 12.4   A Network with Two Switches as the Core Network

Using multiple switches could serve combined purposes of additional connectivity and redundancy.

The heart of any LAN are the switches, which filter and forward packets between LAN segments. Switches operate at the data link layer (Layer 2) and sometimes the network layer (Layer 3) of the OSI Model, which enable them to support any packet protocol. All the individual devices connect to the switch, which then connects back to the core.

Features of Switches

Like any piece of IT hardware, there are a variety of options and considerations when selecting a switch.

Number And Types Of Connections Required   One of the most important considerations is how many devices you'll be connecting to the switch. If you don't have sufficient connections, the device is obviously not going to meet the needs. Similarly, you have to consider the types of connections you'll need (fiber or copper) and the speed of those connections. Not only will you consider the devices you're connecting to the switch, but you'll also consider any uplink(s) to other switches, such as in the core.

Total Throughput   How much total traffic is being pushed through the switch is also a consideration. Even though each of the ports may be able to support a gigabit connection, it doesn't mean that the switch can handle every port simultaneously pushing through gigabit traffic. The total throughput of the switch can be an important factor for determining which ones are right for your environment.

Redundancies   Your network switches are key components since so many devices are dependent on them. Many of the higher end switches have a variety of redundancies to ensure maximum up-time. These can include several redundancies like power supplies, uplinks to the core network, and management modules.

Forwarding Methods   There are three different methods for switches to use for forwarding data:

1. In *store and forward* the switch stores the incoming data until the entire frame is received, and then validates its integrity before forwarding it to its next destination.

2. *Cut-through forward* (often referred to simply as cut-through) is the opposite of store and forward, in that the switch forwards the data before the whole

frame has been received. This technique improves speed, but decreases reliability since it doesn't allow for integrity checking (e.g., validating the checksum) before sending the data on.

3. *Fragment free* is a compromise between store and forward and cut-through. With fragment free, the switch stores the first 64 bytes of the frame before forwarding the frame. The reason for storing only the first 64 bytes is that network errors and collisions generally occur in the first 64 bytes.

A fourth method, called *adaptive switching* automatically switches between the above three methods as conditions on the network change.

Layer 2 or Layer 3   Switches can either function at Layer 2 or 3 of the OSI model, and refer to the layer at which the switch decides how to forward the packet. Layer 2 switches use a table that tracks the MAC addresses and their corresponding port on the switch. Instead of MAC addresses, Layer 3 switches maintain a table of network addresses and switch ports, and make their forwarding decisions based on the network address information found in Layer 3, rather than just the MAC address found in Layer 2. Layer 3 switches function like routers because of the similar Layer 3 forwarding decision handling. However, Layer 3 switches tend to have better throughput because of the hardware processing of the address tables rather than the software.

Since routing occurs at Layer 3 and some LAN switches function at Layer 3, there can be confusion as to the difference between a router and a Layer 3 switch. In truth, the distinction between the two products is becoming grayer and grayer. Layer 3 switching is very similar to routing, with both using the same type of routing algorithms. The main distinction between the two devices is more of a factor of usage. Layer 3 switching is more effective for segmenting a LAN than providing a WAN connection. Layer 3 switching is pretty much a variation on the technology used for determining the efficiency of available paths, and gives you the ability to segment your LAN within itself. The rule of thumb to remember is "route once, switch many." See the section Routers (page 327) later in this chapter for additional information about routers.

Chassis or Stackable   The advantage of a chassis device is that the configuration can be easily altered by swapping components as needed, and if a component fails, it can usually be replaced with minimal disruption to the environment. On the other hand, the up-front cost of the chassis itself can make this architecture expensive if the environment it serves isn't large enough to fully populate most of the chassis's slots. Stackable devices don't require the up-front investment of a chassis. They are available with small numbers of ports (e.g., 12, 24, 48) and can be ideal for a small office or department. As the environment grows, additional units can be added. Stackables are inexpensive and convenient. However, they may lack some of the conveniences of chassis-based

Table 12.4 WiFi standards

Standard	Speed	Frequency	Notes
802.11a	54 Mbps	5 Ghz	
802.11b	11 Mbps	2.4 Ghz	
802.1lg	54 Mbps	2.4 Ghz	Backward compatible with 802.11b

devices (e.g., redundant power supplies, high-end options, and management capabilities).

Wireless LANs

In the past few years, the cost of wireless technology (popularly known as WiFi (for Wireless Fidelity) has become so cheap that it can be easily installed for home use for under $100. The obvious advantage of a wireless environment is that it eliminates the need to run cabling. In the office, many workers find it very convenient to take their laptop to a conference room and wirelessly connect to the network.

As quickly as wireless LANs have taken root, the technology has improved and advanced, resulting in a few different standards. While there are more, three WiFi standards have emerged as the most popular, see Table 12.4.

When WiFi's popularity took off, the "b" version of the standard was virtually the only option available. As other standards came into play, the large installed base of b devices made backward compatibility a key concern, which led to the popularity of the "g" standard. Today, it's easy to find devices that will support all three standards.

Wireless Security

When WiFi was initially deployed, it was considered a very weak technology and easily hacked. In recent years, various security solutions have been developed to help keep wireless networks secure:

✦ **Wired Equivalent Privacy (WEP)**: The first method developed for securing wireless LANs. WEP uses a "key" (either 40 or 128 bits in length) to encrypt and decrypt the data. Some of WEP's deficiencies are that all wireless devices on the network have to use the same key, the key length is considered too short, and the keys can be quickly hacked using readily available utilities.

✦ **WiFi Protected Access (WPA)**: Uses Temporal Key Integrity Protocol (TKIP), and was developed in response to the weakness of WEP. TKIP addresses the encryption weaknesses of WEP by changing the key with each data frame. Another key component of WPA is built-in authentication, which WEP doesn't offer. This allows for easier administration in a large environment.

✦ **Hidden SSID**: Every wireless network has an identifier called the Service Set Identifier (SSID). In a setting where there are multiple WiFi networks accessible (which is becoming increasingly common), the SSID identifies which network is which, allowing you to identify the one you want to connect to. By disabling the broadcast of the SSID, you are essentially hiding the existence of your WiFi network. While this is a good way to keep out the casual or nosey intruder, there are utilities readily available to discover these hidden networks.

✦ **MAC Filtering**: A favorite technique for protecting WiFi networks is to only allow predetermined devices to connect to it by specifying the MAC address of authorized devices. While this helps to prevent intruders, it creates a significant administrative burden to maintain the list of MAC addresses.

✦ **Internet Access Only**: Given the challenge of balancing WiFi security with its convenience, many organizations have decided to find a compromise. Instead of trying to make the WiFi environment more secure with additional technology, they have eliminated some of the security hurdles and decided that instead of connecting their wireless network to their internal LAN, *it will only connect to the Internet*. Essentially, this means that even if an unwanted user does gain access to the WiFi network, the only resources they can get to are those on the public Internet. For authorized users who want to connect to internal company resources, they must then use the approved remote access solutions (such as VPN or Web-based e-mail). See Figure 12.5.

Bluetooth

Bluetooth (named for 10th century Viking King Harald Blåtand, a Danish king who united Denmark and Norway) is another wireless technology. Depending on who you talk to, Bluetooth is either a translation of Blåtand, or a reference to his stained teeth resulting from his penchant for blueberries. Bluetooth technology has a much shorter range (typically 30 feet) than WiFi (up to 300 feet,

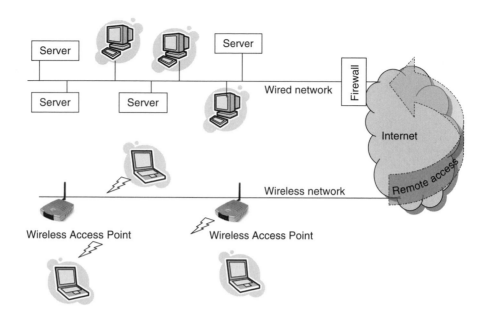

Figure 12.5 Connecting to the Company Network Via WiFi

depending on circumstances). As such, it is generally considered more of an alternative for replacing cables between devices (e.g., between a PDA and a desktop computer) than a networking solution. Similarly, Bluetooth speeds are limited (currently at about 700 Kbps, but faster speeds are expected in future iterations of the technology).

In general, Bluetooth is considered a wireless alternative for USB-type connections, while WiFi is considered a wireless alternative for Ethernet connections.

12.4 Wide Area Networks

A WAN is a network that connects the remote locations via telecommunications facilities (T-1 lines, ISDN, etc.). Unlike a LAN, a WAN can span large distances (such as cross-country). The network resources within the locations of a WAN, by the way, are generally considered to be part of the LAN. Designing a WAN is very similar to designing a LAN: you have to consider geography, traffic flow, and volumes. One of the key differentiators in LAN versus WAN issues is that the vast majority of LAN costs are up-front capital expenditures of cable installation and hardware. On the other hand, the vast majority of WAN costs are often in recurring operating costs for lines.

You'll want to examine the expected traffic load between sites. Very often, the volume of data is directly proportional to the number of devices. But this isn't a hard-and-fast rule. The data center may have just a few devices (compared to the thousands of computers at corporate headquarters in the next state), but the volume of traffic to servers in the data center would be quite high.

Additionally, you need to consider the type of traffic between sites. If the only data going between the sites is data entry from an accounting application, the volume of data will be rather low. However, if large data files are being transmitted (e.g., multimedia or database replication), it could be a very high volume.

Considerations for a WAN

+ The need for high-speed transmissions.

+ The need for 24/7 operations.

+ User needs: Where are your users? If they are all sitting in your remote offices, then a connection from your headquarters to those offices would dictate one kind of design. However, if your users are the sales team, and they are constant travelers trying to connect from hotels, airports, and customer sites, than a different design is called for (discussed more in the later section Remote Access).

+ Backup/fail-over capabilities and facilities: The most critical connections need to be the most reliable. An analog, ISDN, or VPN connection might be sufficient backup. Or you may want to have multiple high-speed connections between your sites so that if one line fails the other continues to provide services.

+ Installation delays: The more sophisticated the line, the more time your telecommunications vendor will need to install it. A simple POTS ("Plain Old Telephone System") line could be installed in 1–2 weeks. However, higher end lines (e.g., T-3) could take months. This could be critical if your WAN requirements are very dynamic.

Your telcos and vendors will probably be eager to help you design an appropriate WAN solution often at little or no cost.

Routers

Just as switches are the primary networking hardware for a LAN, routers are the key devices for a WAN. Routers are the hardware that forward data to another network, using a technique called *routing*, which occurs at Layer 3 (the Network layer) of the OSI 7-layer model. In essence, a router acts as the transfer point between two networks to pass data packets between them. To know how to route the data to its destination, routers communicate with other routers and share information, to create and maintain a routing table, which is constantly being updated.

The routing table is used by the routers to determine the best path to use for each data packet, and serves as a logical map of the network with the address of the next router on the path to a given network destination. Routers periodically broadcast their routing tables to other routers so that they can each update their own tables with the most recent information about the networks and routes. In this way, routing tables are kept current as the network changes.

Some of the same issues that have to be considered when considering a switch (e.g., throughput, redundancies, etc., discussed above in the section Features of Switches on page 322), apply to routers as well.

Key WAN Technologies

When designing a WAN strategy, it's important to know the different connectivity options available. In general, there are several options:

✦ Point-to-point circuits

✦ Dial-up and ISDN

✦ Broadband (cable modems and DSL)

✦ Packet switching (ATM and frame relay)

✦ High-speed Internet

✦ Virtual Private Networks(VPNs)

Some of the solutions overlap; for example, a VPN connection can be (and often is) used with several connection types (such as broadband and high-speed Internet).

Point-to-Point Circuits

Point-to-point circuits, also known as leased, dedicated, and private lines, are facilities from telecom carriers that provide a connection between two locations. Point-to-point circuits can connect sites that are across town or across the country.

The primary advantage of a leased line is that it's always up, 24 hours a day. The cost is fixed and doesn't vary by usage. Since the line is dedicated, when there is a problem with the service the telephone company can investigate, locate, and resolve it. (This is in contrast to a static-y dial-up connection, which is usually only resolved by hanging up and dialing again.)

The most popular leased lines are T-1 and T-3.

- ✦ A T-1 line consists of 24 channels, each of which can provide 64 Kbps, for an aggregate throughput of 1.544 Mbps.

- ✦ A T-3 (often referred to as DS3) line is a leased line that provides data transmission speeds of 44.736 Mbps, via 672 circuits, each of which can support 64 Kbps transmissions.

Quite often, a company will use a fractional T-1 or a fractional T-3. A fractional line is one that uses only a portion of the available channels. While this reduces the throughput, there is also a significant cost savings.

Here is a list of some of the types of lines available:

- ✦ DS0 = 64 Kbps (basic POTS line)

- ✦ ISDN = 128 Kbps (Two DS0 lines)

- ✦ T-1 = 1.544 Mbps (24 DS0 lines at 64 K each, plus signaling (8 Kbps))

- ✦ T-3 = 44.736 (28 T-1s plus signaling)

- ✦ OC3 = 155 Mbps (3 DS3s)

- ✦ OC12 = 622 Mbps (4 OC3s)

- ✦ OC48 = 2.5 Gbps (4 OC12s)

- ✦ OC192 = 9.6 Gpbs (4 OC48s)

Different Overseas Terminology   Outside of the United States, different nomenclature is used. For example:

- ✦ E0 = 64 Kbps

- ✦ E1 = 2.048 Mbps

- ✦ E2 = 8.4 Mbps

- ✦ E3 = 34.368 Mbps

- ✦ E4 = 139.264 Mbps

Dial-Up and ISDN

Everyone is familiar with dial-up lines, like the ones they have at home. While this method used to be the most popular, the availability of high-speed broadband connections has made dial-up the choice of last resort.

Dial-Up/POTS   The best known and most popular type of dial-up line is called a POTS (Plain Old Telephone System) line. A POTS line is what people have in their homes for their residential phone service. POTS lines are also used for fax machines and modems. Because POTS lines are based on analog technology, the highest speed connection available is 56 Kbps, but even connections at this speed are rare. The advantage of POTS is its ubiquity.

POTS lines aren't the most cost-effective (particularly for travelers using dial-up connectivity to make long distance calls from their hotel rooms back to their servers at headquarters). To reduce these charges, some dialers allow you to take advantage of the cheaper fees available via calling-card accounts. Alternatively, if connection to the Internet is what is required, signing travelers up with a nationwide ISP subscription (e.g., Verizon, AT&T, Earthlink) allows them to make local calls (as opposed to long distance) when connecting from remote locations. Taking this idea a step further, vendors like iPass have contracted with providers around the globe, allowing travelers to find connectivity (wireless, dial-up, broadband) options wherever they go, and not be limited to the options of any single ISP.

ISDN   In the 1980s, Integrated Services Digital Network (ISDN) began to become available. ISDN allows for digital transmission over standard copper telephone wire. There are two types of ISDN: the Basic Rate Interface (BRI), usually used in homes and small businesses, and the Primary Rate Interface (PRI), for larger sites. Both types include a number of B (bearer) channels, which carry the actual data, and a D (delta) channel, which is used for signaling. A BRI consists of two 64 Kbps B channels and one 16 Kbps D channel, providing an aggregate throughput of 128 Kbps. A PRI consists of 23 B channels and one 64 Kbps D channel, for a total throughput of 1.4 Mbps. Note that the PRI's capacity is close to that of a T-1. However, since ISDN is billed based on usage and can be used to connect to multiple locations, a PRI can be a more cost-effective solution than a T-1. In fact, ISDN lines are often used as a backup to a leased line circuit.

ISDN popularity seemed to peak in the mid-1990s. Lack of standards, expensive installations, and a relatively small gain in bandwidth for the home consumer (via BRI service) all helped to limit its growth. In addition, with the per-minute charges for ISDN connections, a highly used ISDN line can get very expensive.

ISDN circuits "dial" their calls, similar to the way POTS lines do. As such, ISDN lines can be used to connect to different destinations (assuming, of course, those destinations are properly equipped to receive an ISDN connection). In the mid to late 1990s, as the use of the Internet to provide connectivity took off, and broadband service became increasingly available, ISDN usage waned considerably. Still, it does have a niche for certain needs.

Broadband

Broadband is a term whose definition has somewhat morphed over the years. Technically, it refers to a connection type that can carry more than one signal at a time (as opposed to base-band which can only carry one signal). Lately, however, broadband has come to refer to a "high-speed" connection to the Internet. Of course, high-speed is a relative term, but popular usage would probably put it in the range of 128 Kbps, or higher. Typically, broadband solutions offer a higher "downstream" rate than "upstream" because users are generally doing more downloading than uploading. Another differentiator of broadband from dial-up (also called "narrow-band") is that it's "always on" — there is no number to dial, no busy signals, etc. It's this always-on convenience that has escalated security concerns in recent years, and created the need for personal firewalls on individual devices. Broadband connections are usually priced at a fixed monthly fee and aren't usage based.

Telecommuters are using broadband to connect to the office (as opposed to using dial-up or ISDN connections). In addition, broadband can be a cost-effective alternative for a small office. Combining the use of a cable modem with VPN technology to establish a connection to corporate headquarters provides speed and security.

DSL Digital Subscriber Link (DSL) is a phone company offering for bringing high-speed Internet connectivity to homes and small businesses over standard copper phone lines. Although DSL does run over existing residential lines, it isn't dial-up. DSL provides an always-on connection to your service provider, which is generally the local telephone company. In general, DSL is configured asynchronously (ADSL) to provide high-speed downloads (up to T-1 speeds) and slower speed uploads approximately 128 to 384 Kbps. To be able to use DSL, the home or business must be within a few miles of a telephone company central office.

Cable Modems Cable TV companies all across the country are taking advantage of their existing infrastructure to deliver high-speed Internet access. This is a natural outgrowth of the fact that the technology that brings 100+ TV channels to your home has enormous bandwidth, and that the wire (right to your living room) is already in place. Throughput via a cable modem can vary by cable company and with usage. However, speeds are often in the range of 384 Kbps upstream and 2 Mbps downstream.

Packet Switching

Packet switching technology breaks up a data transmission into small packets. Each packet is then transmitted through the network, generally on different paths, to the destination. At the destination, the packets are reassembled. One of the advantages of using packet switching is that if a portion of the network becomes unavailable (e.g., a resource or segment is down), the packets will find an alternative route through the rest of the network.

ATM and Frame Relay   The two most popular packet switching technologies are frame relay and Asynchronous Transfer Mode (ATM). Frame relay speeds are available between 56 Kbps and 45 Mbps. ATM offers speeds from 25 to 622 Mbps. With ATM's high speed, it is often used for delay-sensitive applications like voice and video, in addition to data. The actual packet switching networks are referred to as clouds. Each of your sites has a line (usually a high-speed leased line) that connects it to the cloud. Then a private virtual circuit (PVC) is established through the cloud to allow your sites to connect to each other. Frame relay and ATM networks are provided by telecom carriers like AT&T and Sprint.

With packet switching, your service is generally priced on a minimum bandwidth. For ATM this is referred to as the Sustained Information Rate (SIR), and for frame relay it is referred to the Committed Information Rate (CIR) — although CIR is the term used with increasing frequency for both technologies.

With a CIR or SIR the carrier is committing that data below this level will be delivered. It's possible that additional traffic may also be delivered, but it's not guaranteed. Of course, when data isn't delivered it has to be re-transmitted until it is, which can impact overall performance. Some vendors offer a CIR of 0, which essentially means that the network will deliver as much data as it can, without any commitments, to a specific throughput.

High-Speed Internet

No organization's technology environment is complete without a connection to the Internet. In fact, it's virtually a necessity and prerequisite to a successful operation. There are a number of alternatives for connecting to the Internet including those solutions discussed in the above section Point-to-Point Circuits, which would probably be used by larger organizations; and the Broadband section, which would be more in line with smaller organizations and the Small Office, Home Office (SOHO) market.

When requesting an Internet connection from a carrier, or ISP, you're generally looking at two types of fees. The first fee is for the physical connection, or the line that comes into your office. The second fee is for the Internet access. For example, the cost for a point-to-point T-1 that connects two of your offices together is just related to the cost of the physical connection. That's because the carrier really is just giving you the line and leaving the use of that line up to you. In short, the carrier isn't adding any value or service to that line. However, if you want a T-1 to the Internet, not only are you paying for the cost of the line, but you also are paying for the "service" of Internet access. Since the carrier has to build and pay for the infrastructure for that Internet access, those costs are passed on to you.

Your ISP or carrier may also be providing you with additional services such as DNS, public IP addresses, etc. (which may be bundled into the costs or priced separately). For smaller organizations, ISPs can offer a full set of services such as Web, e-mail, and FTP servers.

Internet connection alternatives also include "burstable" lines. Essentially, this means that although you purchased a connection of a particular bandwidth, periodic "bursts" of higher throughput can be accommodated. Burstable solutions are very convenient for organizations that have occasional peak demands. Of course, burstable lines are more expensive.

Virtual Private Network

An alternative to ATM and frame relay for a packet switching solution is the Internet. By using various security and tunneling techniques, a VPN can be established via the Internet to connect sites. The advantage of a VPN is significantly reduced costs. However, since the data is traveling over public facilities, specific transmission rates can't be guaranteed. Additionally, even though information is encrypted in the VPN tunnel, it isn't as secure as a "private" connection. Additionally, the encryption and decryption of the data does impact overall throughput.

For remote offices, the concept of "split-tunneling" is often used with their VPN connection. In this situation, each remote office has a connection to the Internet and establishes a VPN back to headquarters to reach the company's systems and applications. However, for local Internet access (e.g., Web surfing), data travels directly from the remote office to the Internet, without first going back to headquarters. While this improves efficiency and throughput, it can also increase the administration since appropriate firewalls must be installed and administered in each remote office.

12.5 Remote Access

Long gone are the days when all work was only done by people sitting at their desks, 9 to 5, Monday through Friday. In a peculiarly vicious circle, we first developed technology that could run 24/7 so that batch processing of transactions could take place while we slept, and a nice report would be waiting for us at 9 a.m. the next morning. Now, we find ourselves striving to keep up with that never-asleep technology, and are constantly chasing the latest innovations for anytime, anywhere access.

At the very minimum, remote access allows employees to access e-mail from home. At the other end of the spectrum, employees need access to all IT resources as if they were in their own office, even if they're in a hotel room in Kuala Lumpur.

Whether it's the CEO wanting to access e-mails, the sales force needing access to warehouse inventories, or the network manager needing to resolve a problem at 3 a.m., virtually every organization has a need for remote access.

The Choices

You have a number of choices for remote access solutions resulting from a combination of two primary considerations: your connection path to your data and applications and what you connect to.

Your Connection Path

- ✦ Internet access
- ✦ Direct access
- ✦ Handheld device

What You Connect To

- ✦ Web-based applications
- ✦ Remote control
- ✦ Remote node
- ✦ Handheld device applications
- ✦ Replication (synchronization)

Before making any decisions, we go back to the same old question: What are the needs of your customers? Some users may need to have access to the full suite of business applications, while others are primarily interested in e-mail.

The Connection Path

One of the two key considerations for remote access is the path you use to connect back to your systems. You primarily have three options for connection:

+ Through the Internet

+ Through a direct connection

+ Through the air waves using a handheld device

Connecting Through the Internet

Using the Internet is certainly the most popular way of providing connectivity for remote users. And that popularity is based on its ubiquity. Almost anywhere you go, be it the neighborhood coffee shop, a hotel, your mother-in-law's house, or a customer site, you can find access to the Internet. Of course, those connections may come through various technologies (dial-up at your mother-in-law's, wireless from the coffee shop, or hard-wired at the hotel).

In many places Internet connectivity is free, or can be purchased for brief periods (e.g., 24-hour increments in hotels, a few hours in airports and coffee shops). Wireless subscriptions can be obtained through services like T-mobile. ISPs like Earthlink and AOL offer the convenience of local numbers for dial-up service across the country. Vendors like iPass have contracted with providers around the globe, allowing travelers to find connectivity (wireless, dial-up, broadband) options wherever they go, and not be limited to the options of any single ISP.

Although the Internet offers convenience, it does expose some security risks. However, these can be mitigated with a number of solutions (SecurID, VPN, etc.), which are discussed later in this chapter and in Chapter 13, Security.

Direct Connections

As late as the mid 1990s, "direct" connections were the method of choice for remote access. And that was primarily a result of the fact that the Internet was in its infancy. The choices for direct connections are pretty limited: dial-up service (slow, but available virtually anywhere you have a telephone), leased lines (fast, expensive), and ISDN (a compromise on both speed and cost). Of course, with ISDN and leased lines you sacrifice some flexibility because each location has to be set up in advance, and it usually just isn't worth the time, money, and effort to set it up in all the places from which your users may need access. The exceptions might be the setup of a satellite office or a special event or project.

Handheld Devices and Wireless Data Networks

Typified by the Blackberry device from Research in Motion (RIM), handheld devices can be highly effective tools for the mobile user. These devices are mostly used for reading and composing e-mails, and lack the ability to run full-scale business applications, although they can run scaled down versions. However, these devices are attractive to many people because they are extremely small and lightweight (they can be carried in a pocket, purse, or belt clip), and usually can serve double duty as a cell phone (thereby eliminating the need to carry a separate device to make phone calls).

In addition to the Blackberry, other examples of handheld devices include Palm's Treo devices, various devices that run Microsoft's Windows Mobile operating system such as the HP iPAQ, or cell phones from a variety of carriers and manufacturers (e.g., Sprint, Motorola, Samsung, etc.).

It's important to note that for handheld wireless devices to work effectively, you'll need the appropriate back-end infrastructure such as Microsoft's Exchange for Windows Mobile Devices, RIM's Blackberry Enterprise Server (BES) for Blackberry devices, or Good Technology's GoodLink.

Depending on the particular solutions, these devices can provide e-mail service, phone service, Internet access, and business applications.

What You Connect To

Previously, we described the different paths available to get to your systems. The next concern is what is available to users via that connection.

Web-Based Applications

Typically, organizations may choose to make some applications accessible on the public Internet. The most popular example of this is a Web interface to electronic mail such as Microsoft's Outlook Web Access (OWA) or iNotes from Lotus Notes. These allow users and employees to access their mailbox from any Internet connected workstation without the need for special software or a specifically configured device.

In some cases other business applications may also be available via the Internet. These may be the same applications available to be customers, but employee IDs provide them with access to additional functions, features, and modules.

Remote Control

With a remote control scenario, the user is essentially taking control of another device on the network that has all the appropriate applications. There are a number of advantages to remote control:

- ✦ The only special software needed on the device the user has at the remote location are for:

  - ✦ establishing the connection (e.g., such as a dialer and/or VPN client), and

  - ✦ establishing the remote control session.

Depending on the circumstances of the particular environment, both of these may be features of the operating systems.

- ✦ The device controlled is usually on the LAN of the user's organization. As such, all the operations (such as file access) happen at the speed of a local user.

- ✦ The only data sent between the two devices are keystrokes, mouse movements, and changes in the screen content.

- ✦ It gives you some ability to mix operating systems. For example, a user with a Macintosh or Unix-based device at home may be able to connect to and control a Windows-based device at the office.

The above list mitigates the importance of the hardware that the user has at the remote end. A user could have a device that is several years old, but during the remote control session she enjoys the performance level of the high-end device she is controlling.

An additional advantage of remote control is that application software doesn't have to be installed on the end users' PCs. Everything is done at the device(s) being controlled. As a result, support demand is reduced since all configuration issues are primarily with the device(s) being controlled, which are generally easily accessible since they are on site.

Remote control is often a convenient solution when a network connection isn't terribly reliable or stable. If you should lose your connection to the remote device, your work isn't lost — it is still on the remote device. Once you regain connectivity, you can reconnect to the remote device and find your work as you left it. If you were running a long request (perhaps generating a report), the processing would also continue when you lost your connection.

Remote control can be a highly effective remote access solution that simplifies administration, management, and support. Many programmers use remote control at home to connect to their own desktop back in the office. This eliminates the need (and burden) to keep their home PC identically configured with their work machine with all of the various tools and utilities they need.

Remote control software is available from a variety of vendors and sources. Elements of remote control are built into Windows with Windows Terminal Services, the Remote Desktop Connection (RDC), and Remote Assistance tools.

Centralized Remote Control Initially, remote control was simply used for users at one device to control another device in a 1 to 1 scenario. However, with the growing popularity of remote control for remote access, it became necessary for IT to be able to better manage and administer all of this remote control activity.

As such, solutions began to appear (most notably, a variety of offerings from Citrix Systems, and Windows Terminal Services from Microsoft) to improve the functionality of remote control and ease the administration. When remote control is centralized, multiple users can simultaneously have their own independent remote control sessions, but those sessions are all running on a common server. These solutions also allow the IT Managers to determine which applications are available to which users. And the server software makes it very easy to administer and manage remote access and distribute new applications and upgrades to all those remote users.

Remote Node

Remote node is essentially the opposite of remote control. With remote node, the remote user's PC acts like any other PC on the internal LAN with one critical difference: instead of a connection speed of 100 Mbps, the user is limited to the throughput of the connection type she is using. For a dial-up connection, this could be a paltry 56 Kbps or a more robust broadband connection of 384 Kbps.

One way to address the speed issues with remote node is to have the applications loaded onto the remote workstation. This way only the data is accessed remotely, while the software itself is loaded from the local hard drive. Of course, this could then create the additional burdens of installing, updating, and supporting software on remote devices.

Handheld Device Applications

In addition to phone and e-mail service, these devices also allow users to view certain attachments and access some Web sites. However, an even greater value may be the applications that can be downloaded to these devices. They can be stand-alone applications, perhaps to help your sales reps figure out how much product your customer should order given certain parameters; or perhaps solutions that interface with your back-end business applications, such as replacing your sales force's paper forms so that the order can be electronically uploaded instead of manually keyed in. In addition, several Enterprise Resource Planning (ERP) vendors such as SAP and Oracle can interface with handheld devices.

Many applications are available for handhelds via free or purchased downloads. However, developing customized applications for handhelds, while growing in popularity, remains a small corner of the traditional application development world.

Replication (Synchronization)

Remote access presents some special concerns. Using the remote control or remote node techniques mentioned above, users can read and write e-mail and access files and applications exactly like they do in the office. However, to do so requires that they be connected at the time they are doing it.

Through a process known as synchronization or off-line replication, users can have their files with them when they travel.

With e-mail, the user can read and compose e-mail while they are disconnected from the network. Then, when they do connect, all the messages they composed are transmitted to the server, and in turn, the server sends to their workstation all the new messages that have come in for that user.

For other types of files (like documents and spreadsheets), the files are also replicated to the local device while connected to the network. When disconnected, the user can then view and edit them, and any changes the user made are automatically replicated back to the server the next time they connect.

Advantages   The advantage of synchronization is that it reduces the amount of time needed (and perhaps the cost) for connecting since the connection is needed only for the transfer of data between the end-user and the server (as opposed to keeping the connection open while e-mails are being written, documents are read and edited, etc.). Equally as important, it allows users to get work done even when they don't have connectivity, such as on a plane, during a dull meeting, in the backyard, or sitting in a waiting room somewhere.

Disadvantage   Replication only really works for remote node solutions. If used in a remote control scenario, the data would be replicated to the device you are controlling, as opposed to the device you are using. Along these lines, replication requires that you have the appropriate application software loaded on the device you have, otherwise you won't be able to do much with the data you're replicating.

Security for Remote Access

Although security is discussed in detail in Chapter 13 on Security (page 349), there are some common techniques for trying to bolster security for remote access.

Firewalls

Typically, the gateways for remote access reside outside your network (so that they can be accessed remotely) in the firewall's demilitarized zone (DMZ). Then, the firewall rules are written so that the traffic coming through the remote access gateway can only get to predetermined internal devices. For example, traffic coming through your Web-based e-mail portal would only be able to communicate with your internal e-mail servers.

VPNs

VPNs are used for connections that come via the Internet to encrypt the data. Since the data is traveling across the public Internet, without encryption, it is at risk for being viewed or intercepted by hackers. VPNs use a variety of techniques to secure the data.

PPTP Point-to-Point Tunneling Protocol (PPTP) was developed in 1996 by Ascend Communications, Microsoft Corporation, 3Com/Primary Access, ECI Telematics, and U.S. Robotics; this group is known collectively as the PPTP Forum.

Although favored by Microsoft, many security experts have criticized the protocol. Like any aged security standard, methods of cracking PPTP have arisen. PPTP is no longer considered a secure protocol, and its use has been declining in favor of other protocols like IPSec and L2TP.

L2TP Layer 2 Tunneling Protocol (L2TP) combines two secure communications protocols: Cisco Systems' Layer Two Forwarding (L2F) and Microsoft's PPTP. L2TP doesn't include encryption or per-packet authentication and must be combined with another protocol, such as IPSec, to provide the data integrity and confidentiality needed for a VPN solution.

IPsec IPsec operates at the Network layer (Layer 3) of the OSI Model and uses algorithms and a public key to encrypt the data. In addition to encrypting the data, it authenticates the two end nodes in the communication session using the Internet Key Exchange (IKE) protocol.

IPsec has two modes:

✦ In transport mode, only the data portion of the packet is encrypted, but not the header

✦ In tunnel mode, both the header and the data are the encrypted

RADIUS

Remote Authentication Dial-In User Service (RADIUS) is a protocol that operates between the client and a remote access server. When a user attempts to dial in to a remote access device, the device first attempts to authenticate the user with a central RADIUS server. If the user is authenticated, the user is routed to the network; otherwise the user is disconnected.

12.6 Network Management

With so much dependency on, and investment in, your network, it's critical to make sure it's managed well. There are entire categories of technologies to manage networks that might run thousands or tens of thousands of dollars. In this section, we'll cover some of the basic technologies of network management.

Ideally, managing a network should be a task that is done proactively. Unfortunately, in practice it's often done reactively: When a problem occurs, you need to go find it and fix it. There are almost certainly problems on your network right now. If you connected a network monitoring device, you might see hundreds of minor problems that could be investigated: collisions, incomplete packets, time-outs, and so on.

Finding Problems

One of the frustrating things about managing a network is that, for the most part, it consists of copper and fiber connections. When data isn't moving, a close look at that copper or fiber won't reveal the cause, and it sure doesn't have a screen displaying error messages. However, you can buy tools that can essentially do that for you.

Vendors of your network hardware (switches, routers, etc.) generally offer some type of management functionality that allows you to gather data about the network. However, very often this is information primarily related to the operation of that particular vendor's hardware. You can also buy products (e.g., Network General's Sniffer) that can connect to your network and allow you to examine the traffic, run traces, trap specific types of problems, and so on.

Products like this are rather complex, though, and a complex tool in the hands of a novice is of little use. On the other hand, there are simpler tools (like those that can test and/or trace a cable to help determine where it is connected, and to see if it is wired properly or cut somewhere that you can't see).

Management Tools

SNMP and RMON are the primary standards and technologies used for network monitoring and management. There have been subsequent enhancements of each, leading to three versions of SNMP and two versions of RMON.

SNMP

Simple Network Management Protocol (SNMP) is the underlying key to network management. It has been adopted by virtually all vendors, not only for network equipment like routers and switches, but for all product types like servers, workstations, and printers. SNMP works by sending messages, called protocol data units (PDUs), to various devices on the network. SNMP-compliant devices, called agents, store data about themselves in Management Information Bases (MIBs) and return this data to the SNMP requesters. The MIB specifies the data managed by the SNMP agents. The MIB defines the data that a manager can request from an agent, and the actions permitted on this data.

Each device on the network running an SNMP agent built into it communicates with an SNMP manager (which is any of a variety of management software applications available from different vendors such as HP's OpenView, IBM's Tivoli, or Computer Associates' Unicenter). The agents on these devices respond to messages from the SNMP managers. Perhaps even more important, the agents can send out unsolicited information, or "traps," to the management tools for an exception condition (such as a failing component). The management tool can then take a predetermined action depending on the severity and the circumstances. These actions might include running a script, sending out alerts to the support staff, or simply creating a log entry.

RMON

Remote monitoring (RMON) takes SNMP to the next level. While SNMP manages devices, RMON can monitor the actual network traffic, collect statistics, and record history. Technically, RMON is an extension to SNMP that was developed to overcome some of the limitations of SNMP, and uses a more complex

MIB. RMON isn't a replacement for SNMP. SNMP can still be used by SNMP management solutions to collect information from RMON devices.

Quality of Service (QoS) and Bandwidth Management

Networking Quality of Service (QoS) refers to a variety of techniques that allow you to prioritize types of traffic or applications. QoS is primarily used to give priority to "time-sensitive" applications. In environments where the network is used for video or audio applications (such as voice-over IP), QoS is used to ensure that that traffic gets priority over other types. QoS mechanisms are built into a variety of hardware and software products (e.g., Cisco and Microsoft), and are also in numerous appliances made by different vendors (e.g., Allot, Packeteer, Juniper Networks). In addition, your carriers and ISPs may have QoS offerings to help you with your Internet and WAN connections.

With QoS you can

✦ Classify different types of traffic (video, audio, data), so that each can be given appropriate treatment and priority

✦ Prioritize mission-critical and time-sensitive traffic

✦ Load balance across multiple resources for redundancy and performance

Because QoS policies are based on specifics of the data (packet types, source and destination address, etc.) it can't be used on encrypted traffic (such as data coming through a VPN tunnel), since the content of the encrypted data can't be inspected.

Not only can these tools help prioritize the traffic you want, they can help you limit (or halt) the traffic you don't want. For example, you can use QoS to ensure that precious bandwidth isn't wasted by your employees making use of file-sharing services (such as Gnutella, Kazaa, etc.). Not only would this help reduce the use of company resources for non-company activities, but in the case of some file-sharing services it could reduce the company's exposure to accusation of violations of copyright and intellectual property laws.

12.7　**Voice and Data Convergence**

The past few years have seen a great deal of progress in the convergence of voice and data. Traditional Time-Division Multiplexing (TDM) phones are slowly losing ground to Voice-Over IP (VoIP) solutions (see Table 12.5).

Table 12.5 Pros and cons of VoIP

PRO		CON	
PRO	You only having to administer and manage one infrastructure.	**CON**	VoIP is still a relatively new technology, and there are concerns about security risks and exposures that it may introduce.
	You can put a handset in any location on the planet as long as it has IP connectivity back to your PBX switch. For example, if your HQ location is in New York, your users in California can easily have handsets connected to the HQ telephone system. When a customer dials the New York number, it rings in California. A Californian can dial the 4-digit extension of a New Yorker without incurring any costs.		There can be issues of audio-quality problems, particularly with network congestion or packet-loss problems.
	Since IP connectivity is generally available anyway, you're not really incurring any additional costs to use it for phone calls.		There is a risk that a network problem (or failure) may interrupt voice service as well as data.
	The use of "soft phones" that turn your telecommuters' or road-warriors' laptops into a telephone, eliminating long-distance charges (especially "hotel" long-distance fees), along with the added convenience of being able to take-and-make calls using their office number no matter where they are.		Since the handsets are now intelligent devices, they may require periodic software upgrades.

(Cont.)

Table 12.5   Pros and cons of VoIP (continued)

PRO	CON
Additional data integration. For example, having the handsets display your company's stock price, or notice of special events. Or, customized applications can be added to the screens of VoIP phones.	With a TDM system, if you could provide power to your PBX during a blackout, users could still make calls. With VoIP, you'd also need to provide power throughout your LAN to ensure that VoIP phones could communicate with the PBX.
	It requires a robust network to ensure that there is no latency.
	Requires your PBX staff to become more knowledgeable about data networking, and your data-networking team to be more knowledgeable about voice issues.

With VoIP, your telephone handsets use your LAN environment to connect to the telephone switch. Instead of the traditional "punch-down" blocks in the wiring closet for connecting phones, you simply plug the handset into the LAN jack on the wall, and it establishes a connection to your central switch. Voice traffic then travels over your Ethernet environment (along-side packets containing e-mail and accounts payable data).

VoIP solutions and products are now offered by major vendors (Avaya, Cisco, Nortel, etc.) The adoption of VoIP has been slow and steady over the past few years, but is expected to continue to grow.

Many companies are using office-relocation projects as an opportunity to implement VoIP.

12.8   Additional Resources

Web Sites

+ *www.allot.com* (network management appliance vendor)
+ *www.apnic.net* (Asia Pacific registry for IP addresses)

- ✦ *www.arin.net* (North American registry for IP addresses)
- ✦ *www.avaya.com* (network hardware and software vendor)
- ✦ *www.bluetooth.com* (industry trade group)
- ✦ *www.cisco.com* (network hardware and software vendor)
- ✦ *www.fluke.com* (cable testing tool vendor)
- ✦ *www.ietf.org* (Internet Engineering Task Force)
- ✦ *www.juniper.net* (network management appliance vendor)
- ✦ *lacnic.net/sp* (Latin American registry for IP addresses)
- ✦ *www.managementsoftware.hp.com/news/about/index.html* (HP's network management solution)
- ✦ *www.mobileinfo.com* (Web site for mobile computing information)
- ✦ *www.netqos.com* (network performance/optimization solution vendor)
- ✦ *www.networkgeneral.com* (network management vendor)
- ✦ *www.nortel.com* (network hardware and software vendor)
- ✦ *www.packeteer.com* (network management appliance vendor)
- ✦ *www.protocols.com* (detailed reference information about standards, protocols, etc.)
- ✦ *www.ripe.net* (Europe/Middle East registry for IP addresses)
- ✦ *www3.ca.com/solutions/Solution.aspx?ID=315* (Computer Associates' network management solution)
- ✦ *www-306.ibm.com/software/tivoli* (IBM's network management solution)

Books and Articles

- ✦ Carlson, Caron, "Alliance Tackles VoIP Threats," *eWeek*, October 24, 2005, p. 22.
- ✦ Della Maggiora, Paul L., and Doherty, Jim, *Cisco Networking Simplified*, Cisco Press, 2003.
- ✦ Erlanger, Leon, "Is VoIP Ripe for Attack?," *Infoworld*, October 17, 2005, p. 31.
- ✦ Farrel, Adrian, *The Internet and Its Protocols: A Comparative Approach*, Morgan Kaufmann, 2004.

✦ Forouzan, Behrouz, *Data Communications and Networking*, McGraw-Hill, 2003.

✦ Keagy, Scott, *Integrating Voice and Data Networks*, Cisco Press, 2000.

✦ Kurose, James F., and Ross, Keith W., *Computer Networking: A Top-Down Approach Featuring the Internet (3rd Edition)*, Addison Wesley, 2004.

✦ Littlejohn Shinder, Deborah, *Computer Networking Essentials*, Cisco Press, 2001.

✦ Liu, Circket, and Albitz, Paul, *DNS and Bind*, O'Reilly Media, Inc., 2001.

✦ Matthews, Jeanna, *Computer Networks: Internet Protocols in Action*, John Wiley and Sons, 2005.

✦ Tannenbaum, Andrew S., *Computer Networks*, Fourth Edition, Prentice Hall, 2002.

✦ Wallingford, Ted, *Switching to VoIP*, O'Reilly Media, Inc., 2005.

Security

Distrust and caution are the parents of security.

—BENJAMIN FRANKLIN

(In)security Is Everywhere. Security is a critical component of an IT Manager's life. Almost every decision he makes will have to be evaluated at some point for its security implications. Hiring a new programmer? How much access should that person have? Installing a new server? Who is allowed to access it? Making sure that authorized people have the access they need, (and *only* the access they need), along with making sure unauthorized people are blocked from access has become one of many security-related themes of IT.

If confidential e-mails about unannounced merger or acquisition plans are posted on the Net, a lot of yelling happens. But security problems do not just cause embarrassing situations. If a laptop containing data with credit card and bank account information is lost, then there are various laws and regulations you have to deal with (particularly related to customer notification). You don't want your CEO

CHAPTER THIRTEEN

349

furiously knocking at your door, but you *really* don't want law enforcement coming to see you.

The topic of computer security has grown so large and complex that a single chapter can't begin to do justice to the topic. Security concerns are now so widespread that it's essentially an industry within an industry, with its own training classes, trade journals, certifications, job definitions, books, Web casts, etc., devoted to addressing the issue.

As a result, the primary goal of this chapter is to provide you with a framework to think about security, to outline the issues, and to point you to places where you can get more information.

13.1   A Quick Note on How We Got Here

It is well understood in the technology community that in the 1980s, but especially in the 1990s, the push was to connect everything and everybody. One of the original goals of Java was to create an operating system so basic it would allow, famously, your toaster to talk to your computer.

Well, now even refrigerators can have Net access, so all that connectivity has been achieved. But it has come at a giant price. Little or no thought was given to the consequences of allowing all those computers to connect to each other. Computers, run by individuals with less-than-ideal motives, can and have joined communities, entered networks, and generally caused havoc all over the planet. The main challenge was once how to share things electronically. The main challenge now is how to keep everything safe, and how to keep your data, your networks, and your company secure.

Get Perspective

First, don't be overwhelmed. Read this chapter to determine which issues you should start examining. Not every threat will affect you; if yours is a virtual company, for example, you may have a different set of security priorities and concerns than someone managing a traditional office setting.

Secondly, read the section on Risk Analysis and Risk Management (page 355) carefully. If it hasn't been done already, perform a risk analysis.

Computer Security Themes

Throughout this chapter, we'll discuss various ideas about security topics. But within these discussions, several themes appear again and again.

Figure 13.1   **Figure 13.2**

Privacy versus Security

In security, the trade-off between privacy and security is a choice made all the time. Radio Frequency Identification (RFID) tags, for example, are an excellent example of this duality. RFID tags are small chips embedded in thousands — soon millions — of products. (They vary in size from tiny chips embedded in razors to larger chips on the outside of shampoo bottles, see Figures 13.1 and 13.2, *www.spychips.com/faqs.html.*)

These tags allow for the electronic identification of people, animals, and objects. Thus a sweater you buy at the department store can carry an RFID tag. With RFID tags, your entire shopping cart could be scanned in an instant at the checkout without having to remove every item to be individually scanned. However, as you go through your day, RFID scanners at other stores could also read those same tags. Perhaps these other stores do this to get a sense of whether you're a big spender or not, what your clothing sizes are, or what their competition is selling.

Shopping lists are generally not held that close to the vest, but you might be surprised at what you value when it's taken away from you. During Super Bowl XXXV in Tampa, all attendees' faces were surreptitiously photographed; those photos were then scanned and compared with images in a police database of criminals and criminal suspects. Many people found news of that action disturbing, both because it was done without permission or notification, and because the technology exists to do something like this.

Intention Matters

White and black hats, "mis-configuration" or "mal-configuration," "adware," or "spam" are all terms discussed in this chapter, but one of the key points in any security discussion is: What was the *intent* behind the event? The results can still be devastating regardless of intent, but knowing the original purpose can sometimes help solve the problem more quickly.

If your system has been breached by a malicious hacker, you need to take specific steps to address the problem. If your system is overwhelmed by adware, you also need to address the problem. In both cases, the entire system can come down. But understanding that one event was the result of malicious intent, and the other may have been the result of innocent user activity can help determine the magnitude of the problem, and how it's addressed.

CIA

The three basic tenets of information security are summarized with a classic acronym: C.I.A. (Like the Culinary Institute of America's acronym, it does not stand for what you think it stands for.) It stands for Confidentiality, Integrity and Availability. Learning about information security means learning about "C.I.A."

+ "Confidentiality" means keeping secret material secret. Techniques for keeping things secret include cryptography, access control, and others. These methods are discussed in the section Encryption, Keys, and Certificates (page 372). You may be protecting corporate data banks or files for next week's presentation to the board. In either case, you want to keep confidential material from getting accidentally or intentionally disclosed. In many cases, confidentially isn't only a professional/ethical obligation, but also a regulatory requirement.

+ "Integrity" in information security means that data isn't intentionally or accidentally altered.

+ "Availability" means the systems are running and useable as they are supposed to be.

The CIA model, adopted from the military, has its strengths and weaknesses. It is a place to start thinking about security, but it isn't the final answer. The Web is full of discussions about the plusses and minuses of the CIA security model.

Security versus Convenience

Security issues now pervade all aspects of computer life and the trade-off between security and convenience will only become more onerous. Previously, systems with little or no security were common; perhaps you had to enter one password, and perhaps that password was your three initials. Now, passwords are often six and ten digits long and have to be changed frequently. If you require "complex" passwords (e.g., mixing upper and lower case, use of special characters, etc.) and require them to be changed frequently, your auditors will probably be thrilled. However, you may find that users end up writing their passwords on Post-It notes attached to monitors in order to remember them. Users complain mightily about issues like this, but the more educated they are about the risks the company faces and their role in mitigating these risks, the less they will protest. This issue is discussed throughout this chapter, in particular, in the section Action 4: Work with Users to Make Everyone More Secure on page 358.

Look Very Closely — It May Not Be What It Appears (Suspicious E-Mails)

Computer security now is often a matter of determining that one innocent-looking item — an e-mail, a log entry, a file change — is actually a sign of something radically different.

Teaching the users to become a lot better about giving out import. info to others.

- ✦ Phishing is e-mail with a carefully disguised intent. If they haven't been already, you need to educate your users on how to behave when they receive those "requests" from their bank for personal information.

- ✦ See the section Some Security Stories (on page 378) for the story of how the research into a $.75 accounting discrepancy led to the dismantling of an international hacking ring.

- ✦ Trojan Horses are applications that appear to be something you want, but in reality they're just disguised files for malicious programs.

- ✦ Social engineering is a technique for gathering confidential or privileged information by simply asking for it. Hackers have discovered that people oftentimes have a general tendency to trust others, and that the hackers can get users to reveal items like passwords, or to do something that's essentially out of policy, by simply phoning the user and pretending to be from tech support, etc.

If you manage the person in charge of security, or you are that person, very close examination of the various elements of your system is required. You have to be able to tell quickly and often what is ordinary and what is even slightly out of the ordinary.

13.2　Managing Security

There are five actions you can take to manage IT security:

- ✦ Action 1: Evaluate your environment's needs, exposures, and defenses
- ✦ Action 2: Get upper level management buy-in

✦ Action 3: Mitigate the risks

✦ Action 4: Work with users to make everyone more secure

✦ Action 5: Security is an ongoing process

Action 1: Evaluate Your Environment's Needs, Exposures, and Defenses

The first step in most problems is to determine how much exposure and vulnerability you have.

Perform a Security Audit

In the world of computer security, determining your exposure and vulnerability is done by performing a computer security audit. An audit like this can range from having your network administrator regularly review logs, current levels of security patches, firewall settings, and policies, to bringing in third party security auditing companies as outside consultants. The latter is often the preferred method, since it eliminates any conflict of interest that could be associated with assessing your own environment. Most companies of any size will use outside firms to assess their security as a means of validation that the controls, policies, and technologies are working as the company had hoped and planned.

The magnitude of your commitment to a security audit depends on two things:

1. How big your company is

2. Which industry and which specific business your company is in

Naturally, a security audit for a garage startup is going to take less time and money than one for a corporation with 5,000 employees. But the first point may not be *less important* than the second: In these days of intellectual property awareness, it isn't hard to imagine how valuable Larry Page and Sergey Brin's company's work was back when they were grad students just out of Stanford. (They are the co-founders of Google.)

And while no company wants to lose data, most would agree that losing sales figures for a small furniture company isn't as disastrous as data lost by some of the private companies doing security contracting for the government.

Regardless of size or industry, the first step you should take is to perform an audit. And the goal of your audit should be to clearly determine the level of risk you are facing now and any potential risks you can identify that you will face in the future.

Risk Analysis and Risk Management

Risk analysis is the process of identifying the security risks throughout your system and the potential loss for every threat that is identified. Risk management is the steps you take to address the risks that are identified as a result of your analysis. Most of this chapter is concerned with risk management; however, the next section discusses risk analysis.

Risk Analysis

There are two types of risk analysis: quantitative and qualitative. As their names imply, each approaches the same data in a different way.

- ✦ **Quantitative:** This method assigns numerical values to both the amount of damage that would occur as well as the costs of prevention to any threats. Formulae include calculating the probability of a threat occurring times the likely loss should one occur. Despite the supposed mathematical rigor of this technique, subjective evaluations creep in.

- ✦ **Qualitative:** This method generates an analysis of the risks facing an organization and is based on experience, judgment, and intuition. While subjective by definition, efforts are made to make these analyses as objective as possible.

Regardless of which method you choose (or, if you have sufficient time and money, you choose both), know there are many companies poised to help you conduct your analysis. As with every component of this chapter, individual companies have arisen that are devoted to even the smallest corner of the computer security world.

The goal of a risk analysis is to provide a clear cost/benefit comparison. The cost of securing an item is compared with the risk of losing it.

Risk analysis is performed throughout corporate America, not only in the computer industry. It's a formal requirement of HIPAA, for example. (HIPAA is the Health Insurance Portability and Accountability Act of 1996 — see Chapter 8, IT Compliance and Controls on page 201). The final Security Rule of HIPAA requires covered entities to "conduct an accurate and thorough assessment of the potential risks and vulnerabilities to the confidentiality, integrity, and availability of electronic protected health information held by the covered entity." In addition, the rule states that the "required risk analysis is also a tool to allow flexibility for entities in meeting the requirements of this final rule…"

The Three Common Weakness I Find After I Do a Security Assessment

When doing a security assessment, there are three major components that companies always suffer from:

#1 Weakness: Weak Internal Controls On People

Companies need stringent controls on their employees. That does *not* necessarily mean watching their every move, tracking their every keyboard stroke, monitoring every Web site they go to—although it *can* mean that, depending on the organization.

What "Internal Controls on People" really means is careful authentication to control who/what/when/and which particular people can access which information. 80% of security breeches occur because of improperly screened people and poor internal controls.

#2 Weakness: Mis-Configured (and Occasionally Mal-Configured) Devices

Most hardware devices, servers, routers, desktops, now come with security controls installed by default. But these devices are often not properly configured, not properly patched, and not properly documented. Security is a 24/7/365 concern, not an "install-the-device-and-forget-about-it" type of activity.

#3 Weakness: Outside "Fingerprints"

As a computer security consultant, I am amazed that corporations don't take advantage of the large number of intrusion detection and intrusion prevention tools that are now available. Hackers are clearly studying these things, why aren't you using them?

—Mark Willoughby
Security Author and Consultant

Risk Analysis Tools

There are many risk analysis tool options, but here are links to two free methods from well-known sources (Carnegie Mellon and Microsoft):

✦ One method of performing a risk analysis is called the Operationally Critical Threat, Asset, and Vulnerability Evaluation (OCTAVE) method.

It's a complete, free, and thorough method. The method was developed by CERT at Carnegie Mellon University (*www.cert.org*) and is federally funded.

✦ A second method is one provided for free by Microsoft. They call theirs the Security Assessment Tool and provide it at *https://www.security guidance.com/*.

Hire White Hats (to Avoid Black Hats)

In general, a hacker is someone who is interested in finding and exploiting security flaws of IT systems and networks. The industry has stolen a paradigm from old cowboy movies to identify the good guys and the bad guys as white-hat and black-hat hackers. Black-hat hackers are those you generally think of with the term hacker — they're interested in security flaws in order to take advantage and abuse them — usually for profit, but oftentimes just to see what trouble they can cause. On the other hand, white-hat hackers are interested in security flaws as a way of identifying how security can be improved, and how systems can be better protected. White-hat hackers are sometimes called "ethical hackers."

Both white- and black-hat hackers have exceptional technical skills, and are experts in operating systems, networks, etc. Many black-hat hackers become white-hat hackers when they realize that their skills should be put to use for good instead of evil. Sometimes, jail time or a fine helps them see the light.

Action 2: Get Upper Level Management Buy-In

Security is an issue that impacts every level and every facet of the organization. CEOs can have their core company data compromised and factory guards can have their keys stolen and their offices broken into. Classically, a top-down approach works better: The policies and procedures are better aligned with the company's overall direction. A bottom-up approach, where IT initiates or needs to drive the direction, will generally not be as successful. Many organizations are now identifying an individual to function as the Chief Security Officer (CSO). Depending on the company and the industry, this role may exist within IT, or it may exist as part of the company's executive team. This individual may tackle issues related to physical security, computer security, IT policies, privacy, investigations, etc.

See Chapter 8, IT Compliance and Controls on page 201 for additional discussion of topics related to security; see Section Action 4: Work With Users to Make Everyone More Secure (page 358) in this chapter for ideas on how to get all employees in an organization to actively participate in making security a part of all corporate activity.

Action 3: Mitigate the Risks

With the risk analysis process, you've identified certain exposures and vulnerabilities in the environment. Now you have to weigh those risks against the cost of mitigating them, along with the trade-offs of security and privacy.

Some of the different technology solutions for reducing risks are addressed below in the section Security Solutions and Technologies (on page 360). However, many things can be addressed with simple solutions, or procedural changes. For example:

- ✦ User education can go a long way; simple things like advising them on effective passwords, or reminding them to log off when leaving for the night, can be very useful.

- ✦ Policies to track security related requests; asking users to submit written requests, for example, for changes in security privileges (instead of a phone call to the network manager) is an effective tool.

- ✦ Carefully tracking all changes to the environment; the change request processes are described in Chapter 10, Operations (page 255).

- ✦ Periodic review of IDs and privileges, and disabling those that are no longer needed, should be a regular process.

- ✦ Being diligent about applying vendor security patches, and best practices.

Action 4: Work With Users to Make Everyone More Secure

If they aren't aware of it yet (and many aren't), you must convince every person in your organization — profit or non-profit—that computer and information security is everyone's job. Safety is everyone's job, and computer security is everyone's job. It's a cliché to you—a computer system is only as secure as its weakest link — but to many other people, that statement counts as wisdom. You must take this message "to the masses."

Your users need to be made aware of security issues. For example, users should be aware of the security concerns associated with storing a file on the LAN versus on their local hard drive. They should be aware of being able to put passwords on files that have sensitive information, and they should be aware of the risks of printing certain information to a network printer. Users should be in the habit of logging off at night or when they'll be away from their desk for an extended period of time.

Training Users

There are books, videos, consultants, and companies that can help you with this task. Like corporate safety, computer security has become an enormous industry in and of itself. Train users about passwords, locking their workstation when they step away, and logging off at the end of the day. Security doesn't have to be strictly about IT — it can include topics like notifying the security guard if they see a stranger wandering the halls unescorted, locking file cabinets, and using shredders for confidential information.

Use the themes in this chapter to regularly train your uses in computer security. Security should be an ongoing theme in the IT department, and users should understand it.

Privacy versus Security

As mentioned above, in the computer security world, the trade-off between privacy and security is a choice made all the time. Users need to be aware of the fact that their computer activity at work is monitored and that that monitoring is done for a variety of reasons, including security — their own security, not just the company's security.

Most companies have policy guides that indicate that company resources (like the phone system and computers) are for corporate use only—even if some personal use is unofficially acceptable. The policies will often also indicate that the company has the right to monitor usage.

Use Care When Surfing

Make your users aware that today's computing world is a complex network that requires a more conscientious computer user. Of course it's certainly possible to accidentally go to an inappropriate Web site — we have all mistyped an address and found ourselves on a very different page from what we were expecting. But repeated travels to those sites will be noticed and acted upon. (See the section Intention Matters on page 351.)

Trade-Off Between Security and Convenience

The long lines at security gates at airports are an excellent metaphor for modern life; you can no longer just walk up to the gate and board your plane. Nor can you just turn on your computer and start working. You need to enter a password, perhaps more than one, to a machine that may be locked to your desk. (See the section Security versus Convenience on page 352.)

Action 5: Security is an Ongoing Process

You'll never be able to say: "OK, we're done, the environment is secure." Security should be looked at as an ongoing, iterative process. The IT staff should always be on the lookout for ways to improve security and audits and compliance activities (see Chapter 8, IT Compliance and Control, page 201) should be viewed as welcome opportunities for continuous reviews of security.

13.3 Security Solutions and Technologies

With entire tomes dedicated to the subject of computer security technologies, a single chapter in this book can't do it appropriate justice. However, there are some basics you should be familiar with.

Tracking and Controlling Access

Carefully control and monitor who goes in and who goes out of your system: who enters your system, what they do there, and when they leave; who enters your facility and who exits it.

Control Access

A critical component of controlling access is to follow the "Rule of Least Privilege": users should only be granted the least amount of access to the system, and for the least amount of time necessary, as is authorized and required for their job. More access and longer access time allows for more potential problems.

The rule originated in the "Orange Book" (part of the "rainbow" series of DoD books on computer security written in the early 1980's) and is officially defined as: "Least Privilege — This principle requires that each subject in a system be granted the most restrictive set of privileges (or lowest clearance) needed for the performance of authorized tasks. The application of this principle limits the damage that can result from accident, error, or unauthorized use (*www.dtic.mil/whs/directives/corres/html2/i85511x.htm*).

The previous method of controlling access was called the "M&M model": the idea was to make your system "hard on the outside and soft in the middle." That model is being replaced by "de-perimeterization" techniques, which make your system secure *throughout*.

One method of achieving security throughout your system is to implement "secure zones." A University of California information security site defines secure zones as "a combination of policies, procedures, and technical tools and techniques that enables an organization to discreetly protect its own information assets. It's a logical and physical environment with strong visible management support in which access privileges to all information assets are clearly defined and followed without exception." (*isecurity.ucsf.edu/main. jsp?content = secure_zones/secure_zones*).

Tracking Activity

There are a variety of methods that you can use to track activity:

- ✦ System log files
- ✦ Monitoring programs
- ✦ Network mapping tools
- ✦ Physical access

System Log Files   Almost every technology (both hardware and software) can generate log files of activities. The level of detail that can be captured can vary tremendously from one product to another, and is often configurable by administrators. Servers, desktops, business applications, operating systems, network hardware, and monitoring and management utilities, all have log files. Log files can indicate who did what, at what time, on which device, and from where. Logs files can be used for basic troubleshooting, or to investigate security issues. These files can be examined and monitored to track user activities.

Log files can be so voluminous that some vendors have utilities to allow for proactive monitoring of them so that pre-defined event types trigger certain types of alerts and actions.

Monitoring Programs   Similar to log files, tools exist that allow you to track all the activity of your network. In addition to the old standard of tracking sites visited, you can now monitor programs used and keystrokes typed. On example of this is a packet sniffer. A packet sniffer is a software package that can examine the data traffic on a network. Typically, a sniffer is used to troubleshoot and isolate network problems. However, it can also be used when investigating security issues. For example, a packet sniffer can be used to "trap" data to and from a particular device. Or it can be used to look for particular content.

Network Mapping Tools   In larger environments, it can be a daunting task just to be aware of everything on the network. While the server side may stay relatively static, activity on the user-device side can be constantly changing with printer and workstations being regularly moved, replaced, and added to. There are tools (like the open source Nmap — "Network Mapper") for network exploration and security auditing. Tools like this can rapidly scan large networks and identify which hosts are available on the network. These tools can usually identify some key aspects of the devices, such as what type of device it may be (printer, workstation, switch), what operating system it is running, etc. Tools like these can help you identify oddities that need to be investigated (e.g., "Why are those workstations running server software?").

Physical Access In addition to obvious building security (door locks, access cards), the physical access to the IT areas should be controlled. Access to the computer room or data center should be limited to those individuals that require it. Other IT areas (e.g., wiring closets) should be locked. Because of the concerns of confidential content, printed report distribution should be controlled, and an industrial-strength shredder (or third party shredding service) should be available to dispose of output that is no longer needed.

Traditional tools for tracking access within a facility, such as security cameras, access card readers, and sign-in sheets, should also be considered part of the arsenal. Periodically reviewing these (particularly sign-in sheets and access cards used for the data center) can be very worthwhile. Simply asking your company's security department to periodically review which employees have access cards that allow entry to the data center demonstrates that you need to partner with them as part of the overall IT security process.

Accounts and Passwords

Account Usage There are some basic principles in setting up accounts that can help ensure that they aren't used for unauthorized activities:

✦ You maybe able to limit an account's usage to certain days of the week and hours. This can be a worthwhile option for temps and consultants' accounts.

✦ You can often set an account to be disabled automatically at a certain date. This is also a good feature to use for temps and consultants since these types of users often leave the company with no notification to IT.

✦ You may want to consider limiting how many times a user can log in simultaneously, or perhaps limit it to two (so the user can log on from home even if they forgot to log out when leaving the office).

✦ Periodically review accounts for usage. If an account hasn't been used, for example, in several weeks, it may be worth investigating. Perhaps the employee is on some kind of leave. After a defined time, you can disable the account. If there is no further inquiry about the account after another few weeks, it may be safe to assume that the account is no longer needed.

✦ Unless otherwise justified and requested, new accounts should be given "plain vanilla" access privileges. Any request for additional access or privilege should be submitted in writing by an authorized individual.

✦ Consider using special naming conventions for temps, interns, and consultants so that security administrators can spot them easily and monitor their activity quickly.

User Terminations   While it's generally easy to ensure that accounts are created when needed (it's easy because the user keeps complaining until it is done), it's more of a challenge to ensure that accounts are deleted/disabled when should be. Too often when an employee leaves the company, the IT security administrator is the last to hear of it. It could be weeks before that employee's ID is terminated. HR should notify IT immediately of any employment terminations so that IDs can be disabled and deleted. When an employee does leave the company, there should be a procedure for moving her files, e-mail, and so on to another employee's ID (perhaps a co-worker, or manager), so that there is no need for maintaining the terminated employee's ID.

Passwords   Passwords should be at least six characters in length (many organizations now insist of passwords of eight characters), should be forced to be changed regularly (but not so often that a user has to write down her current password on a Post-It note attached to the monitor), and shouldn't be the same as the user's ID, nor be a common word. When it's time to change passwords, users should not be able to reuse the same one.

Becoming increasingly popular are "strong" or "complex" passwords. While the definitions of these terms vary, it's easy to understand them in comparison to weak passwords, which are easily guessed, or obvious. A password that is blank, or is the word "password" or is a string of characters (e.g., 12345, or zzzzz), or matches the user's ID, are considered "weak" passwords. Similarly, a password that is the user's date of birth, or pet's name, is considered to be a weak password. Strong or complex passwords are those that aren't words that can be found in the dictionary, often because they include special characters and numbers.

However, a 2005 report by RSA Security, stated that "over a quarter of respondents must manage more than 13 passwords at work, and that nine out of ten respondents are frustrated with the password management challenge. This frustration is leading to behaviors that could jeopardize IT security, as well as compliance initiatives."

In addition, the RSA Security survey also said that "while end-users may attempt to memorize passwords, employees continue to resort to other, less secure means of tracking multiple passwords. The most common risky password management behaviors include:

✦ Maintaining a spreadsheet or other document stored on the PC (25 percent)

✦ Recording a list of passwords on a PDA or other handheld device (22 percent)

✦ Keeping a paper record of passwords in an office/workspace (15 percent)"

(Source: *www.rsasecurity.com/press_release.asp?doc_id = 6095&id = 1034*)

Configure your system to automatically lock out an account after so many failed login attempts. Many systems will automatically lock out an account after 3 failed attempts within a 5-minute period. The system may then be set to automatically unlock the account after another few minutes. While these two steps may seem to be contradictory, the idea is to halt any "brute-force" attempts to guess a password, while still allowing a legitimate user to eventually gain access. Brute-force attacks are done with programs specially designed to try every character combination until the right password is found. Unchecked, a brute-force attempt can try tens of thousands of combinations in a single hour. With these account lockout parameters, the program might only get a handful of attempts.

Special Privilege IDs   Network and system managers usually have special IDs and passwords that provide carte blanche access to the system(s). These are often called root, supervisor, or administrator accounts. Because of their special access, only a handful of people should have accounts like this. System administrators tend to ignore their own security rules and often set these passwords to never expire. It's important that these passwords be changed regularly, and changed immediately when someone who knows them leaves the company.

It's common practice for IT Managers and administrators to use two IDs. One of them has the special privileges they need for certain types of activities. The other isn't privileged, and is what they use for routine tasks like their own e-mail. The reason for two accounts is to minimize the amount of time an IT administrator makes use of privileges, and thereby reducing the risk of their impacting the entire system by accident.

Administrators shouldn't share a common privileged account, and each should have their own non-privileged account. This helps to identify actions and tasks with specific individuals — and is particularly helpful when examining log entries.

Another common practice is to rename, delete, or disable the default privileged account that's installed with operating systems and applications. Since hackers assume these accounts exist on your system, they're usually one of the paths they use to gain access. At a minimum, you must change the default password that is associated with these accounts.

Access Reviews

Large environments might have thousands of users, and hundreds of thousands, if not millions, of files on their computer networks. Usually groups of files are set up that can only be accessed by certain groups of users — and vice versa. It's important that some type of user administrator review these access privileges every now and then (perhaps twice a year) to ensure that unauthorized users haven't mistakenly been given access to the wrong files.

Authorization Levels

Security administrators who process the requests to grant and revoke privileges, change access, and create IDs need to know who is authorized to make these requests. For example, the payroll manager may be authorized to determine who has access to the payroll files, and the VP of sales may be authorized to determine who has access to sales figures. It's up to the IT Manager and the security administrator to make sure it's clear who has authority over what, and that requests are documented — usually via email, and tracked — usually through the Help Desk's call tracking system. HR should alert IT of new employees in advance of their start date so that IDs with basic privileges (e-mail, etc.) can be created.

Authentication

Authentication is the process for determining if someone is authorized for access.

"Two-Factor" Authentication

Typically, access is based on what a user *knows* — usually their ID and password. "Two-factor authentication" bases access not only on what the user knows, but also on what they *have*. The what-they-have component is generally

Figure 13.3   RSA SecurID Devices.

a "token" provided by a device that the user carries with them (small enough to fit into a wallet, or on a keychain). The device operates by displaying a number that changes every minute. The user types in the number when they're logging in, and the number is validated by a corresponding authentication server.

The two-factor authentication helps to prevent unauthorized access resulting from the user telling someone else their password, or by having their password guessed. Many companies use two factor authentication for their remote access security as a way of reducing the exposure associated with connectivity from the public Internet. The SecurID solution from RSA Security is the most popular solution for two-factor authentication, see Figure 13.3.

Single Sign-On

Although the situation is slowly improving, users are still burdened by having to remember a variety of different IDs and passwords. Single Sign-On (SSO) is a solution that allows users to authenticate once, and then have access to all systems and resources for which he has been granted permission. SSO is a convenience for users as it reduces the number of IDs and passwords to remember, and it's a convenience for system managers as it greatly simplifies the administration. Perhaps one of the most valuable aspects of SSO is that once an employee leaves the company, all their access can be removed by disabling their SSO ID. SSO is closely tied to directory services, which are discussed in Chapter 15, Enterprise Applications (page 411).

The challenge with SSO is that the business applications may have to be altered to incorporate the technology. For in-house developed applications, this may be a relatively straightforward change. However, with third party applications, it may be much more complex.

This technique is a classic case of the user convenience versus security trade-off discussed at the opening of this chapter (see the section Convenience versus

Security on page 352). And, should a user gain access to an SSO ID, he then has access to *all* the systems the user is authorized for.

Identity Management

Identity management encompasses a variety of solutions and technologies related to user authentication. These include:

+ SSO (discussed above).

+ Self service: Allowing users to reset their own passwords.

+ Password synchronization: When a user changes their password in one system, the new password is automatically replicated to other applications and system.

+ Account provisioning: The process of creating new accounts, and revoking them when they're no longer needed.

+ Federated identity: A federated identity is a single user ID that can be used for different Web sites because they all belong to a common "federation." While similar to SSO, federated identities are useful when trying to manage authentication to external sites and applications, as well as internal ones. This allows organizations to share user credentials across the network boundaries that normally separate them.

Kerberos

Kerberos is a password scheme developed at MIT. The name, Kerberos, refers to a three-headed dog in Greek mythology. The idea behind Kerberos is to eliminate the need for a password to travel on the network — where they might be intercepted. With Kerberos, the user identifies himself to an authentication server, which then issues an electronic ticket that contains information about what services and resources the user can access. Based on the information in the ticket, the network services will either grant or reject the user's request for access. In addition, the ticket can be time stamped so that it expires at a pre-set time.

Other User Authentication Methods

New methods of confirming a user is who he or she claims, are being created all the time. In addition to the tried and true but sometimes fallible passwords, new (to the computer industry) techniques include fingerprint and retinal scanning; speech, signature and face recognition; and DNA sequencing.

Defending the Perimeter

Firewalls

Firewalls, which could be hardware or software-based, are used to control access between two networks. Typically, a firewall is used to protect your internal network from the public Internet, but could also be used between two private networks. For example, if you have a connection to a vendor, or partner, you could have a firewall between the two. Firewalls are available from a variety of vendors like Cisco, Checkpoint, Juniper Networks, etc.

The Two Sides of a Firewall   Since a firewall controls the flow of information between two networks, it is considered to have two sides: the *private* side (the one that connects to your network) and the *public* side (the one connected to the Internet).

Without a firewall, your network is fully exposed to all the risks, perils, maliciousness, and unknowns of the Internet. With a firewall, you not only can control outsiders' access to your network and its resources, but you can also control what kind of access the users on your network have to the public Internet.

Configuring a Firewall   In general, most firewalls are configured to allow very few types of data streams into your network. Typically, e-mail is allowed in so that your messaging gateway can receive e-mail from the Internet. And, depending on users' needs, file transfers may be allowed.

On the other hand, the firewall may be configured not to allow other traffic types. For example, because of fears that it will clog up your network, you may not want to allow Real Audio data into your network. Similarly, you may be able to configure your network so that only certain users are allowed to surf the Web.

Firewall configurations and polices should follow the Rule of Least Privilege (discussed in the section Control Access on page 360) which dictates that they should allow the minimum access required. This means that unless there is an identified need for particular ports and protocols, they should be disabled.

Proxy Services   A firewall usually provides proxy services. As the term proxy implies, this means that the firewall essentially stands in for your users when they want to access the Internet. When a user wants to access the Internet, the user's request is handed to the firewall, which then executes it. The advantage to this is that the proxy server appears, to the rest of the Internet, as the only source of requests from your network. So, for example, only the proxy server's IP address is seen by the Internet, as opposed to the IP addresses of your entire network. This is very similar to Network Address Translation (discussed in Chapter 12, Networking on page 311). With a proxy server, it is virtually impossible to tell if there is a giant corporation or a mom-and-pop operation behind the firewall.

Stateful Inspection   Stateful inspection is a way of filtering packets and connections on a firewall. Without stateful inspection, the firewall generally only relies on source and destination information in the packet's header to determine if it's allowed through the firewall.

With stateful inspection, the packet is examined down to the application layer. This allows the firewall to not only monitor source and destination, but also context. Stateful inspection helps to ensure that all incoming traffic is the result of a previous outgoing request. This can help reduce attacks that result from IP spoofing and port scanning.

DMZ: Demilitarized Zone   The DMZ is a semi-protected portion of the firewall. It's sometimes referred to as the "third area," or third leg of a firewall configuration (the other two are the public and private sides of the firewall). While devices on the private side of the firewall are fully protected, and the public side is completely exposed, the DMZ offers a middle ground.

For example, your Web site and e-mail gateways would exist in the DMZ. This allows you to provide a level of protection for these devices, while at the same time making them accessible on the public Internet. You can use the firewall's DMZ to allow the types of access and connectivity needed for an e-mail gateway, and block all other types.

Intrusion Detection and Prevention

Intrusion Prevention Systems (IPS) and Intrusion Detection Systems (IDS), offer a layer of protection, in addition to firewalls, against the exposures of the Internet.

✦ An intrusion detection system identifies suspicious traffic based on patterns of activity. Similar to the way anti-virus software works, an IDS compares traffic pattern against various known malicious signatures. Essentially the IDS is evaluating traffic to see if it matches known attacks. When it detects suspicious activity, the IDS system will alert the network administrator.

✦ An intrusion prevention system takes an IDS a step further. Not only does it detect the malicious activity but it takes action (in addition to notifying the administrator). The IPS may drop a packet from the suspicious traffic, automatically close a port, or refuse further traffic from that particular IP address. In the millisecond world of network activity, a network administrator may not be able to react fast enough to a notification from an IDS about a possible attack. An IPS can take preventive action (based on how it's set up and configured) instantly after it detects any suspicious activity.

Malware Prevention

Anti-virus software has long been a cornerstone of protecting the IT environment. Anti-virus solutions are available for workstations, servers, e-mail gateways, and even hand-helds. By regularly downloading the latest pattern and signature files (see the section Ongoing Maintenance on this page), an organization can protect itself against the latest release and developments of viruses. Many organizations will employ virus solutions from multiple vendors as a way of further strengthening their defenses.

Anti-spyware solutions operate very similarly to anti-virus solutions, with signature/pattern files that have to be updated regularly. However, many anti-virus solutions now include anti-spyware functionality as well.

Anti-spam solutions for your e-mail gateway can do more than just reduce the amount of nuisance e-mail. These solutions can provide protection by preventing e-mails that include security risks such as phishing attempts, and code that takes advantage of operating system and browser vulnerabilities. Malware prevention solutions can prevent third party tracking of user activity as well as stopping unnecessary slowdowns in individual systems and servers.

White List and Black List

White List   A White List is a list of sources (e-mail and IP addresses) who you've determined should be able to send you messages *without* being checked for spam. This will prevent their messages from being blocked even if your anti-spam solution determines that the message is spam.

Black List   A Black List is a list of originators (e-mail and IP addresses) who you've determined should *not* be able to send you messages. Any message received from these originators will be rejected no matter the content of the message.

White and Black Lists are primarily used by anti-spam solutions as a way of allowing each organization to tailor it to their needs.

Ongoing Maintenance

In addition to access reviews, as mentioned above, there are activities that should be performed regularly by security administrators to identify and minimize risks.

Log, Account, and Access Reviews

As mentioned earlier, IDs that haven't been used in a predefined period of time should be disabled or deleted. Many systems can report when unsuccessful login attempts have been made; these logs should be reviewed and investigated. System logs should be reviewed for those events and incidents that could identify security threats.

Accounts that have special privileges should be reviewed a few times a year to confirm that the need for the special privilege is still valid and justified.

After discussion with other departments (e.g., Legal, Audit), public areas of the network (places where all users have read and write access) may be regularly purged of files that haven't been accessed in a while. (Not only does this free up space, but it might also remove files with confidential information that users placed there by mistake, or is no longer needed.)

Software Patches and Updates

Security administrators should regularly check with their software vendors to obtain and apply any updates or patches that close security holes. Processes should exist for regularly checking the environment to make sure that systems are current, and for ensuring that unpatched and unprotected systems can't connect.

Following Microsoft's lead, many vendors now have a set schedule for releasing patches. This allows IT departments to set schedules for testing the patches, and implementations to the production environment.

Pattern files updates (for anti-virus, anti-spam, intrusion prevention/detection) are usually released on a much more frequent basis than software security patches. It's common for these files to be updated several times a week, or more. Because of the frequency of these updates, these systems have to be set to regularly download and install new files as they are released.

IT Managers can use various tools and configuration options to manage the distribution of updates to servers and workstations. These allow the IT department to determine if updates should be automatically installed (an increasingly popular and recommended method), or only after they've been tested and validated by the IT department. Similarly, the tools can help you see which devices have the most current updates, and which are behind.

Tunneling

The key to Virtual Private Networks (VPNs) are tunneling protocols. The tunnels make it possible to use a public TCP/IP network, such as the Internet, to create secure connections between remote nodes. The secure connection is called a tunnel. A variety of technologies used with tunneling are discussed in Chapter 12, Networking (on page 311). These include:

✦ IPSec (IP Security)

✦ PPTP (Point-to-Point Tunneling Protocol)

✦ L2TP (Layer 2 Tunneling Protocol)

Encryption, Keys and Certificates

Public and Private Key Cryptography

In public key cryptography, a public and private key are created simultaneously using the same algorithm by a Certificate Authority (CA). The private key is given only to the requesting party and the public key is made publicly available (as part of a digital certificate) in a directory that all parties can access. The private key is never shared with anyone or sent across the Internet. You use the private key to decrypt text that has been encrypted with your public key by someone else (who can find out what your public key is from a public directory). Thus, if I send you a message, I can find out your public key (but not your private key) from a central administrator and encrypt a message to you using your public key. When you receive it, you decrypt it with your private key. In addition to encrypting messages (which ensures privacy), you can authenticate yourself to me (so I know that it is really you who sent the message) by using your private key to encrypt a digital certificate. When I receive it, I can use your public key to decrypt it.

Public Key Infrastructure   Public Key Infrastructure (PKI) enables users to securely exchange data through the use of a public and a private cryptographic key pair that is obtained and shared through a trusted authority. The PKI provides for a digital certificate that can identify an individual or an organization and directory services that can store and, when necessary, revoke the certificates. Although the components of a PKI are generally understood, a number of different vendor approaches and services are emerging.

Digital Certificates   The purpose of a digital certificate is to provide other systems (or users) a level of trust that the public key claimed to belong to a user (or organization) does indeed belong to that user. A digital certificate acts like proof of identity, much the way a driver's license does. Without digital certificates, Alice could impersonate Bob by distributing her own public key but claim that it was Bob's key.

The certificate issued by a CA (such as Verisign, Geotrust, DigiCert, etc.), and binds a particular public key to the name of the entity the certificate identifies (such as the name of an organization or a server). Certificates help prevent the use of fake public keys for impersonation. Only the public key certified by the certificate will work with the corresponding private key possessed by the entity identified by the certificate.

Secure Sockets Layer   Secure Sockets Layer (SSL) is a protocol for encrypting information sent via the Internet. SSL uses a cryptographic system that uses two different keys to encrypt and decrypt data — a public available to everyone, and a private key which is known only to the recipient. Many Web sites use the protocol when asking for confidential user information, such as credit card numbers. URLs that require an SSL connection start with "http*s*:" instead of "http:". When a browser goes to a secure Web page, the browser checks the SSL Certificate to see that (1) the expiration date hasn't passed, (2) it has been issued by a CA the browser trusts, and (3) that it's used by the Web site for which it has been issued. If it fails on any one of these, the browser will display a warning message. Most browsers will support 128-bit key SSL encryption. Some older browsers will only support 40-bit encryption, and should be upgraded.

Pretty Good Privacy   Pretty Good Privacy (PGP) is software that provides encryption and authentication. PGP was initially developed by Phil Zimmerman and was first released in the early 1990s. Later versions have been developed by Zimmerman as well as others. PGP has been so widely embraced that it's now available as an open standard (e.g., OpenPGP, GnuPG). While the name may lead you to think you're settling for a less than ideal solution, it's actually a reference to "Ralph's Pretty Good Grocery" in author Garrison Keillor's stories about the fictional town of Lake Wobegon.

PGP is primarily used for e-mail (although it can be used for any data), and there are plug-ins available for popular e-mail clients to allow for integrated and seamless operation. PGP uses public and privates keys similar to PKI.

AES and DES Encryption Standards   Advanced Encryption Standard (AES) is the standard for encryption adopted by the U. S. Government. AES can use key sizes of 128, 192, or 256 bits. AES replaced Digital Encryption Standard (DES), which was considered too insecure because of its 56-bit key length. However, by using the DES encryption algorithm three successive times (know as Triple-DES), you end up with a key length of 168 bits. Triple-DES was the de facto algorithm standard for encryption until AES was adopted.

Routine IT E-Mail Encryption   Another security behavior that's becoming standard is to encrypt routine e-mail between IT staff members. Not only can IT staff e-mail in aggregate provide more information than it should to a hacker, sending information about a hack in progress via e-mail (as well as a sudden bump in encrypted e-mail) alerts the hacker you are on to him. If encryption between IT team members is done as a matter of course, when an incident occurs, a secure channel already exists, and using it doesn't tip off the intruder.

Staffing

Because many in the IT staff have elevated access privileges, it's important to make sure that the staff members themselves aren't security risks. Many companies and organizations will do background checks on IT staff members, and include specific requirements, accountabilities, and responsibilities related to security in their job descriptions.

Response to Breaches

You should establish procedures for dealing with responses to security breaches. Of course, the type of breach may dictate different types of activities. For example, a rampant virus is going to require a different level of response and urgency than discovering that some phishing e-mails made it past your anti-spam solution.

Many organizations create a formal Security Incidence Response Team (SIRT) to respond to security breaches. A SIRT can be comprised of individuals from all over the organization and are often on 24-hour call. They are responsible for protecting an organization's critical IT assets.

Depending on the circumstances, the situation may call for:

✦ Examining log files and alerts.

✦ Contacting your vendors for assistance in identifying the problem, and determining how to address it.

✦ Shutting down certain resources, services, and network components until the problem has been identified and resolved.

✦ Notifying senior management and the user community. In a heavily regulated industry you may need to involve Legal as well.

✦ Changing all passwords.

✦ Notifying law enforcement.

✦ Performing a security audit.

In all cases, every incident should be documented in a postmortem report. This document should identify what happened and when, what actions were taken, what procedures and tools worked as expected, and what didn't. The document should also include what steps need to be taken to ensure that the incident won't recur. A postmortem document can be an effective summary for senior management that demonstrates that IT security is taken very seriously by your team.

13.4 Types of Threats

The range of possible threats to your business and your information is difficult to gauge. And it changes daily. The most important point about understanding different types of threats is to know that you must constantly stay on top of them. You must have the latest patches, and you must upgrade the operating systems to the latest versions. You don't need to become a guru, but you must either stay up to date or task one or more persons with doing this. A discussion of how to stay current is in the section Stay Informed in this chapter on page 378.

Spoofing

Spoofing essentially amounts to forgery. With spoofing, someone is purporting to have a different identity in hopes that you may trust that identity and allow it access. Most typically, spoofing occurs with e-mail and IP addresses.

With e-mail spoofing, spammers will spoof the sender's address in an attempt to get the recipients to open their e-mails, and hopefully even respond to their offers. Spoofing is also used for phishing (see the section Phishing and Social Engineering on page 377).

With IP address spoofing, the spoofer forges the "source address" of transmitted packets. A number of security attack types are based on IP spoofing including Man in the Middle attacks (also know as session hijacking), Denial of Service (DoS) attacks, and cut-and-paste attacks.

Malware

Malware is a category name to define software that causes problems. This can include viruses, adware, and spyware. Malware can degrade system performance, reveal confidential information, distribute spam, etc. Specific types of malware include:

✦ **Macro Viruses:** Use commands (macros) in application files (e.g., Excel and Word) to replicate themselves and do damage.

✦ **Worms:** Self-contained programs that replicates themselves usually via the network or e-mail attachments.

✦ **Adware:** Software that installs itself on a workstation for the purpose of displaying ads to the user. Users often unknowingly install adware when they download applications from the Web.

✦ **Spyware:** Monitors a user's activity. Spyware often works in tandem with adware as the ads shown may be related to the activity detected by the spyware. Like adware, spyware is also frequently installed by the user unknowingly when downloading applications from the Web.

✦ **Trojan Horses:** Appear to be legitimate programs, but in fact are malicious.

✦ **Backdoor Trojans:** Trojan Horse programs that allow a hacker to control your computer remotely.

✦ **Page Hijackers:** Akin to the purposes of adware, they covertly redirect your browser to specific Web pages.

✦ **Rootkits:** A set of modifications to the operating system that is primarily designed to hide malicious activity. Since the rootkit software essentially resides in a modification of the operating system, it's extremely difficult to detect, and it also continually checks on itself to see that the compromised files are still compromised, and re-infects as needed. In addition to being very difficult to detect, they're equally hard to remove.

✦ **Key loggers:** Small applications that reside on a computer to record key strokes. These are used to capture passwords and confidential information (e.g., credit card numbers).

Of particular concern with malware is what is know as a "Zero-Day" attack, which is malicious code that takes advantage of a security vulnerability before there's a fix for it. In some cases, the malicious code is released even before there is public knowledge of the vulnerability.

Open Relays

An open relay is an SMTP e-mail server that lets third parties send e-mails. An open relay essentially gives spammers a network and mail gateway to distribute spam, and helps the spammer hide their tracks. When this happens, the volume of mail the spammers tries to send via your environment can cause server crashes, network congestion, and can get your mail server blacklisted by other mail gateways. A simple mail server configuration change will disable its ability to operate as an open relay.

Phishing and Social Engineering

Phishing is the process of trying to obtain confidential information (credit card numbers, passwords, social security numbers, bank account numbers, etc.) by fraudulent means. The perpetrator sends out spoofed e-mail messages that appear to come from well-known companies and Web sites. The e-mails will mimic the legitimate company's logos, text style, etc. Typically, the e-mail tells the user that there's some problem with their account, and that they need to log in to confirm/verify some information. The e-mail contains links to sites that can appear virtually identical to the site it claims to be. If successful, the user will click on the link and be fooled into entering the information. Web sites that are frequently spoofed by phishers include PayPal, eBay, MSN, Yahoo, BestBuy, and nationwide banks (although the practice has now filtered down to local companies, too). When phishing is successful, not only will it result in financial loss for the victim, but it could also result in identity theft. *CIO Magazine* reported that in 2005, 73 million consumers received phishing e-mails, up from 57 million in 2004. The situation has gotten so bad that the U. S. Government has developed a site, *www.onguardonline.com*, to help educate individuals about protecting themselves from Internet fraud.

From a technical perspective, phishing relies on spoofing e-mail. From the human perspective, phishing also relies on "social engineering." Social engineering is the practice of trying to get information from people by telling them lies. Social engineering relies on the natural tendency of people to trust, to follow instructions, and to want to help. In this perspective, the adage about users being the weakest link of computer security is certainly true. Typical social engineering tricks include pretending to be an IT administrator and contacting a user to "verify" their account or password. While pretending to be from IT is popular, so is IT as the victim. In the reverse situation, the phisher might call the Help Desk and complain that he's having difficulty logging in. By counting on the Help Desk to provide "help" (including instructions, password resets, etc.), the phisher may be able to gain access to the system.

Some Security Stories

Lost Data ("The dog ate my homework.")

"NEW YORK (CNN/Money) — Bank of America said Friday it lost computer tapes containing account information on 1.2 million federal employee credit cards, among them those of U.S. senators, potentially exposing them to theft or hacking. *http://money.cnn.com/2005/02/25/news/fortune500/bank_ america/index.htm*

A Tiny Clue Leads to Giant Flaw

"What first appears as a 75-cent accounting error in a computer log is eventually revealed to be a ring of industrial espionage . . . Clifford Stoll [Lawrence Livermore lab scientist] becomes, almost unwillingly, a one-man security force trying to track down faceless criminals who've invaded the university computer lab he stewards." *www.amazon.com/gp/product/0671726889/002-0037032-5296037?v=glance&n=283155*

A Classic (and Unfortunate for the Victim) Story of the Damage Lack of Understanding Can Cause

Kevin Mitnick is a famous hacker, one of the first to hone his "social engineering" skills to break into and acquire all kinds of technical information (including code from Nokia and Motorola). After he was arrested, he had the guards so spooked at his federal penitentiary that they put him in solitary confinement for eight months because they were convinced he could launch nuclear missiles by whistling into a phone. *www.cnn.com/2005/TECH/internet/10/07/kevin.mitnick.cnna*

13.5 Stay Informed

If you want to stay abreast of the latest developments in information security, mailing lists (and their archives) are the best method. Excellent sites to check out and sign up with, include the following.

Useful Security Sites

✦ **Bugtraq:** A mailing list for the discussion of computer security issues and vulnerabilities. Bugtraq is hosted by Security Focus (*www.securityfocus. com*). The topics on this site range from Security Basics to Forensics.

✦ **CERT:** This (*www.cert.org*) is a federally funded organization operated by Carnegie Mellon University. CERT is an organization devoted to ensuring that appropriate technology and systems management practices are used to resist attacks on networked systems and to limiting damage and ensure continuity of critical services in spite of successful attacks, accidents, or failures (*www.cert.org/faq/cert_faq.html*).

✦ **Computer Security Resource Center (CSRC):** A division of the National Institute of Standards and Technology, which is an agency of the U.S. Commerce Department's Technology Administration (*csrc.nist.gov/index.html*).

✦ **slashdot.org:** Their motto is "News for nerds."

✦ **spywareinfo.com:** A site for information about spyware.

✦ **blogs.zdnet.com/threatchaos:** A Web log about security.

Computer Security Standards

CISSP

Certified Information Systems Security Professional (CISSP) is a certification for professionals in the computer security field who are responsible for developing the information security policies, standards, procedures, and managing their implementation across an organization.

ISO 17799

Another widely used security standard, the ISO 17799 (*www.iso-17799.com/*) is an internationally recognized information security standard.

13.6 Additional Resources

Web Sites

✦ *blogs.zdnet.com/threatchaos* (a Web log about security)

✦ *bugtraq-subscribe@securityfocus.com* (Bugtrac mailing list)

✦ *computer.howstuffworks.com/workplace-surveillance.htm* (information about workplace surveillance)

+ *csrc.nist.gov/index.html* (National Institute of Standards and Technology's Web site about computer security)

+ *csrc.nist.gov/publications/nistpubs/800-30/sp800-30.pdf* (a risk management white paper from the National Institute of Standards and Technology)

+ *csrc.nist.gov/publications/secpubs/otherpubs/reviso-faq.pdf* (an FAQ from the National Institute of Standards and Technology about ISO/IEC 17799: 2000)

+ *isecurity.ucsf.edu/main.jsp?content = secure_zones/secure_zones* (information about Secure Zones)

+ *netsecurity.about.com/cs/bookreviews/gr/aapr100603.htm* (reviews of various IT security books)

+ *onguardonline.gov* (a U. S. Government site about computer security)

+ *seclists.org/lists/politech/2001/Feb/0009.html* (a Web log about face scanning at the 2005 Super Bowl)

+ *web.mit.edu/kerberos/www* (information about Kerberos)

+ *www.cert.org* (federally funded Computer Emergency Response Team at Carnegie Mellon)

+ *www.checkpoint.com* (security solutions vendor)

+ *www.cisco.com* (security solutions vendor)

+ *www.insecure.org* (nmap utility)

+ *www.iso-17799.com* (ISO site about ISO/IEC 17799:2005)

+ *www.juniper.net* (security solutions vendor)

+ *www.mcafee.com/us* (security software vendor)

+ *www.microsoft.com/technet/security/default.mspx* (Microsoft's security Web site)

+ *www.microsoft.com/technet/security/topics/Serversecurity/tcg/tcgch00.mspx* (Threats and Countermeasures Guide)

+ *www.rsasecurity.com/press_release.asp?doc_id = 6095&id = 1034* (survey by RSA about the risks of multiple passwords)

+ *www.secinf.net* (books about IT security)

+ *www.securityguidance.com* (Microsoft security assessment tool)

+ *www.security-risk-analysis.com/introduction.htm* (introduction to risk analysis)

+ *www.slashdot.org*

+ *www.snpx.com/faq.shtml* (security Web site for IT professionals)

+ *www.spywareinfo.com* (information about spyware)

+ *www.symantec.com* (security software vendor)

+ *www.trendmicro.com* (security software vendor)

+ *www.vnunet.com/vnunet/news/2147200/november-biggest-ever-malware* (malware risks)

Books and Articles

+ Allen, Julia H., *The CERT Guide to System and Network Security Practices*, Addison-Wesley Professional, 2001.

+ Beers, Christopher T., "Beyond Spam Filters," *Network Computing*, February 16, 2006, p. 25.

+ Carlson, Caron, "Alliance Tackles VoIP Threats," *eWeek*, October 24, 2005, p. 22.

+ Carlson, Caron, "Adware Will Need User Consent," *eWeek*, November 21, 2005, p. 27.

+ Dubin, Joel, *The Little Black Book of Computer Security*, 29th Street Press, 2005.

+ Erlanger, Leon, "Is VoIP Ripe for Attack?," *Infoworld*, October 17, 2005, p. 31.

+ Ferguson, Renee Boucher, "RFID World: Searching for ROI," *eWeek*, February 27, 2006, p. 25.

+ Garcia, Andrew, "Anti-Spyware Hones Searches," *eWeek*, October 10, 2005, p. 10.

+ Garcia, Andrew, "Fighting Spyware is a Never Ending Battle," *eWeek*, January 9, 2006, p. 41.

+ Hall, Mark, "Price of Security Breaches," *Computerworld*, November 14, 2005, p. 8.

+ Kalin, Sari, "How to Tackle Identity and Access Management," *CIO Magazine*, December 1, 2005, p. 106.

+ Kelly, Matt, "Betting on Risk Management," *eWeek*, January 9, 2006, p. E1.

◆ Kozoil, Jack, Litchfield, David, Aitel, Dave, Anley, Chris, and Mehta, Neel, *The Shellcoder's Handbook: Discovering and Exploiting Security Holes*, Wiley, 2004.

◆ Krutz, Russell, Vines, Dean, and Stroz, Edward M., *The CISSP Prep Guide: Mastering the Ten Domains of Computer Security*, Wiley, 2001.

◆ McClure, Stuart, Scambray, Joel, and Kurtz, George, *Hacking Exposed, 5th Edition*, McGraw-Hill Osborne Media, 2005.

◆ McWilliams, Brian, *Spam Kings: The Real Story behind the High-Rolling Hucksters Pushing Porn, Pills, and %*@)# Enlargements, First Edition*, O'Reilly Media, October 2004.

◆ Mitchell, Robert L., "Spy Stoppers Fight Back," *Computerworld*, October 31, 2005.

◆ Roberts, Paul F., "Microsoft Moves on Security," *eWeek*, October 10, 2005, p. 9.

◆ Roberts, Paul F., "Phishers Zero in on e-Banking," *eWeek*, October 10, 2005, p. 30.

◆ Schneier, Bruce, *Applied Cryptography, Second Edition*, John Wiley & Sons, 1996.

◆ Tipton, Harold F., Krause, Micki, CISSP (Editors), *Information Security Management Handbook, Fifth Edition* (Hardcover), Auerbach, 2003.

◆ Tynan, Dan, "Identity Management In Action," *Infoworld*, October 10, 2005, p. 23.

◆ Wailgum, Thomas, "50-Cent Holes," *CIO Magazine*, October 15, 2005.

◆ Ware, Lorraine Cosgrove, "Phishing Sinks Confidence in e-Commerce," *CIO Magazine*, October 15, 2005, p. 28.

Software and Operating Systems

*Operating systems are like underwear —
nobody really wants to look at them.*

—BILL JOY, CO-FOUNDER OF SUN MICROSYSTEMS

While software has never been a simple item to categorize, these days there are many more types of software and many more methods of managing those types. In this chapter we'll discuss some of the major types (operating systems, database management systems, enterprise applications, business applications, middleware, productivity tools, utilities, and security) as well as how to successfully manage them (including purchasing, management, licensing, and tracking).

CHAPTER FOURTEEN

14.1 Types of Software

There are many different types of software. In general, software is categorized by the IT industry according to how it's used.

Types of Software

✦ **Database Management Systems (DBMS)**: Data are the heart and soul of IT, and its most valuable asset. While all the data are in a database, a DBMS is used for administering the data. The DBMS is the interface to the database and can control access (so that only certain users have access to certain data), maintain integrity to minimize corruption, adjust the structure of the database to match changing business needs, perform transaction processing (Online Transaction Processing, OLTP), and generate reports (Online Analytical Processing, OLAP). Enterprise DBMS solutions include Oracle, Microsoft's SQL Server, and IBM's DB2. There are also small-scale DBMS offerings like Microsoft's Access, FileMaker Pro, and IBM's Lotus Approach.

✦ **Operating Systems**: There are now essentially three main operating systems: Windows, MacOS, and the family of Linux/Unix variants. See Section 14.2 Operating Systems (page 386) for a full discussion of operating systems.

✦ **Business Applications**: This is a catchall term to refer to those software packages that allow the users and the business to do their job(s). This might be a warehouse inventory system, the payroll application, or a simple application that allows administrative assistants to print mailing labels.

✦ **Enterprise Applications**: Enterprise applications are those that are used by virtually every part of an organization, and act as a way of integrating systems, users, and functions. Enterprise applications may include business applications (like an ERP system), as well as something like company-wide e-mail. They're discussed in detail in Chapter 15.

✦ **Middleware**: This isn't a desktop application, nor an enterprise-wide application. For most of IT, middleware is software that connects other software. This can encompass everything from formal middleware products (such as Oracle's Fusion Middleware software) that are packaged, sold, and installed as distinct units; to a few hundred lines of code custom written to connect one proprietary piece of software to another. Middleware is sometimes referred to as an "interface" or a "hook." There are those in the industry that consider a DBMS or a Web server package to be middleware.

✦ **Client/Server**: This is reference to an application's architecture, and not to its use. A client/server application has two pieces of software associated with it: one that sits on the server and does the vast majority of the processing, and another piece that the user (or client) accesses that serves as the user-interface. E-mail (such as Microsoft's Exchange, or IBM's Lotus Notes) is an example of a client/server. The client portion is the software that allows users to read, write, and manage their e-mails. The server portion is the part that moves mail along between users, provides administration tools for the IT staff, controls security, allows for the creation of policies (like mail retention), etc. Enterprise resource planning (ERP) applications (like Oracle and SAP) are also examples of client/server architected solutions.

✦ **Productivity Tools**: This is the industry-accepted term that refers to common desktop applications like word processing, spreadsheets, presentation, etc. Productivity tools are often sold in suites, or as stand-alone components.

✦ **Utility Tools**: This large category can include items for tasks strictly associated with the IT staff (e.g., backup, monitoring, management, and administration), as well as those that might be used by the end-users (e.g., file compression, file conversion).

✦ **Security**: This category of software can refer to a variety of solutions that protect the environment (firewall, anti-virus, anti-spam, user authentication, encryption, VPN).

✦ **Development Tools**: These items include all elements of software used to create other software such as compilers, linkers, debuggers, source code control systems, languages, etc.

As you can see, some of these categories will overlap. A solution like Oracle Financials could be simultaneously categorized as an enterprise application, a business application, and a client/server solution.

Client Applications

A basic workstation these days is installed with a productivity tool suite, a browser, some basic utilities, and security software.

Productivity Tool Suites   There is a great deal of arm wrestling about exactly which product has what market share; there is little disagreement, though, about the fact that Microsoft's Office has the dominant share. MS Office is available in several editions (e.g., professional, standard, small business, etc.). Microsoft's Office suite has become the *lingua franca* for spreadsheet, word processing, and presentation files. Job seekers are all too familiar with being told to send a "Word version" of their résumé.

OpenOffice is the open source equivalent to MS Office. While hardly a 100%, feature-for-feature match to Office, OpenOffice is a fiery, legitimate contender in the office productivity marketplace. (See *http://www.eweek.com/article2/ 0,1759,1571626,00.asp* for a formal lab test comparison of the two products.) Other offerings in the productivity tool market include IBM's Lotus SmartSuite, Corel's WordPerfect Office, and Star Office from Sun Microsystems.

Regardless of which product and which version your company is using, there are generally viewers for the other products; if you receive a PowerPoint file and your company has no official copies, you can download a viewer from Microsoft to view the file *(http://www.microsoft.com/downloads/details. aspx?FamilyID = 428d5727-43ab-4f24-90b7-a94784af71a4&displaylang = en)*.

Browsers   There are now a variety of options. They're competing to be the new desktop *(http://www.w3schools.com/browsers/browsers_stats.asp)*. Major browsers now include: Microsoft's Internet Explorer, Firefox from Mozilla, Opera, Apple's Safari, AOL, and Netscape.

Utility Software   Typical desktop utilities include Adobe Acrobat Reader (for reading PDF files), a file compression offering (e.g., WinZip), and a media player such as the offerings from Real Networks or Microsoft.

Security Software   Typically, installed desktop products might include anti-spyware and anti-virus tools, as well as a personal firewall, and a solution for encrypting/unencrypting files, etc. See Chapter 13, Security (page 349), for a discussion of security issues.

14.2   Operating Systems

Without an operating system (OS), a computer isn't much more than a door stop. Operating systems have a long and interesting history that includes some familiar names (Unix, Windows, Linux, Mac OS), and some forgotten ones (DOS, CP/M, TRS-DOS, OS/2).

There are three major offerings for operating systems: Windows, Macintosh, and Unix variants.

Windows

Microsoft's offerings dominate both the server market (Windows NT Server, Windows 2000 Server, and Windows Server 2003), and the desktop market (Windows 2000, XP, and Vista). Windows is also making inroads in the hand-held market with Windows Mobile.

Well over 95% of the desktops on the planet are using some version of Windows. Windows 1.0 was released in 1985; and there have been many versions released since. There are flavors of Windows available for servers, desktops, and hand-helds. Because it's so popular, most application vendors will first write their software to support Windows, and many won't even consider writing their application on any other OS platforms.

Real figures about market share are hard to come by, and each OS touts its own Total Cost of Ownership (TCO). (For IBM's analysis of Linux's TCO, see *http://www-1.ibm.com/linux/RFG-LinuxTCO-vFINAL-Jul2002.pdf*. For Microsoft's analysis of Window Server product's TCO, see *http://www.microsoft.com/windows serversystem/facts/default.mspx*.)

Mac

The long-time runner up to Windows for the desktop is the Macintosh Operating System. This operating system has many die-hard adherents; its demise has been predicted unsuccessfully for many years. Mac is the de facto OS used by certain industries — primarily those associated with audio/video media, design, graphic arts, etc. In 2001, with the release of version 10 of the Mac Operating System, Apple has been using Unix as the underlying foundation of its graphical user interface.

Although mostly known as a desktop operating system, there is a server version of the Mac-OS as well.

Unix Variants and Linux

Unix and its variants have quite a history that starts in the 1960s and 1970s at AT&T's Bell Labs. The following family tree from *wikipedia.org* charts Unix history, off-shoots, and derivatives (Figure 14.1):

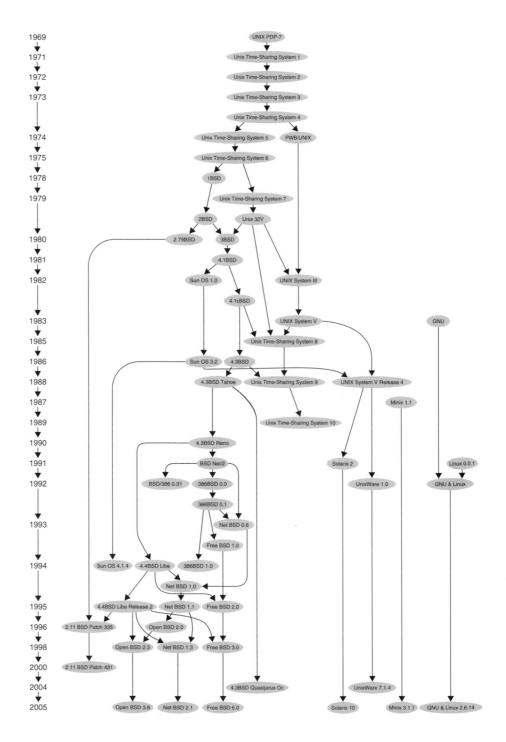

Figure 14.1 A Chart of UNIX HISTORY, OFF-SHOOTS, and DERIVATIVES (Source: *http://upload.wikimedia.org/wikipedia/commons/5/50/Unix_history-simple.png*)

Solaris, from Sun Microsystems, and several other offerings (e.g., HP-UX from Hewlett-Packard, AIX from IBM) compete in this market, but it's Linux that is making real headway in gaining market share. Both IBM and Sun Microsystems now sell and support Linux running on their hardware and with many of their application offerings.

Linux is an open source operating system developed by Linus Torvalds in 1991. The system is a Unix variant and has been freely distributed since its creation, although "free" in this context is a very complicated concept. See the section Open Source (page 393) below for a further discussion of open source software, and the section (page 243) on TCO and Asset Management in Chapter 9, Getting Started with the Technical Environment.

Choosing an Operating System

You probably already have multiple operating systems in your environment. Although it would be nice to standardize on one, it isn't always possible. It's important to keep in mind that you really don't "choose" operating systems directly. It's a decision that is almost made indirectly based on other factors and issues. Specifically, which applications your company uses and what the specific needs of your users are, often determines which operating system(s) you're using.

Applications in Your Environment

Many major desktop business applications are now available on all three platforms. There are equivalent open source applications for Microsoft's Office suite. See the previous section Productivity Tool Suites (page 385) for a discussion of OpenOffice. However, server applications may only run on one or two platforms. For example, the server software for SAP is available to run on Unix or Windows, but not Mac. However, the client front end for SAP *is* available for Mac desktops.

The key issue here is which *non-standard* applications are you going to run? Many companies run custom software applications to manage their inventory or send and receive proprietary data from a variety of sources around the planet. Situations like these make keeping the previous operating system preferable because changing to a new operating system is a difficult task at best.

Typically, most of the operating system choices you face will be related to the server side of the environment, and will come about when consideration is given to bringing a new application in to the organization. Factors to consider here include:

◆ The skill set of your staff, along with the cost, effort, and time involved to develop expertise on a new OS.

✦ Performance/cost concerns: The application may run faster with one operating system as compared to another. But that performance difference could be mitigated with the choice of hardware.

✦ Compatibility with the rest of your environment: If the tools you use to maintain your environment (backup, anti-virus, monitoring, etc.) are operating system specific, the cost and effort of having to support another operating system could be enormous.

Customers' Needs

As we have discussed before, determining who your users are (and who *their* customers are) will make you a much more productive IT Manager. Choosing operating systems is no exception to this rule. Consider what the de facto standard is for your customers. If a user community (e.g., the graphic arts department or the elementary school you are supporting) runs on the Mac platform, it will be much more efficient in both the short and long term if you choose Macs for everyone. This will eliminate problems with sharing files, compatibility, and so on. It will also radically cut down on your training and equipment costs, since users can share their knowledge and their machines among each other.

Multiple Operating Systems

It's common now to have multiple OSs in one company, despite corporate efforts to keep everyone on one platform. Users sometimes go their own way. And supporting three platforms in one environment, of course, can be a difficult task. Here are some issues to mention next time a user wants to put her Linux machine on your Windows system.

Operating System Emulators

A number of tools and products have been developed to allow applications developed for one operating system to run on another operating system. A short list includes:

✦ **WINE** ("Wine Is Not an Emulator"): is GNU licensed software that allows applications written for Windows to run on PCs running variants of Unix (primarily Linux).

✦ **Win4Lin**: Similar to WINE, Win4Lin allows Windows applications to run on Linux-based computers.

✦ **Virtual PC for Mac**: While not exactly an emulator, it does allow you to install Microsoft Windows on to a Mac. (Boot Camp from Apple also allows you to do the same thing.)

✦ **SoftMac**: Software that you install on a Windows PC to allow you to run applications developed for the Macintosh.

While emulators are very convenient, they can create additional challenges for support. Just as there are nuances and idiosyncrasies with applications and operating systems (version, components, setting, hardware, etc.), an emulator can further complicate things by adding another layer into the mix. For example, when an application isn't working right, is it because of the application, the core operating system, or the emulator? Perhaps it's how these are configured, or how they interact with each other.

Virtual Machines

Similar to emulators, there is software that allows you to take a single physical device (e.g., one PC or server) and run multiple instances of operating systems. Each of these instances looks and operates as its own device, but because they co-exist on a single physical device, they are considered to be *virtual machines*. Even if one of the instances should crash, the remaining operating system instances will continue to run. There are a number of virtual offerings available, but some the most popular include:

✦ **VMware Workstation** from EMC allows a workstation to run multiple instances of Windows, Linux, NetWare, or Solaris x86.

✦ **VMWare Server** from EMC allows the running of multiple instances of server operating systems (Windows, Linux, Netware) on a single device.

✦ **Virtual PC** from Microsoft can run multiple instances of Microsoft-developed operating systems (DOS, Windows, OS/2).

✦ **Virtual Server** from Microsoft allows a single server to run multiple instances of Microsoft's server versions of Windows.

Virtual machines take the concept of disk partitioning a step further. With disk partitioning, a computer's hard drive can be partitioned, with each partition running a different operating system. However, with disk partitioning, only one operating system can be running at a time, switching between operating systems requires a reboot of the computer, and it isn't easy to share data among the different partitions. With virtual machine technology, all instances of the various operating systems run simultaneously, and switching among them is fast and easy.

Uses The virtual machine offerings designed for clients are convenient for a number of scenarios: If your environment has to support multiple operating systems, virtual machine software can be used by:

+ Your Help Desk and support staff so that they can use a single piece of hardware to run different operating systems that are comparable to what different users have. In this way, the support staff is enabled to easily replicate the user's environment when providing support.

+ End-users during operating system migration. If a particular business application isn't yet supported by more current versions of an operating system, it can challenge efforts to move the organization to later OS versions. By using virtual machine software, all users can be migrated to the new OS, and legacy applications can be run on an instance of an older OS.

+ The training room PCs can run various instances of operating systems, each configured similarly to various user scenarios. This allows the trainers to easily provide training that replicates the various user environments.

+ Software developers and testers can use virtual machine technology to easily test their applications from varying workstation configurations and environments.

Virtual Machine Benefits Virtual machine offerings for servers also have distinct benefits:

+ More efficient use of hardware via server consolidations.

+ Easily and quickly create new server environments for testing and development without having to buy new hardware.

+ Quickly and easily move virtual-machine images to different hardware (generally accomplished through a management interface tool, as opposed to manually installing/configuring software on new hardware, or doing a restore).

+ Support legacy applications without having to set aside dedicated server environments for them.

Need for Additional Support Labor

Multiple platforms mean you need techs with skills in multiple platforms. In these days of specialization, having a Linux guru who is equally skilled with Windows may be hard to find. It also complicates the life for your Help Desk staff, since they have to know the differences between common operations and software functions among multiple platforms.

Software and File Compatibility

While most applications now run on most major platforms, there are often subtle differences between versions. Sometimes (but not always) you can determine the importance of these problems in advance. If no one in your Sales department even uses Excel macros, then it's a non-issue between using Excel and OpenOffice's Calc program.

Software Versions

Multiple versions of the same software will complicate your administrative burdens in regard to purchasing, upgrades, training, license tracking, maintenance and support arrangements, software distribution, support, etc.

14.3 **Open Source**

For many, many years, there was the Microsoft world of software and then there was everyone else's world. While the Redmond giant still owns a large portion of some very large markets, and lots of individual companies have made inroads into individual markets, it's the Open Source movement that has the largest impact on Microsoft's market share in recent years.

Definition

Open Source Software (OSS) is software created by the worldwide user community. It isn't owned by any one company, much less one person. It isn't developed, supported, or installed by one company. Many individuals, organizations, and companies around the world develop, install, and support OSS. But the software itself isn't theirs, and they don't charge anything for it.

Because the source code for OSS is available for all to see and change at will, there is a certain fear of "who is in control?" In the Open Source movement, the concept of a "benevolent dictator" is recognized as the person in control. While there could be hundreds, or thousands, of people suggesting fixes and enhancements to the product, it's the benevolent dictator that evaluates them and makes the determination as to which will be adopted and when. Of course, that won't stop people from making their own fixes and enhancements; it just means they won't be part of the "official" code. Linus Torvalds is generally recognized as Linux's benevolent dictator. See Table 14.1 for the pros and cons of Open Source.

Table 14.1 Pros and and cons of OSS

PRO		CON	
	Initial cost is low or non-existent.		Depending on how it's obtained in your organization, there might be no formal support for the product.
	Adherents claim many open source products are simpler and easier to use.		Many companies are afraid that without an "identified" owner, or if they haven't paid for the software, there will be no one to turn to when they need help (i.e., vendor support). That's why purchasing "distributions" of Open Source (such as the one from Red Hat) is a common option — the vendor also can provide support, for a fee of course.
	Major corporations — like IBM and Sun — are supporting and offering Linux solutions, bringing legitimacy to the once fledgling movement.		Detractors of OSS say the software is often harder to use and missing important features.
	Because the source code of OSS is available to all, there are more eyes looking at it, which increases the chances that bugs and security flaws will be found (and fixed). In theory, this makes OSS more reliable.		Some are concerned that since OSS code is free (i.e., no "profit"), there is little incentive for anyone to enhance it, add features, etc.
			The success of the product depends on the collaboration of hundreds of people around the planet. This is too much risk for some companies to accept.
			There are many conflicting studies as to which OS is more reliable and secure.

Cost

All OSS is "free;" that is, there is no charge for the software itself. But the costs of software are much more than the initial cost of the purchase; when evaluating the purchase of software, you must consider TCO. This is discussed in more detail in the section TCO and Asset Management in Chapter 9, Getting Started with the Technical Environment (page 243). Typical TCO considerations include the long-term components of a purchase, such as installation, training, financing, etc.

Official Statements

The Official Word on Linux

Linux is an operating system that was initially created as a hobby by a young student, Linus Torvalds, at the University of Helsinki in Finland. Linus had an interest in Minix, a small Unix system, and decided to develop a system that exceeded the Minix standards. He began his work in 1991 when he released version 0.02 and worked steadily until 1994 when version 1.0 of the Linux Kernel was released. The kernel, at the heart of all Linux systems, is developed and released under the GNU General Public License and its source code is freely available to everyone. It's this kernel that forms the base around which a Linux operating system is developed. There are now literally hundreds of companies and organizations and an equal number of individuals that have released their own versions of operating systems based on the Linux kernel. More information on the kernel can be found at our sister site, LinuxHQ and at the official Linux Kernel Archives. The current full-featured version is 2.6 (released December 2003) and development continues.

Apart from the fact that it's freely distributed, Linux's functionality, adaptability, and robustness, has made it the main alternative for proprietary Unix and Microsoft operating systems. IBM, Hewlett-Packard, and other giants of the computing world have embraced Linux and support its ongoing development. More than a decade after its initial release, Linux is being adopted worldwide as a server platform primarily. Its use as a home and office desktop operating system is also on the rise. The operating system can also be incorporated directly into microchips in a process called "embedding" and is increasingly being used this way in appliances and devices.

Source: *http://www.linux.org/info/index.html*

The Official Word from Red Hat: Why Open Source is Better

All software is written with source code. With open source software, the code is protected by a special license that ensures everyone has access to that code. That means no one company can fully own it. Freedom means choice. Choice means power.

That's why we believe open source is inevitable. It returns control to the customer. You can see the code, change it, learn from it. Bugs are more quickly found and fixed. And when customers don't like how one vendor is serving them, they can choose another without overhauling their infrastructure. No more technology lock-in. No more monopolies.

And we believe open source simply creates better software. It multiplies one company's development capacity many times over. Everyone collaborates, the best software wins. Not just within one company, but among an Internet-connected, worldwide community. It's no coincidence that the rise of open source closely followed the rise of the Internet. The perfect breeding ground for collaboration, the Internet moves ideas and code around the world in an instant.

As a result, the open source model often builds higher quality, more secure, more easily integrated software. And it does it at a vastly accelerated pace and often at a lower cost.

The open source model is built on the premise that companies like Red Hat must consistently serve customers through extraordinary value, performance, and ease of integration and management. Or they can choose another vendor.

Open source isn't nameless, faceless, and it's not charity. Nor is it solely a community effort. What you see today is a technology revolution driven ever forward by market demand.

The concept behind open source isn't new. For centuries, universities and research communities have shared their work. Monks copied books by hand. Scientists publish new discoveries in journals. Mathematical formulas are distributed, improved, redistributed.

Imagine if all of this past knowledge was kept hidden or its use was restricted to only those who are willing to pay for it. Yet this is the mentality behind the proprietary software model. In the same way shared knowledge propels the whole of society forward, open technology development can drive innovation for an entire industry.

Source: *http://www.redhat.com/en_us/USA/home/company/whyopensource*

The Official Word from Microsoft on Open Source

Microsoft believes that the future of software will not be the result of the dominance of a single development, licensing, or business model. Future innovation will not come solely from government, private industry, or a loose coalition of individuals acting in the best interests of society at large. Rather, the continued health of the cycle of sustained innovation — the fruits of which we have enjoyed for three decades — will depend entirely on the continued melding of approaches and technologies.

For example, the Microsoft Windows operating system was developed privately and for profit. But the product includes many components born of government and academically funded work and contains implementations of dozens of open industry standards. Furthermore, the publication of thousands of application programming interfaces has created business opportunities for tens of thousands of software businesses and has resulted in innumerable custom applications that address individual needs.

Collaboration is the primary benefit of the OSS development model in that the ideas of the original developer are available for modification and improvement by any other member of the community. It is important to note that simply releasing source code doesn't guarantee the formation of a community. But, the combination of compelling technologies, dynamic project leaders, and a clear sense of direction can result in an active and healthy collaborative community. For consumers, the most obvious benefit of the OSS model is the little to no acquisition cost. Yet, integration, deployment, migration, training, and support costs may exceed other forms of software throughout the life of the software.

The increased competition resulting from the proliferation of OSS has been constructive for the industry as a whole. The implications of OSS within multiple market segments are causing organizations to figure out what is most important to them. It has placed a higher premium on innovation and a drive to deliver greater value for lower costs. The big winner in this equation has been the software consumer, whose choices have increased dramatically.

Source: *http://www.microsoft.com/resources/sharedsource/Articles/MicrosoftandOpenSource.mspx#EKB*

A Word on Richard Stallman and GNU

No discussion of software — certainly "free" software — would be complete without a mention of Richard M. Stallman. The legendary "rms," Richard Stallman founded the free software movement and, among other things, the GNU project.

Other "small" items on his résumé include the invention of the emacs editing utility, and the creation of the Free Software Foundation. His influence on the field of software has been enormous, and his thinking and writing about the nature of the cost and value of software long preceded today's heated debates about open source (*http://en.wikipedia.org/wiki/Richard_Stallman, www.gnu.org*).

14.4   Managing Software

Managing software is a critical component of an IT Manager's work day. There are several key issues and some very useful tools to help the manager cope with those issues. We'll present these issues and suggest some tools — some "free" (shareware) and some that cost money — to help you manage your software issues intelligently.

TCO

Purchasing software is an activity that can range from a simple retail purchase of a graphics tool or a download of a file compression tool to a complex, months-long, meeting-filled, company-wide process of buying an ERP. However, the purchase price isn't the only cost associated with software.

TCO, along with Asset Management, is discussed in much more detail in the section TCO and Asset Management in Chapter 9 Getting Started with the Technical Environment (page 243). It's the concept that when you are considering buying an asset (a computer, a car, a house) you should consider not only the initial purchase price — for example, this business application will cost the department $10,000 — but all the costs associated with that purchase over the life of the asset. There will be costs associated with the time to install the application, as well as hardware associated with it, vendor maintenance/support fees each year, training costs, etc. (For links to sites where Microsoft and Linux claim their server software TCO are lower, see the section Official Statements (page 395) above.)

Software Management Techniques

Deployment

One of the most complicated issues related to desktops and laptops in the large corporate environment is the deployment of software. When there is a new software package to be implemented, or an update (no matter how minor) to an existing application, the manual distribution of files can be a very tedious and labor intensive process.

To streamline this situation, there are several concepts that many environments (small and large) have seized upon. They're gaining in popularity, and quickly becoming standard practice:

✦ Develop a standard disk image

✦ Select a disk cloning package

✦ Implement a software deployment tool

✦ Users download from the IT intranet site

✦ Locking down the desktop

Develop a Standard Disk Image

Every organization should create a disk image that will essentially serve as a way of ensuring that each PC's software is set up and configured as similarly as possible. This can reduce a technician's troubleshooting time significantly. Ideally, there will be only one standard image in an environment. However, it's common to find a need for more than one image. For example, laptops may need to be configured differently to support remote access needs. Or you may find that some business applications aren't fully compatible with the latest version of the operating system. Regardless, the disk image will include the following features.

A Directory Structure for All Programs and Files.   It's the directory structure that will determine where programs and files will be stored. While many environments use each application program's defaults for most directory choices, it's likely that you will have to do some customization, particularly for the directories that hold documents and data files.

An Installation of the Most Common Programs Used.   Many programs, like e-mail and word processing, will be installed on virtually every PC in the company. Other applications, like an inventory management program or an HR system, will have much more limited installations. Depending on circumstances, you can choose not to install these on each PC, or to install them and then "cripple," or hide, them from users who don't need them by deleting a pertinent file or icon. In this way, the more involved effort of installing the software on each PC is simplified because it's the same for each user. Afterwards, the unnecessary applications can be quickly removed for those users who don't need them.

Preset Program Preferences that are Applicable to the Environment. Most programs have many preferences and options that allow the user to customize the look and feel of their program. While many of these can be left to the user's discretion, there are also many that should be set by the IT department. For example, in Microsoft Word it makes sense for IT to set the default document directory, default printer, and AutoSave feature — to name just three. It's best for IT to carefully review each option and determine if the default setting should be changed. The reason for this might be obvious: Default settings for individual programs are set to maximize the performance of that application, and don't consider the disk space, the memory requirements, the power drain, etc., for individual machines that IT then has to manage. It's best to be proactive about these issues.

Select a Disk Cloning Package

A standard disk image is a great way of ensuring consistency in an environment with many PCs. However, the image is only a blueprint. It doesn't provide a way to easily build each PC's disk to match the blueprint's specification. The amount of software on a PC can range from several hundred megabytes to several gigabytes. Even an automated install of all that data can take a fair amount of time.

A disk cloning package uses very sophisticated techniques to quickly copy large amounts of data in a fraction of the time it would take to use conventional methods. Once the master disk image is made, it's possible to duplicate it to other PCs in a matter of minutes. In larger environments, where there is a constant influx of new PCs arriving at the loading dock, a disk cloning package can save an enormous amount of time. And, since it creates an identical duplicate, it virtually eliminates any errors that might crop into a manual effort.

Popular disk cloning packages include:

✦ Symantec's Norton Ghost

✦ Acronis' True Image

✦ IBM's ImageUltra

✦ Miray's HDClone

In addition, there are freeware disk cloning packages, such as Ranish partition manager. Packages exist for MacOS (e.g., Carbon Copy Cloner) and Linux (dolly+) as well. Many PC vendors will also pre-load your image onto PCs they ship to you so they're virtually ready to be put to use out of the box.

Implement a Software Deployment Tool

While a standard disk image, along with a cloning tool, ensures that everyone has a similar software configuration when a new PC is deployed, it does nothing to help with updating software or adding software. There are numerous tools available to help with the deployment of software:

+ Microsoft's SMS (Systems Management Server)

+ Novell's ZENworks suite

+ Symantec's LiveState client management suite

+ Altiris's management suite

+ LANDesk's management suite

These tools operate in a very similar fashion by allowing you to "script" the installation process for a software update — be it as complex as a new company-wide application, or as small as an updated printer driver. For Windows platforms, the process generally includes creating a "package" in the form of an .MSI file. While some applications come with their own .MSI files to aid the deployment, you can create your own using products from vendors like Wise Solutions and Software OnDemand. These .MSI files are basically instruction files that contain all the information an application needs for installation. The .MSI files are then deployed through various delivery mechanisms (like Active Directory's Group Policy Objects, GPOs, or one of the deployment tools listed above).

While the packages provide assistance for creating scripts, it can still be a complex process. Many of the tools allow you to consider many variables and circumstances when the process runs.

For example:

+ You may want to check that the target PC has enough disk space before running.

+ You may only want to deploy to PCs that meet minimum hardware and software requirements that you define.

+ You may want to take different installation steps based on certain circumstances. For example, if a file is to be copied to a PC, you may not want it to do so if a newer version already exists.

+ You may choose whether the deployment runs automatically or by user selection, or to take different actions if the user has a slow connection (like dial-up).

+ You may be able to determine what time of day the deployments occur, in order to minimize network traffic, or user interruption.

+ You can choose what action to take if the installation fails.

As you can see, automated deployments can be a very effective tool, but complex to use. Since there are so many variables and permutations that could occur across hundreds or thousands of machines within an environment, it's best if the job of dealing with automated deployment is given to individuals who have an attention for detail and careful testing.

Without the use of the ideas and tools mentioned above, the effort to deploy software is reduced to an essentially manual one. As the number of PCs in an environment grows, it could easily require a small team of technicians to do the software deployment effort. However, the effort and manpower can be reduced significantly by using the techniques and tools that are readily available. When used effectively, not only can these ideas make the job easier, the end result is likely to be far superior to a manual effort.

Software Patching. In addition to tools for deploying applications, there is the requirement to keep software appropriately patched. This is primarily a security concern as vendors (most notably Microsoft) may release several security patches each month, and it can be a daunting task to get them deployed to all devices in an enterprise.

While some of the above mentioned tools can deal with patch deployment, there are other tools that deal with that task specifically. For example:

◆ Microsoft Windows Server Update Services

◆ HFNetChkPro from Shavlik

◆ PatchLink Update from PatchLink

Alternatively, many programs will periodically check, via the Internet, if updates are available. These programs can be configured to automatically download and install them, or prompt the user to take action. Some IT Managers prefer the automatic downloads as it means that the IT department doesn't have to be as involved. On the other hand, some IT Managers are fearful that with software updating itself, the IT department is no longer in control, and updates can't even be tested by IT before determining if they're safe to be deployed.

Users Download Software from an Intranet

A very common method of deploying software — and one that allows for the user to "pull" the software at their own convenience, rather than have it "pushed" on them when they don't need it — is to have users download software from an intranet. This method is particularly useful for software that not every user needs; every user will need Microsoft Word, for example, but most won't need MS Project, much less that $5,000-per-seat tool the Finance department bought.

You can direct users to your IT intranet site to install these packages. The .MSI files (discussed earlier) will ensure that the software is installed the way you want. Sometimes passwords and user keys are required (if the company has purchased only a specific number of licenses) and sometimes they aren't (the company may have purchased a site license that allows an unlimited number of users). In either case, this method allows IT to very efficiently deploy software that only a percentage of the entire user base will need.

Locking Down the Desktop

Many organizations now try to limit a user's capabilities to make troublesome changes by "locking down" the desktop. Typically, this may mean that the user can't install new programs, alter network settings, or change the way the operating system is configured. Similarly, it prevents the user from deleting key programs and files, and stopping vital operating system services.

However, even with a locked down desktop, the user can still have the flexibility to alter personal settings, such as selection of wallpaper, default printer, screen saver, colors, and fonts, etc.

Software Licensing

There are two general types of software licenses: "free" and "for profit." Initial portions of examples of both types, the GNU and Microsoft licenses, are shown below.

How a Sample GNU License Starts Out

The Opening Paragraphs of the GNU "Free Software" License

We maintain this free software definition to show clearly what must be true about a particular software program for it to be considered free software.

"Free software" is a matter of liberty, not price. To understand the concept, you should think of "free" as in "free speech," not as in "free beer."

Free software is a matter of the users' freedom to run, copy, distribute, study, change, and improve the software. More precisely, it refers to four kinds of freedom, for the users of the software:

+ The freedom to run the program, for any purpose (freedom 0).

(Cont.)

+ The freedom to study how the program works, and adapt it to your needs (freedom 1). Access to the source code is a precondition for this.

+ The freedom to redistribute copies so you can help your neighbor (freedom 2).

+ The freedom to improve the program, and release your improvements to the public, so that the whole community benefits (freedom 3). Access to the source code is a precondition for this.

A program is free software if users have all of these freedoms. Thus, you should be free to redistribute copies, either with or without modifications, either gratis or charging a fee for distribution, to anyone anywhere. Being free to do these things means (among other things) that you don't have to ask or pay for permission. . .

Source: *http://www.gnu.org/philosophy/license-list.html*

How a Sample Microsoft License Starts Out

The Opening Paragraphs of Microsoft's End User License

END-USER LICENSE AGREEMENT FOR MICROSOFT SOFTWARE

IMPORTANT — READ CAREFULLY: This End-User License Agreement ("EULA") is a legal agreement between you (either an individual or a single entity) and Microsoft Corporation for the Microsoft software that accompanies this EULA, which includes associated media and Microsoft Internet-based services ("Software"). An amendment or addendum to this EULA may accompany the Software. YOU AGREE TO BE BOUND BY THE TERMS OF THIS EULA BY INSTALLING, COPYING, OR USING THE SOFTWARE. IF YOU DO NOT AGREE, DO NOT INSTALL, COPY, OR USE THE SOFTWARE; YOU MAY RETURN IT TO YOUR PLACE OF PURCHASE FOR A FULL REFUND, IF APPLICABLE.

1. GRANT OF LICENSE. Microsoft grants you the following rights provided that you comply with all terms and conditions of this EULA:
    1.1 Installation and use. You may:
        (a) install and use a copy of the Software on one personal computer or other device; and
        (b) install an additional copy of the Software on a second, portable device for the exclusive use of the primary user of the first copy of the Software.

(Cont.)

1.2   Alternative Rights for Storage/Network Use. As an alternative to Section 1.1(a), you may install a copy of the Software on a network storage device, such as a server computer, and allow one access device, such as a personal computer, to access and use that licensed copy of the Software over a private network...

Source: Microsoft Word EULA

Licensing Issues

In general, corporations seldom consciously engage in illegal activities. They also generally respect intellectual copyright laws. However, due to complexities of licensing agreements and the volume of purchase activity, it can be difficult for an IT Manager to fully know if his company is properly licensed for all its software.

There are numerous cases of small companies being subjected to a software audit based on a call to one of the software industry trade groups (e.g., Business Software Alliance or the Software and Industry Information Association, which is now a part of the Software and Information Industry Association) from a single disgruntled employee.

Countless hours and resources have been expended by companies to deliver the documentation and proof of appropriate licenses requested. Companies consider themselves fortunate if it's decided that the illegal licensing discovered was unintentional, and that the company had been making a good faith effort to be legal. In cases like this, there may be no fines or punitive damages. But the company will have to pay the license fees for all the unlicensed software that was discovered, or agree to delete all the unlicensed software.

In fact, it isn't unusual for a company to find out that it's over-licensed on some products and under-licensed on others. Under-licensing usually occurs with software that isn't "standard" on every PC. For non-standard software, it's very easy for the purchase of the license to be overlooked and forgotten by the administrative staff. In such a case, the technical staff may seek to satisfy a user's request and install an unlicensed software copy, and neglect to inform the administrative staff to purchase the license.

The process of keeping track of software licenses is often referred to as "software metering." There are some general guidelines that you as an IT Manager should be aware of to avoid putting your company at risk for copyright infringement.

✦   Understand that when you buy a software license, what you're usually buying is the right to use a copy of the software, while the vendor usually remains the actual "owner" of the software.

✦ Read and understand the licenses that come with your software. License terms can change, so review them periodically. If they're complex (and most of them today are very complex), pass them along to the Legal department for review.

✦ Don't expect to be able to negotiate a change with your software's vendor (although very large organizations may have some success here). If the software you're buying isn't an off-the-shelf or shrink-wrapped package, you'll have better chances. See the section Negotiating Licenses below.

✦ Be aware of the difference between different types of licensing.

Multiple Licenses

✦ **Concurrent users:** With concurrent-user licensing, you only have to buy enough licenses to match the number of users who will be logged into the application at the same time. If you have 100 users that use the warehouse inventory application, but only 20 are using it at any one time, you'd only have to buy 20 licenses.

✦ **Per Seat licensing:** With per seat licensing, you have to purchase a license for each user that has access to the application. In the warehouse inventory example above, you'd have to buy 100 licenses.

✦ **Per Server licensing:** With per server licensing, you license the server software, and not the users.

✦ **Multiple Use licenses:** Some licenses allow a single license of the software to be used on each user workstation (e.g., the one in the office, the one at home, and the laptop in her briefcase), as long as these copies aren't used by others, or concurrently.

In many cases, the vendor may require that you buy different types of licenses (e.g., you buy a server license for each server the software will run on, as well as per seat licensing for each user that will use it). In other cases, the vendor may offer licensing alternatives, allowing you to choose the option that makes sense for your environment.

Buy versus Lease

In some cases you "buy" a license, which is yours essentially forever. In other cases, the license is "rented" and must be renewed every few years. Unless you're certain that you're only going to be using a product for a defined amount of time, it's generally wiser to buy the licenses. In addition to the cost implications, there may also be challenges when you must cease use of the software at the end of the rental period.

Maintenance and Support Plans

In addition to buying a license, some vendors sell upgrade or maintenance plans (not unlike the ability to buy extended warranties on a home appliance) that entitle you to upgrade (at little or a reduced cost) to newer versions of the software as they come out. While there is considerable doubt about the value of these plans for your new DVD player, the value of them in regard to software depends on how often the vendor expects to provide new versions, and how often you expect to be interested in these newer versions. Keep in mind that a vendor may also offer a "support" program, which entitles you to technical support on a product but doesn't include providing you with free upgrades. Alternatively, buying into a plan for upgrades may not include free support. Check with your vendor as to what you're buying before you buy it.

Negotiating Licenses

While you probably won't be able to negotiate the terms of the license, it's entirely likely you can negotiate a volume discount based on the license quantities you intend to buy.

Contact the Legal department. Let your company's legal resources review the terms of any software license you buy. In all likelihood, your company's lawyer will say that the license has numerous unfavorable terms, and that he recommends against entering into such an agreement. However, he is also likely to add that he recognizes that there is no real alternative.

Get Organized

Whenever possible, consolidate all your software purchases. Many large software retailers have systems in place designed to help companies keep track of their license purchases, their obligations, expirations, and so on. In a crisis or emergency situation, you may feel that the only solution is to install a copy of a software package that hasn't been paid for. If you choose to go this route, you should ensure that a proper license is ordered and purchased at the same time.

With all the licensing options and permutations available, it can be an administrative chore to track the licenses you have, and to make sure that when you're buying additional licenses, or upgrades, or software and maintenance plans, that you're doing it for the licenses you actually own.

Keep records of your license purchases: quantities, dates, vendors, and so on. For licenses that need to be renewed periodically, keep track of the start and end dates, and the same for support and upgrade plans. Make sure that everyone in IT is fully aware that it's against company policy to pirate software. Advise users that it's against company policy to bootleg software, and any unauthorized software will be immediately deleted when found. (This is a nifty little policy to have around when you encounter games that people have copied from their home PCs.)

Track Your Software

In addition to the above guidelines, there are several tools available to help you track software use in your environment. Software metering packages keep track of how software packages are used in your company. Metering software is generally installed on your LAN's file server(s) and keeps track of which users are using which packages, how often, and when. You can reconcile this information with the records from your software reseller to make sure you have purchased enough licenses for the actual use.

Another tool at your disposal is inventory software. Inventory software can automatically detect what software is installed on each workstation. These data are stored in a database that you can query and generate reports from. Again, this information can be compared to the information from your metering tool, as well as your purchasing records. In IT, software that is no longer needed is rarely removed from the environment. With inventory reports, you can see what software is on each PC, and use it to remove old versions, as well as unauthorized copies.

14.5   Additional Resources

Web Sites

- ✦ *browser.netscape.com/ns8* (Internet browser)

- ✦ *office.microsoft.com/en-us/default.aspx* (productivity tool suite)

- ✦ *sea.symantec.com/content/product.cfm?productid = 28* (software deployment tool)

- ✦ *www.acronis.com/enterprise/products/choose-trueimage* (disk cloning tool)

- ✦ *www.adobe.com/products/acrobat/readstep2.html* (PDF reader)

- ✦ *www.altiris.com/products/clientmgmt* (software deployment tool)

- ✦ *www.apple.com/macosx/features/safari* (Internet browser)

- ✦ *www.bombich.com* (disk cloning utility for Mac operating systems)

- ✦ *www.bsa.org* (trade organization for software publishers)

✦ *www.corel.com/servlet/Satellite?pagename = Corel3/Products/Display&p fid = 1047024307359* (productivity tool suite)

✦ *www.emulators.com/softmac.htm* (Mac emulator for Windows)

✦ *www.gnu.org* ("free" software site)

✦ *www.landesk.com/Products/LDMS* (software deployment tool)

✦ *www.linux.org* (Linux)

✦ *www.microsoft.com/mac/products/virtualpc/virtualpc.aspx?pid = virtualpc* (Windows emulator for Macintosh)

✦ *www.microsoft.com/smserver/default.mspx* (software deployment tool)

✦ *www.microsoft.com/technet/security/topics/AuditingandMonitoring. mspx* (software auditing and monitoring information)

✦ *www.microsoft.com/windows/ie/default.mspx* (Internet browser)

✦ *www.microsoft.com/windows/virtualpc/default.mspx* (virtual machine solution)

✦ *www.microsoft.com/windowsserversystem/virtualserver/default.mspx* (virtual machine solution)

✦ *www.miray.de* (disk cloning tool)

✦ *www.mozilla.com/firefox* (Internet browser)

✦ *www.novell.com/products/zenworks* (software deployment tool)

✦ *www.ondemandsoftware.com/msipak.asp* (software deployment packaging tool)

✦ *www.openoffice.org* (open source productivity tool suite)

✦ *www.opera.com* (Internet browser)

✦ *www.patchlink.com* (patch management solution)

✦ *www.pc.ibm.com/us/think/thinkvantagetech/imageultra.html* (disk cloning tool)

✦ *www.ranish.com* (open source disk cloning tool)

✦ *www.shavlik.com* (patch management vendor)

✦ *www.siia.net* (trade organization for software publishers)

✦ *www.staroffice.com* (productivity tool suite)

✦ *www.symantec.com/home_homeoffice/products/backup_recovery/ ghost10/index.html* (disk cloning tool)

- ✦ *www.vmware.com* (virtual machine solution)

- ✦ *www.win4lin.com* (Windows emulator for Linux)

- ✦ *www.winehq.com* (Windows emulator for Unix)

- ✦ *www.wise.com/wps.asp* (software deployment packaging tool)

- ✦ *www-142.ibm.com/software/sw-lotus/products/product2.nsf/wdocs/ sshome* (productivity tool suite)

Books and Articles

- ✦ Brooks, Jason, "The Rise of the Virtual Machines," *eWeek*, November 7, 2005, p. 39.

- ✦ Garcia, Andrew, "Lock Out Problems: System Lockdown isn't Always Easy, but it's a Powerful Protection," *eWeek*, November 28, 2005, p. 35.

- ✦ Hall, Mark, "Law and Order on the Open Source Range," *Computerworld*, December 5, 2005, p. 29.

- ✦ Koch, Christopher, "Free Code For Sale," *CIO Magazine*, February 15, 2006, p. 48.

- ✦ Mar-Elia, Darren, Melber, Derek, and Stanek, William D. *Microsoft Windows Group Policy Guide*, Microsoft Press, 2005.

- ✦ McAllister, Neil, "Illuminating Server Virtualization," *InfoWorld*, October 17, 2005, p. 14.

- ✦ Meyers, Mike, *Mike Meyers' A+ Guide to Operating Systems*, McGraw-Hill Osborne Media, 2004.

- ✦ Moody, Glyn, "Rebel Code: Linux and the Open Source Revolution," Perseus Books Group, 2001.

- ✦ Overly, Michael, and Kalyvas, James R., *Software Agreements Line by Line: A Detailed Look at Software Contracts and Licenses & How to Change Them to Fit Your Needs*, Aspatore Books, 2004.

- ✦ Tannenbaum, Andrew, *Modern Operating Systems*, 2nd Edition, Prentice Hall, 2001.

- ✦ Torvalds, Linus, and Diamond, David, *Just for Fun: The Story of an Accidental Revolutionary*, Collins, 2002.

Enterprise Applications

The very life blood of our enterprise.
—WILLIAM SHAKESPEARE (*KING HENRY IV*, PT 1., ACT IV, SCENE 1)

An "enterprise application" is an application that is widely used throughout the organization, and integrates the operations of many different departments and functions. Enterprise applications are very valuable but can be very complex pieces of software. They require extensive planning to implement, and can be very expensive.

For large companies, with hundreds and thousands of users, the value of connecting all of their functions is enormous, but so are the tasks of implementing and administering the software. This chapter discusses several enterprise applications: e-mail, directory services, and enterprise resource planning (ERP).

15.1 E-mail

When organizations are doing their disaster recovery planning, one of the applications that is almost always deemed

CHAPTER FIFTEEN

mission critical is e-mail. E-mail has become the lifeblood of communications for virtually all organizations. For a task as simple as seeing if a colleague is free for lunch, many will reach first for the keyboard, as opposed to the telephone.

Usage Statistics

A Hewlett-Packard sponsored white paper by the Radicati Group published in 2005 revealed some staggering information about e-mail.

- ✦ Based on research, corporate users send and receive an average of 133 messages per day, and this number is expected to reach 160 messages by 2009.

- ✦ With the average size of a single message currently around 0.11 MB, the daily e-mail storage requirement for a single user is 14.7 MB. This translates into 294 MB per user, per month (assuming 20 business days per month) for corporations that maintain a standard 30-day e-mail retention period.

- ✦ The average corporate e-mail user sends and receives nearly 15 MB of e-mail per day. For a company with 10,000 e-mail users, that adds up to about 147 GB per day, 735 GB per week, or approximately 2.9 TB per month.

- ✦ Table 15.1 from the white paper shows the projected growth of corporate e-mail traffic from 2005 to 2009.

Table 15.1   Average corporate e-mail user. (Source: *http://h71028.www7.hp.com/ ERC/downloads/5983-2385EN.pdf*)

	2005	2009
Messages Sent/Received Per Day	133	160
Messages Received Per Day	99	109
Messages Sent Per Day	34	51
Messages w/Attachments	22	28
Messages w/o Attachments	111	132
Avg. Attachment Size	469 KB	545 KB
Avg. Message Size (w/o attach.)	38 KB	46 KB
Avg. Total Storage Per User/Day	14.7 MB	21.3 MB

Advantages and Disadvantages of E-mail

In today's world, access to e-mail is as much of a requirement as a telephone. In fact, it's not unusual to do more communication via e-mail than via telephone.

Table 15.2   Pros and cons of e-mail

PRO		CON	
	Since e-mail (unlike face-to-face discussion, instant messaging, or telephone conversations) is not a real-time medium, the recipient can deal with the communication at their convenience — minutes, hours, or days after the sender has sent it.		The tone of a message may be misinterpreted. Virtually everyone has experienced the situation where some intended levity or sarcasm was not picked up by the reader.
	It can be implemented with features to allow for collaborative online work.		Some people are more comfortable with written communications than others, and the extensive use of e-mail may make some feel at a disadvantage.
	It creates a virtual paper trail for who said what, to whom, and when.		There is greater risk of confidential communications getting wider distribution than intended.
	It can easily include additional reference material (file attachments, Web links, etc.).		It can reduce the amount of face-to-face discussions, which may frustrate some people, make the interaction feel impersonal, or lead to confusion.
	Delivery is virtually immediate (even if the recipient doesn't deal with it right away).		Because it isn't interactive, it often doesn't lend itself to the discussion of complex or involved issues.

(Cont.)

Table 15.2 Pros and cons of e-mail (continued)

PRO		CON	
	There is little chance of the communication being lost, although filtering technologies (e.g., anti-virus, anti-spam) can misdirect some messages.		Because it's so convenient, it can easily be overwhelming, possibly even leading to over-communication.
	It allows the recipients to scan the material to find the pertinent information (unlike voice-mail messages, which have to be listened to in their entirety).		
	With integration to hand-helds and cell phones, it's virtually an anytime, anywhere solution.		
	Individuals can be added to, or removed from, a message thread, easily.		
	It can be integrated with telephone systems so that e-mail software can be used to hear voice mail messages, and view faxes, etc.		

E-mail versus Phone Calls

E-mail is often the fastest and most efficient method of making an exchange of information.

+ Phone calls can be faster, but the information exchanged is (for the most part) not recorded.

+ Phone calls aren't in a form that lends itself to re-evaluation.

+ Phone calls aren't appropriate for all exchanges because of the length of some material.

+ Voice mail (v-mail) doesn't lend itself to lengthy messages.

✦ E-mail, on the other hand, can be quite long and very detailed in its content, because the recipient can easily scan the message for the pertinent items, re-read portions as needed, etc.

E-mail versus Faxes

Faxes also are limited in their own way: length can be an issue (nobody likes getting or sending a 20-page fax, although it happens every day), not everyone has a fax machine, the machines can be busy, you can't be sure about the quality at the other end, and so on. Technology exists now to send and receive faxes from the desktop, but this brings faxing closer and closer to e-mail.

The Quality of Communication

It's clear that the growth of e-mail has radically increased communication both within the corporation and between the corporation and its customers. There is no question the *quantity* has increased; the issue commonly is: "Has the *quality* of communication gotten any better?" In other words, we are all getting more e-mail, but is the value increasing? And in general, "Am I better off with e-mail, or is it just another task I need to do during the day?"

Overall, the answer is a qualified "Yes," because e-mail is a tool, and tools can be used well or poorly. It's in your interest as an IT Manager to monitor both the quantity and quality of the e-mail in your company. Keeping tabs on the amount of e-mail being sent is relatively simple since there are tools built into the various programs (as well as third party offerings) that allow you to monitor usage.

How do you track the quality of your company's e-mail? You can't. But you can educate your users about the benefits of better quality e-mail. Often, people only need to be told once and they will alter their behavior. Many people have never been taught how to effectively use e-mail, and they're ripe for a quick lesson or two.

Educate Your Users on the Key Principles of E-mail

You (or the Training department, if you have one) can offer a class on the e-mail system you use and tips for effective communication. And you might have some success getting people to that class, especially if you have upper management buy in. But the truth is, these programs aren't that complex and the basic functions can be easily learned. What you need to get across to all your users are some simple principles of using e-mail that are less software-oriented and more usage-oriented:

✦ **Keep it brief**. If you don't like reading long e-mails, what makes you think others do? Keep it as short as possible. E-mail is fast and efficient, but reading a lot of text online isn't easy. Don't try to cover too many items or areas in a single e-mail.

✦ **Make the subject line count**. Be as clear in this line as possible. Instead of using "meeting" as your subject line, use something more indicative like "operations review status meeting."

✦ **Reply to all e-mails that expect one**. Not every e-mail that is sent needs a reply, but many do. If you send something to somebody, you expect a reply. Provide the same courtesy.

✦ **Differentiate TO and CC recipients**. As a general rule, people on the TO line are people who need to know and/or have to take action with the content of the message. People who are on the line for CC (which stands for carbon copy, a "technology" that pre-dates photocopy machines) are generally getting the information on an FYI basis. (Blind Carbon Copy, BCC, the third line on many e-mail windows, is another term that dates way back. It allows you to send a copy to other people without informing the addressee that you're doing so. Tell your users to use this option only with great care.)

✦ **Use the Reply All button with extreme caution**. This button is probably the largest contributor to e-mail waste. Everyone doesn't have to be copied on every e-mail. Sometimes just replying to the sender suffices. Sometimes a subset of the recipients needs to be informed. Much less frequently, all the recipients of the original e-mail need to be replied to; this occurs less often than people realize. If you can get your users to think before they use this button, the effect on your volume of e-mail will be dramatic. Many users don't know the damage they are causing by routinely using this button and will change their behavior when it's explained to them.

✦ **Spell-check all e-mails**. All e-mail programs now have a function that allows e-mail to be automatically spell-checked. Even though proper spelling, grammar, and punctuation have been early casualties as the world has moved online, you should remember that you're still working in a business environment. And, while the occasional typo or two may be forgiven, they should be avoided. Typos are at the very least annoying, but they can also be devastating and, in general, degrade the value of the message. Automatically spell-checking e-mail is an example of a very useful, everyday software function. Everyone should do it.

✦ **When stressed or angered, don't hit the Send button**. Sometimes people receive an e-mail (or phone call) that angers them, and they fire off a response in the heat of that anger. (E-mails of this kind are often called "nasty-grams," or "poison-pen" e-mails.) When stressed or angered, it's wise to wait until you've had a chance to cool off so that your note isn't overly emotional.

✦ **Define policies and guidelines for saving e-mail**. What do you want your users to do? How do you want them to save their e-mails? Provide your users with a specific plan. Do you want them to store up a month's worth on their hard drive? They need to save only the items that they will need quick access to. Your e-mail system probably has features to help you manage this. You may be able to automatically purge e-mail that reaches a certain age, or you may be able to limit the size of a message, as well as the size of a user's mailbox.

Besides telling users that they can delete their old e-mail, you should tell them that their e-mail is backed up daily so that they don't feel the need to save every little scrap.

E-mail Product Choices

There are many different e-mail programs to choose from, and all rely on industry standards.

Industry Standards

There are many e-mail programs, and many methods of implementing these programs. One of the most important options when considering e-mail is the matter of *industry standards* to ensure that you can exchange messages with users who aren't on your e-mail system. There are many products that adhere to industry standards (IMAP4, POP-3), and a few very popular products (e.g., Microsoft's Exchange, IBM's Lotus Notes, and Novell's GroupWise) that have added their own proprietary enhancements (such as group calendaring and scheduling) in addition to supporting industry standards. These enhancements allow the vendors to add value to their product, as well as support industry standards to ensure messaging interoperability with other products.

By adhering to industry standard protocols, you can mix and match server and client software products and can very often find various products to fit your needs (e.g., Netscape, Microsoft Outlook Express, Thunderbird, Eudora).

Internet Message Access Protocol   Internet Message Access Protocol (IMAP, generally referred to as "IMAP4" to denote its current incarnation) can be thought of as a client/server environment that allows you to view and manipulate e-mail while it's still on the server. The advantage to this is that users' mailboxes are accessible to them from any properly configured workstation. On the downside, it means that the mail server has to have a very large storage capacity.

Post Office Protocol 3   Post Office Protocol 3 (POP-3) can be thought of as a store-and-forward environment. Your mail is held for you on the server until you connect; then it's downloaded to your workstation. So, if you then go to another workstation, you won't see your mail since it's now on the first workstation.

POP-3 is supported by all the major browsers (Internet Explorer, Firefox, Netscape, etc.).

Multipurpose Internet Mail Extensions   The Multipurpose Internet Mail Extensions (MIME) specification is for formatting non-text messages (e.g., graphics, audio, video) so that they can be sent over the Internet. A variation of MIME, called S/MIME, supports encrypted messages.

Proprietary Products

On the other hand, proprietary products from vendors like Microsoft, Novell, and IBM, which support the industry standards, offer additional features (group scheduling and calendaring, full-featured address books, collaborative discussions, bulletin boards, etc.) that make them very attractive as solutions for much more than just e-mail.

The following are some of the most popular e-mail solutions for enterprise environments:

✦ Microsoft Exchange (which uses Microsoft's Outlook as the client)

✦ IBM's Lotus Notes

✦ Novell's GroupWise

Between them, they own the lion's share of the market for e-mail programs in large organizations.

Why You Should Consider Using One of These Products   While the most popular software packages aren't often the best products, there are valid reasons for using products that the market has embraced.

✦ The learning curve isn't as steep; because of their popularity, their use continues to grow. New people joining your company more likely will have experience in one of these packages; they won't need training to get them going.

✦ As with any software, the more people that use it, the more support and third party activity that will be available.

✦ Two of the vendors' products (Microsoft and IBM) have become part of a bundled suite of software. The e-mail program's features are integrated tightly into the features of the other programs.

✦ These products generally offer advanced management and administration tools for their messaging environments.

✦ There are many third party applications available (e.g., anti-virus, anti-spam, monitoring) that can integrate with these e-mail platforms.

✦ It's easier to find IT staff who are skilled with the more popular packages.

Unified Messaging

Unified messaging is the term applied to integrating your voice mail and e-mail systems. In short, you can use your e-mail system to access your v-mail (messages appear in your inbox as audio files), and use your v-mail system to access your e-mail (a synthesized voice reads your e-mail messages to you). Unified messaging can also allow you to send and receive faxes from your e-mail inbox, and can greatly reduce the amount of paper associated with traditional faxing. This technology is just beginning to gain acceptance and is still maturing.

It's also important to note that there are several ways to attack the integration:

1. Your v-mail vendor may sell a system that integrates to your e-mail environment.

2. Your e-mail vendor may have an add-on to integrate with your v-mail.

3. A third party vendor may offer a product to tie the two messaging systems together.

Unified messaging can be complex and may be costly. It also greatly increases the storage requirements since users will have a greater amount of flexibility in saving and forwarding voice mail messages. Even if you aren't planning to implement unified messaging immediately, however, you may want to consider it as an issue if you're evaluating new e-mail systems.

Managing E-mail

Because e-mail can quickly get out of control, it needs to be managed aggressively. Managing it can become a large part of your day; if you have a large company, it can become the sole responsibility of a team of people. A number of vendors offer solutions for monitoring e-mail and to address issues like spam and viruses, etc.

Chapter 13, Security (page 349), covers important aspects related to e-mail, in addition to what is covered below.

Junk Mail (Spam, Chain Letters, Phishing, Jokes, etc.)

While e-mail can be a very valuable tool for circulating vital information very quickly, it can distribute junk just as quickly. If someone receives an e-mail of a joke or a spiritual message that they like, they can circulate it to one person—or thousands—with just a few clicks of the mouse. Although it may seem innocent at first, the growth can be exponential, and it results in massive storage requirements for e-mail servers. It can slow down the delivery of mail because your servers are backed up distributing hundreds or thousands of messages unrelated to work.

E-mail packages now let the user identify the sources of spammers or junk mail senders. With a feature like this, once a source of junk mail is identified, any future mail from the same source is immediately deleted. There are also a variety of anti-spam solutions that are implemented at the e-mail gateway, so that spam never reaches your users' mailboxes. But, even these anti-spam solutions, which are designed to help you mange e-mail, require their own management. Because they aren't foolproof, there may be some issues of false-positives (legitimate e-mail incorrectly identified as spam), and false-negatives (junk mail incorrectly identified as a legitimate message). These issues can lead to more calls to the Help Desk, and your staff tracking down misdirected e-mails. You may also need to maintain white and black lists for your anti-spam solution. White lists identify senders whose mail should always be treated as legitimate, and black lists identify senders whose mail should always be treated as spam. These lists override the determination that the anti-spam solution would make based on its own algorithms.

Harassment

While e-mails with jokes and spiritual messages may seem innocent, they can easily cross the line and some may be seen as offensive or harassment. Your organization should have a clear-cut policy (from senior management, not from

IT) that indicates a zero tolerance for any material (including e-mail) that can be construed as offensive on grounds of sexual harassment, racial discrimination, and so on. It isn't uncommon for e-mail messages to be included as evidence in a various types of litigation. Work with your Legal and HR departments to define, if you haven't done so already, a clear e-mail policy.

Viruses

In the days of yore, computer viruses were most often spread via diskettes, and then through files shared on the LAN. Now, e-mail is one of the most effective methods of spreading a virus. Virus creators, in addition to programming them with disruptive behavior, now also program them to go into your e-mail address book and to re-send themselves to your family, friends, and co-workers down the hall, across the country, and around the globe. An effectively programmed virus can have an enormous global impact in just a matter of days, if not sooner.

Although you should certainly educate your users about messages from unknown sources, a more aggressive posture is also called for. All your workstations and servers should run virus-checking software. In addition, you should have anti-virus software on your e-mail servers that scans messages and their attachments for viruses. Products from Trend Micro, Symantec, McAfee, among others, are relatively inexpensive for the protection they provide. See Chapter 13, Security, for more information regarding viruses and how to defend against them.

Data Size and Retention

Because e-mail is so often used to distribute big files, such as large presentations as well as games and jokes, the amount of storage required to keep it all can be massive. As such, it isn't unusual to have a corporate policy that sets limits on the size of messages, the size of mailboxes, and the age of messages. These limitations are available with the most popular e-mail packages. It's important that users be made aware of these policies, and that the limits be set after considering users' needs.

Another way of addressing space concerns with e-mail is to archive older messages to tape storage. See Chapter 16, Storage and Backup, for a detailed discussion of data storage mechanisms. HR and/or your Legal department may want to get involved in setting these policies, particularly with any related to message retention.

Users should also be aware that limits may be in effect regarding external users with which they send and receive mail. Be clear to your users that just because their e-mail size limit is large, that doesn't mean other companies have the same limit. As such, if you allow your users to send messages of a certain size, there is no guarantee that the message will get through since the recipient's mail environment could very well have a lower limit. You will hear complaints about messages that didn't go through (or messages that your users didn't receive).

Appropriate Use

Just like with the use of the company phones, it's reasonable to expect that not every message your users send will be work related. There will be an occasional personal message. Most organizations expect and tolerate this as long as they aren't oversized and don't contain offensive e-mails. However, it's wise to have a formal policy (just like the one that probably exists for use of the company phones) saying that e-mail is for work-related use only. Some organizations will explicitly state that some personal use of e-mail is okay, as long as it's limited, inoffensive, etc. Similarly, most companies state that the e-mail environment, and its content, are owned by the company, and reserve the right to review e-mail messages that their employees send and receive. Although, the company usually will only invoke that right when a problem or policy violation is suspected.

Along these lines, many organizations automatically add disclaimers to any e-mail messages that are sent outside the company. These disclaimers often assert the confidentiality of the message. But, many industries (e.g., financial, legal) may add statements pertinent to their field.

E-mail Archiving

With regulatory requirements like Sarbanes-Oxley, HIPAA, etc., along with discovery of electronic documents in litigation, finding and accessing specific e-mail messages is becoming a growing requirement. It's becoming increasingly common for the Legal department to contact IT and make a request such as "we need to find all the e-mails that anyone in the Comptroller's group sent or received during 2005 about the merger plans."

Although that seems like a simple request to the Legal department, it's a monumental amount of work for IT. First, we'll need a list of everyone in that department (don't forget people that might have left during the year). The users' online mailboxes are of no use since they no longer contain the items that were deleted. So, the backup tapes have to be recalled, individually restored, and then searched. And, to do the search, someone in Legal is going to have to comeup with a list of keywords that might indicate a message about merger plans.

Archiving solutions can greatly reduce the complexity of requests like the one used in this example. These solutions keep copies of all e-mails sent and received (based on rules you define), and they can easily be searched en masse. While the example above could easily take week or months to fulfill with the restoration and search of backup tapes, the same request could be done within a few days using an archiving solution.

In addition to a sophisticated indexing and searching mechanism, archiving solutions rely on "single instance" storage to reduce the amount of storage required. For example, if HR sent an e-mail to all 1,000 employees, the archiving solution would recognize this and only store a single copy of it (same with attachments) in the archive.

15.2   **Directory Services**

When a new user joins an organization, it's common to find that they may need access to 10 or 20 applications. Sometimes, this means creating a separate account for each application—oftentimes, each with a different ID and password for the user to deal with.

Not only does this become an administrative nightmare for IT (going to each individual application to creating the appropriate IDs), a burden for the user (remembering the different IDs and passwords, changing them, etc.), but it can be a security risk to ensure that all the appropriate IDs are deleted when the user leaves the organization. The issues related to accounts and IDs is referred to as Identity Management.

Moving Toward a Single ID and Password

The goal of directory services is to greatly reduce the administration, user-burden, and security risk that can be associated with multiple IDs.

A directory service is essentially a system application and database that is used by all other applications. By using just a single set of ID and password credentials, called single-sign on (SSO), the user can sign on to the network, e-mail, and all the business applications they will need to access.

Table 15.3 Pros and cons of single sign on

PRO		CON	
	System administrators can now use just one set of administrative tools, and only have to go to one place to create, change, or delete users' access.		Applications may have to be modified to use and access the directory. This may be easy enough for in-house written applications, but may not be an option for third party applications you buy.
	When a user leaves the organization, his access to all systems can be terminated by simply disabling his ID in the directory.		For applications that are hosted externally, users may still need to use different IDs and passwords.
	Users don't have to remember different IDs and passwords for different systems, which may be complicated by different passwords rules (e.g., minimum length, complexity, expiration frequency) employed by each.		The directory usually needs to be modified or expanded to provide the level of granularity of control and access that is required for each application.
	Changes (e.g., a user's name change) only have to be entered once, as opposed to in each individual application.		There may be times when a secondary sign-on is an attractive security mechanism.

Single sign-on and identity management are also discussed in Chapter 13 (pages 366 and 367).

Directory Structure

Directories are set up in a hierarchical or tree fashion, very similar to an organizational chart. Some of the elements found in a directory include:

✦ **Objects (directory entries):** Virtually everything in a directory is an object. An object could be a person (i.e., user), a computer, or a device.

A directory "container," which can hold a collection of objects, is also an object. Objects are often referred to as directory entries.

✦ **Organization unit:** This is comparable to a folder in a file system. It simply holds other objects, and may also hold other organization units.

✦ **Attribute:** Provides some specifics about an object. For example, if the object is a user, there could be an attribute for the user's phone number. If the object is a printer, there might be an attribute for the printer's IP address. Some attributes may have more than one value. In the case of a phone number attribute, it's entirely possible that someone may have more than one phone number. An attribute type is the kind of information (e.g., phone number), while the attribute value refers to the specific content (e.g., 212-555-1212).

✦ **Objectclass:** Defines which attributes are required/optional and allowed in an entry. For example, the objectclass for a printer may indicate that the IP address attribute is allowed and required. Essentially, the object-class defines the rules associated with different types of objects. A directory entry may be assigned to more than one objectclass. For example, a directory entry for a user may be assigned to objectclasses for an e-mail user, an employee, a T&E user, etc. And, each of those objectclasses would have attributes appropriate for its need.

✦ **Distinguished names:** A way of uniquely identifying an entry in the directory. It consists of the name of the entry itself as well as the names, in order from bottom to top, of the objects above it in the directory.

Directory Services Standards

X.500 and Directory Access Protocol

X.500 is a set of several standards for directory services, originally developed to support the needs of the X.400 e-mail standards. The X.500 is actually a series of 10 standards:

✦ X.500 Overview of concepts, models, and services

✦ X.501 Models

✦ X.509 Authentication framework

✦ X.511 Abstract service definition

✦ X.518 Procedures for distributed operation

✦ X.519 Protocol specifications

✦ X.520 Selected attribute types

✦ X.521 Selected object classes

✦ X.525 Replication

✦ X.530 Management for administration

The Directory Access Protocol (DAP) defines the standards for accessing X.500 directories. However, since the DAP and X.500 standards are so complex, a subset known as the Lightweight Directory Access Protocol (LDAP) has been developed and widely adopted.

LDAP

As indicated in the prior section, LDAP is a subset of the X.500 and DAP standards. A key differentiator between DAP and LDAP is that LDAP supports TCP/IP and DAP uses the OSI model as the transport/network layers. From the way the term is used, it would lead you to believe that LDAP itself is a directory (i.e., "let's get that information from LDAP"). But, in truth, LDAP is just the protocol for *accessing* a directory.

The biggest benefit of LDAP is the ability to access the LDAP directory from almost any technology platform, and from LDAP-aware applications (either in-house-developed, or purchased from a third party).

The LDAP directory resides on an LDAP server, which could be one of several products available free as open source, or from commercial vendors. It's also possible to use a relational database with an LDAP interface as the repository. Because of the cross-platform nature of LDAP, application vendors are eager to write the products to support LDAP, as opposed to customizing for proprietary directory services offerings.

Choices in Directory Services

A number of vendors have offerings for directory services. A partial list includes:

✦ Active Directory from Microsoft (*http://www.microsoft.com/activedirectory*)

✦ Sun Java System Directory Server from Sun Microsystems (*http://www.sun.com/software/products/directory_srvr/home_directory.xml*)

✦ eDirectory from Novell (*http://www.novell.com/products/edirectory*)

✦ OpenVMS Enterprise Directory from Hewlett-Packard (*http://h71000. www7.hp.com/commercial/edir*)

✦ Red Hat Directory Server from Red Hat (*http://www.redhat.com/software/ rha/directory*)

✦ Tivoli Directory Server from IBM (*http://www-306.ibm.com/software/ tivoli/products/directory-server*)

✦ Apache Directory Server from Apache (*http://www.redhat.com/en_us/ USA/home/solutions/directoryserver*)

15.3 Enterprise Resource Planning

Enterprise Resource Planning (ERP) has a broad definition; it's used in a variety of ways to mean the set of activities that a company engages in to manage its resources across the entire enterprise. This can mean activities as diverse as product planning, sales programs, materials purchasing, maintaining inventories, and performing classically defined HR functions. Major software companies in the ERP space include SAP, Lawson, SSA Global, and Oracle. ERP is a hot topic in corporate circles. To avoid looking like the naïve ITer in a popular TV commercial, keep in mind that ERP is pronounced "E-R-P," not "erp."

Prior to ERP, companies would use different packages for various business functions: inventory, sales and distribution, financials, HR, and so on. Different packages were used simply because no vendor had a product offering that could cross all these various disciplines. The various packages might be purchased or homegrown. To pass data among the various functions, a company would write numerous interface programs to extract data from one application's database for use in another application.

The Value of ERP Software

With the introduction of ERP, a company can essentially have a single application (or a single set of applications provided by a single vendor) and database for all its vital business functions. The value of this can be enormous. Since all the applications are integrated, a change in activity in one area of the company ripples through the system to all affected departments so that they could react accordingly. A sudden spike in sales notifies the Purchasing department to increase orders of raw materials, the receiving department to look out for these deliveries, the manufacturing department to gear up for increased production, HR that more labor will be needed to fulfill the demands of the increased sales, etc.

ERP solutions for the supply chain (manufacturing, purchasing, logistics, warehousing, inventory, distribution, etc.) are a large portion of the market. Solutions for the supply chain often extend to include links and interfaces with suppliers and partners. ERP vendors also have different offerings for different industries.

General ERP Implementation Issues

There are several elements of ERP to keep in mind when considering implementing an ERP system:

+ ERP isn't a trivial-sized activity. True ERP systems run across the entire enterprise and as such, they literally affect every aspect of a company's business.

+ Because the scope of an ERP implementation can be so far reaching, it acts as a magnifying glass. Problems are quickly seen throughout the organization. And, problems no one knew about suddenly become very exposed.

+ Implementation of an ERP system is a gut-wrenching experience for a corporation. Some companies thrive on the new system, embrace it as the salvation of their business, and explode forward. Others find the difficult medicine of ERP a very hard pill to swallow, and eventually bail in midstream, leaving unhappy employees, customers, and vendors screaming in their wake (to say nothing of opening the gate of lawsuits). Trade journals are equally filled with success and failure stories of companies that have gone through ERP implementations.

Costs of Implementing ERP

In addition to the upheaval an ERP implementation can cause, the cost of implementing ERP will easily be in the hundreds of thousands of dollars, and could go to the tens of millions for larger and more complex environments. Usually, the biggest costs of an ERP implementation are the consultants that you will need to assist in the implementation. Because of the complexity of installing an ERP package, it's common for consulting costs to total two to three times the cost of the actual software package. Many very large consulting firms (e.g., PricewaterhouseCoopers, Accenture, Ernst & Young) have entire divisions dedicated to ERP implementations.

In addition to consultants, a good portion of the budget will also go to training, support, and a large investment in additional hardware.

Major Changes Required

In many cases, the organization may find that it actually has to change the way it does business in order to implement an ERP package. While the traditional approach of implementing a package is to tailor it to your organization's needs, it's not uncommon to have to use the reverse approach when implementing an ERP package.

There are many core activities associated with ERP that are software related, although the thrust of the implementation is often not only software. It can include changing the way departments function, organization, procedures, employees' roles, and a sea of change in the way the company operates.

As the person responsible for a large part of the software and hardware health and well-being of the corporation, your job, your responsibilities, and your entire skill set are going to be radically affected by any ERP motions your company undertakes.

It Isn't Only IT's Decision

It's likely that you won't be the only one consulted before your company decides to implement an ERP system. Most likely, you will be part of a group or committee making that decision. Because implementing an ERP system is almost always a multi-year adventure, you will likely join a company in mid-implementation. Your decisions won't be "Should my company do this?" as much as "How can I help my company do this in the most efficient manner possible?"

ERP may be the single largest IT project your company has ever undertaken. Its success or failure may lead to the success or failure of many executives and departments. Stories abound of ERP implementations that led to enormous cost overruns, 20-hour days, 7-day weeks, loss of key team members, implementation delays, and more.

If you're involved in an ERP implementation, chances are you will be making more use of some of the topics in this book (project management, budgeting, etc.) than with any other project you'll ever be involved in.

You, as well as everyone else involved, should look at an ERP implementation as the single greatest opportunity to re-engineer the way your organization works, and to have a huge beneficial impact that will probably live on for many years.

Disadvantages to ERP

ERP isn't without its risk and detractors. There can be disadvantages and pit-falls to it.

✦ The very rigid structure of an ERP solution oftentimes makes it difficult to adapt to the specific needs of individual organizations.

✦ Because ERP software is enormously sophisticated, there is often a tendency to implement more features and functions for a particular installation than is actually needed. This drives up costs and may reduce usage if the system proves to be too complex to use.

✦ The cost to implement and maintain ERP systems is very high, and can challenge ROI calculations.

✦ Some departments and users may be hesitant to agree to the implementation if they feel they're giving up control of their data by switching from a department application to an enterprise-wide solution.

15.4   Additional Resources

Web Sites

✦ h71028.www7.hp.com/ERC/downloads/5983-2385EN.pdf (white paper on e-mail usage)

✦ *www.brightmail.com* (e-mail management vendor)

✦ *www.eudora.com* (e-mail software vendor)

✦ *www.f-secure.com* (anti-virus software vendor)

✦ *www.ironport.com* (e-mail management vendor)

✦ *www.lotus.com* (e-mail software vendor)

✦ *www.mcafee.com* (anti-virus software vendor)

✦ *www.microsoft.com/exchange* (e-mail software vendor)

✦ *www.novell.com/groupwise* (e-mail software vendor)

✦ *www.oracle.com* (ERP software vendor)

✦ *www.radicati/com* (market research firm)

- ✦ *www.sap.com* (ERP software vendor)

- ✦ *www.ssaglobal.com* (ERP software vendor)

- ✦ *www.symantec.com* (anti-virus software vendor)

- ✦ *www.trendmicro.com* (anti-virus software vendor)

- ✦ *www.tumbleweed.com* (e-mail management vendor)

Books and Articles

- ✦ Anderegg, Travis, *ERP: A-Z Implementer's Guide For Success,* Resource Publishing, 2000.

- ✦ Beers, Christopher, T., "Beyond Spam Filters," *Network Computing Magazine,* February 16, 2006, p. 59.

- ✦ Carter, Gerald, *LDAP System Administration,* O'Reilly Media, Inc., 2003.

- ✦ Hamilton, Scott, *Maximizing Your ERP System: A Practical Guide for Managers,* McGraw-Hill, 2001.

- ✦ Sheresh, Doug, and Sheresh, Beth, *Understanding Directory Services,* Sams, 2001.

- ✦ Wallace, Thomas F., and Kremzar, Michael H., *ERP: Making It Happen: The Implementers' Guide to Success with Enterprise Resource Planning,* Wiley, 2001.

Storage and Backup

...all you need in life is a little place for your stuff...

—GEORGE CARLIN

Even though the name of the entire field is *Information Technology*, the heart of that information is *data*. And the growth in the amount of data is proceeding at an exponential rate. It isn't uncommon for a presentation or word processing document to be several megabytes in size. Where once the transmission of a file that size would be considered prohibitive, it's now commonplace and routine.

In addition, individuals are more reluctant than ever to delete files, preferring to keep copies of everything just in case they may need it again. Certainly, compliance and regulatory requirements have encouraged this posture.

CHAPTER SIXTEEN

16.1   Managing the Data

If you're responsible for all that data, the first thing you need to know is where it all is. The easy issue is the servers: they're easier to identify and locate. More complex are the issues surrounding the workstations that users have — some in the office, and some in remote locations — and the data that is stored on those C: drives with no management and backup. Some user education and policies will help.

Data Retention

Working with your company's Legal department, you may want to establish some data-retention policies. Very often, the first item addressed regarding data retention is e-mail. Many companies are now setting specific periods of time for retaining e-mail, after which the items are automatically deleted. You may permit users to get around the auto-purge by moving items to another location, but this requires that the user take a specification.

One of the Reasons Data Retention Got a Bad Name

Everyone first understood the real value — and the danger — of computer data retention during the Federal Government's anti-trust suit against Microsoft in the late 1990s. David Boies, the government's lead attorney, "consistently used e-mail and other documents to impugn the credibility of Microsoft witnesses." Old e-mails suddenly became not only sources of historical interest but weapons to be used against their authors.

Source: *http://news.com.com/2100-1001-241335.html*

Related issues about the age of data include:

✦ How long should the files of a user that has left the company be kept?

✦ How long should backup tapes be kept?

✦ What happens to files in "shared" areas of the network (see the section Shared Data Storage on page 436)? If a file hasn't been touched in several years it could be pretty unlikely that anyone is aware the file is there, or would even think to look for it.

Many organizations are now using retention levels as an opportunity to minimize their risk of culpability in legal matters. If the data isn't there, then it can't be found. However, this is a double-edged sword in that retention levels may work to eliminate files you need, as well as those you don't.

IT has to work with user departments in setting data-retention practices. It is important — and often difficult — to remember that the users are generally considered the "owners" of data, while IT is the "custodian." While all sales data may look the same to you, all hardware looks the same to them.

User Education

It's important to educate users about good practices with their data:

◆ Users have to understand that unless data is stored on the network, it won't be backed up. Many organizations have implemented desktop configurations that prevent users from storing files locally.

◆ For users who travel, the use of off-line replications of network files can give them the best of both worlds — network storage and local access. See the section on Replication (Synchronization) on page 339 in Chapter 12, Networking.

◆ Users should be advised about removing large attachments from e-mail messages and saving them to a network drive. Multiple copies of large attachments in e-mail can waste enormous amounts of space.

◆ Some technically savvy users like to periodically back up their workstations, and they find that the network is a convenient place to do so. Since a backup like this would also include the operating system, and software applications, the vast majority of this would be unnecessary (since those items are easily restored from the original media). Work with the users to show them how to use a CD or DVD burner to back up their data, or explain to them that their network files are already backed up each night.

Users often don't understand the issues of storage. They know that disk drives with hundreds of gigabytes of space are fairly cheap at their local PC store. While that fact is true, cost isn't the only issue in a corporate environment, and the cost of high-end drives used in corporate environments is considerably more expensive than the disk drive in the family PC. Users usually don't understand that while disks are cheap, their IT department isn't in the position of making unlimited space available. IT departments know that when storage space grows, it impacts the backup procedures (number of tapes, drives, and time required), and in the event of a disaster, it impacts the amount of time needed for recovery.

It's common for IT departments to periodically scan servers for "junk," which could be:

+ Files with extensions or prefixes that indicate they're temporary files, created by applications, that weren't properly deleted

+ Copies of software installation images

+ Games

+ Music

+ Personal photos and videos

+ Backups of workstations

Shared Data Storage

For data stored in a user's private directory, or data stored in application databases, it's generally pretty easy to identify who owns that data. However, most networks also include space for shared data which might be for a team, a department, or a specific project. These shared areas can easily deteriorate into dumping grounds over time.

While it probably isn't possible (or desirable) to eliminate the use of shared directories, there are procedures to help manage them:

+ Users shouldn't be allowed to create shared areas on their own; they should be required to submit a request to IT for that.

+ The request should identify which specific users are allowed which type of access to that area.

+ The request should identify who will serve as the overall manager of that space, so that when IT has questions or concerns about it or its files, they have a specific individual they can work with.

You might get pushback from some users (who have, for example, worked at other companies where users could create whatever shared spaces they wanted). But the days of limitless access and almost limitless disk space are over; while abuse of network disk space isn't the most pressing item on an IT Manager's agenda, it can be one that easily gets out of hand.

Quotas

Disk quotas are annoying, but they can be an effective tool for helping to manage disk space. The most common types of quotas put in place include the size of

✦ A User's mailbox

✦ A Network directory

✦ The total amount of space available to an individual user in all locations

Of course, as with any policy, there will be some exceptions for some users. However, quotas, along with occasional messages about exceeding them, as well as having users request more space from IT, can all be a great way of keeping users conscious of the fact that space is an issue.

16.2   Disk Storage Technology

Disk drives are the nuts and bolts of data storage, and they come in many shapes and sizes.

Direct Attached Storage

Direct Attached Storage (DAS) is the term used for storage that is part of a server. The primary difference between DAS and other storage configuration (like network attached storage and storage area network, discussed below) is that DAS storage is directly connected to (or part of) a server, while the others are essentially stand-alone units that attach to a network. For larger amounts of storage, DAS is considered to be an inefficient use of hardware since a considerable investment has to be made in servers, which may end up going under-utilized.

Network Attached Storage

Network Attached Storage (NAS) refers to storage hardware that connects directly to your Ethernet network. NAS combines traditional disk array technology with "intelligence." This intelligence comes from a processor and small operating system, embedded in the NAS unit. To a certain degree, since a NAS device does include a small operating system, it could technically be considered a server. However, the entire unit is optimized for storage and ease of use. NAS units can be installed very easily and quickly, right out of the box, without a lot of the complex configuration needs of a "traditional" file server.

NAS solutions are based on file-level access, unlike storage area networks, (below) which are based on block-level access. Files on the NAS are made available over the LAN using file-sharing protocols such as NFS or Microsoft's CIFS. Users on the network are able to access files from the NAS without having to go through a traditional server.

Storage Area Network

There is some debate within the industry as to what characterizes a Storage Area Network (SAN). At a minimum, most agree that SANs do block-level access, as opposed to file-level access of NAS solutions. Data traffic on SANs is very much akin to the traffic used with internal disk drives, like ATA and SCSI. In a SAN, the server issues a request for specific blocks of data from the disks. This method is known as "block storage."

However, there are some that say SAN solutions are also characterized by a fibre channel network, as opposed to TCP/IP and Ethernet, which is discussed below in the section Storage Network Connectivity (iSCSI and Fibre Channel).

Just a Bunch of Disks

Just a Bunch of Disks (JBOD) is a term that has been developed to differentiate lower level storage solutions from higher level ones (like SAN and NAS). There are some in the industry that will say that JBOD is synonymous with DAS, and others say that JBOD refers to "unprotected" storage (e.g., no RAID or mirroring, see page 440 for the section on RAID).

Storage Network Connectivity (Fibre Channel and iSCSI)

Fibre Channel

Traditionally, SAN environments have used Fibre Channel (FC) for connectivity, which can provide gigabit speeds and has become the most common connection method for SANs. Despite its name, FC can be implemented on copper cabling as well as fiber-optic cables.

Since FC is considerably faster, it's often used as an alternative to SCSI for connecting servers with storage devices. FC requires an investment in specialized hardware, which is a deterrent for many users. Each server must have an FC host-bus adapter (HBA) to allow it to connect to an FC switch (which is analogous to a traditional network switch). The combination of FC cabling, HBAs, and switches is commonly referred to as the Fiber Channel, or SAN, "fabric." FC can provide speeds of 2 Gbps, and is considered the ultimate solution for enterprise and mission critical needs.

A variation of the Fibre Channel, known as Fibre Channel over IP (FCIP) is bridging the gap between traditional IP networking and FC. Intended for connecting geographically distant SANs, FCIP can only be used with FC technology, and associated special hardware; in comparison, iSCSI will run over existing Ethernet environments.

iSCSI

iSCSI (IP SCSI) overcomes many of the limitations of traditional Small Computer Systems Interface (SCSI) (such as distance limitations and number of devices) by using traditional Ethernet, which would then allow an almost limitless number of devices, and extends the geography dramatically — essentially to any device on the LAN or WAN. In addition, with traditional SCSI, the disk drives can only communicate with the device that has the SCSI controller. However, an iSCSI device can be shared by multiple servers. iSCSI has a significant advantage in that it can leverage your existing Ethernet infrastructure for your SAN solution. However, the trade-off for that convenience is speed. iSCSI provides about half the speed of FC technology.

Although iSCSI can use traditional Ethernet hardware, some installations are making use of iSCSI HBAs in their servers. These HBAs are specialized cards that can off-load TCP/IP and iSCSI processing from a server's CPU, and increase overall performance.

Disk Drive Types

There are a number of different disk drive technologies available on the market:

✦ **ATA** (also known as IDE) is the type of drive most often used in desktop and laptops, and uses a 16-bit parallel interface. The latest iteration of the standard supports transfer rates of 133 MB/sec and is believed to be about the maximum available.

✦ **Serial ATA (SATA)** picks up where ATA ends. Its transfer rate is 150 MB/sec, and future iterations are expected to see transfer rates of 300 and 600 MB/sec. In addition, the SATA devices draw less power and are easier to install.

✦ **SCSI** has gone through a number of iterations and enhancements, with the latest being SCSI Ultra/320 with a transfer rate of 320 MB/sec. An SCSI environment consists of a controller and a cable, with all the disk drives connected to the same cable. Of course, it's common to have multiple controllers and multiple cables to ensure redundancy and eliminate single points of failure.

Factors that Impact Disk Drive Performance

While picking the right disk drive technology is one part of the process for optimizing performance, it isn't the only item to consider. The transfer rate that a disk can deliver depends on a variety of factors:

✦ **Rotation speed**. This is the speed the disk spins at and ranges from 5,400 to 15,000 rpm. The higher the speed the more often the data on the disk will be in the right position to be read by the drive heads, and the faster data can be transferred.

✦ **Average Access Time**. This is the average time is takes to position the heads so that data can be read. The faster the better.

✦ **Cache Size**. This is the size of the cache built into the disk drive hardware. Just like the cache on a chip or system board, the bigger the better. However, cache is expensive and reaches a point of diminishing returns beyond a certain size.

✦ **Internal Transfer Rate**. This is the speed that data can be transferred *within* the drive. This will be a bit faster than the actual transfer rate of data to other system components because of associated overhead.

In addition to the above issues, other factors like network performance, server performance, application efficiency, traffic loads, etc., can impact the overall result of how long it takes to access the data you need.

Redundant Array of Inexpensive/Independent Disks

Because protecting your data is such a vital concern, a number of technologies have been developed to ensure that the loss of a disk drive doesn't mean the loss of your data. Redundant Array of Inexpensive/Independent Disks (RAID) defines different levels of protection, each having various trade-offs of performance and cost. These trade-offs are shown in Table 16.1, below.

Table 16.1 RAID levels (Source: *www.digidata.com*)

Common RAID Levels (Note that RAID level numbers indicate different types of data layouts, not higher performance or availability)

RAID Level	Description	Data Reliability	Performance	Application Strength	Cost
RAID 0	Data striped across multiple disks	Not true RAID; any disk failure causes loss of data	Faster than single disk for reads because data striped across several disks can be read simultaneously; similar to single disk for small writes	General	Low; because there is no redundancy
RAID 1	All data copied onto two separate disks	Very high; can withstand selective multiple disk failures	Faster than single disk for reads because data mirrored on two disks can be read simultaneously; similar to single disk for small writes	General	High; requires twice as many disks for redundancy
RAID 10	Two copies of data striped across disks	Very high; can withstand selective multiple disk failures	Very high; for reads, access is very fast because data is both mirrored and striped (i.e., there are two disks from which to read any piece of data, and striping spreads data across more disks)	High data reliability and performance applications such as ERP and image processing	High; requires twice as many disks for redundancy
RAID 2	Data bit striped across disks with error correcting codes on additional disks	Very high; can withstand multiple disk failures	Slowest of all the RAID levels due to bit striping	Slow speed makes RAID 2 unattractive; it is not used commercially	

(Cont.)

Table 16.1 RAID levels (continued)

RAID Level	Description	Data Reliability	Performance	Application Strength	Cost
RAID 3	Data striped across disks on separate channels with dedicated parity disk	Much higher than single disk; can withstand single disk failure	Faster than a single disk, owing to parallel disk accesses	Video, prepress, medical imaging, and other large file applications	Low; requires only one disk per RAID group for redundancy
RAID 30	Data striped across disks on separate channels with dedicated parity disk and across disks on the same channel	Much higher than single disk; can withstand single disk failure	Faster than RAID 3	Video, prepress, medical imaging, and other large file applications	Moderate; designed for large arrays
RAID 4	Data block striped across disks on separate channels with dedicated parity disk	Much higher than single disk; can withstand single disk failure	Faster than a single disk, owing to parallel disk accesses	Video, prepress, medical imaging, and other large file applications	Low; requires only one disk per RAID group for redundancy
RAID 5	Data and parity striped across multiple disks	Much higher than single disk; can withstand single disk failure	High compared to single disk for reads but lower than single disk for writes	OLTP, e-mail, ERP, Web, CRM	Low; requires only one disk per RAID group for redundancy
RAID 50	Data and parity striped across multiple disks and across disks on the same channel	Much higher than single disk; can withstand single disk failure	Faster than RAID 5	Transaction processing with high read to write ratio	Moderate; designed for large arrays

16.3 Tape Storage and Backup

While disk is the technology for online storage, tape is the preferred method for backup solutions (see Table 16.2 below for pros and cons).

Table 16.2 Pros and cons of tape as a storage medium

PRO		CON	
	It's very inexpensive. As such, multiple copies (such as having complete sets for different points in time, or copies in different locations) can be easily kept without incurring enormous expense.		It's much slower than disk.
	It's easily transportable. This makes it convenient for storage at an off-site location and easy to retrieve, if needed, to a recovery site.		It's a "sequential" medium; that is, if the file you need is at the end of the tape, you have no choice but to read through the entire tape to get to it.
			It's a more fragile medium than disk; is more susceptible to deterioration over time.

Tape and Tape-Drive Technologies

Just as there are different kinds of disks, there are different kinds of tapes (see Table 16.3).

Variations on Backup

Although tapes are the standard for backup, there are a number of variations on this solution that have been adopted.

Disk-To-Disk-To-Tape

Because tape is a slow medium, and because backup does impact overall performance of the production environment, some environments have implemented

Table 16.3 Tape drives (Source: *www.govconnection.com*)

Tape Drive Comparison Chart

Type	Vendors	Formats	Capacities (GB): Native/Compressed*	Transfer Rates (GB/h): Native/Compressed*
Travan	Certance	Travan 20, Travan 40	10/20, 20/40	3.5/7, 7/14
AIT	HP, Sony	AIT-1, AIT-2, AIT-3	35/91, 50/130, 100/260	14/37, 16/43, 33/86
DAT	Certance, HP, Sony	DDS-4, DAT72	20/40, 36/72	10/20, 12.6/25.2
DLT vs80/160	HP, Quantum	DLT vs80, DLT vs160	40/80, 80/160	11/22, 29/58
DLT 8000	Quantum, HP	DLT 8000	40/80	22/44
Super DLT	HP, Quantum	SDLT220, SDLT320, SDLT600	110/220, 160/320, 300/600	36/72, 58/116, 130/260
LTO/Ultrium	Certance, HP	LTO-1, LTO-2	100/200, 200/400	54/108, 108/216
Super AIT	Sony	S-AIT	500/1300	108/280

*All AIT/S-AIT speeds and capacities assume 2.6:1 compression. All other speeds and capacities assume 2:1 compression.

a backup solution where the disk storage is first copied (often referred to as taking a snapshot) to another disk environment, and that second disk environment is then backed up to tape. This offers a number of benefits:

✦ Because disk performance is much faster than tape, a disk-to-disk backup can happen very quickly. As such, the impact to the production environment (e.g., shutting down databases during backup) is minimized.

✦ Because the disk-to-disk backup happens fast, the performance hit to the production environment is also reduced.

✦ The backup of the snapshot image happens faster since the backup process isn't competing with any other processes or users for performance. The snapshot image exists only for the benefit of the backup environment.

✦ If a user needs a file restored and that file is still available from the snapshot image, it can be restored easier and faster than it could be restored from tape.

The cost of the device that holds the snapshot image is the only downside to this alternative. And, since it really doesn't have to be a high-end device (i.e., no redundancy is really needed since it's only an interim copy of the data), it may be quite affordable for small and mid-size environments.

Disk-to-Disk

Because there is a certain security risk with a portable medium like tape, some organizations have tried to eliminate the use of tape altogether by using disk as an alternative. However, there are some significant factors to consider with the elimination of tape:

✦ Because tapes are often used for "archival" purposes (i.e., allowing you to have complete copies of your environment from different points in time), the cost of doing the same with disk can be prohibitively expensive.

✦ Disk storage isn't as portable, so it could impact the flexibility of your disaster recovery plans.

✦ Because of the risk of having your live data and the backup copy in the same location, it's worth considering doing the disk-to-disk copy over a WAN connection to a remote site (perhaps your disaster recovery site). The cost of a line with sufficient bandwidth could be very expensive. And, while the need for replicating only the "deltas" to your backup site (as discussed in the section Data Replication in Chapter 20) may make for relatively fast backups, restoring an entire server over a WAN connection may take an extensive amount of time.

Data Encryption

Again, because tape is a portable medium, there are certain security risks associated with it. Citigroup and Bank of America are just two of the companies that have had to deal with lost backup tapes that contained confidential personal data (see Chapter 8, IT Compliance and Controls and Chapter 13, Security). To limit the risks of backup tapes falling into the wrong hands, many organizations have started to encrypt their backup. Decru and Neoscale Systems are two companies that offer solutions for encrypting a backup.

A key up to 256-bits in length is commonly used to encrypt the data on the tape. When using encryption for your backup tapes, you must have copies of the key stored in multiple locations, most important at your disaster recovery site. Without the key, you won't be able to decrypt your backup tapes, and you will be unable to restore any data.

Dedicated Network

Another alternative for backup solutions is to set up a dedicated network for it. Because of the volume of data that travels across it, network performance could be adversely impacted as it competes with users and application traffic for network bandwidth and throughput.

By providing a dedicated network for backups, it allows the backup to perform faster, and eliminates any impact it may have had on the users and the production environment.

Backup Schedule

Backup traditionally comes in three flavors:

- ✦ **Full**. Captures everything in the environment, regardless of when the data was last modified or backed up.

- ✦ **Differential**. Captures those files that have changed since the last *full* backup.

- ✦ **Incremental**. Only captures those files that have changed since the last backup of *any* kind.

Traditionally, IT environments have done a full-complete backup of everything over the weekend, followed by differential backups on weeknights. However, with the incredible growth of data storage, backup has become almost a non-stop process. Operations managers are constantly juggling the backup scheduling of different systems in order to maximize the efficiency of all resources, and ensure that backup procedures don't interfere with other applications and activities.

Full

A full backup is a complete copy of everything in the environment, regardless of when files were last backed up, accessed, or modified. Full backups take the longest amount of time to complete and tie up the most resources such as tapes and tape-drives. A full backup is the handiest when a total restore is needed, since it has a complete image.

Differential

With differential backups, a complete restore of an environment would require the last full backup to be restored, followed by a restore from the last differential backup.

Incremental

Incremental backups execute the fastest, since they capture the smallest number of files. However, they make the restoration more complex. For a full restoration, the last full backup needs to be restored, along with each incremental backup, in order, that was taken since the full backup.

You should also check with your application and database vendors about the integrity of backups that are performed when files are open. You may need to shut down the application and/or database to get a reliable backup.

Backup Storage

Backup tapes are usually stored at an off-site location. The thinking is that if a disaster wipes out your primary facility, you don't want to lose your backup tapes at the same time. If you do, then you lose any ability to recover data.

Some companies may choose to store their tapes at another company location, most opt to use dedicated records storage facilities that have appropriate security and climate controls.

One of the challenges with off-site storage of the backup tapes is determining when to send them off site. For the highest level of protection in case of disaster, the tapes should go off site immediately after they are created. However, chances are that any requests you get for a restore will require the most recent backup tapes, so there is some convenience and cost efficiency involved in leaving them on-site for a short period of time.

The intermediate disk storage discussed in the disk-to-disk-to-tape backup solution (see section above) can also be used for restoring data when the tapes are sent off site. Another alternative is to make two sets of backup tapes, one kept on site for any restores that are needed, and the other sent off site to be used in case of disaster.

16.4 Information Lifecycle Management

Information Lifecycle Management (ILM) is one of the more recent topics to warrant a large amount of attention in the storage industry. In a nutshell, ILM reflects the fact that the value and use of data and information change over time. The cafeteria lunch menu isn't as important as the payroll data. And, whatever value the cafeteria menu has this month, it will be negligible next month; while the payroll data will be valuable for quite some time. Similarly, ILM recognizes that there are aged data (e.g. files that haven't been modified in some time), as well as static data (e.g. files that generally don't change, such as graphics and multimedia files). How data's use and value changes can vary greatly from industry to industry and from organization to organization.

With ILM, an organization has to define different use classes of data (e.g., critical, static, archival, transactional, etc.), and the needs of that data over time (high-speed access, real-time replication, etc.). With those two items, you can then define different classes of storage solutions (online disk, tape, DVD/CD, on-site/off-site, etc.).

Since the needs and use of data will change over time, an ILM solution (which is a combination of hardware and software) allows you easily manage the data and seamlessly migrate it to different storage solutions during the data's lifetime. With a comprehensive ILM solution, you're ensuring that you're not wasting a very expensive storage solution for aged data that is hardly ever accessed or neglecting to back up critical data that change radically over the course of a day. An ILM solution also ensures that you don't lose track of where the data is during its lifetime.

ILM has grown in popularity just as compliance issues (see Chapter 8, IT Compliance and Controls) have become a more serious concern in IT. To comply with various rules and regulations regarding the retention of data, organizations have begun to adopt ILM solutions as way of helping to ensure compliance (i.e., the tracking of data). At the same time, companies are making cost-effective and cost-conscious decisions as to what technology to use to store data with different needs, so that the high-cost, high-performance, and high-availability storage solutions are used only for the data that needs it.

ILM versus Hierarchical Storage Management

The discussion of ILM may sound suspiciously like Hierarchical Storage Management (HSM). They both have some common elements in that data is moved to other storage forms at certain points.

The key difference between the two concepts is that HSM primarily relies on the measure of access frequency and/or age to determine when a file should be moved to another storage medium. HSM also is primarily one-directional, in that it generally moves data from primary to secondary, and from secondary to tertiary storage solutions. ILM, on the other hand, can move data based on a number of policies (in addition to age and access frequency) and to/from any storage solutions.

16.5 Additional Resources

Web Sites

+ *www.ca.com* (backup software vendor)

+ *www.decru.com* (storage security vendor)

+ *www.emc.com* (storage solution vendor)

+ *www.hitachi.com* (storage solution vendor)

+ *www.hp.com* (storage solution vendor)

+ *www.ibm.com* (storage solution vendor)

+ *www.neoscale.com* (storage security vendor)

+ *www.netapps.com* (storage solution vendor)

+ *www.quantum.com* (storage solution vendor)

+ *www.veritas.com* (backup software vendor)

Books and Articles

◆ Apicella, Mario, "Fibre Channel vs iSCSI," *Infoworld*, September 8, 2005, p. 32.

◆ Baltazar, Henry, "iSCSI takes on Fibre Channel," *eWeek*, February 13, 2006, p. 39.

◆ Laird, Campbell, "The Virtues of Virtualized Storage," *InfoWorld*, January 16, 2006, p. 37.

◆ Mearian, Lucas, "Cleaning Out the Attic," *Computerworld*, October 17, 2005, p. 62.

◆ Mearian, Lucas, "Storage: Round 2," *Computerworld*, November 14, 2005, p. 54.

◆ Venezia, Paul, "iSCSI SANs Unleashed," *Infoworld*, October 3, 2005, p. 37.

User Support Services

I get by with a little help from my friends.
—LENNON/MCCARTNEY

Whether it goes by the name of Help Desk, Support Center, User Services, or any of a variety of other names, your IT department needs some kind of support organization to provide assistance to your user population — employees, clients, customers, or business partners.

In general, IT Help Desks are designed to be one-stop shopping for all computer-related requests. For many users, your support organization is the only interaction they will have with IT. For these users, the IT department is only as good as their last call to the Help Desk.

Managing a Help Desk well is a difficult task, but a task with key specific rewards:

✦ The company will be able to see a visible portion of IT's efforts. Installing a new server isn't a trivial task, but users generally only see the results; they see a whole new range of applications and storage but generally don't go and check out the shiny new hardware.

✦ You get to help people. IT departments in general, and Help Desks in particular, are service centers.

✦ A well-run Help Desk can collect a multitude of data and metrics. You will therefore be able to more clearly and concretely justify your need for manpower, training, hardware, software — the types of resources you need — when budget time rolls around. In this chapter we'll talk about how to quantify the Help Desk's performance, and how, for example, you can use the fact that it took on average 15 minutes to answer incoming calls to justify the hiring of three new analysts. In some cases, that data can be shared with various department heads so that they can identify how systems are being used, where training is needed, etc.

✦ Insight into the entire company. IT support staff work with virtually every level of the company from the loading dock to the CEO's office. If building key relationships is one of your goals (and as an IT Manager, it should be), you can't ask for a better opportunity than running a Help Desk.

17.1 Value of Help Desks

Help Desks are often the user's first line of assistance, and often their last, too. So it's best to view this situation as an exciting opportunity, not a large problem. You must manage it well.

You don't want:

✦ Users wandering into your office whenever they have a question, as opposed to using the process that was designed to help them

✦ Users yelling at your staff

✦ The reputation of the entire department having to suffer because of poor support

Rather than assign two random people to answer any calls that come in, take proactive control of the Help Desk activity.

Typical Help Desk Activities

A Help Desk's responsibilities can include:

✦ Requests for new equipment

✦ Password resets

✦ Providing users with documentation and Web links

✦ Requests for new IDs and setting up new employees

✦ Coordinating the process and activities related to a new-hire

✦ Computer supplies (toner, CDs)

✦ Installation and move requests

✦ Taking the appropriate steps when an employee leaves the organization — recovering equipment, disabling accounts, etc.

✦ Scheduling training

✦ Tracking each request to make sure that it doesn't fall into a black hole, and that someone always has ownership

✦ Generating reports for management on the types and volume of calls

✦ Keeping current databases of users, inventory, etc.

✦ Routing and coordinating requests with other IT groups (application development, operations, networking, etc.)

✦ Maintaining a knowledge base of fixes and resolutions so that repeat problems can be more quickly addressed

✦ Providing application support

✦ Reporting and resolving hardware problems

✦ Helping remote users with connectivity issues

17.2 Components of a Help Desk

Two Critical Help Desk Issues

In setting up a Help Desk, you need two essential items:

1. A centralized way for users to reach you — usually a phone extension and/or e-mail address

2. Sufficient staffing to answer and deal with requests for support

Centralized Method of User Contact

The Help Desk is more of a set of resources than a physical place. In a small environment, staffing the Help Desk may be something done in addition to an individual's regular assignments. In a large environment, it may consist of an entire department staffed around the clock dedicated to the function. When you think of the functions of a Help Desk, one of the common assumptions is that it provides support for applications like Word and Excel. In truth, questions like these generally represent a small portion of the calls that go to the Help Desk. More typical are calls about network issues, program crashes, hardware problems, security requests, and requests for new software or upgrades.

Staffing

Staffing the Help Desk with the right individuals is vital to its success. Not only must they have appropriate technical expertise, but they also must have excellent interpersonal and telephone skills. They have to be adept at diagnosing problems based on a telephone conversation and walking users through resolution procedures. They must possess a high degree of professionalism to deal with users at all levels of the organization. They must have a great deal of patience. And lastly, they must convey a certain degree of calm and confidence to the users to prevent an irate user from trying to escalate the problem up the corporate organizational chart.

Help Desk staffing is discussed in detail in the section Specific Considerations When Hiring for a Help Desk (page 461) later in this chapter.

Telephone System

The majority of requests to the Help Desk will probably come via telephone. You should take care that a user never gets a busy signal. Voice mail messages should be acknowledged (with a call back to the user) as soon as possible to avoid the user assuming that their request will never be addressed. Consider an Automatic Call Distribution (ACD) system; ACDs can route calls to technicians based on menu prompts and can provide you with detailed reports about activity.

Call center ticket systems are also common. Regardless of how a user contacts the Help Desk — phone, e-mail, PDA, etc. — each contact is given a specific ticket number. All contacts are entered by Help Desk personnel into a tracking system that generates a ticket number for each item. The user is then given that number; both the caller and the Help Desk can then use it to reference the particular problem. See the section Call Tracking (page 459) later in this chapter for more information.

Procedures

Analysts at the Help Desk need clear procedures for handling different call types. They should know how to route different types of calls, how to escalate, when to follow up, etc. These procedures should include detailed contact information of various internal and external resources. If your company offers 24/7 support, contact information should include times when personnel from other departments will be available. Call tracking software, intranets, etc., can aid in ensuring that procedures are followed. These procedures should also be shared with other departments within the company.

Access

The more a Help Desk analyst can do, the more effective she'll be, and the more likely she'll be able to resolve a problem on that initial call. Consider giving your analysts various degrees of administrative access so that they can reset passwords, edit e-mail distribution lists, change access levels, see users' files/data, and so on. Of course, this type of access has to be carefully considered first before it's granted. Analysts should be made aware of the capabilities they have, and warned about the privileges they have, and that it must not be abused. They also need to be aware that special access means they can cause problems as easily as they solve problems.

Various tools from software vendors allow you to delegate specific administrative tasks to the support staff, without giving them the "keys to the kingdom."

Self-Service

Today, every service-based organization is looking to allow its customer to perform some basic functions on their own (e.g., tracking their package at *www. fedex.com*) to avoid tying up support staff resources. The same expectations are true for Help Desk organizations.

IT has started to embrace and incorporate some self-service ideas to address Help Desk type user needs. Some common self-service techniques that have been put into place include:

- ✦ E-mailing requests to the Help Desk instead of talking to an analyst on the phone
- ✦ Allowing users to see the status of their tickets
- ✦ Setting up knowledge bases for users to browse through on their own (either on the Net or on an intranet)
- ✦ Setting up online forms for common requests (supplies, moves, etc.)
- ✦ Resetting their own password (although this has been commonly implemented, there are security concerns that you should consider)

♦ Allowing users to see what messages have been identified as spam if they are trying to track down an e-mail that hasn't been delivered

♦ Online forms to request file restores; these are then passed on to the backup software and the files can be restored without human intervention if the tape library has the proper tapes

These self-service tools can be particularly helpful for those Help Desks that aren't staffed around the clock.

As in other aspects of our society, some people are quite fond of self-service since it allows them to feel that they have more control and involvement. Others are more comfortable with personal interaction. Self-service options shouldn't be considered as a wholesale replacement for personal interaction or other existing methods. Instead, self-service should be thought of as an alternative.

Tools

Help Desk tools number in the hundreds — *www.helpdesk.com* lists over 350 different Help Desk software applications alone. But that software can be divided into three relevant classes:

Knowledge Management

Since no Help Desk analyst can be expected to know everything, a knowledge base of information can be a valuable resource. This might be something developed internally, or part of a call tracking system or an external resource.

Remote Control

Very often an issue may go unresolved during the initial phone call because the user was unable to accurately describe the problem or couldn't follow directions provided by the Help Desk analyst. Using a remote control package (e.g., PC Anywhere from Symantec, SMS from Microsoft, Remote Control from Dameware, etc.), a Help Desk analyst can see exactly what the user sees on their PC, and even take control of the user's PC, all without ever leaving the Help Desk chair. (Of course, the support staff should always ask for the user's permission before accessing their workstation this way.) This remote control/access saves time, increases user satisfaction, and tremendously improves the effectiveness of the Help Desk.

Installation Tools

Many calls to the Help Desk result in a request for some type of installation (printer drivers, new software, upgrades, patches, etc.). By using various software tools, for example, remote control mentioned above, as well as solutions for the automatic deployment of software the Help Desk, can fulfill a request without having to dispatch a technician or walk a user through a complicated process.

See Chapter 14, Software and Operating Systems (page 383), for a more detailed discussion of software deployment.

Call Tracking System

A mid-size environment can receive hundreds of calls a month; a large environment can receive hundreds of calls each day. A call tracking system can serve many functions in addition to just keeping track of calls. It can route calls to the right person for resolution, schedule activities, set priorities, automatically escalate, generate reports on the types of activities, and track call history (both by user and by equipment or resource).

See the section Call Tracking Software (page 459) later in this chapter for more information on call tracking packages.

Service Level Agreements

Service Level Agreements (SLAs) represent a declaration to the user community of what type of service your Help Desk can provide, and how quickly it hopes to provide it. SLAs help to set the users' expectations, as well as define the performance criteria upon which you, your staff, and your Help Desk organization will be judged.

SLAs are discussed in detail in Section 17.5 on page 463.

User Surveys

While reports from your ACD system and call tracking software can give you all kinds of statistics, they often don't tell you if your customers are satisfied. It can be very helpful to periodically survey a sample of users who have called your Help Desk and ask them a small handful of questions.

The survey can be done in person, over the phone, or via e-mail or weblink. A sample survey might include questions such as:

✦ How was your initial call to the Help Desk answered . . . by a person, by voice mail, or by e-mail?

- ✦ If your request was submitted by e-mail or by voice mail, how long was it before you received a reply?

- ✦ How long did it take before your problem was completely resolved?

- ✦ Did it require multiple visits to your desk or multiple phone calls to resolve your problem?

- ✦ Did the analysts who worked to resolve your call act in a professional and courteous manner?

- ✦ Overall, how would you rate this specific call to the Help Desk (using a scale of 1 to 10, with 10 being perfect)?

- ✦ Please feel free to make any additional comments, complaints, or suggestions you may have regarding the Help Desk.

You may find that a survey yields very different numbers than the statistics you get from other tools. Your call tracking software may report that the average call is resolved in 3.2 hours. However, the user survey may indicate that the average is 4.5 hours. Even if the call tracking statistics are more accurate, as an IT Manager it is often more important to deal with the users' *perception*. Regardless of the results, the act of taking the survey will help users to believe that you're concerned about the quality of service being delivered. After each survey, statistics should be compiled and decisions made about what the results indicate, and what actions should be taken to improve service levels. When you do surveys periodically, you can then evaluate trends and patterns.

Measuring the Help Desk Workload

Tracking the performance of your Help Desk is important because, as discussed earlier, this department is often the only face of the IT department that the rest of the organization knows.

Within most call tracking applications, tools exist to monitor typical Help Desk activities. You can track:

- ✦ Service ticket submissions

- ✦ Service ticket categorization

- ✦ Activities by technician (volume of tickets, resolution time, etc.)

- ✦ Busy periods (by hour, day, month)

- ✦ Service tickets due and completed

- ✦ Volume of calls in different categories (e.g., password resets, hardware, software)

+ Service ticket billing (if you chargeback for services)
+ Reporting and performance charts
+ Billable time/expense tracking
+ E-mail ticket volume

17.3   Call Tracking

In a small environment that only receives a handful of Help Desk calls each day, tracking the call can be done through any number of simple means (whiteboard, spreadsheet, etc.). However, in larger environments that receive hundreds, thousands, or tens of thousands of calls per month, a more sophisticated solution is required.

Call Tracking Software

Call tracking is a software category designed specifically for managing calls at call centers. (This category includes more areas than just traditional corporate IT Help Desks.) There are call tracking solutions that are available for a few hundred dollars, up to those that may cost a few hundred thousand dollars. Since most offerings are licensed based on the number of concurrent users, however, the size of your staff may be the greatest factor in determining how much your implementation will cost. Since there are a surprisingly large number of offerings in this product area, a good resource to start narrowing your search is the Help Desk Institute (*www.helpdeskinst.com*). This organization, which you may want to consider joining to keep abreast of developments in the area of support services, can be a good resource to learn about call tracking software offerings, and other aspects of Help Desk operations, etc.

Specific Issues

There are a variety of factors to consider when evaluating this category of call tracking packages:

+ Ease of customization. Some packages can be customized using a point-and-click type interface; others require scripting.
+ Client, server, and database platforms supported.
+ Auto-escalation (beeper, e-mail, alerting management, etc.).
+ Integration with your e-mail environment.

+ Ad hoc queries and reports; the ability to define and generate customized reports.

+ Integration with handheld devices to allow technicians to view calls while away from their desks.

+ Access from a Web browser interface. This could be helpful for technicians who work from non-supported platforms (e.g., Macintosh or Linux) or to allow technicians to access the database from any workstation without having to install the full client software package.

+ Integration with third party desktop management tools (Microsoft's SMS, LANDesk's Management Suite, Altiris's Client Management Suite, etc.).

+ Integration with third party knowledge base packages.

+ Ability to build an internal knowledge base of calls.

+ Support for international use. If your organization will use the package in countries outside the United States, you may want to make sure the package can be configured for multi-language support, and that the vendor has a presence in the countries you will be operating in.

+ How usable the package is out of the box. You may not have the resources available to dedicate for customizing the package to your exact needs.

+ Extent of the implementation effort in terms of time, training, and need for consultants.

The Value of Selecting Appropriate Help Desk Software

Selecting a Help Desk package is a critical decision since you will be using it for several years. In addition to the standard practices of checking references, investigating the vendor, and so on, you should also consider getting the input from some (if not all) of the staff that will be using the package. You may want to solicit their assistance in narrowing down the field of candidates to a few finalists. And, when you're down to deciding among the last two or three vendors, you may want to have some of the staff sit in on the vendor demos so that they can see how the packages operate and ask questions.

17.4 Staffing

It's important to remember that a Help Desk is essentially a complaint desk — people only call when there is a problem. As such, callers to the Help Desk are likely to be frustrated and impatient.

Accordingly, one of the most vital prerequisites for Help Desk analysts is their interpersonal skills. The staff on the Help Desk has to be sensitive to callers' needs; remain calm, mature, polite, and professional; and demonstrate confidence. The last item is of particular importance. If a caller to the Help Desk feels that the analyst isn't qualified or capable, the caller is likely to become more frustrated. On the other hand, if the caller believes (whether it's true or not) that the analyst is confident and capable of finding a resolution, the caller will immediately feel better. Confidence is contagious.

A user is likely to appreciate and value a quick, courteous, and helpful response to a basic support question more than they would appreciate major upgrades and investments to your infrastructure. A friendly voice helping a road warrior through a hotel connectivity issue (which helps only one person) will usually generate more goodwill than an operating system upgrade to a file and print server (which helps the whole company). Both are required for a successful organization, but the former will probably be more popular than the latter.

In addition to interpersonal skills, individuals at the Help Desk need to have skills in whichever technologies they're supporting. Since you're unlikely to find someone who knows everything, it's important that they're also resourceful enough to find solutions to problems they haven't seen before, and be able to think through problems and explore alternatives on their own.

Specific Considerations When Hiring for a Help Desk

Chapter 3, Staffing Your IT Team (page 43), covers staffing and recruiting in detail, but when hiring for a Help Desk, you should especially consider how they perform in a telephone screening. This call should give you some feel for the candidates' telephone personality.

Develop a set of representative questions that might come into the Help Desk, and see how the candidate handles them. The questions should be ones that don't draw on technical skills exclusively, but also allow you to get a glimpse as to how the candidate thinks through troubleshooting, and how she reacts when the answers aren't clear-cut.

✦ Look for evidence that the candidate can learn on his own. Have all his technical skills been developed through formal training or self-taught?

✦ Is the candidate prepared for full shifts answering phones?

✦ If the candidate sees the Help Desk as a stepping stone to a higher level position in IT, you and she should agree on a minimum time commitment at the Help Desk before such a transfer is possible.

Size of Support Staff

How many people you need supporting your Help Desk depends on the number of calls that come in a given period, your service level targets, average length of each call, and so on. A Help Desk that has multiple shifts will obviously need more analysts than one that runs just a single shift. You'll probably need to be flexible in your staffing: you'll want more analysts during peak periods, and fewer during quiet periods. Statistics from your ACD and your call tracking software can help you evaluate call patterns.

Staff Burnout

Taking calls at the Help Desk for eight hours a day can be exhausting and may be a short path to quick burnout. Consider rotation of assignments with other positions. Or schedule the shifts so that each analyst has some time away from the phone, perhaps, to research questions that might normally have been escalated to some sort of second level. The section Avoiding Burnout in Chapter 2 (page 23) addresses staff burnout in more detail.

Staff Training

Ongoing training for your staff is critical to the success of your Help Desk. In addition to the obvious training of applications, there are a number of training ideas you want to incorporate:

✦ Training on IT policies and procedures. When the staff is familiar with the policies, they're more likely to apply them consistently

✦ Training from other IT teams (systems development, networking, etc.) on what those teams do, and how they interact with each other, the Help Desk, and the users

✦ Discussions with vendors: Innovative ways to use their products, for example, or in-depth training on particular features

✦ Training on trends in the industry; this could be a discussion you lead based on headlines in trade journals

✦ Training on security issues; this discussion could be led by your internal networking team and could be a great way to inform your team about "social engineering" and how to be on the look-out for it

◆ Sharing knowledge with other Help Desk members; if one member encounters an unusual question or problem from a user, have the member share both the problem and its resolution with the team

Remember that training is an ongoing process. Periodic refresher courses are just as important as the initial training.

Escalating a Call

Escalating calls that are beyond the skills or authority of your Help Desk personnel is an important part of the Help Desk's function.

Escalating a call occurs when an issue is too complex for the first level support; many companies have several levels of support designed to have the correctly skilled people taking the right calls. You don't want your very technical people answering simple calls about how to use Windows, nor do you want your first-level personnel addressing system architecture calls.

A call can also be escalated when the customer has an issue whose resolution requires more authority than the Help Desk person has. Approving a non-standard request, or addressing a security concern, are examples of issues a person further up the Help Desk ladder generally deals with. Similarly, a call may be escalated when the ticket has been open too long, as defined by the SLAs, or when the user is a VIP and should be getting extra special attention.

In both types of situations, clear policies should be put in place so that the personnel can know when and where to re-route the calls.

17.5 Service Level Agreements

When a user calls the Help Desk, they're hoping for immediate service and resolution. Of course, that may not be possible in all cases; a technician may have to be dispatched, it may be a problem that has to be researched or escalated to a specialist, and so on. If it's a hardware problem, a part may need to be ordered. When this happens, the user will usually ask: "How long will it take?"

Service level agreements (SLAs) give you, and them, the answer to that question.

Specific Issues

SLAs are your targets for delivering service. There can be many different types of SLAs.

+ System up-time

+ Hours of Help Desk operation

+ How many rings before a phone is answered, or how long before a voice mail message is returned

+ Time until call resolution

+ Turnaround time for different types of tasks like:

+ Creating an ID

+ Restoring a file

+ A password reset

+ Break/fix repairs

+ Obtaining new hardware

+ Installations and/or moves

Positive Values of SLAs

By defining and publishing your SLAs, you can help reduce anger and frustration — yours as well as the users'. For example, if you tell users that it takes 24 hours to create an ID, you are likely to get users in the habit of requesting them in advance versus those emergency requests that come on Monday mornings because HR never informed IT about the new hires.

There will always be exceptions, emergencies, and special cases, but published service levels can be an enormous help in keeping a support organization from constantly operating in crisis mode. Of course, it's important that the service levels you set be ones that you can meet and that are reasonable for the user community. For example, don't tell users that voice mail messages will be returned within 15 minutes unless you have a very high degree of confidence that you can do so consistently. On the other hand, promising a return call in 24 hours may be a target that you can meet, but one that your users are likely to find unacceptable.

Ask for Help from Your Staff

When setting service levels, solicit input from your support staff, as well as users, as to what is reasonable and what is feasible. Then, before publishing your service levels, have your staff work with them for a while to see how well they meet them. Then, when you're confident you have service levels that are both reasonable and feasible, let the users know. Post them on your intranet, or distribute them via e-mail. Afterwards, monitor how well you're meeting them. They aren't carved in stone. It's okay to adjust them if they aren't working. And you may need to add to them as your support organization takes on additional responsibilities or types of services.

Writing Good SLAs

Good SLAs have several things in common:

✦ The levels of service should be clearly defined (Write "remote access to the database shall be 99.99% available during normal business hours," not "the database will be available M-F, 8 a.m.–5 p.m.")

✦ SLAs should first be written for the most requested tasks.

✦ Measuring SLA performance should be easy, and preferably automated.

✦ SLAs should be written clearly so they are understood by all.

✦ SLAs should be focused on metrics that have meaning for the customer. Your customers may not be interested in a router's up-time, but they are interested in the reliability of Internet access.

✦ Consider SLAs for end-to-end tasks, as opposed to individual components. For example, consider the availability of the finance application to the end-user, as opposed to individual SLAs for the network, the server, the database, the application, etc.

17.6 User Training

There are many options available for user training, as well as training for your staff. The ones you choose to use depend on the size and budget of your organization, as well as the skills you need to develop in your users.

In-House Classes

If you're able to have your own training staff and facilities, you can tailor course content, schedule, and class size exactly to your needs. The costs are readily identifiable in terms of staff and equipment needed for the training room.

Third Party Training Providers

These organizations can provide quality training in popular skill sets. The downside is that they're somewhat inflexible in regard to schedules and curricula. Alternatively, you can usually arrange (at an additional charge) for these providers to deliver classes customized to your needs. Training providers usually have a staff of professional and highly experienced trainers, and the curricula for many classes usually adhere to outlines established by the appropriate vendor (e.g., Microsoft) to maintain their authorizations.

Computer-Based Training

Computer-Based Training (CBT) applications are often multimedia based, and sometimes include exams to gauge the students' progress and adjust the pace accordingly. On the plus side, CBT can be very inexpensive, very flexible (students can use it at their convenience, rerun specific portions, or jump ahead as needed), and convenient (no travel or time away from the office required). On the other hand, students can't ask the instructor questions and may rush through the program if it doesn't hold their interest or it's presented at the wrong level. Students may also hold CBT in less esteem than a formal instructor-led course. And, if done while in the office, the student may be easily distracted by phone calls, e-mails, and other interruptions — especially if the course doesn't hold their interest.

Web-Based Training

Web-based training has exploded in recent years; "e-learning" is now a standard — not unusual — offering for most training situations; giants like Microsoft, Sun and Intel offer e-learning options. There are many different varieties of Web training that you can customize to your particular staffing and budget needs, and there are many companies that now either develop their own Web-based training (because the tools are so easy to use) or have a company develop courses just for their needs. See Table 17.1 below for the pros and cons of Web-based training.

Table 17.1   Pros and cons of Web-based training

PRO		CON	
PRO	Easier delivery than standard classroom training. No need to set up classrooms, equipment, and schedule an instructor.	**CON**	Less personal. Depending on the system—such as some "whiteboard systems" where all the user sees is an electronic whiteboard—a human may never appear on the screen, or all the user will hear is a voice directing him through the "class."
	Size of the class isn't an issue—you can train one or hundreds at the same time.		If the material doesn't hold their interest, students may spend the time answering e-mails, taking phone calls, and doing other work.
	Some of the classes are instructor led, allowing the students to ask questions (via a chat window).		Sometimes less effective. A user new to a system may have basic questions that are technically answered by the training but can't be answered to the user's satisfaction because no interaction with a teacher is possible.
	Scheduling isn't an issue. "On demand" classes allow the users to start and stop the training on their own timetable.		Initial training (on the training system) will be required. More users are getting used to the concept, but there are still many people who have never taken an online class and need some training on how to take the class.
	Negligible cost, since all the student generally needs is a workstation connected to the Internet.		

17.7 Additional Resources

Web Sites

- ✦ *crm.ittoolbox.com/topics/t.asp?t=490&p=490&h1=490* (CRM site)

- ✦ *www.cio.com* (*CIO Magazine* site)

- ✦ *www.e11online.com* (help desk software vendor)

- ✦ *www.helpdesk.com* (help desk support)

- ✦ *www.helpdeskinst.com* (Help Desk Institute)

- ✦ *www.help-desk-world.com* (help desk software vendor)

Books and Articles

- ✦ Bruton, Noel, *How to Manage the IT Helpdesk — A Guide for User Support and Call Center Managers*, Butterworth-Heinemann, 2003.

- ✦ Czegel, Barbara, *Running an Effective Help Desk, 2nd Edition*, John Wiley, 1998.

- ✦ Dawson, Keith, *The Call Center Handbook, 4th Edition*, CMP Books, 2001.

- ✦ Jaffe, Brian D., "Maturity Is a Help Desk Prerequisite," *PC Week*, February 7, 2000.

- ✦ Jaffe, Brian D., "Taking the Measure of Customer Service," *PC Week*, June 5, 1998.

- ✦ Knapp, Donna, *A Guide to Help Desk Concepts*, Course Technology, 2003.

- ✦ Mohr, Julie, *The Help Desk Audit: Blueprint for Success* (Spiral-bound), Blueprintaudits.com, 2003.

- ✦ Sanderson, Susan, *Introduction to Help Desk Concepts and Skills*, McGraw-Hill/Irwin; 2003.

- ✦ Wooten, Bob, *Building & Managing a World Class IT Help Desk*, Osborne Publishing; 2002.

Web Sites

On the Internet, no one knows you're a dog.

—PETER STEINER CARTOON, THE NEW YORKER MAGAZINE, 1993

A company's online presence is a critical component of most organizations. And that online presence includes not only its face to the *external* world — its Web site(s) for customers, potential clients, suppliers, etc. — but its face to its *internal* world, its intranet, for use by its employees.

18.1 The Internet

The Internet is a global network of computers — the "network of networks" — that connects companies, universities, and individuals all over the planet. "Man is a tool-making animal," wrote Benjamin Franklin. And the Internet is one of the most flexible, ubiquitous, powerful, and useful tools ever created.

A Little History

Before we get to *why* the Internet is all these things, we want to add a few sentences on *how* the Internet got to be all these things.

In 1969, working on funding from the U. S. Department of Defense, a company called BBN connected individual computers at UCLA, SRI in Palo Alto, University of California at Santa Barbara, and the University of Utah into a single network (*http://en.wikipedia.org/wiki/ARPANET*). The network has grown to a point where Google stopped counting after nearly searching 5 *billion* Web pages. See Figure 18.1 for a "map" of the Internet.

Papers detailing the history of the Internet are available at *www.isoc. org/internet/history.*

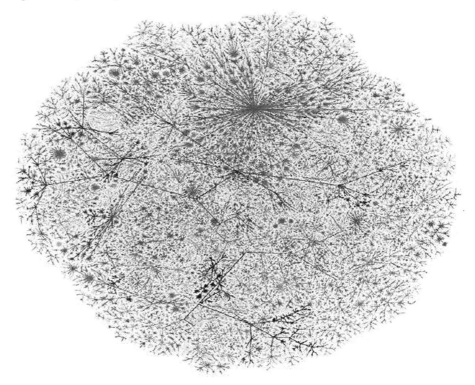

Figure 18.1   A Cool Map of the Internet (Source: *http://www.mathaware.org/mam/04/ 6_Internet_structure.html*). Patent Pending & Copyright © Lumeta Corporation 2006. Reprinted with permission

What to Say When Someone Asks the Difference between the World Wide Web and the Internet

Though often used interchangeably, there is a subtle difference.

The World Wide Web
The Web is the widely used *graphical interface* to the Internet. Web sites are a collection of files that can be viewed graphically on the Internet using an Internet browser.

The Internet
The Internet is comprised of much more than just the World Wide Web, though. It contains millions of files and lots of data that can't be seen graphically but can still be accessed. The Web is exciting, but the Internet is bigger. You may do business over the Web, but a lot of work is done and a lot of information is exchanged over the Internet without the use of graphics of any kind. The Internet is often referred to as "the Net."

Your company's Web site is on the Internet, but also on the World Wide Web. Your department may have older files on the Internet server that are no longer active; they may not be accessible by the Web (because they are not viewable with a browser) but they may still be accessible through the Internet.

Nonetheless, if you choose to use Internet and Web synonymously, it's unlikely you'll ever be corrected, or misunderstood.

Types of Users

Academic

Universities around the world are connected to the Net. In fact, academicians were the original ones to embrace the idea of easy connectivity. Originally conceived as a method for researchers at universities to quickly and easily exchange information, the Internet now provides a wide range of teaching solutions. There is also "Internet 2," a network designed, used, and moderated only by academic and research institutions (*http://www.internet2.edu*, for more information).

Corporate

Virtually all companies and organizations are now connected to the Net; see the discussion below in the section Specific Examples of What the Web Can

Do for Your Company (page 473) for a range of ideas about how companies use the Net.

Personal

Originally a tool for academic institutions and then corporations, the creation of Web browsers (the graphic interface to the Net) as well as the availability of broadband has made personal Internet usage soar. While interesting, that subject isn't relevant to most IT Managers (although, the fact that it's so widely used and available, is very relevant to IT Managers). However, it's worth pointing out that when Marie in accounting can create a family Web site in an evening, and make it available on the Internet for $9.95 per month, she picks up just enough knowledge to ask why it's taking months to get the new company Web site launched.

Value as a Tool

Of course, users use these Web site creation tools for a variety of reasons. The professor who sells his inventions (which he has co-licensed with his university), teaches online classes, and also consults with a corporation, uses the Internet in multiple ways. When he sends his daughter e-mail from his university account asking her for the name of the head of the research division for the company she works for, he is using the Internet for personal, academic, and corporate reasons — all at the same time.

Flexible

The Net is one of the most flexible, multi-purpose tools ever invented. For a relatively low cost you can run a virtual business; run a virtual division; and manage employees, suppliers, and distributors across the planet.

Everywhere

There only a few places on earth where you can't access the Internet, and those places are shrinking in number.

Strong

The Internet came into being in the late 1960s as a U.S. Defense Department experiment designed to test networks under wartime conditions. As such, it was designed to be particularly resilient. If a portion of the network is damaged, or out of service, there are numerous alternate paths. The most sensitive portion of the Internet is that which is called the "last mile." The last mile is the telecommunications facility that connects your Web server, or your users, to the Internet. Typically, this is a single facility that disrupts your connectivity if damaged. Today, since Internet connectivity is so critical, many companies have multiple paths for access to the Internet.

Powerful

With the Internet, users in your Sales department can immediately send up-to-the-minute sales data to management when one group is in a meeting room in Sydney and the other is at the home office in London. It facilitates communication and interaction when individuals are separated by distance, providing a way to share information, exchange ideas in real time, converse, and collaborate.

Complex

The diagram below (Figure 18.2) illustrates *some* of the connections between *some* of the nodes on the Web.

Specific Examples of What the Web Can Do for Your Company

The ways that the Web can benefit your company are probably only limited by your imagination. However, some of the more successful efforts include the following:

+ **Increase product, brand, and company recognition.** Best Buy and Circuit City (among many others), for example, use their Web sites to encourage retail stores' location purchases, while their retail stores encourage visits to and purchases from the Web site. Many retailers are adopting this model; retail stores can increase the inventory they can claim to "have available" and online stores can promise quick "delivery" of products. In both cases, the brand name is strongly reinforced.

+ **Provide product information** (description, specifications, uses) or company data (financial, executive biographies, press releases) directly into the hands of your consumers. Most large corporations use their Web sites (e.g., *www.chrysler.com* and *www.kraftfoods.com*) for this reason, among others. Web pages like this are sometimes referred to as "brochure ware."

474

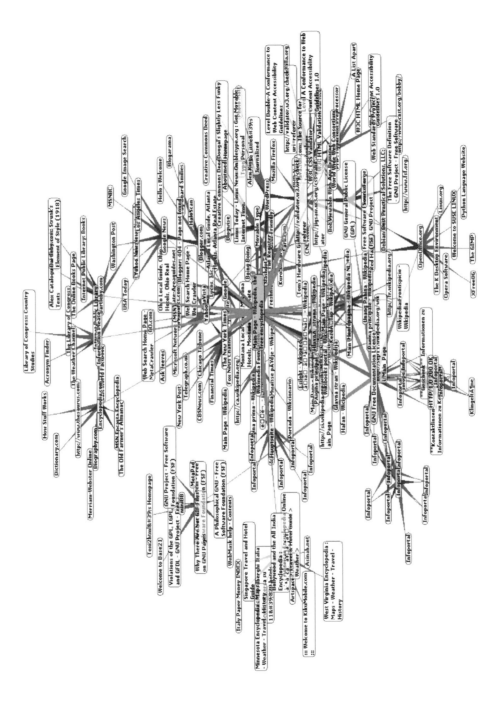

Figure 18.2 Wikipedia Example of How Some of Its Pages are Linked (Source *http://en.wikipedia.org/wiki/Image: WorldWideWebAroundWikipedia.png*)

✦ **Keep your "doors open" 24 hours a day.** Airline sites, such as *www.ual. com* and *www.americanairlines.com,* as well as retail sites, for example, use the Web for this reason. Also, companies designed from the outset to be e-commerce-only companies — *www.amazon.com* — exploit this significant advantage they enjoy over their traditional brick-and-mortar competitors.

✦ **Improve profits with direct sales** by eliminating distributors and unnecessary layers of middlemen. (This process of eliminating the middleman is often referred to as *disintermediation.*) This strategy can backfire if it alienates your critical channel partners, so you need to address these concerns directly. For example, Merrill Lynch, one of the largest Wall Street stock brokerage houses, began offering the ability for consumers to buy stocks online, without consulting a Merrill Lynch broker (*www. ml.com*). The company is convinced that consumers who want to trade online will do so, while those who want the advice of a broker will continue to contact their broker. They made a painful decision to embrace the new business model of the Web, but without abandoning their long-established broker network. On the other hand, some companies are so thrilled with the idea of conducting business on the Web, that they charge a fee to their customers who want a more traditional means of doing business. In 2006, the Trio cable TV network stopped broadcasting on cable TV and moved to an Internet-only delivery model (*www. triotv.com*).

✦ Alternatively, a Web site can **bring together a buyer and seller** that might not otherwise transact with each other (e.g., *www.ebay.com*). Assembling or reassembling components of the traditional supply chain like this is called *reintermediation.*

✦ **Improve customer service** via e-mail communications with customers. Virtually all companies provide options for feedback and questions. Most common (usually via a "contact us" link) is the ability to send e-mail feedback. However, many companies are also employing an online chat option for customer service. For organizations dedicated to customer service, these sites are staffed to respond very quickly to feedback and customer service inquiries.

✦ **Receive more precise and immediate market research** by tracking customer activity on the Web, as well as Web-based surveys and direct marketing via e-mail. While this is a controversial and quickly changing aspect of the Web, the ability of the medium to provide much more targeted consumer information is undisputed. Issues such as tracking customer activity, and what is done with customer information are highly controversial. There are groups that study vendor and Web site privacy statements the way baseball fans study box scores.

✦ **Adjust to changing market conditions almost instantaneously** with price adjustments, sales incentives, product placement, and so on. Dell, for example, changes its product promotions every few days. This technique is both in response to market demands as well as a way of generating buyer interest by always having something new and different.

The potential advantages to virtually any company are almost unlimited.

18.2 Corporate Web Sites

Corporate Web sites are often the "faces" of corporations. Customers and the public may form opinions about a company simply based on the look of a company's Web site, how easy it is to navigate, how much information it provides, and how functional and helpful it is. As discussed earlier, it can be used to generate brand loyalty, product awareness, sales, and improve profits.

A corporation's primary goal is to make a profit. And the Net can radically change the way companies try to achieve that goal.

Examples of the Old Model

✦ Business travelers called their travel departments with their travel requests. The departments controlled the information about flight times and hotel availability.

✦ Suppliers called the company to determine what inventory the company needed and when. The data presented was anywhere from several days to several weeks old.

Examples of the New Model

✦ Business travelers go directly to the airplane and hotel sites and book the reservations themselves or receive updated flight information on their cell phones. Travelers save the company money by "cutting out" the middlemen.

✦ Suppliers go on to the company Web site themselves (which are often updated in real time) and determine the most efficient order for themselves.

> **Example of a Site That Successfully Charges a Fee:** *The Wall Street Journal*
>
> The *Wall Street Journal's* site is one of the glowing successes of publishing on the Web. They do so well that they charge a fee for a subscription to their site, one of the few content sites that has been able to do so successfully. Their site contains not only material found in their daily newspaper, but also content specific to the up-to-the-minute medium of the Web.

18.3 Intranets

Company's use intranet sites, sometimes called portals, for many of the same reasons that they use an Internet site: for convenience, ease of use, enhanced offerings, and to reduce costs. Depending on the capabilities of the site, it can also help employees feel good about the company they work for.

Uses

Intranet sites have been most popular for functions of the HR departments, but that is rapidly expanding. Other intranet uses include:

+ **Posting of the company's policy manual:** Putting the policy manual on the intranet eliminates the hassle of distributing periodic updates to the old three-ring binder. Plus, it ensures that everyone has immediate access to the latest version.

+ **Payroll information:** Employees can use the intranet to view and update their tax information (e.g., W-4 type) and view their pay stubs. These two functions alone can eliminate a great deal of paper and phone calls.

+ **Time sheets:** A convenient replacement for the paper forms to track hours, sick days, vacation days, etc. An automatic feed to the payroll system can reduce a lot of paper-movement and keying errors.

+ **Benefit plan enrollment:** In addition to viewing information about the differences in plans, employees can sign up, identify beneficiaries, and authorize payroll deductions.

+ **Employee discounts:** An intranet can provide information on getting employee discounts on the company's own products.

✦ **Annual budget planning:** Department managers can see their department's spending history, and plan next year's budget. All budgets are then rolled up automatically to create a company-wide budget. It sure beats e-mailing spreadsheets all around.

✦ **T&E submissions:** Through the intranet (often in partnership with a third party software vendor), employees can submit travel and expense information. Not only is the submission done online (including receipts, by scanning them to electronic files), but managers can approve the requests online, and accounting can review/audit them online, and authorize reimbursement (which is often a direct deposit to the employee's bank account). Transactions from the company credit card can be automatically posted, and reimbursed by electronic transfer to the card issuer.

✦ **Job postings:** Many companies will post job openings on their intranet before they post them on the public Web site or job boards. By filling jobs with internal candidates (or referrals from employees), the company can save money on recruiting and advertising fees, and employees feel better about the potential for promotion and career growth.

✦ **Requesting supplies:** Virtual catalogs from approved vendors can be posted, and employees can submit their requests, which are often delivered to their desks the next day.

✦ **Company announcements:** The intranet (sometimes coupled with e-mail) can be used to make employees aware of everything from the year's holiday schedule to the plans for the company picnic, and from changes in management to the cafeteria menu.

See Figure 18.3 for an example of a page from a company's intranet.

18.4 Creating and Managing Web Sites

Creating a corporate Web site, whether an Internet or intranet site, has become a complex endeavor. When the Web was new, in the mid-1990s, businesses could create their own Web sites, typically just basic brochure information, and have them running — and used — in a day. Now, the abilities of the software are so great, the standards for design and functionality are so high, and the expectations of the users are so large, that it's no longer possible to toss up an effective website in your spare time.

In particular, you and your company need to carefully focus the purpose of your Web sites. Are you doing business-to-consumer? Business-to-business?

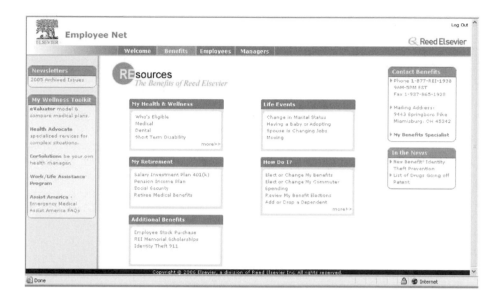

Figure 18.3   Sample Intranet Site

Both? Have you thought about who your users are, what they want, and how you want them to contact you?

As complex and daunting as its challenges are, though, so are its potential rewards. There are millions of people now using the Internet, and more are joining daily. And those people are looking to be informed, entertained, and, most important to the corporate side of life, they are looking to buy.

There are five issues you need to consider when setting up a Web site:

1. Technical considerations

2. Content and function

3. Design

4. Development

5. Hosting

Technical Considerations

The attention span of a Web surfer is notoriously short. If users have to wait too long (a time span usually measured in seconds), they may avoid your site, or may go there once but never return. If you are depending on your site to draw new customers, or to offer you an advantage over your competitors, this is a serious consideration.

Infrastructure Issues

One of the most critical decisions in setting up a server is sizing it to ensure that it's fast enough. However, the size of the box is only half the equation. The other consideration is to make sure that the network connection has enough bandwidth to ensure that a bottleneck isn't created. Bandwidth is covered in more detail in the section Internet Service Providers on page 487. The size of the server and the pipe are areas of detail that are beyond the scope of this book. However, there are many resources available to guide you on this subject.

The hardware for a Web site can be as small as a PC purchased at a retail store, or as large as a roomful of servers. If you expect your Web site to be highly complex, with a lot of activity, you want to invest in selecting the hardware and software that will provide the performance you need. On the other hand, if the Web site isn't expected to draw a lot of visitors, your hardware and software choice might be based on whatever equipment is readily available, or available at minimal cost.

When building your Web site's infrastructure, you also have to give consideration to cyclical use. What is sufficient for 11 months of the year, may come to a grinding halt under the deluge of holiday shopping in December. There are plenty of stories in the industry of sites coming to their knees because the traffic generated during a new advertising campaign (e.g., a Super Bowl commercial) was much more than expected.

Server Issues

There are many issues to think about when setting up an environment for Web access.

✦ If the server is going to be functioning as a public Web site, you need to make sure that it's connected to the Internet, and on the public side of your firewall. Intranet sites are generally not connected to the Internet. If the server is going to be hosting your intranet site, it's almost certainly on your own premises and needs to be connected to your network on the private side of the firewall — just like any other file and print server, PC, or printer you might have.

✦ Depending on the criticality of the site, you may want to have redundancies of Internet connections, servers, and network equipment (firewalls, routers, etc.). These redundancies may be in the same room, or you may even have redundant computer rooms geographically dispersed.

✦ There are, of course, serious security issues with any Web site. Because they are outside of the firewall, not only are they prime targets, many times they have hooks into back-end databases, etc., to serve up information — and these make them increasingly useful for hackers as a way into the systems.

✦ There are two operating systems that have the bulk of the Web server market: Linux/Unix variants and Microsoft Windows IIS Server. Which one you use could depend upon your staff's skill sets, as well as the applications and tools you will use on your Web site. (For a further discussion of operating systems, see Chapter 14, Software and Operating Systems on page 383.)

✦ You need to give the site a name so that people with their browser software can get to all the information you've posted. If you've set up an Internet or extranet site, you need to register the domain name (e.g., *www.yourcompany.com*). Your ISP will probably do this for you, or help you do this at little or no charge. Or you can do it yourself by going to one of several services on the Web. If all goes well, within 24 hours after registering, users will be able to type *www.mycompany.com* and discover the information you've posted for all the world to see. Domain names are discussed on page 486 of this chapter.

✦ Match your efforts and cost to the value you expect to get from the site; if you're not looking to build, or don't need a complicated, interactive site, match your hardware and software purchasing decisions accordingly. There are several important Web page design tools, as well as issues regarding the Web server that you need to consider.

As mentioned above, the only technical difference between an Internet and intranet Web site is which side of the firewall they're connected to — the public side or the private side. Other than that, all Web sites are developed with the same tools and run on the same kind of server hardware and software. However, even though there are no technical differences among them, there are important issues you should consider when setting them up. The issues primarily revolve around performance and response time.

Web Pages and Databases

If the plans for the Web site call for queries, or updates, against your legacy databases (inventory, order processing, etc.), there may be a need for special tools and utilities to marry your state-of-the-art Java Web code with your been-around-the-block mainframe routines. There are tools that allow you to make this link. However, this is a growing and complex field, filled with companies that will help you write the custom software often required to make this typically complicated connection.

Like all types of computer programming, there is more to creating good code than simply meeting the specifications. Optimized performance is of particular concern to Web sites, given the average Web users' intolerance for slow response times.

Content and Function

You should determine content and function based on your company's overall goals, and their expectations of the Web site. If they're planning a major e-commerce initiative, you will need to verse yourself not only on what your company's products are, but what your company's competition is doing with their Web site. The larger your company, the more likely that you will need and benefit from having both an Inter- and an intranet site.

Overall Company Goals

What do you want to do with your site? There are four general activities that you can use your Web site for: informing, entertaining, selling products or services, and generating sales leads. Determine which of these — either one or a combination of several — you want or need to do on your Web site. By "need to do," we're referring to the decisions companies have been forced to make lately about Web sites due directly to actions their competitors have performed.

Informing

During the early history of the Web, providing information was the primary function of most Web pages. The nickname "brochureware" was used to describe this idea. "Brochureware" isn't a compliment.

Information broadcasting is an ideal use of Web pages: it's easy to set up, easy to maintain, and useful for your customers. Information on Web sites can range from simple material like your company hours and location to more sophisticated offerings like product specifications and online copies of manuals: *www.microsoft.com* contains thousands of different Web pages with many different uses (product information, instruction, technical support, etc.).

Informing can also be more dynamic than simply showing product specifications and manuals. FedEx, for example, allows you to track your package delivery, even allowing you to view the recipient's signature. Communications to and from customer service would also fall into the category of informing. Of course, news Web sites (e.g., *www.cnn.com*) have informing as their primary objective.

Entertaining

If your goal is to entertain, the Web is rapidly providing you with plenty of methods to do so. You can have games, audio, and video on your Web site, as well as sophisticated graphics that are pleasing to the eye. Entertaining Web sites tend to be those that not only have valuable content, but that change content frequently. Sophisticated graphics and audio components can be difficult to create, and it's more work to maintain a fresh site with this kind of material. Sites that are focused on entertainment often generate their revenue with online ads at the Web sites.

Generating Leads

Selling and pre-selling over the Web have become a very sophisticated enterprise, and the days of throwing up a site in a day or two using shareware and a programmer in your garage are gone.

There are two key elements to designing a site that will generate sales leads:

1. Make it clear what your company does and what products/services it offers. Have information on the Web site to help make this apparent. This helps to ensure that the leads that are generated will more likely result in a sale.

2. Make clear what potential customers should do if they're interested. Do you want them to call you? Make your phone number (it should be a toll-free number) obvious. Want them to fax you a complete form? Make the form easy to get to and your fax number available 24 hours a day. But, if the person is online and at your Web site, why make them use another medium (like phone or fax) to reach you? Allow them to click a link to send an e-mail, chat with a rep, or complete an online form.

Once you have collected this information, it's up to you and your company to respond to these requests. Leads may be passed to different sales representatives, or generate mailings, and so on.

Sell Products or Services

This topic is the subject of entire books — it has become a complex and exciting area of the global marketplace. Many companies now use the Web for a significant portion of their sales. For the 2005 holiday season, L. L. Bean reported that its online sales surpassed catalog sales for the first time ever.

Some companies (Amazon and eBay, for example) rely exclusively on Internet sales for revenues.

Ideas for Content: Static versus Dynamic Web Sites

What you put on any Web site is generically called "content." If you simply have static content such as the company address and phone number on your Web site, it won't be very exciting and may not draw visitors.

Major sites like *www.dell.com* and *www.amazon.com* change a portion of their sites regularly to keep them fresh and to keep customers coming back to look at the new features. At the other extreme, if the content is designed to be more dynamic (e.g., the constantly changing information at a newspaper's Web site), you have to deal with the burden of keeping the content updated. A static Web site may be created once and updated by a single person with some spare time a few times a year. A more dynamic site may require an entire department to continuously develop, post, and update the content, like *www.cnn.com*. Of course, the decision about content is a reflection of the decision about what functionality you want your Web site to provide and who your intended audience is.

Changing the content is a double-edged sword. New content keeps the site looking fresh, but you have to be careful not to make the changes so drastic that users lose a sense of familiarity. That's why many sites are very careful about making design changes to the site, like altering menus and navigation, but allow the content to change.

Design

The design of a Web site refers to everything involved in a site, including colors, placement of graphics, menu structure, navigation, etc. Anything that covers what the Web pages look like or how a user navigates through the site is part of its design. The site's design is critical because it affects its ease of use, and may be as important (sometimes more important) as the site's content in determining if a user will return or how often. Fortunately, the World Wide Web offers us many examples of the best and worst of Web design. And, just like keeping content fresh, even the best designed Web sites are constantly tweaked for improvements, or simply to keep them looking new.

Development

Whether your company creates a site internally or has it outsourced, the steps to get the task accomplished are the same. Both options, as you can guess, have their strengths and weaknesses.

Why You Should Outsource Web Site Development

✦ To create useful and important sites, you're going to need a high level of skill. Web development used to be for amateurs, and even companies paid for sites designed by "developers" with no real experience but with a tiny bit of HTML knowledge. Those days are gone. The skill set required to develop Web sites has matured: It's common now for Web site development team members to have human factor skills, user analysis and design, and commercial art in their backgrounds.

✦ Web site development can create massive political infighting, dividing companies into warring parties about which division gets which menu item priority. Having a third party implementing the site can sometimes provide a welcome outside group to blame/praise, and provide some impartiality and objectivity.

Why You Should Do Web Site Development Internally

✦ If in your company security concerns are paramount (such as in the finance and healthcare industries), internal development may be the better choice. Some companies don't care, but many aren't the slightest bit interested in external groups ever looking at their data, much less having access to it.

✦ You have more control over the entire process. Using an outside developer to make periodic minor tweaks to the Web site can be cumbersome and expensive. Also, the process to change outside developers (or to bring the process inside) may be painful.

Hosting

Many companies don't want, or don't have, the resources to keep their own Web site up and running 24 hours a day, 7 days a week. They may not want to spend the money on the hardware (particularly if a great deal of redundancy is required), or they may lack the appropriate staffing levels or technical skills. For companies like this, an entirely separate industry has sprung up. There are numerous companies, from giants like AT&T, Sprint, and Cogent Communications to your local ISP, that are ready, willing, and anxious to run and manage your Web site for you. These hosting companies will rent you space on their own hardware, in their own facilities, and provide the skills and resources to make sure the site runs around the clock. In addition to these facilities, these providers offer very high-speed Internet access.

Mirrored Sites

If your needs are justified, hosting companies can generally offer mirrored sites. Mirrored sites are generally for very active and very critical Web sites. In essence, a mirrored site is a copy of your Web site in another location. There are two primary reasons why you might need this service:

✦ First, a mirrored site ensures that your Web site continues to function even if there is some type of disaster (e.g., power failure) at the first site.

✦ In addition, by having multiple locations, response time is likely to be improved for end-users, since special technology directs the user's request to the site that will provide the best performance. Often, due to the fewer number of "hops," the site that is physically closer to the user may offer the best response time. However, that isn't *always* the case. A user's request may actually travel faster to a site that is further away because that route has lighter traffic — just like when you take side streets because of rush hour congestion on the highway.

FTP Sites

Many companies also have "ftp sites." These are sites on a server that are provided for customers to either get or place data files. Sometimes companies password-protect these sites, and sometimes they don't. Using ftp sites requires some technical knowledge but can also be very useful to both the company and the customer. If you have ever had to download a printer driver that didn't come with your system, you probably used an ftp site.

FTP sites provide faster throughput than moving files via HTTP. They are convenient for up- and downloading of large files, and for files that are exchanged via automated batch processing.

Domain Names

The Domain Name System (DNS) helps users find their way around the Internet. Every computer on the Internet has a unique address called its "IP address" (Internet Protocol address). Because IP addresses (which are strings of numbers) are hard to remember, the DNS allows a familiar string of letters (the "domain name") to be used instead. So rather than typing "192.0.34.163" (for example), you can type *www.icann.org*. See Chapter 12, Networking (page 311), for a more detailed discussion of IP addressing and DNS.

ICANN

The Internet Corporation for Assigned Names and Numbers (ICANN) is an internationally organized, non-profit corporation that has responsibility for IP address space allocation, DNS management, and root server system management functions.

ICANN is responsible for managing and coordinating the DNS to ensure that every address is unique and that all users of the Internet can find all valid addresses. It does this by overseeing the distribution of unique IP addresses and domain names. It also ensures that each domain name maps to the correct IP address.

ICANN is also responsible for accrediting the domain name registrars. "Accredit" means to identify and set minimum standards for the performance of registration functions, to recognize persons or entities meeting those standards, and to enter into an accreditation agreement that sets forth the rules and procedures applicable to the provision of Registrar Services.

ICANN's role is very limited, and it isn't responsible for many issues associated with the Internet, such as financial transactions, Internet content control, spam (unsolicited commercial e-mail), Internet gambling, or data protection and privacy.

ICANN's glossary can be found at *http://www.icann.org/general/glossary. htm*.

You can register domain names for just a few dollars with registrars like *Register.com*, Network Solutions, Verio, etc. The process is relatively simple and straightforward and takes just a few minutes with a credit card.

Consider "locking" your domain name as soon as you register it. Locking a domain name prevents any changes from being made to it, including changing the contact information or name servers. Once a domain name is locked, unlocking it involves a multistep verification process.

Internet Service Providers

Internet Service Providers (ISPs) are companies that provide the connections to the Internet. There are three key issues that you need to consider when evaluating ISPs: speed, reliability, and cost.

Speed

When considering ISP speeds, it's tempting to focus only on the speed (or bandwidth) of the line between your company and the ISP. At the low end are broadband connections that may be sufficient for smaller offices of perhaps up to 50 people. Larger offices may have pipes with more bandwidth up to T-1 lines, which run at 1.54 Mbps. Some large sites have T-3 lines at 45 Mbps. See

Chapter 12, Networking (page 311), for more discussion about Internet connectivity options.

However, it's important to note that not all ISPs, nor all lines, are created equal. It's entirely possible that two different ISPs will provide different levels of response times, even if the line speeds to your site are identical. This is due to a variety of reasons, including the number of lines they have, the speed and traffic volume of those lines, and the number of other users of that service. It's important to remember that while lines connect you and your users to the ISP, there are additional lines that connect your ISP to a Network Access Point (NAP), which is in essence the Internet itself (see Figure 18.4). NAPs are the connection points for Tier-1 providers such as AT&T, Sprint, and MCI WorldCom.

An ISP has many customers and has to ensure that its own connection to the Internet can support the combined activity of its customers. So, while the Internet performance you experience is dependent on the speed of your line to the ISP, it's also dependent on the speed of the line from your ISP to the NAP, and your ISP's own internal network infrastructure. The last two items are important because your ISP has many customers, and while your company's traffic is the only data traveling on your line to the ISP, it then has to merge with the other customer data on that ISP and wait its turn to be moved along — just like multiple roads merging together to form a highway. In fact, it's possible for a large ISP to provide Internet services to several smaller ISPs, which in turn

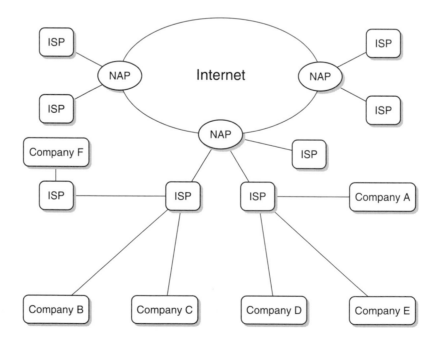

Figure 18.4   ISP Connections

provide access to consumers and businesses. Many factors affect Web response time: hardware, software, line speed, traffic, demand, Web site design, and so on. Accordingly, each can be fine-tuned to optimize performance. There are various products available on the market to help you monitor and improve performance. Caching products, which store frequently accessed pages so that subsequent requests for the page can be retrieved much more quickly, can also boost performance.

Reliability: Define Your Tolerance for Risk

If your need for Internet access is primarily traditional surfing and e-mail, you may be easily able to tolerate a few hours of downtime as a result of a line outage or problems at the ISP. On the other hand, if your business lives and dies by the Internet, and runs "mission-critical" applications with customers around the country or around the globe, an outage means a loss of significant business. You have much more significant concerns over reliability. Many companies now expect and demand that their sites are up and running 24/7.

You need to carefully define your tolerance for risk. You need to quantify, as carefully as possible, how important your ISP is. How long can you run your business without it? How long can you tolerate your Web site being down? Determine how much money it will cost your company when/if your connection to the Internet is broken. If your Web site is down for a couple of hours, do you care? Some companies don't really mind while others go to enormous lengths to ensure that they have 100% connectivity. Once you have these numbers and once you have determined how much per hour and per day without connection to the Internet will cost your company, you can then decide how best to deal with the risk.

In general, there are two components to consider in regard to ISP reliability. The first is the stability of the line from your site to the ISP. This line is provided by the phone company, not your ISP (although, they may very well be one and the same). Secondly, you have to consider the reliability of the services the ISP provides.

While telecomm line outages are rare, they aren't unheard of. And the complexity that occurs when computers meet telephones is increasing, not decreasing. If the connection to your ISP suddenly goes down, whose fault is it? It could be your computer, your network, the phone line, or it could be the ISP itself.

Multiple Lines   Some companies lessen their risk by having more than one line to their ISP, and some have each line from a different ISP. When choosing multiple ISPs, they may even choose providers that are geographically distant from each other. If a disaster (weather, power outage) strikes one area of the country, companies increase their chances that at least one of the ISPs will continue to provide service. For companies that have multiple offices throughout the country, which are networked together, they may choose to have certain offices in different parts of the country with lines to local ISPs.

Cost

Cost is always a factor in any business decision. Unfortunately, comparing costs between ISPs can be difficult. ISPs offer different levels of service, some with many variables of their own. For example, since the cost of the leased lines is based on speed and distance, you may find one ISP to be more expensive than another because of its distance to your company. If you ask an ISP for firewall services, you may be faced with choices about buying, leasing, or renting the appropriate technology at your site. If you don't have the expertise on site, you may have to pay the ISP for maintaining and supporting the firewall, often with pricing based on hours of coverage and response times. Costs for other site services (hosting, design, programming, etc.) can vary significantly with factors like complexity, size of the site, hardware required, and so on.

Some ISP fees have little room for negotiation of some services (e.g., connectivity and hosting) since the ISP is simply passing on its fixed costs. Other services (design and programming) may be highly negotiable. Regardless, your leverage increases with the total projected revenue stream and by bundling multiple services together.

Changing ISPs

As a general rule, changing ISPs is relatively easy. If the only service your ISP provides is the pipe to the Internet, changing ISPs may be as simple as ordering a line to your new provider and giving the old one notice of termination.

The only planning required might be to make sure that you have the new service in place before terminating the old service. If your ISP provides hosting services, changing is a little more complicated, but not much. You can copy all the program logic and Web pages to servers at your new ISP; a simple notification to the domain name registrar is all it takes to have your domain name point to the new provider, and your users will probably never notice the change.

There is also a propagation issue: Typically it takes 24 hours for the change to be replicated throughout the Internet.

18.5   **E-commerce**

The advent of the Web has transformed a network of computers originally designed for research and military purposes to one that allows mom-and-pop operations to compete with corporate giants in selling goods and services all over the planet. IT cares because much of this e-commerce now requires very sophisticated technical operations, including elements such as electronic shopping carts, credit card authorization and acceptance, and online inventory verification.

Main Components of E-commerce

E-commerce has two main components:

+ Business-to-consumer

+ Business-to-business

While the former gets a lot of headlines, the latter is where the money is.

Business-to-Consumer

The principal advantage e-commerce offers business in their relationship with the consumer is the exponential increase in speed and convenience the Internet offers both parties. There are other benefits, but these two are the most important. You can search for the exact airline ticket you want, which airline, when you want to shop for it, and even specify how much you are willing to pay for it. An airline can change airfares and availability on a minute-by-minute basis (and they do). Both parties gain a tremendous advantage over the old way of doing business.

In short, e-commerce allows consumers to purchase your company's goods and/or services directly via the World Wide Web. In its simplest form, e-commerce could be sending an e-mail message that says, "Please ship 2 boxes of widgets." More complex e-commerce transactions allow the consumer to fill out some sort of electronic order form at your Web site, perhaps by browsing through an online version of your catalog and clicking on the items they want, entering information for payment and shipping, and so on. When the consumer clicks OK, the order is sent directly to the warehouse or to regional distribution centers, and so on. The customer gains in speed and efficiency: They ordered when they wanted to from the convenience of their computer. Your business gains by not only shipping your products faster, but by having detailed customer data in digital form; you can use that data later for sales and marketing plans.

Business-to-Business

Although most people associate e-commerce with the Internet, in truth it has been around long before the World Wide Web reached its current popularity.

Six Initial Questions to Ask Before Embarking on an E-commerce Initiative

✦ What measurement systems are currently in place and being utilized within the organization?

✦ What are the important criteria to the company and its constituencies and stakeholders?

✦ What does the company desire to accomplish with the e-commerce initiative?

✦ What is the anticipated time frame associated with the e-commerce program?

✦ Who are the parties involved in implementing the e-commerce project, and who will be affected by the results?

✦ What critical processes are associated with the successful execution of the e-commerce project?

Source: "Start to Measure Your E-commerce Success," by Marc J. Epstein
Working Knowledge for Business Leaders,
http://hbswk.hbs.edu/item.jhtml?id=4401&t=managing_recovery

Years ago, standards were set for Electronic Data Interchange (EDI) to allow companies, vendors, manufacturers, suppliers, and customers to transmit purchase orders, invoices, and so on, to each other electronically. Initially, EDI information was transmitted over standard telephone lines (dial-up, leased, etc.). With the connectivity of the Internet, the same EDI data and files can be transmitted among the same organizations over the Web. The content and process is the same, only the transmission medium has changed. E-commerce offers several distinct advantages in the business-to-business model. A critical one is that a company can reduce, if not eliminate, the need to have brick-and-mortar stores, offices, and so on, in all the areas it wants to serve. Instead, they can move most of their operations to warehouse facilities in parts of the country with reduced labor, real estate, and operating expenses. In addition, by having the order placed by the customer directly into your company's order fulfillment systems, you can greatly reduce the labor normally involved in taking and processing a customer's order.

Some companies are now using their Web sites to allow suppliers and vendors to compete. A company can post an RFP stating they need to buy 10,000 widgets. Vendors can submit proposals and bids in what essentially amounts to a reverse auction (lowest price wins).

Businesses can also use the Web much like consumers do, to buy goods and products. But, instead of ordering in quantities of one or two, they are ordering by the case, or gross, or pallet. And, instead of using a credit card, a purchase order is issued.

Difficulties in Starting and Implementing E-commerce

While all those advantages make e-commerce sound like the greatest invention since pockets, there are some significant difficulties in implementing and executing a successful e-commerce plan.

Security Concerns

✦ In addition to being the victim of classic fraud schemes, e-commerce firms must also deal with the wealth of online scams that have proliferated at an exponential pace. Just as the Net allows you to sell your products to customers in Cairo, it allows hackers in The Netherlands to send orders using fake credit cards.

✦ Hacking is often compared to physical theft, as if stealing the cash in a cash register were similar to breaking into a company's HR records. The two may seem similar, but security measures haven't yet caught up to electronic methods of theft.

Demand

✦ The same ability to keep your doors open 24/7 can cause an overflow of demand. Many companies routinely under- or overestimate the online demand for their products. Not having enough green sweaters in the XXL size in a retail outlet can be pretty easily seen; not having enough of those sweaters in your online store may not be immediately apparent, cause many delayed orders, and generate a lot of ill-will.

Advertising

✦ Getting the word out on the advantage of your particular product is hard enough in the "real world," but getting noticed in the cyber world is very hard. It's much harder than it initially appears, often because people are told that "putting up a Web site isn't expensive." Putting up a Web site can be inexpensive, but it can also be very costly. But putting a site up isn't the big problem for most companies; getting it noticed and generating traffic, is.

✦ Using traditional advertising, as well as online search engines can help your (potential) customers, be they companies or individuals, know that your site is up and running and can be used for placing orders.

Staffing

✦ Creating a Web site is difficult enough, but maintaining one is much harder. Does your company have the resources to constantly and efficiently update your site? You might have a site that sells items: prices, quantities, shipping costs all change frequently. Perhaps you sell services and someone has to update the site to reflect the new offerings you have come up with. Maintaining a Web site is hard work. We all know how hard it is because we constantly go to sites that don't get updated regularly.

The Value of Selling over the Internet

There are several issues to consider when thinking about your e-commerce Web site:

✦ Your site has to be of a high quality. If customers are frustrated by slow response time, have difficulty figuring out how to place an order, encounter error messages, etc., they may not trust your site enough to fork over their credit card number, or their company's business. And given the short attention span and low annoyance threshold for users on the Web, you generally only have one chance to make that e-commerce sale to that customer. That's not so bad if they just decide to drive to the mall and visit your regular store instead, but perhaps they'll just visit your competitors' Web sites. If a customer encounters a rude clerk in your store, they still might come back. If a customer has a problem on your Web site, you may never see that e-customer again.

✦ You must be ready to handle the business, both from a computer traffic perspective as well as a product availability and shipment perspective.

✦ You must provide adequate security for the users of your site. Comfort is a large part of the selling process, and you need to provide your customers with confidence that the security that will protect their privacy. See Chapter 13, Security (page 349), for a more complete discussion of security issues. Not only is security important to protect things like your customers' credit card numbers, but it's also important to make sure your site stays up and running.

Is E-commerce Worth It?

Girding up for e-commerce isn't easy. On the front side, you need to make sure your customers and potential customers are aware of your Web site. On the back end, you need to be sure you have the inventory and other traditional mechanisms required for fulfilling the customer's request. But the excitement comes in the middle as your Web site connects these two sides and tries to do all the things that your sales representatives, store clerks, and phone operators normally do.

Although building a Web site can be fairly uncomplicated, the task of adding e-commerce functionality to your site is significantly more complicated. The other side of that issue, however, is that the rewards for creating and executing a successful e-commerce initiative are astronomical. Entire new markets, new buyers and sellers, and new business models emerge quickly in what has become known as the "digital economy."

The rules of this new economy are evolving rapidly, but the rewards to be reaped are often orders of magnitude larger than the old ones. It's interesting to note that a study by Ipsos Insight reported that 20 million Americans made online purchases of $2.00 or less in 2005. This shows that in addition to books, DVDs, clothing, and electronics consumers are willing to use the Net for very small purchases as well as large ones.

Value of E-commerce

"E-commerce ... is another vehicle — not the only one, but another one — that allows businesses to interact with their customers. Companies that have been using the Net for years (some have been regular users for over a decade) understand the power of personalization that selling on the Internet provides. No other medium provides the flexibility and the individualization."

—Nils Davis
Product Manager, NetIQ, San Jose, CA

Some Important Elements of an E-commerce Web Site

Some of the functions required of an e-commerce application are listed below.

- ✦ **Shopping cart:** This is the function that allows users to browse your "store and "catalog" and keep track of each item that they select for purchase.

✦ **Payment processing:** Since most e-commerce is paid for via credit card, you need to be able to accept credit card numbers, validate them to be sure they aren't fraudulent or stolen, forward the payment information to the credit card company for collection, and so on.

✦ **Shipping and handling calculations:** Because most Web purchases are sent directly to the consumer, you need to calculate the cost of the shipment (often giving the customer several choices in regard to speed of delivery) and include it in the total cost of the order.

✦ **Security provisions:** This is the way of encrypting critical data (e.g., credit card numbers) to minimize the chances of them being stolen while the information is sent over the World Wide Web, or from the database on your server. This is usually done using SSL, which is discussed in detail on page 373 in Chapter 13, Security.

✦ **Data exchange with other business applications:** Since the information is already in computer form after the customer enters the order, you'll want this data to feed into your business databases and applications. This might include accounts receivable, inventory, and shipping and receiving. In addition, you'll probably need to share this data with your business partners like credit card companies, fulfillment centers, and various carriers.

Many hosting companies can provide you with the above services. Of course, you can't even begin to consider getting into e-commerce until you've developed your Web site and created "catalog pages" or "store aisles" that will allow your customer to locate and select what they want. And, for some companies, e-commerce may be a complete change of business model. For example, it would be an enormous change for an appliance maker to get into e-business. If you think about it, appliance makers generally ship truckloads of their products to various appliance retail centers. The switch to e-commerce would require them to now ship units, one at a time, to individual consumer homes. This would have an enormous impact on their normal logistical operations. They might have to dispense with their fleet of trucks and partner with some of the existing nationwide carriers. It would also impact their invoicing and receivables operations since they'd now have a greater volume of transactions, each for a much smaller amount. In the end, it might generate more business and profits for the company, but it would be a significant change in business operations. And, it would alienate their stores and resellers, a different take on the situation discussed earlier in the chapter regarding Merrill Lynch's Web site and their brokers.

18.6 **Additional Resources**

Web Sites

- ✦ *manage.directi.com/kb* (Reseller Club Support knowledge base)
- ✦ *www.ecommercetimes.com* (e-commerce news)
- ✦ *www.icann.org* (information about Internet domain names, registrars, etc.)
- ✦ *www.intranet.com (pre-packaged intranet applications)*
- ✦ *www.isoc.org/internet/history* (Internet history)
- ✦ *vwww.mathaware.org/mam/04/6_Internet_structure.html* (A visualization of the network structure of the Internet)
- ✦ *www.online-commerce.com* (e-commerce primer)

Books and Articles

- ✦ Addison, Doug, *Web Site Cookbook: Solutions & Examples for Building and Administering Your Web Site*, O'Reilly Media, Inc., 2006.
- ✦ Alhadeff, Roni, *Succeeding in E-commerce, Insider Advice And Practical Tips*, Lulu Press, 2005.
- ✦ McDonald, Matthew, *Creating Web Sites: The Missing Manual*, O'Reilly Media, Inc., 2005.
- ✦ Microsoft Corporation, *Improving Web Application Security: Threats and Countermeasures*, 2003.
- ✦ Reynolds, Janice, *The Complete E-Commerce Book: Design, Build, and Maintain a Successful Web-Based Business*, CMP Books, 2004.
- ✦ Tredinnick, Luke, *Why Intranets Fail And How To Fix Them*, Chandos Publishing (Oxford) Ltd., 2004.
- ✦ Viney, David, *The Intranet Portal Guide (How to Make the Business Case)*, Mercury Web Publishing, 2005.

User Equipment

Computers are useless. They can only give you answers.

—PABLO PICASSO

Hardware technology advances rapidly. Each day brings newer buzzwords, stranger acronyms, and faster processors. What you buy today will probably be with you for several years, but you can't be sure the *manufacturer* will still be around at that time. One of the reasons the IT budget is so large is because of all the hardware you will be buying. This chapter offers you specific information on how to make intelligent and cost-effective decisions on technology solutions for your users such as desktops, laptops, and handheld devices.

19.1 User Equipment Issues You'll Face

You will face a variety of issues regarding IT equipment:

- ✦ Who gets what equipment
- ✦ Should you upgrade their equipment or not

CHAPTER NINETEEN

✦ Business versus personal use

✦ What to do if equipment is lost or stolen

One of your goals as the IT Manager is to define and document policies addressing issues such as these. The primary reason for documenting isn't for the user community (although that can be a real value). The real benefit of documenting policies is so that they are available to everyone in IT, which then means that they can be applied consistently across every decision. There will be exceptions to every policy, of course. But having policies documented is the first step in having standards. But it's not the policies alone that define behavior, it's the application of them that really makes it clear that the policy is in force.

Don't feel that your policies are carved in stone. It's not uncommon for policies and procedures to be defined, only to find that they need to be adjusted because they aren't working out as planned. And, it's certainly to be expected that circumstances will change over time, and that a policy that made sense two years ago just doesn't make sense today.

Wide Range of Policies

It is important to note that there is a wide range of corporate concerns about these four issues. Some companies don't care about mixing personal and business; often they are small companies, sometimes run out of garages, where the "company hard drive" is also the family hard drive.

If your company has this relaxed attitude about mixing personal and business equipment, and you aren't in a decision-making capacity, you should raise the issue anyway. If you're in a decision-making capacity, make sure everyone understands the consequences of these actions and try to get corporate policy to be explicit about this issue quickly. The stakes have risen dramatically in recent years for this kind of action — and inaction.

Who Gets What

The key word for this issue is "demonstrable." Does the person really need this? Sometimes it's your call, sometimes they have to get their manager's approval. If it's your call, be as polite as possible in determining the demonstrable need.

Don't turn things into an unnecessary power play. First try and determine *exactly* what the employee is asking for.

✦ They may have said they deserve a "new laptop," but what they mean is they want their computer to run faster. Maybe they really only need more memory, or to have you take all those illegal games off of their machine, or you need to remove all that spyware and adware that has taken up residence on their laptop.

✦ They may have said they need a "new operating system," but they really meant they need a half-day class in how to use MS Office.

After the exact need has been determined, articulate the time and money involved. Whose department is paying for this upgrade? (Some IT departments pay for all computer equipment, but many other companies have complex chargeback processes.) A new laptop may be in the storeroom (you keep five around for the revolving door that is the Sales department), or it may be a week before your supplier can get one to you.

As you go forward about the who-gets-what issues, you may want to consider allowing for a greater degree of flexibility over the issues that a number of users are very sensitive to. For example, a user may not care about how much RAM they get, but they could be extremely concerned about having an ergonomic keyboard.

Other items along these lines could include:

✦ Type of mouse (trackball, optical, wireless, etc.)

✦ Flat screen or tube, and the size of the monitor

✦ Anti-glare screen for monitor

✦ Privacy screen for monitor

✦ Wrist-rest devices

The above items might be considered "incidentals" in terms of the cost, and have virtually no bearing on the core technology. Offering the user their choice of these items may make them more agreeable to meeting other, more meaningful standards. (Besides, HR probably wouldn't want to hear that a user was complaining of carpal tunnel syndrome because IT was inflexible about buying a non-standard $49 ergonomic keyboard.)

Also see the section Issues that Users Care About (page 248) in Chapter 9, Getting Started with the Technical Environment, for more discussion on this topic.

To Upgrade or Not

You will be inundated with requests to upgrade user equipment, both hardware and software. Here are a few ideas about how to handle these situations.

✦ Decide whose call it is; the person requesting the new laptop may need their manager's approval, for example, or there might be other (more politically powerful) users ahead in line.

✦ Determine if there are financial issues; who is going to pay for the new hardware, and has the old item been fully depreciated yet.

✦ Run the numbers. Because of budget constraints, maybe only one user out of many can get a new desktop right away, but perhaps that person is the top sales guy.

✦ Figure out if it's a *predictable purchase* (like routine replacement of aged desktops and laptops), *semi-predictable purchase* (such as "the new company Web site is such a success, we need to upgrade the server in order to ensure appropriate performance"), or *completely unpredictable purchases* (like the VP of Finance suddenly telling you he has 10 new people starting on Monday and they all need equipment).

✦ Set the schedule. Many software installations are now handled centrally from the IT department and not on that department's schedule. When and how fast a company goes to a new operating system isn't an individual's call, but the IT department's call. The reasons are straightforward: It isn't about simple power plays ("who controls what") but about overall reliability and the complexities of all the users on one network being able to continue to work together. Entire systems have been brought down by one user introducing an unauthorized personal laptop into a corporate environment.

Business versus Personal

There will be widespread confusion about what the organization's policies are regarding this issue. As computers become omnipresent — everywhere at work and everywhere at home — the line between work and home becomes blurred.

It Can Be Confusing

It's important for the organization — generally led by you as the IT department manager — to help clearly define the organization's policies regarding using work equipment at home and vice versa.

The best idea is to write a policy (one that you make widely known and update regularly) that clearly outlines the company positions on these matters. Be as specific as possible. This chapter discusses individual hardware items such as cell phones, flash drives, and laptops.

The best idea for a policy is to be as clear as possible. Try not mix business and personal use if at all possible. This, of course, is easier said than done.

If a company provides an employee a cell phone, and the employee calls back to the office while on a trip, that is a company expense. But what if an employee uses a company cell phone to call a friend? Or talk at length while at work with a former co-worker about a potential job at another firm?

Even something as simple as employees using their own personal computer at home for work activity can get confusing. They may need to install applications on it (which will raise licensing issues), or perhaps they will want to upgrade the hardware to make those applications perform better. In general, those could be simple issues, but they could raise difficult questions: Who pays for that upgrade? What happens to it when the employee leaves the company? If that upgrade causes the rest of the system to malfunction, who is responsible for resolving the problem?

Limiting the use of company resources to company business is a common policy that most companies have spelled out somewhere. It's a policy that is often ignored for routine offenses (use of the copy machine, the occasional personal phone call and e-mail), but it's a convenient policy to have when more serious infractions arise.

See the individual items below for further discussions on particular items.

It Can Be Embarrassing

Mixing business and personal items can be embarrassing both for the individuals named as well as the entire organization. Boeing fired a CEO "because, among other things, he had the bad judgment to detail his actions and desires in a series of very explicit e-mails" to a co-worker with whom he was having an affair (*http://www.careerjournal.com/myc/killers/20050314-murray.html*).

It Can Raise Accountability Issues

Large business transactions (in fact, many business transactions, regardless of size) require auditability. If you or one of your employees has been using corporate equipment for personal reasons, you have legal problems. (See Chapter 8, IT Compliance and Controls, Section 8.2 Sarbanes-Oxley, page 203.) One example of where this problem can exist is with government contracts: After a disaster that brought on the need for large external contractors, the governor of the state pledged to have "auditors auditing auditors." That isn't an environment where you want to have any questions about personal use of corporate assets.

Security

Since security is such a driving concern, many organizations have policies in regard to desktop and laptop standards. For example, some may prohibit the use of CD and DVD drives to prevent the loading of unauthorized software. Some may allow these drives but for read-only, not for writing (to minimize the risk of company data being copied).

Another security issue occurs if the hardware is stolen and suddenly the data it contains is compromised. Careful backup and encryption are required to head this problem off at the pass.

Of course, with technology the way it is today with anywhere/anytime connectivity, and pocket-size devices like PDA and USB flash drives, it's becoming more and more difficult to limit a user's activities. With many handheld devices, a password can be implemented, and some of them (like Blackberry units) can be remotely erased and disabled when they are reported lost.

Who Is Liable When It's Lost/Stolen?

While this is more an issue for portable equipment (see the section Laptops, Hand-helds, and Other Portable Equipment on page 506), it's still something to consider in advance. Of course the company will pay for a desktop that stops working or a monitor that quits. The company will probably pay for the corporate cell phone that was lost on vacation. But who pays if the laptop is stolen during a personal visit to a place the employee wasn't supposed to be at, such as a competitor's site for a job interview? Similarly, what if the item is lost due to the employee's own negligence (like leaving a laptop in a cab, or giving it to the airline as checked baggage instead of carrying it on the plane)? Or, if the company expects the employees to use personal cell phones for business calls, but the phone is lost on a business trip. Who pays for the replacement? As much as possible, these issues need to be discussed in advance of the problem occurring.

19.2   Desktops

Factors to Consider

Typically, many organizations consider three years to be the expected life of a PC (although, depending on the circumstances, you may be able to get 4 or 5 years out of some). The driving force for the rapid aging of these machines is that as the available hardware gets more powerful, applications are developed for them, and the newer applications run too slow on older units. In fact, some have said that with faster and faster hardware getting cheaper and cheaper, software developers see no need to write "efficient" code; hence, the birth of "bloatware."

Specifications for Individual Components

When considering desktops, consider the following:

- ✦ Price
- ✦ Service
- ✦ Long-term vendor relationship
- ✦ Component consistency
- ✦ Performance
- ✦ User considerations
- ✦ Depreciation
- ✦ Recycling policy

Price   Obviously this is the first choice, but not the only issue. The real price (see Chapter 9, Getting Started with the Technical Environment, the section TCO on page 244) may be tough to judge with new models and configurations being announced weekly. Leasing is now a common option for PC purchases. Leasing is discussed on page 172 of Chapter 6, Budgeting.

Service   Many vendors, especially those selling to the corporate market, include on-site service as a standard (or as an inexpensive option) part of the warranty coverage. Also, check the quality of the tech support (24/7, hold time, expertise, etc.).

Long-Term Vendor Relationship   Will the vendor be around in three years? If you're tempted to buy no-name or "white-box" devices, you risk that the off-brand components may cause problems with future versions of operating systems and application software. See Chapter 7, Managing Vendors.

Component Consistency   Corporate environments are often leery of equipment marketed at consumers, primarily because the manufacturer may switch brands of components depending on source availability and pricing. This leads to PCs that are identical in model number, but could be very different in regard to the makeup of the internal components. This technique can cause support head-aches among your staff in regard to repairs, hardware drivers, configurations, and so on.

Performance   With hardware specifications varying widely, and PCs priced as low as $500 and up to $3,000 or more, it's difficult to know whether to buy a bargain at the low end, or to buy at the high end in hopes of getting the most bang for the buck. There is no right or wrong answer to the question; it's part financial and part philosophy of technology. The difference between the low end and the high end really amounts to how much useful life you think you can get out of a PC. A $500 device might be considered a disposable machine that you replace every 18–24 months. On the other hand, a $2,000 unit should serve you a lot longer.

User Considerations   Some users like getting new equipment ("technology envy"), even if the new hardware has no impact on how they do their job. On the other hand, some users fear the disruption of new equipment, thinking that they just got the old one working the way they like, and now it's being taken away.

Depreciation   Your finance department may not like the idea of corporate assets being replaced too often — especially if it's replaced before it has been fully depreciated on the corporate books.

Recycling Policy   What do you do with the old PCs? Many vendors (notably Hewlett-Packard) have very robust recycling policies.

19.3 Laptops, Hand-helds, and Other Portable Equipment

Mobile devices, by their very nature, allow users to use them in a variety of locations and for a variety of uses. Some of those locations and some of those uses will be work related, but some won't. See the section Wide Range of Policies earlier in this chapter for a discussion of this issue and the importance of setting clear company policies on the use of corporate equipment.

Laptops

IT Managers need (as has been mentioned often in this book) to carefully define the requirements of users — which is a process that must involve discussions with those users. If your company doesn't have people who travel a great deal and work from home or work from remote locations, laptops may make little sense for your user base. A laptop's primary advantage is its portability; it allows the knowledge worker to be a mobile worker. Some users want laptops to do some e-mail or basic word processing while away from the office. Others may want their laptop for doing presentations. Many of the factors that go into choosing a workstation also apply to choosing a laptop.

Specifications for Individual Components

- ✦ CPU speed
- ✦ Screen size
- ✦ Battery life
- ✦ Connectivity options
- ✦ Weight
- ✦ Number and types of slots
- ✦ Docking station/port replicator
- ✦ Service
- ✦ Price

CPU Speed   Sometimes you can lose CPU speed when you move from a desktop to a laptop. Desktops are always the fastest machines available; laptops lag behind. You lose speed but you gain portability. You can work on a laptop in an airport, but you can hardly carry your desktop around with you. If you find that users are requesting laptops even though they don't have a real justification for them, you may find you can dissuade them with a simple reference to the fact that laptops are slower than desktops.

Screen Size   Laptop screens generally range from about 12 inches (diagonally) to 17 inches. Many users will prefer the smaller screen since it generally means a smaller, lighter, and more portable device. Others may prefer a larger screen because it's easier to work with, or if they're using the device to give ad hoc presentations at customer sites.

Battery Life   The Holy Grail of battery life is the cross-country airplane ride — 5 to 6 hours. If the battery can last that long, it will garner 100% of the market. Unfortunately, no one has nabbed it yet. (Although they are definitely getting closer.)

 Don't believe the numbers listed in the specs in the ads; those numbers for battery life are only relevant if the user simply turns the machine on and leaves it sitting alone. If the user actually uses the machine, opens applications, saves to disk, and so on, the inflated numbers in the ads can be cut by one-half or one-quarter. Don't forget: The battery life is significantly impacted by the use of the computer and the power management configuration settings. As the use of the laptop increases, the battery life drops faster.

One bright spot to this issue is that many airlines are now installing power outlets on their planes, so the Holy Grail of battery life isn't as important as it once was.

Connectivity Options   Virtually every laptop comes with a modem and Ethernet network connection as a standard. Many are now also coming with integrated wireless services as standard, or available as an option. Even if your office doesn't have a wireless network, the convenience of wireless outside the office at coffee shops, hotels, and airports makes it a worthwhile feature.

Weight   This is an issue that can appear less important to the (typically non-traveling) IT Manager than to her users. A couple of ounces or a pound may not seem much to someone who goes to a conference once or twice a year, but to a person who travels weekly with that bag over her shoulder, that number is important. Find out just how important it is to your user base. And remember, the "carry weight" (the amount pulling on that shoulder) is more than the weight of the laptop. It may include cables, adapters, the charger, and external devices (floppy/CD drive, etc.). Today, 4 lbs for a laptop is on the light side, 7 lbs is considered heavy.

Writeable CD and DVD drives are now common options in laptops. For the smaller devices, these optical drives are external to the laptop and are connected by a cable. In the larger laptops, the optical drive is built-in to the unit. This also comes in as a personal preference. Some users may not like the external devices because it's another piece to be tracked and possibly misplaced. Others may prefer the external device because it means they don't have to carry the extra weight if they don't need to.

Number and Types of Slots   Laptops usually support a slot or two for expansion cards. These were originally referred to as the Personal Computer Memory Card International Association (PCMCIA) cards, and then later known as PC Cards and CardBus. The latest iteration of this is the Express Card. While popular and important when first introduced, the use of these expansions cards is waning with the growing popularity of USB devices, and more features being built-in to the base unit.

Docking Station/Port Replicator   Once rare items, these units are now almost standard items when buying corporate laptops. A replicator is a small device that allows a user to "dock" their laptop into it; once docked, the laptop can then be used just like a desktop. The cables are connected to the replicator and don't have to be unhooked each time the laptop is undocked.

Service Laptops are more prone to problems, in part from being bounced around when being carried, in part because the advanced technology inside a small space makes them more delicate than desktops. Many IT departments have had repeated success with one laptop manufacturer, and they stick with what works. The manufacturer knows this and tries to encourage it by allowing generous volume discounts, letting the company in on non-advertised specials, giving them advance notice on upcoming products, and so on. Find out about service options available from your vendor. Is the technical support staff knowledgeable? How are repairs handled? Overnight exchange? Return to factory? What about damage from accidents (e.g., being dropped, spilled coffee)?

Price This shouldn't be your only, nor should it be your last, criterion for how to buy a laptop. Get a number and use it along with the other criteria mentioned above to make the decision. If you're buying multiple machines, factor in a discount. But try to achieve a number that you can use with other criteria to arrive at the machine you want to buy.

Bluetooth

Bluetooth is an industry standard that allows wireless communication between devices. Each device must be "Bluetooth compatible." If they are, communication can occur at up to speeds of 1 Mbps and above. It has become the standard for communication between portable devices; servers don't connect using Bluetooth standards, but a cell phone and a PDA do. Bluetooth is also discussed in more depth in Chapter 12, Networking (page 325).

Handheld Equipment

The range of equipment that IT could be responsible for can include, but isn't limited to, the following:

+ Hand-helds/Portable Digital Assistants (PDAs)
+ Cell phones
+ Flash drives

Hand-helds/PDAs

We've come a long way from room-sized computers (the ENIAC weighed 30 tons) to today's multi-purpose handheld computers (PDAs now weigh in the 4 to 7 *ounce* range). Back then, you could only compute ballistic tables for the Air Force; now you can access the Web, get e-mail, download the latest PowerPoint presentation, take a phone call, listen to music, and perform an innumerable series of other functions, including look-up the address book, check the calendar, take a picture, etc.

More and more functions that used to be performed by a variety of pieces of hardware, including laptops, cell phones, and PDAs, are now being merged into a single device.

Hand-helds now carry the burden pagers carried when they appeared; at first, there was some excitement about being important enough to merit your company buying you one. But that excitement soon fades as you realize the new hardware makes the task of separating work life and non-work life almost impossible. The *New Yorker* cartoon in the mid-1990s of the father taking a (obviously work-related) cell phone call while swinging his toddler on the swing set now no longer seems all that funny.

Handheld devices have a particular array of burdens for IT policies:

+ Users can be quite emphatic about which device they want, often based on issues like appearance, size, weight, fads, etc., without any concern as to function or technology.

+ Each handheld device has its own set of accessories, such as belt clip, batteries, cables, styli, carrying cases, etc.

+ In addition to choosing the hardware, there are also various choices for service carriers, service plans, and coverage issues, which are all further complicated by the fact that not all devices will work with all service carriers.

One Example of How PDAs Are Being Used in the "Real World"

"While applications and application development for hand-helds are still somewhat limited, some stunning developments have already been made that clearly demonstrate the power of hand-helds. I develop apps for healthcare professionals, so I see firsthand the changes that are taking place.

Most of the general public is only slowly beginning to realize the difference between a laptop and a hand-held. Handheld devices provide the opportunity to use technology in new ways and in new places. Hand-helds are real-time devices with increasing computing power and data storage capacity. Their abilities are just now being truly demonstrated.

(Cont.)

Everyone knows about the tablets the UPS guy and the oil change guys use. You may have even had your food order taken by a stewardess on a plane with a mobile device. But in the medical world, the changes have been more significant than just mere convenience. They have dramatically improved the quality of care that is being delivered along with the standardization of care.

The Health Professional is at the Bedside with a PDA and can follow Consensus Treatment Algorithms/Guidelines.

In other words, he isn't trying to remember (or figure out) what the most current treatment modality is — because his PDA provides instant access to all of the approved and recommended methodologies, methodologies that were arrived at by many expert doctors' research and consensus, not one doctor's opinion.

A direct consequence of using a PDA like this is that the quality of care is raised and a "Standard of Care" is developed; all medical practitioners are now walking down the same path and the overall continuity of care is proportionally improved.

In addition, all of the patient information is now available: he has immediate access to patient's medical information regardless if he is in his office or not. If a doctor gets a call over the Thanksgiving weekend, he can access the patient's chart, history, etc., while out of the office.

Medical care now becomes much more accountable, of course, because up-to-the-minute data allows for better and more timely decisions; rather than wait for a paper report to be mailed to the doctor. With wireless technology and digital photography, now the doctor can see a digital photo of a wound taken by a nurse in the patient's home with a PDA while he sits in front of his PC in his office.

Other applications include disease management programs, patient medical record management, risk and clinical assessments, scheduling, and billing.

Using Wireless Technology with an Internet-Based, Shared Secured Server in a Group Medical Practice or Hospital Setting

PDA technology, databases, and cross-platform applications allow data to be collected by multiple users using either the PDA or a desktop computer. Data (patient health information) that is collected out in the field (home care, nursing homes, assisted living facilities) by multiple health professionals can be transmitted wirelessly via a smart phone to a secure server allowing access to the aggregate data of all patients served by all health professionals or billing coordinators that are provided with such access."

Stephen Feldman, Chief Developer
Hand-Medical.com

Cell Phones

You may be given the task of buying, organizing, tracking, and distributing cell phones for your organization. While many IT tasks are thankless (often because no one outside IT understands how difficult they are — upgrading 220 desktop operating systems isn't just "popping in a CD and letting it run," for example), managing cell phones is a particularly thankless job. Almost everyone has one at home now, and many expect one at work as well. Many need one at work and many don't. And no one is ever going to say "Thank you for doing such a great job of managing all of the company's cell phones."

Then there's the complexity of tracking usage. Usage of this asset is difficult to monitor carefully; even the most conscientious user (and there aren't many of those) can be tripped up by the unknown factor of the cost of incoming calls. And if you have ever seen a home cell phone bill, try to imagine what a corporate bill looks like: It isn't a pretty sight — they can be several hundred pages long.

Also, mixing business and pleasure (or "company" and "non-company" use) is most pronounced when it comes to cell phones. Examples earlier in this chapter point to the difficulties: Are calls to home while traveling a company expense? And, even more challenging is going through the bills and attempting to identify company versus personal calls.

With cell phones there is a question of who owns the device (some companies buy the phones for the employees to use, others reimburse for use of the employees' own cell phone), as well as the question of who is liable for the charges (some companies pay the bills directly, others expect the employees to pay, and submit T&Es for reimbursement). Policies vary widely from company to company, and are often decided with input from HR, IT, and Accounting.

See Chapter 7, Managing Vendors (page 179), for a detailed discussion on how to evaluate different vendors' products. Regarding cell phones, the old adage "give them the razor and sell them the blades" applies. The overall cost-per-minute charge is the most relevant, not the thirty free phones they give you. And, as in any complex purchase, the more you understand about your current needs, the better a buyer you will be. (Anticipating future phone use, however, is very, very difficult. Be warned.)

Flash Drives

While all computers may some day talk to all other computers (that's the theory, anyway), many computers still don't talk to each other. Some don't for perfectly good reasons: Security considerations, for example, are making systems more closed, not more open. Or, as is more likely the case, just when you need to network your computer, you don't have a convenient network connection available.

But sometimes the issues are more mundane such as Jane is at the meeting with her laptop and Tom arrives with the changes he made last night to the presentation. If her laptop wireless card was working, she could retrieve the changes he sent her from her e-mail. But she's sitting in a corner of the building where there is no wireless coverage. Covering all of his bases, Tom has shown up with the presentation on his flash drive, too, thereby saving the day.

Flash drives are small, very portable, easy to use, and easy to lose hard drives. They plug directly into USB ports and have rapidly become the "sneakernet" tool of the new century. (Webopedia refers to sneakernet as "the channel by which electronic information is transmitted from one computer to another by physically carrying it stored on a floppy disk, CD, or other removable medium.") Flash drives are the new "removable medium."

19.4　Additional Resources

Web Sites

✦ *whatis.techtarget.com* (IT-specific encyclopedia)

✦ *www.bluetooth.com* (short range connectivity standard)

✦ *www.brighthand.com* (news and reviews of handheld devices)

✦ *www.cnet.com* (tech community with product reviews, articles, etc.)

✦ *www.dell.com* (desktop and laptop product manufacturer and vendor)

✦ *www.gateway.com* (desktop and laptop product manufacturer and vendor)

✦ *www.idg.com* (IT trade journal publisher)

✦ *www.lenovo.com* (desktop and laptop product manufacturer and vendor)

✦ *www.palm.com* (handheld product manufacturer and vendor)

✦ *www.rim.com* (handheld product manufacturer and vendor)

✦ *www.techrepublic.com* (tech community)

✦ *www.wired.com* (tech publication)

✦ *www.ziffdavis.com* (IT trade journal publisher)

Books and Articles

✦ Garcia, Andrew, "Lock Out Problems: System Lockdown Isn't Always Easy, but It's a Powerful Protection," *eWeek*; November 28, 2005, p. 35.

✦ Wailgum, Thomas, "Mastering Mobile Madness," *CIO Magazine*, December 1, 2005, p. 74.

Disaster Recovery

. . . I have always found that plans are useless, but planning is indispensable.

—DWIGHT D. EISENHOWER

It's no secret that the daily routine of everyday life is highly dependent on information technology. And incidents like September 11, 2001, hurricanes Katrina and Rita in 2005, the blackout of the Northeast in August, 2003, and many other crises serve as regular reminders that we have to be prepared for the worst. This is where disaster recovery comes in.

Disaster recovery is like buying insurance; you're planning for the worst, but all the time hoping that it doesn't happen. IT disasters come in all shapes and sizes, from hardware failures and computer viruses, to blizzards, floods, and terrorist attacks.

Today, IT environments are replete with all kinds of solutions to deal with various outages and failures: redundant servers, transaction logs, backups, RAID disk drives, and so on. The problem with these kinds of solutions is that each can only handle the failure of a specific

CHAPTER TWENTY

component. This leaves IT Managers with the issue of what to do if the *entire* environment fails.

As you will see in this chapter, the key to good disaster recovery is the involvement of as many components of the organization as possible. IT can be the leader or motivator (even that isn't required, but it's a common situation), but all facets of a company must be involved in the planning of a disaster. The reason is simple: Disasters of every size (from brief power outages to city-wide blackouts) affect every department and affect every employee and possibly your customers and suppliers, too. Everyone should be ready.

20.1   Defining the Scope

The extent to which you as an IT Manager have to, or can, plan for a disaster is directly related to how much your organization is dependent on IT for its core business operation — and how much money your organization is willing to invest to protect it.

When you start to think about disaster recovery, and the infinite combination of things that could go wrong and what you might have to plan for, you can easily find yourself in a cold sweat, thinking there is simply no way you have it all covered.

Key Questions

One of the most important steps in disaster recovery planning is trying to define the scope. While it's inconceivable to think of every scenario, you can help put things in perspective with questions like:

- ✦ Which exactly are the critical applications and services?

- ✦ How quickly do you have to recover those critical applications and services (Seconds? Minutes? Hours? Days?)

- ✦ What are the different scenarios to plan for?

  - No access to the building (e.g., snow storm)

  - Loss of data center (flood, fire)

  - Loss of building (fire, hurricane, collapse)

  - Loss of some public services (mass transit, phone service, electricity, etc.)

- Geographic impact (a blackout that effects just a few blocks in your city, or one that effects 50 million people across several states such as the blackout in August of 2003)

✦ How long of an interruption should be planned for? (Days? Weeks? Indefinitely?)

✦ How quickly do I need access to my data and systems? And, is last week's backup good enough, or do we need to be able to restore more current data?

Notice the range of disasters you need to think about: one-to-three day events like snow storms all the way up to events like terrorist attacks that have permanently changed the way we think about certain things.

Obviously, these are questions you can't answer alone, and can be the subject of endless discussion. The answers will vary greatly depending on the size of your organization, the industry you're in, and probably most critically, the cost of the required resources.

Once the scope is agreed to by the key departments (HR, IT, Facilities, Legal, etc.), it's critical that it have the support of company executives. At a minimum, this would probably include the CIO and CFO. But there are others that should be considered. For example, the Legal department and the departments that deal with regulatory compliance may need to weigh in with their thoughts. It is not unheard of for the scope to be presented to the Board of Directors, or perhaps one of the Board's committees.

During the process of defining the scope, you can expect to be educating others about your IT environment. Some of the people you're working with may assume that since they hear the word server so often, they think that the company has just one, not 100. They may think of the computer room as that rack they saw in a closet 5 years ago, and have no idea that it's now a 2,500 square foot facility with dedicated environmental services. In short, you'll be explaining to them what is a mountain, and what is a mole hill.

Scope Definition Phase

As part of the scope definition phase, you'll want to determine two key objectives:

1. Recover Time Objective (RTO) — The amount of time between the disaster, and when services are restored.

2. Recover Point Objective (RPO) — the age, or "freshness," of the data available to be restored.

RPO and RTO are sometimes best illustrated graphically (see Figure 20.1).

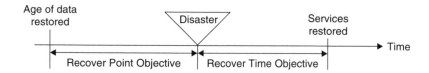

Figure 20.1   RPO and RTO

Disaster Recovery Committee

To get the answers to the questions posed above, you'll need to work closely with others. Although it relies heavily on IT, disaster planning and recovery isn't a function of IT alone. It requires the involvement of a number of other departments, including:

+ Finance

+ Human Resources

+ Legal

+ Key user departments (Manufacturing, Customer Service, etc.)

+ Building Facilities

A committee like this can also help determine what the priorities are in the event of a disaster. What about Customer Service? Financial stability? Regulatory compliance? Health and Safety? These answers can vary greatly depending in the organization's industry. A Web-based e-tailer may consider continued customer service as its key priority as a way of protecting its financial stability. A publicly traded financial services company may place a high priority on investor relations, regulatory compliance, and financial stability. A hospital may be willing to sacrifice all those things because it's focusing on the health and safety of its patients.

There are no standard answers to these questions and issues. Each organization must consider them and come to a decision about their own priorities. And the answers won't come easily or quickly. It could easily take months just to determine the answers, and all this must happen before you can begin to formulate the actual disaster recovery plans. Because of questions like these, and many more, it's important that the planning not be limited to IT alone.

The committee can serve not only to develop the plan, but also, in the event of a disaster, serve as a decision-making body — one that provides leadership and guidance to the rest of the organization for the duration of the disaster recovery effort.

Application Assessment

In Chapter 9, Getting Started with the Technical Environment (page 231), we talked about inventorying your applications. This inventory will be a critical tool for disaster recovery planning. With this list, you can begin to assess, along with other departments, the criticality of your business's applications.

You'll want to set up some guidelines for the assessment, probably along the framework of your organization's priorities (see the section above, Defining the Scope). For example, if continued customer service is a key priority, you'll have to identify those applications that are associated with customer service.

In all likelihood, you'll probably end up with several priorities of applications.

An example of those applications, as shown in Figure 20.2 below, might be:

✦ Priority 1: Those applications that need to be returned to service within 6 business hours.

✦ Priority 2: Those applications that need to be returned to service within 24–48 hours.

✦ Priority 3: Those applications that need to be returned to service within 3–7 days.

✦ Priority 4: Those applications that need to be returned to service within 1–2 weeks.

✦ Priority 5: Those applications that can wait more than 2 weeks to be returned to service.

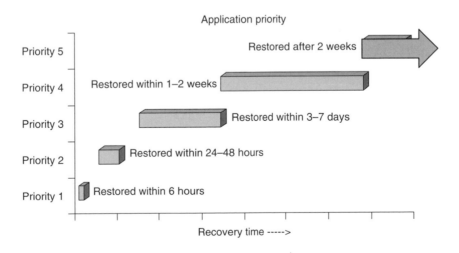

Figure 20.2   Sample Application Recovery Priorities

Again, the specifics of the application prioritization, as well as the number of priorities, will vary tremendously from organization to organization.

At the same time you're considering application priorities, you have to consider how much data loss you can tolerate. For example, in a payroll system, it may not be that much of a problem if the last two days of changes have to be re-entered (because the last backup available was taken 48 hours prior to the disaster, and not many changes occurred since then). In a brokerage house trading system, the tolerance for data loss might be at zero, necessitating real-time replication of all data. And, the volume of data change in these two scenarios are very different.

You may choose to define a Priority Zero for your applications, which would include the core services. This could include items like a network environment, remote connectivity, Internet access, DNS and DHCP services, etc. For many organizations, e-mail might be considered a Priority Zero application, along with telephone services, etc.

20.2 Create a Disaster Recovery Plan

Once you have the scope, and identified the critical applications, you can begin to develop a plan. If you expect to have any hope for any level of success in the event of a disaster, there are several key items you must have:

+ **Communication plan:** A plan for contacting key personnel, customers, vendors, and so on.

+ **Documentation:** Written material describing the existing environment, procedures for declaring a disaster, procedures for re-establishing services in a disaster recovery mode, etc.

+ **Real estate and IT facilities:** Where will people meet if the facility is suddenly off-limits, inaccessible, or out of commission? Where can you set up servers?

+ **Off-site storage of data:** If your facility is destroyed, or inaccessible, you'll want to be sure you have an up-to-date copy of your data at an off-site facility.

+ **Hardware availability:** You want to make sure that you can get replacement hardware if yours is destroyed. This list could include workstations, servers, routers, switches, storage (disk and tape), etc.

+ **Regular updating and testing:** Your environment changes regularly (technology, people, needs, organization, procedures, etc.). You need to regularly test and update your disaster recovery plan to make sure it retains its value.

Each of these items is discussed in detail below.

Communication Plan

The hallmark of a good disaster recovery plan is good communications. Disasters don't necessarily happen when everyone is sitting at their desk. They can happen on weekends or in the middle of the night. People may be on vacation, at off-site meetings, or in transit.

To ensure you can get word to people in an emergency, you should have a call list that includes information such as:

◆ Home phone number(s)

◆ Cell phone number(s)

◆ PIN number(s) for handheld devices

◆ Non-work e-mail address(es)

You may also want this list to include the geographic location of each person's home, as well as cell phone carrier(s). This information could be useful to quickly identify those people that may (or may not) be impacted in an isolated disaster, or those using a carrier struggling with restoring service.

Your list should include individuals from within the company and from outside the company.

◆ All members of IT

◆ Key executives

◆ Individuals from key departments (Facilities, HR, etc.)

◆ Key partners and suppliers (vendors, telecomm carriers, off-site storage facility)

◆ Appropriate regulatory agencies

For some contacts (like vendors and suppliers), you should also be sure that your contact list includes appropriate identifying information (like account numbers) to help avoid delays and confusion.

The list should exist in electronic form (such as on your PC, hand-held, USB memory drive, etc.) as well as in paper form in multiple locations (home, office, car, predetermined off-site meeting locations). In a situation where a large number of individuals have to be contacted, you may want to define a phone tree. Alternatively (or in addition), you can consider using a third party service like Send Word Now (*www.sendwordnow.com*) that can facilitate communications to very large groups of people quickly through multiple mechanisms.

Documentation

Thorough and up-to-date disaster recovery documentation is the foundation of an effective disaster recovery plan. Although the document can be distributed in electronic form (Web posting, word-processing document, USB memory drive), it should also be distributed on hard copy. After all, in the event of a disaster, there is no certainty that you'll be able to access the electronic version. (We don't like to admit it, but sometimes that note you scribbled on the back of a restaurant receipt ends up being more accessible than that Outlook reminder you sent yourself last Thursday.)

Every key member should have at least two copies — one copy in their office and one in their home — since there is no guarantee that a disaster will happen between 9 and 5 on a business day. Lastly, keep a copy with your off-site backup tapes.

This document will become an indispensable resource. Memories fail, particularly in a crisis. In fact, aside from your backup tapes, your disaster recovery plan may be the only resource available to you during a disaster. As such, it's in your best interest to make it as useful as possible by including as much information as possible in this document. This should include documentation about the existing environment, such as those areas discussed in Chapter 9.

All documentation should be reviewed and updated at least once a year to reflect changes to the environment, operations, procedures, etc. These review opportunities can be a great time to keep key people current on the plans — don't assume that everyone will read the plans on their own.

Real Estate and IT Facilities

One of the first questions that has to be considered in regard to disaster recovery planning is: "Where should we go now?" If you're unable to use your organization's facilities, where will everyone go when disaster strikes? If your organization is very small, you might be able get away with operating for a small time out of someone's residence. A slightly larger organization might be able to use a meeting or banquet room at a nearby hotel, assuming that the same disaster hasn't wiped out those facilities. Other alternatives might include a nearby branch office of your organization, or perhaps the office of a sister, subsidiary, or parent company.

However, if your IT organization is of any size, you're probably going to need specialized facilities with sufficient space, air conditioning, electricity, telecommunications resources, and so on. This may be the case even if you're only supporting a portion of your normal operation, even for just an interim period.

There are many companies that offer disaster recovery facilities. They can generally tailor their offerings to your needs, perhaps just providing space, or at the other extreme, provide specified computer hardware, telecommunications, and perhaps even some staffing. There are several disaster recovery service providers listed in the Additional References section at the end of this chapter.

Of course, the ultimate in disaster recovery facilities is for an organization to maintain its own standby site with redundant hardware. In the most critical situation, the standby site is always live, with a mirrored copy of the database, applications, and so on.

Disaster Recovery Facilities Considerations

When looking at companies that provide disaster recovery facilities, you have to consider several issues:

✦ **Proximity to your location:** You generally want a nearby location in order to get to it easily, but not so close that the facility is likely to be hit by the same disaster that affects yours. You may need to consider a facility that is reachable by mass transit if you're in a large metropolitan area where not everyone has their own car.

✦ **Costs:** The more services and facilities you want to be ready for your needs, the more it will cost. Contracts for disaster recovery usually last at least two years and are billed monthly. However, there are several aspects to disaster recovery fees:

– Standby fees: The monthly fees you pay to have contracted facilities available for your use

– Activation fee: A fee you pay when you decide that you have a disaster that warrants use of the facilities

– Use fee: The rate (weekly, monthly) that you pay while you're using the facilities during a disaster

– Test fee: A fee that is paid when you want to make use of the facilities while testing your disaster recovery plans

✦ **Number of Clients:** You want to make sure that the provider you're working with hasn't contracted with more clients than it can provide services for. If there is a regional disaster, and all the provider's customers suddenly need to use the facilities, will there be enough to go around?

✦ **Other Required Services:** Space, hardware, staff, telecommunications, air conditioning, electricity? Don't forget basics like furniture, phones, and so on.

In the event of a disaster, one of the critical decision points is when to fail-over to the recovery site. In the event of a catastrophe like an earthquake that destroys your primarily facility, the decision is pretty easy. But, in the case of a blackout, it is reasonable to think that the power will be back on soon enough, and the time, cost, and effort to bring the disaster recovery facility (along with the reverting back to the primary facility) does not outweigh the benefits of being down for a few hours.

Because of this, many environments don't configure their hardware and software to automatically fail-over to the backup facilities if a problem is detected at the primary site. Often, the fail-over process is something that has to wait for a human decision and be specifically initiated.

Off-Site Storage of Data

Backup Tapes

If you need to activate a disaster recovery plan, make sure that you can get your company's systems and data up and available. Most likely, you'll have to do some sort of restore from your backup tapes. If your regular facility is destroyed or inaccessible, you'll have to retrieve the backup tapes from your off-site storage vendor.

To get those tapes, you'll need several items:

✦ Contact information for your off-site location

✦ A method of identifying which set of tapes you want retrieved

✦ A customer ID, account number, and possibly a password as a way of identifying yourself to the off-site location as someone authorized to request that the tapes be retrieved

✦ The address (and probably directions to the location) of where the tapes should be delivered. (You most likely won't want them delivered to your usual facility)

Getting the tapes is the first step. Then you have to begin the restore process. You'll need to make sure that you have access to compatible hardware and software that can read those tapes, and that you have procedures for doing the restore. And, if you normally encrypt your backup tapes, you'll need to make sure that your recovery site has the appropriate technology and copies of the "encryption keys" to ensure that the backup tapes can be unencrypted.

Data Replication

If you have a dedicated disaster recovery facility, with hardware, there are a number of options, in addition to backup tapes, that you can use for making data readily available in an emergency.

✦ A number of storage vendors (e.g., EMC, NetApps, Hewlett-Packard, etc.) have solutions for replicating data between sites. These utilities don't duplicate the entire data set, but merely the changes (usually referred to as the "deltas"), which results in the two copies being in synch. Similarly, there are third party utilities that can do the same thing (Double Take, PowerSync, XOsoft, Neverfail, etc.).

✦ Database vendors (e.g., Oracle, Microsoft SQL Server) have features and utilities for keeping multiple copies of databases in synch. Similar to the data replication feature discussed in the previous bullet, this is strictly for databases.

✦ Transaction logs can be regularly replicated to your secondary site where they can be imported into the copy of the database.

Hardware Availability

If your regular computer hardware is unusable for any reason (e.g., power outage or destruction of your facilities), you'll have to quickly get your hands on some computer hardware before you can even begin rebuilding your environment.

Size of Your Environment

The smaller and more generic your environment is, the more solutions you'll have. For example, if your environment is based on Intel PCs and servers, you may be able to rely on local retailers or your regular reseller. Or you can contract with your disaster recovery facility to keep a quantity of these units on hand for you.

With larger or more complex environments, it will be more difficult (and more expensive) to make sure the equipment will be available. You may want to purchase some of this equipment yourself to have in an emergency, or your disaster recovery provider may do this and pass the cost on to you. Your manufacturer may also have options and provisions available to allow for you to receive emergency delivery of specified equipment in the event of a disaster.

For larger environments you may consider having a dedicated facility, either at your own site, or from a disaster recovery provider, that is a running environment with all your necessary hardware.

Duplicating Your Entire Environment

In case of a disaster, you may not need to duplicate your entire environment. You probably just want to plan for bringing up the systems that are the most critical to the continued operation and survival of the organization (as discussed in the section Application Assessment on page 519). To make sure your recovery operation is as smooth as possible, you'll want to ensure that you're using equipment as comparable and similar to possible to your existing environment. The middle of a crisis isn't the time to find out that the emergency tape drive you have isn't compatible with the backup tapes you use, or that you don't have the proper drivers for the network interface cards you're using, or that your application software has to be recompiled before it will run on the hardware you have.

Equipment at Home

If your plan includes people working from home, be sure they have what they need.

- ✦ Workstation with appropriate software (either the application they need, and/or software for remote access to reach those applications and data). If it's a laptop you gave them strictly to be used in the event of a disaster, you'll want to periodically check the laptop to make sure it's still functioning, has up-to-date software, etc.

- ✦ Will broadband access be available in a disaster, or will they have to use dial-up?

- ✦ Familiarity with procedures for connecting remotely (especially for connecting to a recovery site).

Regular Updating and Testing

A disaster recovery plan needs to be regularly reviewed and updated. Just as important is periodically testing the plan. (See the next section, Testing, for details on testing your plan.)

Review and Update

At least once a year you should review your plan for the following:

- ✦ Is the emergency contact list current? Check it to verify it doesn't contain individuals who have left the company or are no longer relevant to the plan, and that the information on the list is accurate.

- ✦ Are your own internal safety nets still working? You've probably installed a number of redundant resources to use in case of emergency. However, too often, when an emergency strikes, the backup facility fails because it isn't working either. Perhaps it hasn't been used for so long that it's fallen into disrepair. Or, perhaps it hasn't been kept up to date with upgrades. Regular testing of your redundant resources is important. A spare tire is of no use if there's no air in it.

- ✦ Can the backup tapes be read by the equipment at the backup site?

- ✦ Do you have copies of the media and installation instructions for the requisite software (operating systems, backup software, etc.) that may have to be installed before you can begin restoring your data from tape?

- ✦ Do you have current critical passwords?

Testing

To make sure your plan is of value, you need to periodically test it. This can be an enormous task, and requires a fair amount of planning of its own:

- ✦ You'll need a way to take your primary site off line (or at least have it seem off line). You may be able to power down your environment, or disconnect its WAN connections. Regardless, your monitoring and management solution will start sending a number of alerts.

- ✦ You want to develop a test plan and script to run through to make a determination if things are working as expected.

- ✦ You'll need to coordinate with all parts of IT and user department representatives to prepare for and participate in the test.

- ✦ To make sure you get the most value from the test, you want to have a rigorous postmortem process to evaluate what aspects didn't work, why they didn't work, and what has to be changed so that they'll work the next time.

If there is simply no way to plan downtime to your production environment (perhaps because your organization runs 24/7), you may have to consider doing tests in phases, just a few systems or components at a time. In very large environments, it can take months to plan out a single test of a disaster recovery plan.

Don't be surprised if your testing isn't 100% successful. Developing and testing disaster recovery plans is an iterative process. And, better to identify problems during a test, than during a real crisis.

After the Disaster

An often forgotten aspect of disaster recovery planning is the steps required once the disaster abates and things can return to normal. While in disaster-recovery mode, you've been running critical systems and applications out of your disaster recovery facility. When the disaster is over, and you can return to your primary facility, you now need to have a plan to get the data from the disaster recovery facility (which now has the most current data) back to your primary site.

The process will probably be somewhat similar to the one you used to get then-current data to your disaster recovery facility (duplication of transaction logs, tapes, data replication, etc.). Of course, this process has to be done after you've repaired any damage that may have occurred to the primary facility, or the systems it contains.

Regional and Catastrophic Disasters

Many disasters are often a result of the forces of nature (e.g., Hurricane Katrina in 2005). As such, if your organization suffers a disaster, it's entirely likely that many other organizations in your geographic area will also suffer, and they may be scrambling for the recovery resources that you're planning to rely on.

+ The local computer retailer may be rushed by other organizations trying to get their hands on hardware.

+ Hotel rooms may be sold out.

+ Telephone companies will be working around the clock to get regular services restored, so your plans to install temporary lines may not pan out.

+ The very vendors and service providers you had planned on may not be functioning because of the same disaster you're suffering from.

A key issue to keep in mind in this regard when crafting your disaster recovery plan is to incorporate some non-local options for each category in the plan.

As a final reminder that even the best of intentions and planning can go awry, it's important to remember that in the event of a truly catastrophic disaster, employees' priorities will quickly shift from trying to aid their employer to trying to aid their families. For dealing with the human side of disasters, see the next section.

The ACT Model

Most of the chapter has focused on the mechanics and technologies of dealing with a crisis. However, it's also wise to plan for individuals (staff, employees, etc.) during a crisis.

Consider the guidelines of the ACT model:

✦ **A** — Acknowledge and name the trauma. Have the courage to use names and the true words describing what happened, including the word "death," (if warranted, of course). It's important to validate the accuracy of information and share only what is known for sure. Know the facts, and don't speculate. (New York City Mayor Rudy Giuliani's refusal to speculate on the cost in human lives of the 9/11 disaster was an excellent example of the value of waiting until all the facts were in. He was asked about the toll repeatedly for many days, but refused to give a number until he knew the facts.) Straying from the script can be very harmful. Personally acknowledge the incident in order to position leadership as also being impacted by the event, thereby aligning leaders with the staff.

✦ **C** — Communicate both competence and caring. Competence and caring aren't mutually exclusive! Demonstrate expertise in dealing with the issue and express compassion for the personal impact to those assembled and others affected.

✦ **T** — Transition. Communicate an expectation of recovery. Show sensitivity and flexibility as people return to life and return to work. Communicate clearly that leadership will take steps to help people transition back to health and productivity. Identify internal and external resources for additional information and support. Be especially visible and accessible to employees for support and information.

The ACT model focuses on direct and honest communications and demonstrating sensitivity. For further information on ACT, see *http://www.crisisinterventionnetwork.com/intervention_act.html* and the complete articles by Albert R. Roberts.

20.3 A Word About Business Continuity

Business Continuity Planning, and Disaster Recovery are often used as inter-changeable terms. Although the two types of planning are similar, there are differences:

✦ **Business Continuity Planning:** Business Continuity Planning (BCP) is a methodology used to create a plan for how an organization will resume partially or completely interrupted critical function(s) within a predetermined time after a disaster or disruption. BCP may be a part of a larger organizational effort to reduce operational risk associated with poor information security controls, and thus has a number of overlaps with the practice of risk management.

✦ **Disaster Recovery:** Disaster Recovery (DR) is the ability of an infra-structure to restart operations after a disaster. While many of today's larger computer systems contain built-in programs for disaster recov-ery, stand-alone recovery programs often provide enhanced features. Disaster recovery is used both in the context of data loss prevention and data recovery.
(Source: *Wikipedia*)

These two areas do overlap, and to a certain degree are interdependent. To help differentiate between the two, it's best to think of disaster recovery as those areas and issues related to the IT environment and infrastructure (data center, servers, access, data, applications, etc.). The remaining items would generally fall into the area of Business Continuity Planning (BCP).

Business continuity essentially picks up where disaster recovery leaves off. In a perfect world you have a parallel data center that is a mirror image of everything in your primary data center. When disaster hits, you can invoke your disaster recovery plans to bring the parallel data center online with all applications and no loss of data. Then business continuity comes into play as the user departments attempt to continue functioning. "Continuing their normal function" becomes quite challenging if there is no electricity and/or phones, travel is severely curtailed, people can't get to the office, etc.

For example, while disaster recovery planning would cover the issues below:

✦ Secondary data centers

✦ Off-site storage of backup tapes

✦ Redundancy of technical resources

✦ Replication of data

✦ UPS and generator solutions

BCP, on the other hand, would cover issues such as:

✦ Communication plans

  – Lists of phone numbers

  – Plans for communicating to the employee population at large, as well as those critical in a disaster scenario (emergency phone numbers, Web sites)

✦ Where people will meet to continue to conduct business if the office is unavailable

✦ Locations of nearby hotels, restaurants, and other services if the need arises

✦ Plans for continuing key business operations and working with critical partners (e.g., banks, suppliers, etc.) during a crisis

✦ Copies of vital files and information

✦ Availability of cash

✦ What would the sales department do? Could/should they continue to try to sell products? How would they reassure customers?

✦ How would the accounting department make sure that the company's supplies are paid, and that receivables are collected?

✦ How would customers, suppliers, partners, clients, investors, and employees be kept informed?

✦ Could payroll continue to pay employees during the disaster?

As a general rule, the IT department's greater priority is disaster recovery, while user departments are generally concerned about BCP.

20.4   The Hidden Benefits of Good Disaster Recovery Planning

One seldom understood value of good disaster recovery planning is that it often helps tremendously with regular, everyday corporate process execution. Good disaster recovery makes for good everyday business performance.

✦ You need to know exactly where every piece of hardware in your company is anyway. Where is it, how old is it, whose department is paying for it? (See Chapter 9, Getting Started with the Technical Environment.) But if you can't find the time to do this kind of inventory on a regular basis, you should find the time to do it for a formal disaster recovery plan.

✦ If you don't have current contact lists for people outside your direct reports, here is a chance to create one and keep it current. (You'll be shocked at all these people you have never heard of who work for your company.)

✦ Naturally, you should have very complete data backup procedures. (See Chapter 16, Storage Backup on page 433.) But if you haven't yet set up off-site backup, creating a disaster recovery plan can force you — or higher ups, once you put it in the context of disaster recovery — to get the time and money to make this basic need happen.

Like the Dwight Eisenhower quote that opened this chapter indicates, never underestimate the value of planning.

20.5 **Additional Resources**

Web Sites

✦ *h20219.www2.hp.com/services/cache/11358-0-0-225-121.html* (HP Business Continuity and Availability Services)

✦ *www.capsbrs.com* (Computer Alternative Processing Sites, CAPS)

✦ *www.drj.com* (*Disaster Recovery Journal*)

✦ *www.drs.net* (Disaster Recovery Services, DRS)

✦ *www.neverfailgroup.com* (data replication software)

✦ *www.nsisoftware.com* (data replication software)

✦ *www.recovery.sungard.com* (SunGard Recovery Services)

✦ *www.rentsys.com* (Rentsys Recovery Services)

✦ *www.sendwordnow.com* (Send Word Now)

✦ *www.weyerhaeuser.com/disaster-recovery* (Weyerhaeuser Recovery Systems)

+ *www.xosoft.com* (data replication software)

+ *www-1.ibm.com/services/continuity/recover1.nsf* (IBM Business Continuity and Recovery Services)

Books and Articles

+ Carlson, Carol, "Agencies Under Fire for Disaster Recovery Plan," *eWeek*, September 26, 2005, p. 37.

+ Fulmer, Kenneth, *Business Continuity Planning: A Step-by-Step Guide with Planning Forms,* on CD-ROM, Rothstein Associates; 2004.

+ Larstan Editors, *Larstan's The Black Book on Business Continuity and Disaster Recovery*, Larstan Publishing; 2006.

+ Matthews, Carrie, "How to Involve the Business to Create a Solid Continuity Plan," *CIO Magazine*, October 1, 2005, p. 102.

+ National Fire Prevention Association NFPA 1600, *Standard on Disaster/ Emergency Management and Business Continuity Programs. (http:// www.nfpa.org/categoryList.asp?categoryID=628&URL=Research%20& %20Reports/Fact%20sheets/Homeland%20Security).*

+ Rittinghouse, John, and Ransome, James, *Business Continuity and Disaster Recovery for InfoSec Managers*, Digital Press; 2005.

+ Toigo, Jon, *Disaster Recovery Planning: Strategies for Protecting Critical Information Assets*, Prentice Hall, 2002.

+ Wallace, Michael, Webber, Lawrence, *The Disaster Recovery Handbook: A Step-by-Step Plan to Ensure Business Continuity and Protect Vital Operations, Facilities, and Assets*, AMACOM, 2004.

Bibliography

Web Sites

- *aicpa.org/sarbanes/index.asp* (Sarbanes-Oxley)

- *blogs.zdnet.com/threatchaos* (Web log about security)

- *browser.netscape.com/ns8* (Internet browser)

- *bugtraq-subscribe@securityfocus.com* (bugtrac mailing list)

- *careerplanning.about.com/cs/firstjob/a/new_job.htm* (first day tips from *about.com*)

- *computer.howstuffworks.com/workplace-surveillance.htm* (information about workplace surveillance)

- *crm.ittoolbox.com/topics/t.asp?t=490&p=490&h1=490* (CRM site)

- *csrc.nist.gov/index.html* (National Institute of Standards and Technology's Web site about computer security)

- *csrc.nist.gov/publications/nistpubs/800-30/sp800-30.pdf* (a risk management white paper from the National Institute of Standards and Technology)

- *csrc.nist.gov/publications/secpubs/otherpubs/reviso-faq.pdf* (an FAQ from the National Institute of Standards and Technology about ISO/IEC 17799: 2000)

- *datacenterdynamics.com* (trade association for data center managers)

- *en.wikipedia.org/wiki/Patriot_Act* (Patriot Act)

- *europa.eu.int/information_society/policy/ecomm/site_services/faq/index_en.htm* (Privacy and Electronic Communications Directive)

- *ftp://www.apcmedia.com/salestools/NRAN-69ANM9_R0_EN.pdf* (white paper on "Guidelines for Specification of Data Center Power Density")

- *h20219.www2.hp.com/services/cache/11358-0-0-225-121.html* (HP Business Continuity and Availability Services)

- *h71028.www7.hp.com/ERC/downloads/5983-2385EN.pdf* (white paper on e-mail usage)

◆ *hbswk.hbs.edu/item.jhtml?id=2647&t=finance* (a Harvard Business School article on corporate budget problems, specifically typing budgeting to compensation)

◆ *humanresources.about.com/od/360feedback* (360 reviews)

◆ *info.sen.ca.gov/pub/01-02/bill/sen/sb_1351-1400/sb_1386_bill_20020926_chaptered.html* (SB-1386)

◆ *isecurity.ucsf.edu/main.jsp?content=secure_zones/secure_zones* (information about Secure Zones)

◆ *itmanagement.earthweb.com* (IT management site)

◆ *knowledge.wharton.upenn.edu/index.cfm?fa=viewfeature&id=693* (article on outsourcing back-office functions)

◆ *lacnic.net/sp* (Latin American registry for IP addresses)

◆ *manage.directi.com/kb* (Reseller Club Support knowledge base)

◆ *nasd.complinet.com/nasd/display/display.html?rbid=1189&element_id=1159000466* (U. S. Securities)

◆ *netsecurity.about.com/cs/bookreviews/gr/aapr100603.htm* (reviews of various IT security books)

◆ *news.findlaw.com/hdocs/docs/gwbush/sarbanesoxley072302.pdf* (Sarbanes-Oxley)

◆ *office.microsoft.com/en-us/default.aspx* (productivity tool suite)

◆ *onguardonline.gov* (a U. S. Government site about computer security)

◆ *register.consilium.eu.int/pdf/en/02/st03/03636en2.pdf* (Privacy and Electronic Communications Directive)

◆ *rules.nyse.com/NYSE/Help/Map/rules-sys454.html* (U. S. Securities)

◆ *rules.nyse.com/NYSE/Help/Map/rules-sys552.html* (U. S. Securities)

◆ *sea.symantec.com/content/product.cfm?productid=28* (software deployment tool)

◆ *searchcio.techtarget.com* (product technical information)

◆ *searchwebservices.techtarget.com/gDefinition/0,294236,sid26_gci927714,00.html* (trouble ticket defined)

◆ *seclists.org/lists/politech/2001/Feb/0009.html* (a Web log about face scanning at the 2005 Super Bowl)

◆ *software.isixsigma.com/newsletter* (Six Sigma — quality control implementation methodology)

✦ *techrepublic.com.com/5138-10878_11-729776.html* (360 review templates)

✦ *thomas.loc.gov/cgi-bin/bdquery/z?d107:h.r.03162:* (Patriot Act)

✦ *web.mit.edu/kerberos/www* (information about Kerberos)

✦ *whatis.techtarget.com* (IT-specific encyclopedia)

✦ *www.3m.com/novec1230fluid* (vendor Web site about Novec 1230 fire suppression)

✦ *www.acronis.com/enterprise/products/choose-trueimage* (disk cloning tool)

✦ *www.adobe.com/products/acrobat/readstep2.html* (PDF reader)

✦ *www.agmaglobal.org* (gray market alliance)

✦ *www.allot.com* (network management appliance vendor)

✦ *www.altiris.com* (technology management solution vendor)

✦ *www.altiris.com/products/clientmgmt* (software deployment tool)

✦ *www.amanet.org/index.htm* (industry organization for managers)

✦ *www.ansul.com* (vendor Web site about Inergen fire suppression)

✦ *www.answers.com* (general information source)

✦ *www.apcc.com* (vendor of data center power and cooling products)

✦ *www.apcc.com/prod_docs/results.cfm?class=wp&allpapers=1* (variety of white papers on data center power and cooling)

✦ *www.apnic.net* (Asia Pacific registry for IP addresses)

✦ *www.apple.com/macosx/features/safari* (Internet browser)

✦ *www.arin.net* (North American registry for IP addresses)

✦ *www.asic.gov.au/asic/asic_polprac.nsf/byheadline/CLERP+9?open Document* (CLERP-9)

✦ *www.asktheheadhunter.com/hastartjob.htm* (tips from a headhunter)

✦ *www.avaya.com* (Network hardware and software vendor)

✦ *www.bangaloreit.in/index.asp* (India offshoring resources)

✦ *ww.bis.org/bcbs/index.htm* (Basel II)

✦ *www.bluetooth.com* (short range connectivity standard)

✦ *www.bombich.com* (disk cloning utility for Mac operating systems)

✦ *www.brighthand.com* (news and reviews of handheld devices)

✦ *www.brightmail.com* (e-mail management vendor)

✦ *www.bsa.org* (trade organization for software publishers)

✦ *www.buzzle.com/editorials/4-10-2005-68350.asp* (White Box testing strategy)

✦ *www.ca.com* (technology management solution and backup software vendor)

✦ *www.capsbrs.com* (Computer Alternative Processing Sites, CAPS)

✦ *www.cert.org* (Federally funded Computer Emergency Response Team at Carnegie Mellon)

✦ *www.cheatingculture.com/resumepadding.htm* (resume cheating info)

✦ *www.checkpoint.com* (Security solutions vendor)

✦ *www.cio.com* (*CIO Magazine* site)

✦ *www.cisco.com* (network management, security solutions, hardware and software vendor)

✦ *www.cmp.com* (consulting vendor)

✦ *www.cnet.com* (tech community with product reviews, articles, etc.)

✦ *www.compliancepipeline.com* (online journal for IT compliance-related issues)

✦ *www.computerworld.com* (IT technical journal)

✦ *www.corel.com/servlet/Satellite?pagename=Corel3/Products/Display&pfid=1047024307359* (productivity tool suite)

✦ *www.cse.mrt.ac.lk/lecnotes/cs5162/08-lan-cabling.ppt* (presentation on LAN cabling)

✦ *www.datacenterdynamics.com/Portals/e5b81c2f-f780-4e59-88fc-068dccab9568/SF04%20Liebert.pdf* (presentation on data center cooling)

✦ *www.decru.com* (storage security vendor)

✦ *www.dell.com* (technology management, desktop and laptop product manufacturer and vendor)

✦ *www.destinationcrm.com/articles/default.asp?ArticleID=4354* (CRM)

✦ *www.discover6sigma.org* (information about Six Sigma)

✦ *www.dobetterdeals.com* (Web site for Joe Auer, who has written frequently for *Computerworld* on the issue of IT vendors and contracts)

✦ *www.drj.com* (*Disaster Recovery Journal*)

✦ *www.drs.net* (DRS Disaster Recovery Services)

✦ *www.e1.greatlakes.com/wfp/product/jsp/faq.jsp* (vendor FAQ about FM-200 fire suppression)

✦ *www.e11online.com* (help desk software vendor)

✦ *www.ecommercetimes.com* (e-commerce news)

✦ *www.ecommercetimes.com/story/42781.html* (article about India's offshore outsourcing)

✦ *www.emc.com* (storage solution vendor)

✦ *www.emulators.com/softmac.htm* (Mac emulator for Windows)

✦ *www.epic.org/privacy/fcra* (FACTA)

✦ *www.epic.org/privacy/glba* (Gramm-Leach-Bliley Act)

✦ *www.epic.org/privacy/terrorism/hr3162.html* (Patriot Act)

✦ *www.eudora.com* (e-mail software vendor)

✦ *www.eweek.com* (IT technical journal)

✦ *www.fastcompany.com/magazine/77/walmart.html* (article about Wal-Mart's offshore practices)

✦ *www.federalreserve.gov/generalinfo/basel2/default.htm* (Basel II)

✦ *www.findtech.com/keyword,Problem+Ticket+Management/search.htm?&* (problem ticket management)

✦ *www.fluke.com* (cable testing tool vendor)

✦ *www.f-secure.com* (anti-virus software vendor)

✦ *www.ftc.gov/os/statutes/fcrajump.htm* (FACTA)

✦ *www.ftc.gov/privacy/glbact/glboutline.pdf* (Gramm-Leach-Bliley Act)

✦ *www.ftc.gov/privacy/privacyinitiatives/glbact.html* (Gramm-Leach-Bliley Act)

✦ *www.gateway.com* (desktop and laptop product manufacturer and vendor)

✦ *www.gnu.org* ("free" software site)

✦ *www.helpdesk.com* (help desk support)

✦ *www.helpdeskinst.com* (Help Desk Institute)

✦ *www.help-desk-world.com* (help desk software vendor)

✦ *www.hhs.gov/ocr/hipaa* (HIPAA)

- *www.hipaacomply.com* (HIPAA)

- *www.hireright.com* (background checking company)

- *www.hitachi.com* (storage solution vendor)

- *www.hp.com* (technology management solution vendor)

- *www.hp.com* (storage solution vendor)

- *www.ibm.com* (technology management, storage solution vendor)

- *www.icann.org* (information about Internet domain names, registrars, etc.)

- *www.idg.com* (IT trade journal publisher)

- *www.ietf.org* (Internet Engineering Task Force)

- *www.informatics.indiana.edu/news/news.asp?id=131&careers=true* (IT Career Growth News)

- *www.informationweek.com/805/budget.htm* (article on budgeting software)

- *www.infoworld.com* (IT technical journal)

- *www.insecure.org* (nmap utility)

- *www.intel.com/standards/execqa/qa0904.htm* (Craig Barrett on the Importance of Global Standards)

- *www.intranet.com* (pre-packaged intranet applications)

- *www.ipswitch.com* (technology management solution vendor)

- *www.ironmountain.com* (records storage facility)

- *www.ironport.com* (e-mail management vendor)

- *www.isaca.org* (trade association for IT governance professionals)

- *www.isixsigma.com* (information about Six Sigma)

- *www.iso.org* (information about the International Organization for Standards, and ISO 9000)

- *www.iso-17799.com* (ISO site about ISO/IEC 17799:2005)

- *www.isoc.org/internet/history* (Internet history)

- *www.itaa.org/business/it* (IT Industry association)

- *www.itgi.org* (trade association for IT governance professionals)

- *www.itil.co.uk* (information about ITIL)

✦ *www.itmanagersjournal.com* (IT technical site)

✦ *www.juniper.net* (security solutions and network management appliance vendor)

✦ *www.landesk.com* (technology management solution vendor)

✦ *www.landesk.com/Products/LDMS* (software deployment tool)

✦ *www.lenovo.com* (desktop and laptop product manufacturer and vendor)

✦ *www.liebert.com* (vendor of data center power and cooling products)

✦ *www.LinkedIn.com* (professional networking site)

✦ *www.linux.org* (Linux)

✦ *www.lotus.com* (e-mail software vendor)

✦ *www.managementhelp.org* (library of resources for managers)

✦ *www.managementsoftware.hp.com/news/about/index.html* (HP's network management solution)

✦ *www.mathaware.org/mam/04/6_Internet_structure.html* (A visualization of the network structure of the Internet)

✦ *www.mcafee.com* (anti-virus software vendor)

✦ *www.mcafee.com/us* (security software vendor)

✦ *www.mercury.com/us/products/it-governance-center/project-management* (enterprise project manager tool vendor)

✦ *www.mgeups.com* (vendor of data center power products)

✦ *www.microsoft.com* (technology management solution vendor)

✦ *www.microsoft.com/exchange* (e-mail software vendor)

✦ *www.microsoft.com/india/indiadev* (Microsoft development in India)

✦ *www.microsoft.com/mac/products/virtualpc/virtualpc.aspx?pid=virtualpc* (Windows emulator for Macintosh)

✦ *www.microsoft.com/office/project/prodinfo/epm/overview.mspx* (enterprise project manager tool vendor)

✦ *www.microsoft.com/smserver/default.mspx* (software deployment tool)

✦ *www.microsoft.com/technet/security/default.mspx* (Microsoft's Security Web site)

◆ *www.microsoft.com/technet/security/topics/AuditingandMonitoring. mspx* (software auditing and monitoring information)

◆ *www.microsoft.com/technet/security/topics/Serversecurity/tcg/tcgch00. mspx* ("Threats and Countermeasures Guide")

◆ *www.microsoft.com/windows/ie/default.mspx* (Internet browser)

◆ *www.microsoft.com/windows/virtualpc/default.mspx* (virtual machine solution)

◆ *www.microsoft.com/windowsserversystem/virtualserver/default.mspx* (virtual machine solution)

◆ *www.miray.de* (disk cloning tool)

◆ *www.mobileinfo.com* (Web site for mobile computing information)

◆ *www.mozilla.com/firefox* (Internet browser)

◆ *www.naceweb.org/press/display.asp?year=2005&prid=216* (association of college employers)

◆ *www.neoscale.com* (storage security vendor)

◆ *www.netapps.com* (storage solution vendor)

◆ *www.netiq.com* (technology management solution vendor)

◆ *www.netqos.com* (network performance/optimization solution vendor)

◆ *www.netsupport-inc.com* (technology management solution vendor)

◆ *www.networkgeneral.com* (network management vendor)

◆ *www.neverfailgroup.com* (data replication software)

◆ *www.niku.com* (enterprise project manager tool vendor)

◆ *www.nortel.com* (network hardware and software vendor)

◆ *www.novell.com* (technology management solution vendor)

◆ *www.novell.com/groupwise* (e-mail software vendor)

◆ *www.novell.com/products/zenworks* (software deployment tool)

◆ *www.nsisoftware.com* (data replication software)

◆ *www.ondemandsoftware.com/msipak.asp* (software deployment packaging tool)

◆ *www.online-commerce.com* (e-commerce primer)

◆ *www.openoffice.org* (open-source productivity tool suite)

◆ *www.opera.com* (Internet browser)

+ *www.opsware.com* (technology management solution vendor)

+ *www.oracle.com* (ERP software vendor)

+ *www.oracle.com/applications/projects/intro.html* (enterprise project manager tool vendor)

+ *www.organicconsumers.org/clothes/nike041505.cfm* (article about Nike's offshore practices)

+ *www.packeteer.com* (network management appliance vendor)

+ *www.palm.com* (handheld product manufacturer and vendor)

+ *www.panduit.com/products/WhitePapers/103681.pdf* (white paper on "Facility Considerations for the Data Center")

+ *www.patchlink.com* (patch management solution)

+ *www.payscale.com* (salary survey information)

+ *www.pc.ibm.com/us/think/thinkvantagetech/imageultra.html* (disk cloning tool)

+ *www.peregrine.com* (technology management solution vendor)

+ *www.pfdf.org/leaderbooks/drucker/bio.html* (Drucker quote)

+ *www.pipedainfo.com* (PIPEDA)

+ *www.planview.com* (enterprise project management tool vendor)

+ *www.pmi.org* (Project Management Institute)

+ *www.primavera.com* (enterprise project manager tool vendor)

+ *www.privcom.gc.ca/legislation/02_06_01_e.asp* (PIPEDA)

+ *www.protocols.com* (detailed reference information about standards, protocols, etc.)

+ *www.quantum.com* (storage solution vendor)

+ *www.radicati/com* (market research firm)

+ *www.ranish.com* (open source disk cloning tool)

+ *www.raycomm.com/techwhirl/employmentarticles/contractorsupto-speed.html* (tips for getting contractors up to speed in their new job)

+ *www.raycomm.com/techwhirl/magazine/gettingstarted/tipsforstartin-ganewjob.html* (tips for starting your new job)

+ *www.recovery.sungard.com* (SunGard Recovery Services)

- *www.remedy.com* (technology management solution vendor)
- *www.rentsys.com* (Rentsys Recovery Services)
- *www.rim.com* (handheld product manufacturer and vendor)
- *www.ripe.net* (Europe/Middle East registry for IP addresses)
- *www.rsasecurity.com/press_release.asp?doc_id=6095&id=1034* (Survey by RSA about the risks of multiple passwords)
- *www.salary.com* (salary survey information)
- *www.sap.com* (ERP software vendor)
- *www.scism.sbu.ac.uk/law/Section5/chap3/s5c3p23.html* (Black Box and White Box testing compared)
- *www.sec.gov/rules/final/34-44992a.htm* (U. S. Securities)
- *www.secinf.net* (books about IT security)
- *www.securityguidance.com* (Microsoft security assessment tool)
- *www.security-risk-analysis.com/introduction.htm* (introduction to risk analysis)
- *www.sei.cmu.edu/cmmi* (information about CMMI)
- *www.sendwordnow.com* (Send Word Now)
- *www.shavlik.com* (patch management vendor)
- *www.siia.net* (trade organization for software publishers)
- *www.slashdot.org* (IT news site)
- *www.snpx.com/faq.shtml* (security Web site for IT professionals)
- *www.spywareinfo.com* (information about spyware)
- *www.ssaglobal.com* (ERP software vendor)
- *www.staroffice.com* (productivity tool suite)
- *www.sunflowersystems.com* (technology management solution vendor)
- *www.symantec.com* (security software, anti-virus software, disk cloning tool vendor)
- *www.techrepublic.com* (IT technical site)
- *www.theiia.org/itaudit/index.cfm?fuseaction=forum&fid=5501* (SB-1386)
- *www.theregister.co.uk* (IT technical site)

✦ *www.treas.gov/offices/enforcement/ofac* (OFAC)

✦ *www.treas.gov/offices/enforcement/ofac/articles/abamag.pdf* (OFAC)

✦ *www.treasury.gov.au/contentitem.asp?NavId=013&ContentID=403* (CLERP-9)

✦ *www.trendmicro.com* (security software vendor)

✦ *www.tumbleweed.com* (e-mail management vendor)

✦ *www.uptimeinstitute.com* (industry group for data center management)

✦ *www.veritas.com* (backup software vendor)

✦ *www.vmware.com* (Virtual Machine solution)

✦ *www.vnunet.com/vnunet/news/2147200/november-biggest-ever-malware* (Malware risks)

✦ *www.wageweb.com* (salary survey information)

✦ *www.weyerhaeuser.com/disaster-recovery* (Weyerhaeuser Recovery Systems)

✦ *www.win4lin.com* (Windows emulator for Linux)

✦ *www.winehq.com* (Windows emulator for Unix)

✦ *www.wired.com* (tech publication)

✦ *www.wise.com/wps.asp* (software deployment packaging tool)

✦ *www.wisegeek.com/what-is-budgeting.htm* (article on budgeting)

✦ *www.wisegeek.com/what-is-six-sigma.htm* (brief article about Six Sigma)

✦ *www.workopolis.com/servlet/Content/tprinter/20001014/TS27929* (tips from Canada's biggest job site)

✦ *www.xosoft.com* (data replication software)

✦ *www.ziffdavis.com* (IT trade journal publisher)

✦ *www.zoominfo.com* (professional networking site)

✦ *www-1.ibm.com/services/continuity/recover1.nsf* (IBM Business Continuity and Recovery Services)

✦ *www-142.ibm.com/software/sw-lotus/products/product2.nsf/wdocs/sshome* (productivity tool suite)

✦ *www3.ca.com/solutions/Solution.aspx?ID=315* (Computer Associates' network management solution)

✦ *www-306.ibm.com/software/awdtools/portfolio* (enterprise project manager tool vendor)

✦ *www-306.ibm.com/software/tivoli* (IBM's network management solution)

Books and Articles

✦ [No Author Identified], "Hiring and Keeping the Best People," *Harvard Business School Press*, 2003.

✦ *A Guide To The Project Management Body Of Knowledge*, (PMBOK Guides), Project Management Institute (2004).

✦ Addison, Doug, *Web Site Cookbook: Solutions & Examples for Building and Administering Your Web Site*, O'Reilly Media, Inc., 2006.

✦ Alger, Douglas, *Build the Best Data Center Facility for Your Business*, Cisco Press, 2005.

✦ Alhadeff, Roni, *Succeeding in E-commerce, Insider Advice And Practical Tips*, Lulu Press, 2005.

✦ Allen, Julia H., The *CERT Guide to System and Network Security Practices*, Addison-Wesley Professional, June 7, 2001.

✦ Anderegg, Travis, *ERP: A-Z Implementer's Guide For Success*, Resource Publishing, 2000.

✦ Anthes, Gary H., "ITIL Catches On: British-Bred Quality Framework is Becoming the Tool of Choice in US Data Centers," *Computerworld*, October 31, 2005, p. 39.

✦ Apicella, Mario, "Fibre Channel vs iSCSI," *Infoworld*, September 8, 2005, p. 32.

✦ Baltazar, Henry, "iSCSI takes on Fibre Channel," *eWeek*, February 13, 2006, p. 39.

✦ Barnett, David, Groth, David, and McBee, Jim, *Cabling: The Complete Guide to Network Wiring*, Sybex, 2004.

✦ Beers, Christopher T., "Beyond Spam Filters," *Network Computing Magazine*, February 16, 2006, p. 25.

✦ Beers, Christopher T., "Beyond Spam Filters," *Network Computing Magazine*, February 16, 2006, p. 59.

✦ Bender, Stephen A., *Managing Projects Well*, Butterworth-Heinemann, 1998.

✦ Berglas, Dr. Steve, "Serenity Found: How to Inoculate Yourself Against Stress and Burnout (Once You Understand the Difference)," *CIO Magazine*, December 1, 2005, p. 42.

✦ Black, Rex, *Managing the Testing Process: Practical Tools and Techniques for Managing Hardware and Software Testing*, Wiley, 2002.

✦ Blitzer, Roy J., Reynolds-Rush, Jacquie, *Find the Bathrooms First!: Starting Your New Job on the Right Foot*, Crisp Learning, Inc., 1999.

✦ Bossidy, Larry, and Charan, Ram, *Execution: The Discipline of Getting Things Done*, Crown Business, 2002.

✦ Bradbary, Dan, and Garrett, David, *Herding Chickens: Innovative Techniques for Project Management*, Jossey-Bass, 2005.

✦ Broadwell, Martin M., and Carol Broadwell Dietrich, *The New Supervisor: How to Thrive in Your First Year as a Manager*, Perseus Publishing, 1998.

✦ Brooks, Frederic, *The Mythical Man-Month*, Addison-Wesley Professional, 1995.

✦ Brooks, Jason, "The Rise of the Virtual Machines," *eWeek*, November 7, 2005, p. 39.

✦ Bruton, Noel, *How to Manage the IT Helpdesk — A Guide for User Support and Call Center Managers*, Butterworth-Heinemann, 2003.

✦ Carlson, Carol, "Agencies Under Fire for Disaster Recovery Plan," *eWeek*, September 26, 2005, p. 37.

✦ Carlson, Caron, "Alliance Tackles VoIP Threats," *eWeek*, October 24, 2005, p. 22.

✦ Carlson, Caron, "Adware Will Need User Consent," *eWeek*, November 21, 2005, p. 27.

✦ Carter, Gerald, *LDAP System Administration*, O'Reilly Media, Inc. 2003.

✦ Ciampa, Dan, and Watkins, Michael, *Right from the Start: Taking Charge in a New Leadership Role*, Harvard Business School Press, 1999.

✦ Coffee, Peter, "Set Expectations for Outsourcing," *eWeek*, September 26, 2005, p. D1.

✦ Computerworld Special Report, "Knowledge Center Outsourcing," *Computerworld*, November 14, 2005, p. 61.

✦ Czegel, Barbara, *Running an Effective Help Desk, 2nd Edition*, John Wiley, 1998.

◆ Dawson, Keith, *The Call Center Handbook, 4th Edition*, CMP Books, 2001.

◆ Della Maggiora, Paul L., and Doherty, Jim, *Cisco Networking Simplified*, Cisco Press, 2003.

◆ Droms, William G., *Finance And Accounting For Nonfinancial Managers: All The Basics You Need to Know*, Perseus Publishing, 2003.

◆ Dubin, Joel, *The Little Black Book of Computer Security*, 29th Street Press, 2005.

◆ Duncan, Les, *They Made You the Boss, Now What?: A Practical Guide for New Leaders*, PublishAmerica, 2004.

◆ Erlanger, Leon, "Business Process Outsourcing: Putting IT in the Director's Chair," *InfoWorld*, February 27, 2006, p. 23.

◆ Erlanger, Leon, "Is VoIP Ripe for Attack?," *Infoworld*, October 17, 2005, p. 31.

◆ Farrel, Adrian, *The Internet and Its Protocols: A Comparative Approach*, Morgan Kaufmann, 2004.

◆ Ferguson, Renee Boucher, "RFID World: Searching for ROI," *eWeek*, February 27, 2006, p. 25.

◆ Fields, Ed, *The Essentials of Finance and Accounting for Nonfinancial Managers*, American Management Association, 2002.

◆ Finney, Robert G., *Office Finances Made Easy: A Get-Started Guide to Budgets, Purchasing, and Financial Statements*, Amacom, 1999.

◆ Flynn, Nancy, and Kahn, Randolph, *E-Mail Rules: A Business Guide to Managing Policies, Security, and Legal Issues for E-Mail and Digital Communication*, American Management Association, 2003.

◆ Forouzan, Behrouz, *Data Communications and Networking*, McGraw-Hill, 2003.

◆ Fournies, Ferdinand F., *Why Employees Don't Do What They're Supposed to Do and What to Do about It*, McGraw-Hill, 1999.

◆ Fulmer, Kenneth, *Business Continuity Planning: A Step-by-Step Guide with Planning Forms*, on CD-ROM, Rothstein Associates, 2004.

◆ Gallegos, Senft, Manson, Gonzales, *Information Technology Control and Audit*, Auerbach Publications, CRC Press, Boca Raton, FL, 2004.

◆ Garbaczeski, Paul, "Inside the Software Testing Quagmire," *CIO Magazine*, November 15, 2005, p. 38.

✦ Garcia, Andrew, "Anti-Spyware Hones Searches," *eWeek*, October 10, 2005, p. 10.

✦ Garcia, Andrew, "Fighting Spyware Is a Never Ending Battle," *eWeek*, January 9, 2006, p. 41.

✦ Garcia, Andrew, "Lock Out Problems: System Lockdown isn't Always Easy, but it's a Powerful Protection," *eWeek*, November 28, 2005, p. 35.

✦ Garton, Coleen, and McCulloch, Erika, *Fundamentals of Technology Project Management*, Mc Press, 2005.

✦ Geer, David, "Measuring Project Risk," *Computerworld*, January 9, 2006, p. 38.

✦ Gibson, Stan, "IT 101 Switches Gears," *eWeek*, September 26, 2005.

✦ Gincel, Richard, "The Awful Truth About Compliance," *Infoworld*, December 12, 2005, p. 29.

✦ Gladwell, Malcolm, "Getting In: The Social Logic of Ivy League Admissions," *The New Yorker*, October 10, 2005, p. 80.

✦ Gomes-Cassere, Ben, "Outsource, Don't Abdicate," *CIO Magazine*, October 1, 2005, p. 36.

✦ Hall, Mark, "Law and Order on the Open Source Range," *Computerworld*, December 5, 2005, p. 29.

✦ Hall, Mark, "Price of Security Breaches," *Computerworld*, November 14, 2005, p. 8.

✦ Hamilton, Scott, *Maximizing Your ERP System: A Practical Guide for Managers*, McGraw-Hill, 2001.

✦ Hayes, Jim, Rosenburg, Paul, *Data, Voice, and Video Cabling*, Thomson Delmar Learning, 2004.

✦ Hill, Linda, *Becoming a Manager: How New Managers Master the Challenges of Leadership*, Harvard Business School Press, 2003.

✦ Hoffman, Thomas, "Double Dipping on Sarb-Ox," *Computerworld*, November 7, 2005, p. 42.

✦ Hoffman, Thomas, "New Obstacles Dogging Outsourcing Customers," *Computerworld*, October 24, 2005, p. 10.

✦ Hoffman, Thomas, and Thibodeau, Patrick, "Working through the Pain, After Rocky Starts, Some US Clients are Learning How to Get Better Results Offshore," *Computerworld*, December 5, 2005, p. 46.

✦ Holton, Ed, and Naquin, Sharon, *So You're New Again: How to Succeed When You Change Jobs*, Berrett-Koehler Publishers, 2001.

◆ Jaffe, Brian D., "Following a Few Simple Rules Can Ease the Pain of Employee Reviews," *InfoWorld*, January 26, 1998.

◆ Jaffe, Brian D., "Maturity Is a Help Desk Prerequisite," *PC Week*, February 7, 2000.

◆ Jaffe, Brian D., "Taking the Measure of Customer Service," *PC Week*, June 5, 1998.

◆ Jayaswal, Kailash, *Administering Data Centers: Servers, Storage, and Voice over IP*, Wiley, 2005.

◆ Kalin, Sari, "How to Tackle Identity and Access Management," *CIO Magazine*, December 1, 2005, p. 106.

◆ Keagy, Scott, *Integrating Voice and Data Networks*, Cisco Press, 2000.

◆ Kelly, Matt, "Betting on Risk Management," *eWeek*, January 9, 2006, p. E1.

◆ Kemp, Sid, and Dunbar, Eric, *Budgeting for Managers*, McGraw-Hill, 2003.

◆ Knapp, Donna, *A Guide to Help Desk Concepts*, Course Technology, 2003.

◆ Koch, Christopher, "Free Code For Sale," *CIO Magazine*, February 15, 2006, p. 48.

◆ Kozoil, Jack, Litchfield, David, Aitel, Dave, Anley, Chris, and Mehta, Neel, *The Shellcoder's Handbook: Discovering and Exploiting Security Holes*, Wiley, 2004.

◆ Krutz, Russell, Vines, Dean, and Stroz, Edward M., *The CISSP Prep Guide: Mastering the Ten Domains of Computer Security*, Wiley, 2001.

◆ Kurose, James F., and Ross, Keith W., *Computer Networking: A Top-Down Approach Featuring the Internet (3rd Edition)*, Addison Wesley, 2004.

◆ Laird, Campbell, "The Virtues of Virtualized Storage," InfoWorld, January 16, 2006, p. 37.

◆ Larstan Editors, *Larstan's The Black Book on Business Continuity and Disaster Recovery*, Larstan Publishing, 2006.

◆ Levinson, Meredith, "Inside an IT Marketing Campaign," *CIO Magazine*, February 1, 2006, p. 47.

◆ Levinson, Meredith, "Testing 1, 2, 3 . . . ," *CIO Magazine*, November 15, 2005, p. 63.

◆ Lewis, Bob, *Bob Lewis's IS Survival Guide*, Sams, 1999.

◆ Lientz, Bennet P., and Rea, Kathryn P., *Breakthrough IT Change Management: How to Get Enduring Change Results*, Butterworth-Heinemann, 2003.

◆ Littlejohn Shinder, Deborah, *Computer Networking Essentials*, Cisco Press, 2001.

◆ Liu, Circket, and Albitz, Paul, *DNS and Bind*, O'Reilly Media, Inc., 2001.

◆ Lynch, C. G., "Most Companies Adopting ITIL Practices," *CIO Magazine*, March 1, 2006, p. 18.

◆ Mar-Elia, Darren, Melber, Derek, Stanek, and William D., *Microsoft Windows Group Policy Guide*, Microsoft Press, 2005.

◆ Margulius, David L., "10 Ways to Get Offshoring Right," *InfoWorld*, August 28, 2005, p. 33.

◆ Margulius, David L., "Breaking Away: When IT Puts Business In the Lead," *InfoWorld*, December 5, 2005, p. 28.

◆ Maslach, Christina, and Leiter, Michael P., (Contributor), *The Truth about Burnout: How Organizations Cause Personal Stress and What to Do about It*, Jossey-Bass Publishers, 1997.

◆ Matthews, Carrie, "How to Involve the Business to Create a Solid Continuity Plan," *CIO Magazine*, October 1, 2005, p. 102.

◆ Matthews, Jeanna, *Computer Networks: Internet Protocols in Action*, John Wiley and Sons, 2005.

◆ McAllister, Neil, "Illuminating Server Virtualization," *InfoWorld*, October 17, 2005, p. 14.

◆ McAllister, Neil, "You Can't Kill TCO," *InfoWorld*, August 29, 2005, p. 40.

◆ McClure, Stuart, Scambray, Joel, and Kurtz, George, *Hacking Exposed, 5th Edition*, McGraw-Hill Osborne Media, 2005.

◆ McDonald, Matthew, *Creating Web Sites: The Missing Manual*, O'Reilly Media, Inc., 2005.

◆ McWilliams, Brian, *Spam Kings: The Real Story behind the High-Rolling Hucksters Pushing Porn, Pills, and %*@)# Enlargements*, First Edition, October 2004.

◆ Mearian, Lucas, "Cleaning Out the Attic," *Computerworld*, October 17, 2005, p. 62.

◆ Mearin, Lucas, "Storage: Round 2," *Computerworld*, November 14, 2005, p. 54.

✦ Meyers, Mike, *Mike Meyers' A+ Guide to Operating Systems*, McGraw-Hill Osborne Media, 2004.

✦ Meyers, Michael, *Mike Meyers' Network+ Guide To Managing and Troubleshooting Networks* (Mike Meyers' Guides), McGraw-Hill/Irwin, 2004.

✦ Microsoft Corporation, *Improving Web Application Security: Threats and Countermeasures*, 2003.

✦ Mitchell, Robert L., "Redefining Cool," *Computerworld*, October 31, 2005.

✦ Mitchell, Robert L., "Spy Stoppers Fight Back," *Computerworld*, October 31, 2005.

✦ Mohr, Julie, *The Help Desk Audit: Blueprint for Success* (Spiral-bound), Blueprintaudits.com, 2003.

✦ Moody, Glyn, "Rebel Code: Linux and the Open Source Revolution," Perseus Books Group (2001).

✦ Mornell, Pierre, and Hinrichs, Kit, *45 Effective Ways for Hiring Smart!: How to Predict Winners and Losers in the Incredibly Expensive People-Reading Game*, Ten Speed Press, 2003.

✦ National Fire Prevention Association NFPA 1600: *Standard on Disaster/Emergency Management and Business Continuity Programs, (http://www.nfpa.org/categoryList.asp?categoryID=628&URL=Research%20&%20Reports/Fact%20sheets/Homeland%20Security)*.

✦ Neff, Thomas, and Citrin, James, *You're in Charge — Now What?: The 8 Point Plan*, Crown Business, 2005.

✦ Overby, Stephanie, "Simple Successful Outsourcing," *CIO Magazine*, October 1, 2005, p. 51.

✦ Overly, Michael, and Kalyvas, James R., *Software Agreements Line by Line: A Detailed Look at Software Contracts and Licenses & How to Change Them to Fit Your Needs*, Aspatore Books, 2004.

✦ Potter, Beverly, et al., *Overcoming Job Burnout: How to Renew Enthusiasm for Work*, Ronin Publishing, 1998.

✦ Pratt, Mary K., "Finding the T in TCO," *Computerworld*, November 11, 2002.

✦ Rapoza, Jim, "The Game of IT Management: How to Avoid Hearing 'You Sank My Project,'" *eWeek*, October 3, 2005, p. 43.

✦ Reynolds, Janice, *The Complete E-Commerce Book: Design, Build, and Maintain a Successful Web-Based Business*, CMP Books, 2004.

✦ Rittinghouse, John, and Ransome, James, *Business Continuity and Disaster Recovery for InfoSec Managers*, Digital Press, 2005.

✦ Roberts, Paul F., "Microsoft Moves on Security," *eWeek,* October 10, 2005, p. 9.

✦ Roberts, Paul F., "Phishers Zero in on e-Banking," *eWeek*, October 10, 2005, p. 30.

✦ Robinson, William, *Your First 90 Days In A New Job (How To Make An Impact)*, Lulu, Inc., 2004.

✦ Sanderson, Susan, *Introduction to Help Desk Concepts and Skills*, McGraw-Hill/Irwin, 2003.

✦ Schiesser, Rob, *IT Systems Management: Designing, Implementing, and Managing World-Class Infrastructures*, Prentice-Hall PTR, 2001.

✦ Schneier, Bruce, *Applied Cryptography*, Second Edition, John Wiley & Sons, 1996.

✦ Sheresh, Doug, and Sheresh, Beth, *Understanding Directory Services*, Sams, 2001.

✦ Siciliano, Gene, *Finance for Non-Financial Managers*, McGraw-Hill 2003.

✦ Snedaker, Susan, and Hoenig, Nels, *How to Cheat at IT Project Management*, Syngress Publishing, 2005.

✦ Snevely, Rob, *Enterprise Data Center Design and Methodology*, Prentice Hall PTR, 2002.

✦ Stallings, William, *Data and Computer Communications*, Prentice Hall, 2003.

✦ Stettner, Morey, *Skills for New Managers*, McGraw-Hill, 2000.

✦ Strassman, Paul A., "GAAPHelps Whom?," *Computerworld*, December 6, 1999.

✦ Straub, Joseph T., *The Rookie Manager: A Guide to Surviving Your First Year in Management*, Amacom, 1999.

✦ Surowiecki, James, "Sarboxed In," *The New Yorker*, December 12, 2005, p. 46.

✦ Tannenbaum, Andrew, *Modern Operating Systems*, 2nd Edition, Prentice Hall, 2001.

✦ Tannenbaum, Andrew S., *Computer Networks*, Fourth Edition, Prentice Hall, 2002.

- Thibodeau, Patrick, "Gov't IT Execs Seek Software Accountability," *Computerworld*, October 18, 1999.

- Thibodeau, Patrick, "Sarbanes-Oxley Adds to IT Costs But Pushes Companies to Prepare," *Computerworld*, October 24, 2005.

- Thibodeau, Patrick, "Water Returns to the Data Center," *Computerworld*, August 22, 2005.

- Thompson, Robert Bruce, and Thompson, Barbara Fritchman, *PC Hardware in a Nutshell*, 3rd Edition, by R, O'Reilly & Associates, 2003.

- Tipton, Harold F., and Krause, Micki, CISSP (Editors), *Information Security Management Handbook, Fifth Edition* (Hardcover), 2003.

- Toigo, Jon, *Disaster Recovery Planning: Strategies for Protecting Critical Information Assets*, Prentice Hall, 2002.

- Torvalds, Linus, and Diamond, David, *Just for Fun: The Story of an Accidental Revolutionary*, Collins, 2002.

- Tredinnick, Luke, *Why Intranets Fail And How To Fix Them*, Chandos Publishing (Oxford) Ltd., 2004.

- Trulove, James, *LAN Wiring*, McGraw-Hill Professional, 2000.

- Tynan, Dan, "Identity Management In Action," *InfoWorld*, October 10, 2005, p. 23.

- Tynan, Dan, "Proving Your Project's Worth," *InfoWorld*, November 21, 2005, p. 25.

- Uchitelle, Louis, "College Still Counts, Though Not as Much," *New York Times*, October 2, 2005.

- Vacca, John R., *The Cabling Handbook*, Pearson Education, 2000.

- Venezia, Paul, "iSCSI SANs Unleashed", *InfoWorld*, October 3, 2005, p. 37.

- Viney, David, *The Intranet Portal Guide (How to Make the Business Case)*, Mercury Web Publishing, 2005.

- Wailgum, Thomas, "Mastering Mobile Madness," *CIO Magazine*, December 1, 2005, p. 74.

- Wailgum, Thomas, "50-Cent Holes," *CIO Magazine*, October 15, 2005.

- Wallace, Michael, and Webber, Lawrence, *The Disaster Recovery Handbook: A Step-by-Step Plan to Ensure Business Continuity and Protect Vital Operations, Facilities, and Assets*, AMACOM, 2004.

✦ Wallace, Thomas F., and Kremzar, Michael H., *ERP: Making It Happen: The Implementers' Guide to Success with Enterprise Resource Planning*, Wiley, 2001.

✦ Wallingford, Ted, *Switching to VoIP*, O'Reilly Media, Inc., 2005.

✦ Ware, Lorraine Cosgrove, "Phishing Sinks Confidence in e-Commerce," *CIO Magazine*, October 15, 2005, p. 28.

✦ Watkins, Michael, "The First 90 Days: Critical Success Strategies for New Leaders at All Levels," Harvard Business School Press, 2003.

✦ Wendover, Robert, *Smart Hiring at the Next Level*, Sourcebooks, Inc., 2006.

✦ Whittaker, James A., *How to Break Software: A Practical Guide to Testing*, Addison Wesley, 2002.

✦ Wideman, R. Max, *A Management Framework for Project, Program and Portfolio Integration*, Traddford, 2004.

✦ Wooten, Bob, *Building & Managing a World Class IT Help Desk*, Osborne Publishing, 2002.

✦ Worthen, Ben, "ITIL Power," *CIO Magazine*," September 1, 2005, p. 47.

✦ Yate, Martin, *Hiring the Best: Manager's Guide to Effective Interviewing and Recruiting*, Adams Media Corporation, 2005.

Glossary

"360" Reviews A performance review in which employees receive feedback from not only their direct supervisor, but from other individuals as well, including peers and subordinates.

7-Layer OSI model Open System Interconnect; an abstract model that describes procedures for transferring data in a network environment.

ACD Automatic Call Distribution; software that can route calls to technicians based on menu prompts and can provide detailed reports about activity.

ACT Model A method of managing a crisis; (A)cknowledge and name the trauma, (C)ommunicate both competence and caring, and provide (T)ransition.

Adaptive switching Data forwarding method that automatically switches between store-and-forward, cut-through forward, and fragment-free forwarding methods.

Advanced Encryption Standard AES; the standard for encryption adopted by the U. S. Government. AES can use key sizes of 128, 192, or 256 bits. AES replaced DES (Digital Encryption Standard).

Adware Software that installs itself on a workstation for the purpose of displaying ads to the user. Adware is generally unwanted and often installed without the knowledge of the user. It is considered to be malware.

AES Advanced Encryption Standard; the standard for encryption adopted by the U. S. Government. AES can use key sizes of 128, 192, or 256 bits. AES replaced DES (Digital Encryption Standard).

AGMA Alliance for Gray Market and Counterfeit Abatement.

ANSI/EIA American National Standards Institute/Electronic Industries Alliance. Standards coordinating organization.

APNIC Asia Pacific Information Centre; Internet registry for Asia Pacific.

ARIN American Registry for Internet Numbers; Internet registry for North America.

Asset management Processes and techniques employed to minimize TCO (total cost of ownership).

ATA The type of drive most often used in desktop and laptops; uses a 16-bit parallel interface. (Also known as IDE.)

ATM Asynchronous Transfer Mode; a high speed networking technology.

Automatic Call Distribution ACD; software that can route calls to technicians based on menu prompts and can provide you with detailed reports about activity.

B2B Business-to-Business e-commerce marketing direction.

B2C Business-to-Customer e-commerce marketing direction.

Backbone The high-capacity portion of the network that carries/transfers data collected from other portions of the network that interconnect with it.

Basel II International agreement that sets out the details for adopting more risk-sensitive minimum capital requirements for banking organizations.

BCC Blind Carbon Copy; allows you to send a copy of an e-mail (or letter) to individuals without informing the other addresses of the message that you're doing so.

BCP Business Continuity Planning; a methodology used to create a plan for how an organization will resume partially or completely interrupted critical function(s) within a predetermined time after a disaster or disruption. BCP differentiates from disaster recovery in that DR is primarily associated with resources and facilities, while BCP is primarily associated with processes.

Black List A list of originators (e-mail and IP addresses) whose messages should always be considered spam.

Bluetooth Wireless technology standard used for transmitting data between devices in close proximity.

BTUs British Thermal Units; heating and cooling measurement.

Burstable lines A connection of a particular bandwidth that allows periodic "bursts" of higher throughput.

Business Continuity Planning BCP; a methodology used to create a plan for how an organization will resume partially or completely interrupted critical function(s) within a predetermined time after a disaster or disruption. BCP differentiates from disaster recovery in that DR is primarily associated with resources and facilities, while BCP is primarily associated with processes.

C Programming language that was very popular (i t was used to write many of the Unix operating systems) but has now been supplanted in many areas by C++ and Java.

CIA   Confidentiality, Integrity, and Availability; tenets of information security.

C++   Programming language that gained popularity with the advent of object-oriented programming. It's a successor of the C programming language and still widely used.

Call tracking   A software application designed specifically for managing large volumes of calls at call centers.

Capital expenditure   A financial expenditure for an asset: an item that will have a useful life of several years such as a piece of hardware. Many companies consider software to be a capital expenditure.

CardBus   Standard for expansion cards used in laptops.

CAT   Short for "category;" ANSI/EIA (American National Standards Institute/Electronic Industries Alliance) specifications for twisted pair wiring used in local area networks.

CBT   Computer-Based Training; software-based (stand-alone or on the Web) education that trains the user in a particular product set.

CERT   Research and development center at Carnegie Mellon University (funded U.S. Department of Defense and the Department of Homeland Security) that coordinates communication among security information experts.

Certified Netware Engineer   Certification for Novell Netware product.

Change Request   CR; change management notification for a change in current process/environment.

Chief Security Officer   CSO; individual at a corporation in charge of defining and implementing security policies.

Chiller   In an air conditioning system, the piece of equipment that produces the chilled water which is then circulated.

CIFS   Common Internet File System; protocol for sharing data and files between different platforms.

CIR   Committed Information Rate; metric used by frame-relay carriers as a guarantee that data below this level will be delivered.

CISSP   Certified Information Systems Security Professional; security certification.

CLERP-9   Australian legislation similar to U.S. version Sarbanes-Oxley.

Client/server   An application architecture that has two pieces of software associated with it: one that runs on the server and does the vast majority of the processing, and another piece that the user (or client) accesses that serves as the user-interface.

CMMI Capability Maturity Model Integration; a methodology for process improvement.

CNE Novell Certified Netware Engineer.

COBIT Control Objectives for Information and related Technology; a set of documents developed by the Information Systems Audit and Control Association and the IT Governance Institute that provide guidance for computer security. Much of COBIT is available at no cost.

Compressed OSI Model Alternative of the 7-layer OSI-model in which some of the layers are combined.

Computer-Based Training CBT; software-based (stand-alone or on the Web) education that trains the user in a particular product set.

COSO Committee of Sponsoring Organizations; "is a private sector organization dedicated to improving the quality of financial reporting through business ethics, effective internal controls, and corporate governance."

CR Change Request; change management notification for change in current process/environment.

CSO Chief Security Officer; individual at a corporation in charge of defining and implementing security policies.

Cut-through forward Data forwarding method used by networking equipment in which the switch forwards the data before the whole frame has been received.

DAP Directory Access Protocol; defines the standards for accessing X.500 directories. (See X.500 directories.)

DARPA Defense Advanced Research Projects Agency; federal agency originally responsible for the network that became the Internet.

DAS Direct Attached Storage; the term used for storage that is part of a server, or directly attached to it.

Database Management System DBMS; sophisticated software system that controls the databases.

DBMS Database Management System; sophisticated software system that controls the databases.

Defense Advanced Research Projects Agency DARPA; federal agency originally responsible for the network that became the Internet.

DHCP Dynamic Host Configuration Protocol; used for assigning IP addresses.

Digital Certificates   A method of providing other systems (or users) a level of trust that the public key claimed to belong to a user (or organization) does indeed belong to that user.

Directory Services   A system application and database, for tracking and administering resources (users, devices, etc.), that is used by all other applications. Frequently used for IDs and passwords in single sign on applications.

Disaster Recovery   DR; the ability of an infrastructure to resume operations after a disaster. Disaster Recovery differentiates from Business Continuity Planning in that Disaster Recovery is primarily associated with resources and facilities, while BCP is primarily associated with processes.

DMZ   Demilitarized Zone; Used to host devices that are accessible via the Internet, but are still protected by the firewall.

DNS   Domain Name Servers; translates alphanumeric resources names to IP addresses.

DR   Disaster Recovery; the ability of an infrastructure to resume operations after a disaster. Disaster Recovery differentiates from Business Continuity Planning in that Disaster Recovery is primarily associated with resources and facilities, while BCP is primarily associated with processes.

DSL   Digital Subscriber Link; high-speed Internet connectivity for homes and small businesses over standard copper phone lines.

E-commerce   A term to describe the many activities involved in buying and selling over the Internet.

ECR   Emergency Change Request; change request processed outside the normal channels and procedures of change management because of time constraints, or urgent requirements

Emergency Change Request   ECR; change request processed outside the normal channels and procedures of change management because of time constraints, or urgent requirements.

Enterprise Resource Planning   ERP; set of applications and systems that a company uses to manage its resources across the entire enterprise.

EPO switch   Emergency Power Off; a switch found in data centers to be used when an emergency situation requires that all electrical power be immediately shut down.

EPS   Emergency Power Supply; usually a diesel-powered generator, usually outside the building, oftentimes on the roof.

ERP   Enterprise Resource Planning; set of applications and systems that a company uses to manage its resources across the entire enterprise.

Ethernet   10, 100 (a.k.a. fast Ethernet), 1,000 (a.k.a. gigabit) is the most popular LAN topology.

Expense item   A financial expenditure for something whose value is gone in a short period of time, typically less than a year. Also used for items that have a longer life, but are relatively inexpensive (below a threshold set by Accounting).

Extranet   An extranet site is similar to an Internet site except that it's specifically designed for use by the company partners (suppliers, customers, etc.).

FACTA   Fair and Accurate Credit Transactions Act; a consumer rights bill that became fully effective June 1st, 2005, and is an extension of the Fair Credit Reporting Act (FCRA). The rule says that in regard to consumer information (such as name, social security number, address, etc.) you must "take reasonable measures to protect against unauthorized access or use of the information."

FASB   Financial Accounting Standards Board; organization for establishing standards of financial accounting and reporting.

FCRA   Fair Credit Reporting Act; extended by FACTA.

FDDI   Fiber Distributed Data Interface; the protocol for transmitting data on fiber-optic cable.

Fibre Channel   The most common connection method for storage area networks.

Firewall   A device that is used to control access between two networks. Typically used when connecting a private network to the Internet as a way of protecting and securing the internal network from threats, hackers, etc. Also used when connecting two private networks (e.g., supplies, partners, etc.).

FireWire   Apple Computer IEEE standard for connecting devices.

Fiscal year   Twelve-month period used for budgeting. Frequently, the fiscal year that a budget tracks isn't the January–December calendar year. The year that the budget tracks can be any 12-month period, although it generally begins on January 1, April 1, July 1, or October 1.

Fractional T-1   Refers to using one, or more, of the 24 channels available in a T-1 circuit. While this reduces bandwidth, there is also a cost savings.

Fragment free   Data forwarding method for networking hardware where the switch stores only the first 64 bytes of the frame before forwarding the frame.

Frame relay   A cost-effective method of connecting distant points in a WAN using packet switching technology with packets of variable sizes.

FTP   File Transfer Protocol; an application protocol that transfers files from the source where they were created to a server that makes them accessible to users on the Internet.

GnuPG   Open source computer program that provides encryption and authentication.

Gramm-Leach-Bliley Act   An act passed by Congress that has provisions to protect consumers' personal financial information held by financial institutions.

Gray Market   Brand name items sold outside of the producer's official distribution channels. Gray market goods are usually not backed by the manufacturer's warranty.

HBA   Host-Bus Adapters; used for connecting servers to storage area networks.

HIPAA   Health Insurance Portability and Accountability Act; regulations passed by Congress promoting the privacy and security of medical records.

HRIS   Human Resources Information System; HR software.

HSM   Hierarchical Storage Management; a data storage solution that moves data to secondary and tertiary storage media based on access frequency and/or age.

HTTP   Hyper Text Transfer Protocol; transfers displayable Web pages.

Hub/concentrator   A generic term for a device that interconnects several nodes on a network.

HVAC   Heating, Ventilation, and Air-Conditioning.

ICANN   Internet Corporation for Assigned Names and Numbers; an internationally organized, non-profit corporation that has responsibility for IP address space allocation, domain name system management, and root server system management functions.

IDE   The type of drive most often used in desktop and laptops; uses a 16-bit parallel interface (also known as ATA).

IDF   Intermediate Distribution Frame/Facility; essentially a network wiring closet.

IDS   Intrusion Detection Systems; security hardware/software that identifies suspicious traffic (i.e., potential security threats) based on patterns of activity.

IEEE   Institute of Electrical and Electronics Engineers; a key standards-setting body.

IKE   Internet Key Exchange; a method for automating the provisioning of authenticated keys for IPsec.

ILM   Information Lifecycle Management; storage methodology that reflects the fact that the value and use of data and information change over time. Incorporates software and hardware to move data to different storage media to make the most effective use of resources.

IMAP4   Internet Message Access Protocol; an e-mail standard for accessing e-mail messages on a server without having to download them to a workstation.

Information Lifecycle Management   ILM; storage methodology that reflects the fact that the value and use of data and information change over time. Incorporates software and hardware to move data to different storage media to make the most effective use of resources.

Intermediate Distribution Frame/Facility   IDF; essentially a network wiring closet.

Internet Corporation for Assigned Names and Numbers   ICANN; an internationally organized, non-profit corporation that has responsibility for IP address space allocation, domain name system management, and root server system management functions.

Internet Key Exchange   IKE; a method for automating the provisioning of authenticated keys for IPsec.

Internet Protocol suite   IP suite; a set of communications protocols that define how devices connect to the Internet.

Interoperability   The ability for two (or more) components of technology to interface and work together.

Intranet   A private Web site available only to those within a company or organization.

Intrusion Detection Systems   IDS; security software that identifies suspicious traffic (i.e., security threats) based on patterns of activity.

Intrusion Prevention System   IPS; security software that not only detects malicious activity (like an IDS), but also takes action to halt it.

IPng   IP Next Generation; alternate name for version 6 of IP addressing.

IPS   Intrusion Prevention System; security software that not only detects malicious activity (like an IDS), but also takes action to halt it.

IPsec   Internet Protocol Security; a protocol for ensuring data security with IP connectivity; includes encryption and authentication technologies.

IPv6   Version 6 of IP addressing, also known as IPng (IP Next Generation)

iSCSI   IP SCSI; within storage networks, uses IP networking to connect servers to SCSI devices.

ISDN   Integrated Service Digital Network; a way of transmitting digital signals over standard telephone company copper lines.

ISO 17799   An internationally recognized information security standard.

ISO 9000   A standard; framework for quality management throughout the processes of producing and delivering products and services.

ISP   Internet Service Provider; a company that provides connectivity to the Internet.

ITIL   IT Infrastructure Library; a set of guidelines for developing and managing IT operations and services.

Java   Popular programming language for developing software; used to create many of the applications that run on Web sites.

JBOD   Just a Bunch of Disks; a term used to differentiate lower level storage solutions from higher level ones like SAN (Storage Area Network) and NAS (Network Attached Storage).

Kerberos   Password security scheme.

Kernel   The core components of an operating system.

Key loggers   Small applications that reside on a computer to record key strokes, usually installed without the knowledge or consent of the user, and considered to be malware and spyware.

L2TP   Layer 2 Tunneling Protocol; a tunneling protocol (developed by Cisco and Microsoft) used in virtual private networks (VPNs).

LACNIC   Latin American and Caribbean Internet Addresses Registry.

LAN   Local Area Network; a network of computers that are physically connected within a single site (or campus) without the use of telecomm lines.

LDAP   Lightweight Direct Access Protocol; a subset of the X.500 and DAP standards for directory services.

Leased line   Dedicated circuit (a.k.a. private line, point-to-point-circuit) provided by the telecommunications carriers that connects two locations.

M&M security model   Security model designed to make a system "hard on the outside and soft in the middle."

MAC address Media Access Control address; a unique identifier for any device connected to a network. MAC addresses are generally created and assigned during manufacturing.

Malware General term for software designed to damage a computer or computer system. Spyware, adware, viruses, etc., are considered forms of malware.

Middleware Software that connects other software.

Milestone A point in a project that represents the completion of an important sequence of key tasks and activities.

MIME Multipurpose Internet Mail Extension; for formatting non-text messages (e.g., graphics, audio, video) so that they can be sent over the Internet.

Multimode A less expensive (compared to singlemode) type of fiber cable that is often used within a building or small campus, since its maximum distance is about 2 km.

NAP Network Access Point; in the United States, one of several major Internet connection points that connect all ISPs together.

NAS Network Attached Storage; refers to storage hardware that connects directly to your Ethernet network.

NAT Network Address Translation; a method for allowing all on a LAN to share the same IP address when accessing devices on the Internet.

Object-Oriented Programming OOP; a methodology or a method that defines how you write a software program in a very specific way. Rather than have a series of commands that specify certain actions, objects interact with each other. C++ is an object-oriented programming language; C is not.

OCTAVE Operationally Critical Threat, Asset, and Vulnerability Evaluation; a method of performing a risk analysis developed by CERT.

OFAC Office of Foreign Assets Control; part of the U. S. Department of Treasury that administers and enforces economic sanctions programs primarily against countries and groups of individuals, such as terrorists and narcotics traffickers.

Offshore Outsourcing The process of a domestic company arranging with one or more overseas third parties to provide services that the first company could provide but chose not to.

OOP Object-Oriented Programming; a methodology or a method that defines how you write a software program in a very specific way. Rather than have a series of commands that specify certain actions, objects interact with each other. C++ is an object-oriented programming language; C is not.

Open Relay An SMTP e-mail server that lets third parties send e-mail messages.

Open Source Software OSS; software created by the worldwide user community. Open source software is generally free, can be modified by anyone, and usually doesn't have any single "owner."

OpenPGP Open source computer program that provides encryption and authentication.

OSS Open Source Software; software created by the worldwide user community. Open source software is generally free, can be modified by anyone, and usually doesn't have any single "owner."

Outsource The process of a company arranging with one or more third parties to provide services that the first company could provide but chose not to.

Packet Switching Technology that breaks up a data transmission into small packets. Each packet is then transmitted through the network, often on different paths, to the destination. At the destination, the packets are reassembled.

Passive/active hubs A passive hub (a.k.a. dumb) is a hub device that does nothing more than pass all the data and signals it receives to all the devices connected to it. It's an inexpensive device for interconnecting network nodes. An active hub (a.k.a. intelligent) adds value to its general function of interconnecting network nodes.

Patriot Act U.S. legislation that has a number of requirements for financial institutions in regard to verifying customers' identities and determining whether the customer appears on any list of known or suspected terrorists or terrorist organizations.

PC Cards Standard for expansion cards used in laptops.

PCMCIA standard cards Personal Computer Memory Card International Association; standard for expansion cards used in laptops. Later known as PC Cards and CardBus.

PDA Portable Digital Assistant; handheld electronic device that can be used as a phone, scheduler, e-mail client, etc.

PDCA Plan, Do, Check, Act; continuous improvement cycle originally developed by Walter Shewhart in the 1930s.

PDU Power Distribution Unit; equipment in a data center for distributing power to individual equipment cabinets and devices.

Perl   Programming language that uses primarily scripts. It has certain very specific strengths, and Perl programmers tend to be very devoted to their language.

PGP   Pretty Good Privacy; a computer program that provides encryption and authentication.

Phishing   The process of trying to obtain confidential information (e.g., credit card numbers, passwords, social security numbers, bank account numbers, etc.) by sending e-mails that appear to be from legitimate organizations but are in fact fraudulent.

PII   Personal Identifying Information; term used frequently in a number of compliance regulations and legislations to refer to types of protected information.

PIPEDA   Personal Information Protection and Electronic Documents Act; a Canadian law that regulates the collection, use, and disclosure of personally identifiable information.

PKI   Public Key Infrastructure; enables users to securely exchange data through the use of a public and a private cryptographic key pair that is obtained and shared through a trusted authority.

PMO   Project Management Office; department within an organization that oversees all project activity.

POP-3   Post Office Protocol 3; a protocol for downloading e-mail messages from an e-mail server.

Port replicator   A device for easily connecting external peripherals (keyboard, monitor, printer, etc.) to a laptop.

Position Description   A relatively detailed description of a specific job function.

POTS line   Plain old telephone system; a single line analog jack usually found in homes and is typically used for fax machines, modems, etc.

PPTP   Point-to-Point Tunneling Protocol; a tunneling protocol used in virtual private networks (VPNs). Has lost favor in recent years to alternatives like L2TP and IPSec.

Pretty Good Privacy   PGP; computer program that provides encryption and authentication.

Private side   A reference to the internal local area network as it relates to its connection to a firewall.

Production environment   The environment that contains the actual production systems, application, and data.

Protocol A set of rules and standards that ease the interconnectivity of devices of different platforms and from different vendors.

Public side A reference to the Internet as it relates to its connection to a firewall.

QoS Quality of Service; a technology for managing network performance.

RADIUS Remote Authentication Dial-In User Service.

RAID storage Redundant Array of Independent Disks; a method of storing on multiple disks so that data are still available even if one of the disks malfunctions.

RAS Remote Access Servers.

Recover Time Objective RTO; in disaster recovery planning, the expected amount of time between the disaster, and when services are restored.

Recovery Point Objective RPO; in disaster recovery planning, the age, or "freshness," of the data available to be restored in a disaster scenario.

Reintermediation Assembling or reassembling components of the traditional supply chain, such as connecting remote buyers and sellers on eBay.

RFID Radio Frequency Identification; technology used to identify and track items (e.g. inventory, consumer products) using very small components known as tags.

RIPE NCC Réseaux IP Européens Network Coordination Centre; Internet address registry for Europe.

RMON Remote Monitoring; a technology for managing networks.

Rootkits A set of modifications to the operating system that is primarily designed to hide malicious activity.

Router A device that connects two networks.

RPO Recovery Point Objective; in disaster recovery planning, the age, or "freshness," of the data available to be restored in a disaster scenario.

RTO Recovery Time Objective; in disaster recovery planning, the expected amount of time between the disaster, and when services are restored.

Rule of Least Privilege Users should only be granted the least amount of access to the system, and for the least amount of time necessary, as is authorized and required for their job.

S/MIME Secure Multipurpose Internet Mail Extension; a variation of MIME that supports encrypted messages.

SAN Storage Area Network; a type of network that connects servers to storage devices and provides block-level access, as opposed to file-level access of NAS solutions. (See Network Attached Storage.)

Sarbanes-Oxley Law passed by the United States Congress to regulate the integrity of financial statements.

SATA Serial ATA; type of disk drive.

SB-1386 California state law requiring organizations that maintain personal information about individuals to inform those individuals if the security of their information is compromised.

SBA Small Business Administration; government agency that manages small business definitions, loans, lobbying, etc.

SCAMPI Appraisal process for the CMMI process improvement methodology.

SCSI Small Computer Systems Interface; type of disk drive.

Secure Sockets Layer SSL; a protocol for encrypting information sent via the Internet.

Service Level Agreement SLA; a statement to customers or the user community about the service the IT department will provide. It can refer to a variety of metrics, such as performance, up-time, resolution time, etc.

Seven Layer OSI Model An abstract model for transferring data in a network environment.

Single Sign-On SSO; a security solution that allows a user to authenticate once, and then have access to all systems and resources for which he has been granted permission. Eliminates the need to remember multiple IDs and passwords. Considered a convenience not only for users, but for system administrators as well.

Singlemode A more expensive (compared to multimode) type of fiber cable that is used for longer distance runs such as 20 km.

SIR Sustained Information Rate; used by ATM carriers as a guarantee that data below this level will be delivered. Often used as a synonym for CIR.

Six Sigma Process improvement methodology.

SLAs Service Level Agreements; a statement to customers or the user community about the service the IT department will provide. It can refer to a variety of metrics, such as performance, up-time, resolution time, etc.

SNMP Simple Network Management Protocol; technology for monitoring and managing devices on a network.

SOHO Small Office, Home Office.

SONET   Synchronous Optical Network; technology for providing very high-speed connection (from 51.84 Mbps to 2.4 Gbps) for geographically distant connections (hundreds and thousands of miles).

Spoofing   The process of forging an e-mail address or IP address. Usually used by hackers for illicit purposes like fraudulently entering a computer or computer network.

Spyware   Software placed on a computer that monitors a user's activity. Usually installed without the knowledge or consent of the user, and considered to be malware.

Structured Query Language   Used for creating and maintaining databases.

SSID   Service Set Identifier; an identifier for wireless networks.

SSL   Secure Sockets Layer; a protocol for encrypting information sent via the Internet.

SSO   Single Sign-On; a security solution that allows users to authenticate once, and then have access to all systems and resources for which he/she has been granted permission. Eliminates the need to remember multiple IDs and passwords. Considered a convenience not only for users, but for system administrators as well.

Stackable devices   An alternative solution for the chassis architecture. Stackable devices (so named because they can be easily stacked on top of each other and are often rack-mountable) don't require the upfront investment of a chassis.

Storage Area Network   SAN; a type of network that connects servers to storage devices and provides block-level access, as opposed to file-level access of NAS solutions. (See Network Attached Storage.)

Store and forward   Data forwarding method where the switch stores the incoming data until the entire frame is received, and then validates its integrity before forwarding the data to its next destination.

T&M Service   Time-and-Material service; a hardware/software support model that requires the customer to pay for both the technician's time as well as any parts required.

T-1   A leased line that provides data transmission speeds of 1.544 Mbps. A T-1 line consists of 24 channels, each of which can support 64 Kpbs transmissions.

T-3   A leased line that provides data transmission speeds of 44.736 Mpbs. A T-3 line consists of 672 circuits, each of which can support 64 Kpbs transmissions.

TCO   Total Cost of Ownership; refers to the fact that there are many more items related to the cost of technology besides the initial price of the hardware and the software (e.g., training, support, etc.)

Telcos   Telecommunication companies.

Time-and-Material service   T&M service; a hardware/software support model that requires the customer to pay for both the technician's time as well as any parts required. Similar to a car repair bill.

Token-Ring   A star topology networking environment that was popularized by IBM in the 1980s, with speeds of 4 Mbps and 16 Mbps. However, Token-Ring lost considerable popularity beginning in the early to mid-1990s, and is rarely used anymore. Ethernet is far more popular and is available with higher speeds.

Topologies   The architecture of how network nodes are connected (e.g. ring, star, bus).

Total Cost of Ownership   TCO; refers to the fact that there are many more items related to the cost of technology besides the initial price of the hardware and the software (e.g., training, support, etc.)

Trojan Horse   Software that appears to be an application but is, in fact, a destructive program.

Ts and Cs   Terms and Conditions; Section of a contract with a vendor that deals with items such as service level guarantees and hardware and software specs.

Tunneling   A method for creating secure connection over the Internet between remote nodes.

Twisted pair   A somewhat generic term for the copper cabling that connects devices to the network.

Unified messaging   The term applied to integrating voice mail and e-mail systems.

UPS   Uninterruptible Power Supplies; a device for conditioning electrical power (smoothing out intermittent drops and spikes); may also provide electrical power, via batteries, during power interruptions.

URL   Uniform Resource Locator; the global address of Web pages.

USB   Universal Serial Bus; a standard used for connecting small devices (e.g., digital camera, flash memory, headset).

VAR   Value Added Reseller; a company that provides additional services (e.g., installation, upgrade) to product they sell.

Virtual Machine   Software that allows you to take a single physical device (e.g., one PC) and run multiple instances of operating systems on it.

VoIP   Voice over IP; a technology for using IP networking for phone calls.

VPN   Virtual Private Network; a method of establishing a secure connection between two devices over the public Internet.

WAN   Wide Area Network; a network that connects devices over long distances using telecomm facilities.

War room   A room provides team members a place to work on a project that is separate from their work area.

WEP   Wired Equivalent Privacy; a method for securing wireless networks.

White List   A list of sources (e-mail and IP addresses) who you have determined should be able to send you messages and that should never be flagged as spam.

WiFi   Wireless Fidelity; Wireless networking.

WPA   WiFi Protected Access; a method for securing wireless networks.

X.500 Directories   A set of several standards for directory services, originally developed to support the needs of the X.400 e-mail standards. (See DAP.)

Index